SAGE was founded in 1965 by Sara Miller McCune to support the dissemination of usable knowledge by publishing innovative and high-quality research and teaching content. Today, we publish over 900 journals, including those of more than 400 learned societies, more than 800 new books per year, and a growing range of library products including archives, data, case studies, reports, and video. SAGE remains majority-owned by our founder, and after Sara's lifetime will become owned by a charitable trust that secures our continued independence.

Los Angeles | London | New Delhi | Singapore | Washington DC | Melbourne

INDIA HIGHER EDUCATION REPORT 2018

Thank you for choosing a SAGE product!
If you have any comment, observation or feedback,
I would like to personally hear from you.

Please write to me at **contactceo@sagepub.in**

Vivek Mehra, Managing Director and CEO, SAGE India.

INDIA HIGHER EDUCATION REPORT 2018

Financing of Higher Education

Edited by

N. V. Varghese

Jinusha Panigrahi

Los Angeles | London | New Delhi
Singapore | Washington DC | Melbourne

First published in 2019 by

SAGE Publications India Pvt Ltd
B1/I-1 Mohan Cooperative Industrial Area
Mathura Road, New Delhi 110 044, India
www.sagepub.in

SAGE Publications Inc
2455 Teller Road
Thousand Oaks, California 91320, USA

SAGE Publications Ltd
1 Oliver's Yard, 55 City Road
London EC1Y 1SP, United Kingdom

SAGE Publications Asia-Pacific Pte Ltd
18 Cross Street #10-10/11/12
China Square Central
Singapore 048423

**National Institute of Educational
Planning and Administration (NIEPA)**
17-B, Sri Aurobindo Marg
Opposite Adchini
New Delhi–110016

Published by Vivek Mehra for SAGE Publications India Pvt Ltd. Typeset in 10.5/13pt Bembo by Zaza Eunice, Hosur, Tamil Nadu, India.

Library of Congress Cataloging-in-Publication Data Available

ISBN: 978-93-532-8311-7 (HB)

SAGE Team: Rajesh Dey, Guneet Kaur Gulati, Arushi Jain and Ritu Chopra

Contents

Part I: State, Market and Financing of Higher Education

Part II: Responses to Declining Public Funding

Part III: Student Financing in Higher Education

Part IV: Private Higher Education

List of Tables

List of Figures

List of Abbreviations

AFRC	Admission and Fee Regulation Committee
AFRCUP	Admission and Fee Regulation Committee of UP
AGF	Annual Guarantee Fee
AICTE	All India Council for Technical Education
AIDS	Acquired Immune Deficiency Syndrome
AISHE	All India Survey of Higher Education
AIU	Association of Indian Universities
APSCHE	Andhra Pradesh State Council of Higher Education
ATO	Australian Taxation Office
BA	Bachelor of Arts
BAF	Bachelor of Accounting and Finance
BBA	Bachelor of Business Administration
BBI	Bachelor of Banking and Insurance
BBM	Bachelor in Bank Management
BCom	Bachelor of Commerce
BCs	Backward Communities
BE	Budget Estimate
BEd	Bachelor of Education
BHA	Bachelor in Hospital Administration
BIBF	Bachelor in International Business & Finance
BLib	Bachelor of Library Science
BMM	Bachelor of Mass Media
BMS	Bachelor of Management Studies
BRICs	Brazil, Russia, India, China and South Africa
BSR	Basic Science Research
CABE	Central Advisory Board of Education
CAGR	Compound annual growth rate

CAP	Certified accounts professional
CAS	Career Advancement Scheme
CBSE	Central Board of Secondary Education
CELAF	Common Education Loan Application Form
CET	Common entrance test
CGDAN	Credit Guarantee Demand Advice Note
CGFSEL	Credit Guarantee Funds for Educational Loans
CII	Confederation of Indian Industry
CoA	Council of Architects
CPRHE	Centre for Policy Research in Higher Education
CSR	Corporate social responsibility
CSS	Centrally sponsored scheme
CSW	Commission of the Status of Women
DA	Dearness allowance
DDE	Department of Distance Education
DFID	Department for International Development
DIB	Diploma in International Business
DIET	District Institute of Education and Training
DMLT	Diploma in Medical Laboratory Technology
DNYS	Diploma in Naturopathy and Yogic Sciences
DOST	Degree Online Service, Telangana
DPEP	District Primary Education Programme
EAMCET	Engineering and Medical Common Entrance Test
EBCs	Economically Backward Communities
ECE	Electronics and Communication Engineering
EFA	Education for All
EGB	Education gender budgeting
EMI	Easy monthly instalment
EU	European Union
FICCI	Federation of Indian Chambers of Commerce and Industry
FRS	Fee reimbursement scheme
FTM	Foreign Trade Practices and Management
GATE	Graduate Aptitude Test in Engineering
GB	Gender budgeting
GBS	Gender budget statement
GDI	Gender Development Index

GDP	Gross domestic product
GEMR	Global Education Monitoring Report
GER	Gross enrolment ratio
GIS	Geographic information system
GM	Gender mainstreaming
GNI	Gross national income
GoI	Government of India
GRB	Gender responsive budgeting
GPAT	Graduate Pharmacy Aptitude Test
GPI	Gender Parity Index
GSDP	Gross state domestic product
HC	Human capital
HE	Higher education
HECS	Higher Education Contribution Scheme
HEFA	Higher Education Finance Agency
HEIs	Higher education institutions
HELP	Higher Education Loan Program
HIV	Human immunodeficiency virus
HMRC	Her Majesty's Revenue and Customs
HRD	Human Resource Development
HRM	Human resource management
IBA	Indian Banks' Association
ICHR	Indian Council of Historical Research
ICL	Income-contingent loan
ICSE	Indian Certificate of Secondary Education
ICSSR	Indian Council of Social Science Research
ICT	Information and communication technology
IGNOU	Indira Gandhi National Open University
IHER	India Higher Education Report
IIIT	Indian Institute of Information Technology
IIM	Indian Institute of Management
IIPCs	Institute–industry partnership cells
IISER	Indian Institute of Science Education and Research
IIT	Indian Institute of Technology
IMC	Integrated Marketing Communication
INC	Indian Nursing Council
IoE	Institute of Eminence

IRPM	Industrial Relationship and Personnel Management
ISRO	Indian Space Research Organisation
IT	Information technology
JRF	Junior Research Fellowships
LLB	Bachelor of Law
LLM	Master of Law
MA	Master of Arts
MArch	Master of Architecture
MBA	Master of Business Administration
MBBS	Bachelor of Medicine, Bachelor of Surgery
MCA	Master of Computer Applications
MD	Doctor of Medicine
ME	Master of Engineering
MFAM	Master of Finance and Management
MFC	Master of Finance and Control
MFC	Master of Finance and Control
MHRD	Ministry of Human Resource Development
MHRM	Master of Human Resource Management
MIM	Master in Management
MLib	Master of Library and Information Science
MLIs	Member Lending Institutions
MOOC	Massive open online course
MPharma	Master of Pharmacy
MPhil	Master of Philosophy
MS	Master of Science
MSc	Master of Science
MSW	Master of Social Work
MTech	Master of Technology
NAAC	National Assessment and Accreditation Council
NBCFDC	National Backward Classes Finance and Development Corporation
NCGTC	National Credit Guarantee Trust Company
NET	National Eligibility Test
NHFDC	National Handicapped Finance and Development Corporation
NIEPA	National Institute of Educational Planning and Administration

NIRF	National Institutional Ranking Framework
NIT	National Institute of Technology
NKC	National Knowledge Commission
NMDFC	National Minorities Development and Finance Corporation
NMEICT	National Mission on Education through Information and Communication Technology
NPM	New public management
NRI	Non-resident Indian
NSCFDC	National Scheduled Castes Finance and Development Corporation
NSCS	Non-Special Category States
NSFAS	National Student Financial Aid Scheme
NSKFDC	National Safai Karamcharis Finance and Development Corporation
NSQF	National Skill Qualification Framework
NSS	National Sample Survey
NSSO	National Sample Survey Office
NUEPA	National University of Educational Planning and Administration
OBC	Other Backward Class
ODA	Official development assistance
ODL	Open and Distance Learning
OECD	Organisation for Economic Co-operation and Development
PAYE	Pay as You Earn
PCI	Pharmacy Council of India
PG	Postgraduate
PGDCA	Postgraduate Diploma in Computer Applications
PGDEL	Postgraduate Diploma in Environmental Law
PGDHRL	Postgraduate Diploma in Human Rights Law
PGDMM	Postgraduate Diploma in Marketing Management
PGD-THM	Postgraduate Diploma in Tourism and Hotel Management
PGPSEM	Post Graduate Programme in Software Enterprise Management
PH	Physically Handicapped

PPP	Public private partnership
PRAGATI	Providing Assistance for Girls' Advancement in Technical Education Initiative
PSBs	Public sector banks
PSUs	Public sector undertakings
R&D	Research and development
RBI	Reserve Bank of India
RE	Revised estimate
RFD	Results Framework Document
RISE	Revitalising Infrastructure and Systems in Education
RMSA	Rashtriya Madhyamik Shiksha Abhiyan
RTE	Right to Education
RTF	Reimbursement of tuition fee
RUSA	Rashtriya Uchchatar Siksha Abhiyan
SAP	Structural adjustment programmes
SBMS	Social Benefit Management System
SCs	Scheduled Castes
SCS	Special Category States
SDG	Sustainable development goals
SDTP	Skill Development Training Programme
SIP	Study India Programme
SLC	Student Loans Company
SMU	Sikkim Manipal University
SRF	Senior Research Fellowship
SSA	Sarva Shiksha Abhiyan
SSR	Self Study Report
SSS	Self Supported Scheme
ST	Scheduled Tribe
TDP	Telugu Desam Party
TEFSA	Tertiary Education Fund of South Africa
TEQIP	Technical Education Quality Improvement Programme
TISS	Tata Institute of Social Sciences
TRS	Telangana Rashtra Samithi
TSCHE	Telangana State Council of Higher Education

UG	Undergraduate
UGC	University Grants Commission
UIDAI	Unique Identification Authority of India
UIS	UNESCO Institute for Statistics
UKIERI	UK India Education and Research Initiative
UNESCO	United Nations Educational, Scientific and Cultural Organization
UNPF	United Nations Population Fund
UPE	University with Potential for Excellence
USIS	United States Information Service
UT	Union territories
WCD	Women and Child Development

Preface

Higher education plays an important role in promoting economic growth, social progress and human development and in the overall development of the nations. While higher education is clearly an important source of economic growth, it can also be a source of inequalities in income and wealth if opportunities for higher education are not equally distributed.

The recent decades experienced an unprecedented expansion of higher education, both globally and in India. The emergence of knowledge economy has enhanced skill requirements and qualification levels for job entry to a minimum of post-secondary levels. Similarly, the anti-poverty initiatives and EFA programmes have contributed to the massive expansion of education at the school level, leading to increased social demand for higher education. These two factors necessitate the formulation of meaningful and sound approaches and policies towards massification of higher education in most countries.

India experienced its ever-highest rates of growth in higher education at the turn of this century. With more than 900 universities, 39,050 colleges and 36.6 million students, India has the second largest higher education system in the world. It can be expected that the expansion will continue given the favourable demographic dividend reflected in the growing social demand for higher education. It is expected that India will have the largest youth population in the 2020s.

The present *India Higher Education Report* is fourth in the series initiated by the Centre for Policy Research in Higher Education (CPRHE) of the National Institute of Educational Planning and Administration (NIEPA). The series is envisaged to provide an in-depth analysis of some of the critical dimensions of higher education in India, with contributions from eminent scholars engaged in research, policy and planning in the area of higher education. The first report—IHER 2015—provided a comprehensive account of the higher education situation in the country, focusing on various challenging issues facing the higher education sector in India. The subsequent reports—IHER 2016 and IHER 2017—focused on equity in higher education and quality and teaching–learning in higher education.

The present IHER 2018 is devoted to the theme of financing of higher education. The aspects covered in the volume include issues related to state, market and financing of higher education, responses to declining public funding, student financing in higher education and private higher education. The chapters in the report deal with state market dynamics in higher education, university–industry linkages, foreign aid, gender budgeting, self-financing courses in public institutions, changing sources of funding of public higher education institutions, scholarship schemes, student loans and fee reimbursement schemes, growth and expansion of private higher education, and financing of private higher education.

We are grateful to the authors of various chapters for their valuable contributions and for their continued support. I take this opportunity to place on record my deep appreciation for the efforts made by my colleague at CPRHE, NIEPA, Dr Jinusha Panigrahi, in bringing out this important volume.

N.V. Varghese
Vice Chancellor, NIEPA, New Delhi

Acknowledgements

The CPRHE published the first issue in the *India Higher Education Report* (IHER 2015) series. We are happy to present the fourth volume IHER 2018, titled *Financing of Higher Education in India*. The IHER 2018 discusses various aspects of financing in higher education in India, focusing on public and private financing and emerging student financing in India. This volume, as the previous ones, is the outcome of support received from various intellectuals and institutions and the efforts put in by the CPRHE

IHER 2015 was a comprehensive volume covering various issues and challenges facing higher education in the country. It was felt that the subsequent issues should focus on specific themes. The theme considered for the current IHER is financing. This proposal was discussed and approved in the Executive Committee (EC) meeting of the CPRHE in 2017. We would like to express our sincere thanks to members of the EC of the CPRHE.

The volume includes chapters by some of the leading academics and policymakers in higher education. They not only contributed their individual chapters but also contributed substantially to shape the current volume through their extensive comments on chapters by others. We gratefully acknowledge the valuable contribution of all the authors.

We are grateful to the registrar, NIEPA, Professor Kumar Suresh, and his team for their support in facilitating the publication process and procedures. We also thank Dr Pramod Rawat and his colleagues in the NIEPA publication department for their help at different stages.

We thank Mr Rajesh Dey and his entire team at SAGE for their help in the processing of this manuscript for publication.

We are also grateful to all our colleagues in CPRHE, namely Professor Mona Khare, Dr Nidhi Sabharwal, Dr Garima Malik, Dr Anupam Pachauri, Dr Malish C. M. and Dr Sayantan Mandal, for their continuous support and several rounds of comments.

Ms Anjali Arora, Mayank Rajput and Monica Joshi extended all logistics support to organize peer review meetings and contact the authors. We gratefully acknowledge their support in the preparation of this volume.

N.V. Varghese
Jinusha Panigrahi

Chapter 1

Financing of Higher Education
An Introduction

N. V. Varghese and Jinusha Panigrahi

INTRODUCTION

This century experienced one of the fastest reductions in out-of-school children, a leap in enrolment at all levels of education, especially in less developed countries, reduced dropout rates, improved gender parity, retention rates and stage transition ratios. The higher education sector, too, experienced unprecedented progress resulting from the accelerated rates of growth in the sector in this century. The pace of progress has accelerated in education resulting from the benefits gained from the increased investment in education following the reaffirmation of the Education for All (EFA) goals and the millennium development goals (Steer & Smith, 2015). Public investment by national governments and international agencies and private investments by households and enterprises, in the recent past, have indeed increased the total resource availability in the education sector. Needless to add, the increased resource availability has contributed to accelerated growth and expansion of the system.

While the international declarations and national commitments helped improve allocations to primary education, the private sector played a significant role in boosting private investments in higher education. The Right to Education (RTE) Acts, in many countries, compelled states to allocate a sufficient proportion of the national budget to education to ensure equity in the provision of education facilities and learning outcomes. According to the Jomtien statement of 2011, the state is expected to spend at least 6 per cent of their gross domestic product (GDP) and at least 20 per cent of their national budgets on education. In some countries such as Brazil and Indonesia, the national education budget is guaranteed by the constitution and legislation. These progressive public actions protected, if not promoted, state investments in education.

The state financing of higher education is supported and opposed by many scholars and policymakers. Their views essentially follow from the vision and understanding they hold with regard to the nature of education.

STATE FINANCING OF HIGHER EDUCATION

Who should finance higher education has become a contentious issue and is continuously debated in the present context. While some argue for continued state-dominated financing of higher education, others argue for more market-mediated financing of higher education. It was argued in the 1960s (Musgrave, 1969) that the extent of public expenditure will depend on the level of economic development attained by the economy. It is expected to have higher levels of public investment at lower levels of development and lower levels of public investment at higher levels of economic growth when private expenditure will be able to complement, if not substitute, public investment in several areas.

The arguments for or against the level of public investment in higher education depend on the way the sector and its contribution to development is valued. It is, very often, argued that knowledge is a public good (Samuelson, 1954) or a global public good (Stiglitz, 1999). However, opinions vary when discussions are centred around institutions producing knowledge. It is argued at times that the private benefits outstrip the social benefits from higher education and hence higher education should be treated as a private good for individuals who get it.

If one applies two critical properties of a public good, namely, non-rivalrous consumption and non-excludability in distribution (Samuelson, 1954), higher education may, perhaps, not fully qualify to be a pure public good. As Marginson notes, many goods, including higher education, may have one or the other quality in part or full (Marginson, 2011). Higher education has more of a non-rival goods property than non-excludable goods property. It can exclude people from consuming it when it is priced, even then it can remain non-rivalrous in a stage of massification or universalization.

The benefits from higher education cannot be confined to those who pursue it because of its externalities. Therefore, some (Cemmell, 2002) argue that higher education is a merit good whose benefits are neither totally public nor all private. Given the externalities of higher education, state investment is necessary for its promotion and expansion. In the absence of state investment, higher education will be under-provided and profits cannot be the sole criterion to decide the optimum level of investment in the sector (Tilak, 2008). These arguments in favour of continued state support for higher education found favourable audience when state-led development was an accepted strategy and the idea of a welfare state was commonly accepted. However, arguments for state support have become less acceptable in policy discussions in the present context, primarily due to the growing influence of market forces in decision-making in higher education.

Some others not only accept the fact that individuals benefit from higher education but also argue that society also benefits from it and increased income leads to increased tax amount from individuals. 'Graduates are more likely to more than pay for their education over their working life via the tax system, so that the onerous fees that immediately recover the cost of providing higher education are not needed' (Heaton, 1999). In general, the equity considerations justify continued state support to institutions of higher education in the developed world, even during the massification phase (Neave, 2000).

A more acceptable argument, in the context of market-mediated strategies for higher education development, is that higher education benefits the individuals through enhancing their capacity to get better jobs, higher earnings and improved social status. Given these benefits, the individuals need to invest rather than looking towards state subsidies to pursue higher education. Further, some believe that the fiscal and monetary policies, necessary to sustain a high level of public subsidy, have a damaging effect on growth of national income (Williams, 1992). They argued that subsidies in higher education and public funding of higher education have regressive effects (Psacharopoulos, 1994) on national income and economic development.

The era of State-sponsored expansion of higher education came to an end with the ascendancy of market-friendly reforms in the 1980s and expansion of the globalization process to developing countries. Cost-cutting strategies, cost recovery measures and income-generating activities became common strategies for higher education development. The idea of entrepreneurial universities (Clark, 1998) emerged as a more acceptable model of higher education development in the developed world.

GLOBAL TRENDS IN PUBLIC FINANCING OF HIGHER EDUCATION

The budgetary allocations to education as a share of national income and the share of higher education in the education budgets show interesting trends. The global trends in resource flows to education, in the 1980s, show that the share of education in the overall budgets in the developed countries declined. However, higher education sector received a larger share of the education budgets in the developed world. There are examples of the share of higher education in the education budgets doubling in the developed world and halving in the developing world during the period of transition from state funding to markets (Varghese, 2001). Between 1985 and 1995 the share of higher education to total educational expenditure more than doubled in Norway and it almost halved in the case of Nepal.

The resource flows in developing countries were different from the pattern experienced in the developed countries. The share of education budgets improved in many developing countries. However, the share of allocations to higher education declined in many instances. It seems that the structural adjustment programmes (SAP), while helping to maintain the share of education budgets, were also instrumental in diverting resources from higher to primary levels of education.

The per student expenditure on higher education was several times higher than that on basic education in many developing countries. The per student expenditure on higher education was also much higher than the per capita income in developing countries. The per student expenditure on higher education was less than the per capita income in developed countries. In other words, while higher education became a service of mass consumption in the developed world, it remained an exclusive privilege of the well-to-do and elite in the developing world. The public funding was not sufficient to alter this balance of power and authority.

NON-STATE FUNDING OF HIGHER EDUCATION

The declining public funding of higher education resulted in seeking alternative strategies for financing of higher education. The strategies included cost-saving measures, cost-sharing or cost recovery measures, including increasing tuitions, introducing student loans (Woodhall, 1991; World Bank, 1994) and income-generating activities. Student loans are increasingly being introduced in many countries. Venezuela, Jamaica, Mexico, Hungary and China are some of the countries which introduced student loans in the 1990s (Johnstone, Arora, & Experton, 1998). However, loan recovery seems to be a formidable task in many countries. One of the most common strategies followed in many countries is introduction of tuition fees. The student fee is becoming an important form of non-state funding. The advantages with student fees are that they are a regular source of flow of income and a sustainable source of income.

The major reforms related to reliance on non-state funding in higher education are privatization of public institutions and promotion of private higher education (Varghese, 2004a). Privatization implies applying market principles in the functioning of public institutions of higher education. The ownership and management of the institutions remain with the public authorities, while the operating principles are mostly market-oriented. Privatization is very often facilitated through transferring the governance to public institutions (autonomy). Many public institutions introduce cost recovery measures and for-profit activities.

An analysis of public universities in many countries shows that many public universities have started entrepreneurial activities. The market-friendly reforms in public institutions in United Kingdom and Australia are examples of privatization measures. The United States has one of the highest tuition fees among Organisation for Economic Co-operation and Development (OECD) countries (OECD, 2017). It needs to be noted that the student support systems, especially student loan schemes, have become very common in many of these countries. It seems that the OECD countries relied more on public institutions and on privatization measures than on private higher education institutions (HEIs) to massify, and later to universalize, higher education. The private sector surge is experienced mostly in the developing countries.

The private sector implies the non-state sector in higher education. The institutions are owned and operated by private individuals or trusts or groups. In most cases, this sector does not receive funding from the government and in any case, it does not rely on state funding for its growth and expansion even when they receive partial public funding support in some countries (Varghese, 2004b). Private HEIs can be universities or non-university institutions. Private universities offer courses leading to a degree, while courses offered in the non-university private HEIs, very often, lead to a certificate or a diploma.

The empirical evidence shows that developed market economies relied on public institutions to massify their higher education systems, while less developed economies relied on the market to massify higher education. It is important to note that in many less developed countries, a major share of growth in enrolment is accounted by the private segment of the public institutions and private HEIs. The private students in the public universities and students in the private universities helped the state to offload its financial burden to households. Interestingly, households have been willing to invest in private higher education, either in public institutions or in private institutions, for various reasons. First, the income levels of the families improved and capacity to pay of the households increased. Second, the courses offered on payment were more market-friendly and employment-oriented. In other words, the public policies found these measures—privatization and promotion of private institutions—attractive because of their effectiveness in reducing public funding to meet the growing social demand for higher education. The households found these measures acceptable since they felt that they get good rewards for their investment in private higher education.

The emergence and expansion of private universities and private higher education is an important trend that became dominant from 1990s onwards. Many countries have changed rules and regulations to encourage opening of private universities. At present, the private sector accounts for a respectable share of global enrolment in higher education and in many countries it accounts for a major share of enrolment.

Many universities initiated income-generating measures which included income from overseas students and entrepreneurial activities initiated by the universities. United Kingdom is a classic example of utilizing the overseas student market to generate income for the universities. Until the 1980s, education of overseas students in Britain was highly subsidized. In the 1980s, the government decided to charge full fees from the overseas students. Going a step ahead with entrepreneurial universities (e.g., Africa), is introduction of innovations leading to patented products, which licensing to manufacture would generate revenues for the institution and, likewise, using physical facilities such as guest house and hotels (e.g., Tanzania and some other countries in Africa) would generate additional resources for the university concerned (Varghese & Panigrahi, 2017).

FOREIGN AID

The governments in the post-Second World War period recognized the importance of the state in development. It was argued that the developing countries need to develop markets to catch-up with the developed world. However, in the absence of developed markets, the market-based operational principles cannot be applied to formulate and develop policies. Taking into account this reality and the expansion of influence of the centrally placed economies, many in the developed countries believed that foreign aid is an important modality to help develop the less developed countries to access capital, expand markets and accelerate economic development (Van de Walle, 2005) to facilitate the 'catch-up'. The success of the Marshall Plan further reinforced the belief in governments' role in developing markets.

Apart from the economic rationale, aid support was always linked to the foreign policy of the donor countries. The political reason for providing foreign aid was to maintain colonial links and 'contain communism'. It was believed that aid was a good instrument to promote democracy, prosperity and peace, and to contain communism through accelerated economic development (Coleman & Court, 1993). The two economic and political blocks (Soviet and The United States) were, in a sense, competing to extend funding support to the third world countries during the Cold War period. The pattern of aid flows indicates that European foreign aid went more to their former colonies and the US aid more to those countries that were aligned with them (Moyo, 2009). Soviet aid flowed more to countries that supported them politically.

It was realized in the 1990s that the initial argument for aid—catch-up—did not materialize. Further, the decade also marked the end of Soviet Union which reduced the political incentive to extend foreign aid. These factors reduced the space for aid and expanded the scope of trade. The share of aid as a share of national income declined in many developed countries. The sub-Saharan African countries used to receive the highest share of education aid followed by the East Asia and Pacific region and, South and West Asia (8.2%) (Varghese, 2010). It is important to notice that a major share of aid in Africa was for basic education while that in East Asia and Pacific was devoted to higher education.

FINANCING OF HIGHER EDUCATION IN INDIA

Higher education in India depended on public policy and state investment for its expansion. This is more so when the private universities were not established. With the emergence of private universities and private higher education in public and private institutions, the expansion of the sector is partly divorced from the public expenditure incurred by the government on higher education. The governmental commitment and priority in allocation of resources can be assessed on the basis of three indicators: (a) the share of resources invested in education or higher education as a share of national income, (b) the share of resources allocated to education as part of the public expenditure or national budgets and (c) the share of higher education in the education budgets.

Following the recommendations of the Education (Kothari) Commission (1966) and the National Policy on Education (1968), the national government was supposed to increase the allocation to education to at least 6 per cent of the national income. However, in 2014–2015 only 4 per cent (4.04%) of the GDP was being spent on education. A committee of the Central Advisory Board of Education (NUEPA, 2005) has recommended that at least 1.5 per cent of GDP needs to be allocated to higher education—1 per cent to university and higher education and 0.5 per cent to technical education (Tilak, 2006). The allocations fall very much short of the expected level of 6 per cent of the GDP.

The share of higher education in the total government expenditure is an indication of its commitment to the sector. The share of higher education in total expenditure of the central government declined over a period of time from 2 per cent in 2000–2001 to 1.38 per cent in 2011–2012. In other words, priority given to higher education as a whole has been very low and it has declined over the years. Another indicator of priority in allocations is the share of higher education in education budgets since it reflects the share relative to other levels of education. What one finds is a relative decline of the share of higher education in the total education budget. In fact, the higher education share declined from 18.8 per cent in 2000–2001 to 17 per cent in 2010–2011. University and higher education suffered more than technical education (Tilak, 2016).

As noted previously, a major share of the expenditure on education is accounted for by the states. Although nearly 75 per cent of the total public expenditure on education is spent by the states, the state's share declined to 61 per cent in higher education (MHRD, 2012). A major share of the central government expenditure is allocated to central universities and institutions of national importance as grants. Similarly, a major share of grants from the technical education budget goes to institutions like the IITs.

Total expenditure on higher education consists of plan and non-plan expenditure, the latter forming a high proportion in the total. As a percentage of the total non-plan budget of all sectors, non-plan expenditure on university and higher education constitutes about 14 per cent, while in the plan budget, the share is relatively small. According to the Planning Commission documents, the plan expenditure on higher education increased to ₹39,647 crores in the eleventh plan and to ₹110,700 crores in the twelfth plan (Planning Commission, 2013).

A state-wise public expenditure on higher education by levels of education is given in Table 1.1. The table shows, most of the educationally backward states allocate a larger share of their resources to elementary education. In some cases, the share of resources allocated to elementary level of education exceeds half of the total resources for education. For example, Jharkhand invested more than 70 per cent of its resources on primary education in 2010–2011 and in 2012–2013. States such as Arunachal Pradesh, Chhattisgarh, Jharkhand, Madhya Pradesh and so on invest more than 60 per cent of their budgeted expenditure on primary education whereas more than 50 per cent of the resources of Punjab and Goa are invested at the secondary level.

The expenditure on higher education is highest in Manipur at 20 per cent of the budgeted expenditure. Nearly 10 states allocated less than 10 per cent of their expenditure on higher education, while another 10 states allocated to higher education a share between 10 per cent and 15 per cent of their total expenditure on education. The public expenditure on higher education varies partly also due to the presence of private providers in some of these states. Some of the educationally backward states such as Assam and Bihar started enhancing their share of allocations to higher education.

Table 1.1 Public Expenditure on Education in 2010–2011 and 2012–2013

State/UTs	Elementary(%)		Secondary(%)		Adult(%)		Higher(%)		Technical (%)		Others(%)	
	2010–2011 (A)	2012–2013 (BE)	2010–2011 (A)	2012–2013 (BE)	2010–2011 (A)	2012–2013 (BE)	2010–2011 (A)	2012–2013 (BE)	2010–2011 (A)	2012–2013 (BE)	2010–2011 (A)	2012–2013 (BE)
Andhra Pradesh	41.44	42.09	36.30	36.64	0.34	0.26	15.68	14.88	5.48	5.48	0.55	0.46
Arunachal Pradesh	63.52	61.86	25.25	26.85	1.14	1.16	7.31	8.02	1.08	0.90	1.70	1.22
Assam	52.37	51.00	29.58	28.20	0.38	0.38	13.74	17.43	1.50	1.86	0.28	0.31
Bihar	62.54	61.60	20.35	17.68	0.31	0.42	14.89	18.19	0.50	0.50	0.19	0.63
Chhattisgarh	62.37	59.46	24.18	28.58	0.01	0.02	11.01	9.36	1.35	1.29	1.05	1.24
Goa	20.11	20.00	55.27	57.95	0.18	0.25	17.61	13.93	5.78	6.70	0.86	0.79
Gujarat	58.69	59.60	28.96	28.48	0.56	0.03	8.07	7.20	2.47	3.08	1.20	1.58
Haryana	52.75	58.25	31.51	27.70	0.04	0.14	12.19	10.28	3.38	3.63	–	–
Himachal Pradesh	58.61	58.54	32.88	32.87	0.03	0.04	7.16	7.18	0.84	0.91	0.25	0.22
Jammu and Kashmir (J&K)	43.56	49.10	42.57	36.98	0.00	0.32	11.31	10.68	2.31	2.26	0.25	0.65
Jharkhand	75.93	73.51	11.84	12.10	0.04	0.18	9.78	11.16	2.04	2.57	–	–

(Continued)

Table 1.1 (Continued)

State/UTs	Elementary(%)		Secondary(%)		Adult(%)		Higher(%)		Technical (%)		Others(%)	
	2010–2011 (A)	2012–2013 (BE)	2010–2011 (A)	2012–2013 (BE)	2010–2011 (A)	2012–2013 (BE)	2010–2011 (A)	2012–2013 (BE)	2010–2011 (A)	2012–2013 (BE)	2010–2011 (A)	2012–2013 (BE)
Karnataka	51.31	54.46	29.70	28.29	0.13	0.15	13.82	12.45	2.63	2.79	2.21	1.69
Kerala	40.41	37.22	38.60	39.79	0.09	0.13	15.11	15.89	4.80	5.82	0.50	1.06
Madhya Pradesh	63.34	64.62	24.89	23.41	0.01	0.01	8.65	8.92	2.11	1.96	0.91	0.98
Maharashtra	46.09	44.51	39.70	41.35	0.10	0.09	10.28	9.77	3.49	3.90	0.33	0.38
Manipur	45.33	44.97	34.54	31.18	0.89	1.07	15.51	20.02	2.09	1.05	1.39	1.54
Meghalaya	58.37	50.47	27.82	31.55	0.63	0.57	8.81	12.03	1.00	2.31	3.37	3.06
Mizoram	51.47	48.22	26.92	24.57	0.57	0.53	10.23	14.74	0.98	1.23	1.74	2.27
Nagaland	54.48	56.98	35.78	32.91	0.04	0.14	8.26	8.45	1.36	1.44	–	–
Odisha	52.94	54.36	24.15	27.23	0.05	0.13	20.50	15.57	1.39	1.41	0.43	0.42
Punjab	23.04	28.35	65.93	61.09	0.01	0.01	8.64	8.36	1.65	1.48	0.45	0.46
Rajasthan	59.27	54.80	32.86	38.11	0.08	0.13	6.01	5.18	0.69	0.80	0.14	0.13
Sikkim	3.66	4.23	87.07	84.37	0.02	0.01	4.67	5.79	0.20	0.49	4.37	5.03
Tamil Nadu	44.58	43.45	36.69	40.47	0.05	0.04	10.70	8.51	3.96	5.41	2.25	1.92
Tripura	39.21	45.48	49.83	42.74	3.93	3.50	5.02	6.15	0.98	1.19	0.74	0.69
Uttarakhand	47.77	45.42	41.37	45.52	–	–	7.25	5.49	2.31	2.35	0.80	0.78

Uttar Pradesh	59.49	58.78	31.25	31.71	–	–	7.17	7.85	0.94	0.80	0.47	0.32
West Bengal	35.67	36.95	48.42	45.41	0.05	0.17	12.30	12.96	2.04	2.61	1.25	1.59
Total states	50.40	50.60	34.53	34.47	0.15	0.15	11.09	10.88	2.51	2.77	0.79	0.79
Andaman and Nicobar Islands	54.98	54.04	32.29	31.48	0.37	0.29	6.39	5.53	3.34	3.11	2.43	5.30
Chandigarh	24.26	34.84	15.60	22.63	0.17	0.39	51.79	27.69	7.28	13.24	0.56	0.82
Dadra and Nagar Haveli	72.77	62.50	18.50	16.48	0.13	0.10	0.04	14.00	3.32	2.82	5.24	4.10
Daman and Diu	46.00	33.91	38.02	43.15	0.24	0.21	6.19	9.50	6.55	9.05	3.01	4.18
Delhi	21.95	23.12	65.61	63.74	2.33	2.32	3.08	3.11	4.86	4.49	2.07	3.11
Lakshadweep	9.55	0.00	40.50	1.09	–	–	9.40	0.00	–	–	40.54	98.91
Puducherry	36.98	35.35	33.41	33.54	0.13	0.31	16.84	19.00	10.67	10.07	1.87	1.57
Total UTs	25.99	27.09	54.84	55.04	1.73	1.83	9.29	6.38	5.49	5.41	2.52	4.11
Total (states UTs)	49.71	49.96	35.10	35.03	0.20	0.19	11.04	10.76	2.59	2.84	0.84	0.88
Total centre	56.47	51.73	12.91	13.20	0.91	0.96	17.58	21.11	11.50	12.36	0.22	0.26
Grand total	51.21	50.36	30.17	30.04	0.36	0.37	12.49	13.12	4.57	5.02	0.70	0.74
Total (rupees in crores)	119581.4	163103.8	70450.7	97276.2	832.4	1188.5	29169.4	42504.6	10673.3	16250.0	1636.1	2387.3

Source: Varghese (2015).

ALTERNATIVES TO PUBLIC SOURCES OF FUNDING

The public policy and institutional strategies are directed towards seeking alternative channels to public sources to mobilize resources. The measures adopted by institutions are in line with the reforms introduced globally, namely, cost-saving measures, cost-sharing strategies and income-generating activities.

The most common cost-sharing strategy has been cost recovery from students in the form of student fees. The committees appointed by the government in the 1990s and after strongly recommended cost recovery in higher education. For example, cost recovery through fees has been recommended by Punnayya Committee and Swaminathan Committee in the early 1990s. These committees recommended that the cost recovery in higher education should be to the tune of 15 per cent initially and 25 per cent, and eventually the full cost of higher education. The Ambani–Birla Committee favoured cost recovery and promotion of private institutions. Yash Pal Committee argued for affordable education either through scholarships or loans.

Student loan is another popular method to share the cost of higher education with students/parents. India initiated interest-free student loan scheme in 1963 which was revised in 2001, in 2004–2005 and a new Loan Guarantee Authority covering bank loans for accredited universities of India and abroad in 2008. The amount provided as loans to students has gone up several times in the past. The loans are relied on for studies within the country and also for study abroad programmes. In 2000–2001, the total number of loans taken was 1.12 million and it increased to 2.59 million in 2013–2014. The released education loan amount increased from ₹1,028 crores to ₹70,282 crores in 2013–2014 which was more than the total central allocation to higher and technical education (Rani, 2017).

Important strategies followed by many institutions of higher education for additional mobilization of resources include introduction of self-financing courses, promotion of consultancy services, mainly through research, contributions from alumni associations and other income-generating activities.

The most commonly relied on policy to reduce costs is to save on the teacher salaries. An unfortunate trend which is spread wide in the public universities is replacement of permanent teaching positions by ad hoc, temporary and guest lecturers (Panigrahi, 2018). The emoluments given to these temporary faculty members is at times 20 per cent of that of the regular faculty members. The teacher shortage in institutions of higher education in the public sector is very high. This form of cost-saving is not favoured since it goes against any efforts to improve quality.

NEW INITIATIVES BY GOVERNMENT OF INDIA (GOI)

A new centrally sponsored scheme (CSS)—Rathriya Ucchathar Sikhsa Abhiyan (RUSA)—was introduced in 2013 to provide funding for public HEIs. The state universities and colleges are provided resources to improve their infrastructural facilities based on the plans prepared by institutions.

The GoI set up a Higher Education Financing Agency (HEFA) with a view to mobilize funds from the market as per requirements of the centrally funded higher educational institutions. HEFA has been set up in 2017 as a non-profit, non-banking financing company (NBFC) for mobilizing extra-budgetary resources for building crucial infrastructure in the higher educational institutions. The Budget 2018–2019 called for increased investments in research and related infrastructure in premier educational institutions. The launch of RISE (Revitalizing Infrastructure and Systems in Education) with a total investment of ₹100,000 crore in next four years is a step in that direction. The funds mobilized through HEFA will be used to finance quality infrastructure, research labs and other facilities in the centrally funded institutions such as IITs, NITs, IIITs and IISERs, and central universities.

The Ministry of Human Resource Development (MHRD) prepared a Bill—Higher Education Commission of India (Repeal of University Grants Commission Act) Bill 2018. This Bill seeks to repeal the University Grants Commission (UGC) Act and provides for setting up of Higher Education Commission of India (HECI). This Act envisages that UGC's role will be confined to maintenance of standards and the funding responsibility will be taken away from the UGC to the MHRD or other agency. The implications of this Bill for funding arrangements for public institutions will be clearer when the provisions of the Bill are implemented.

It becomes clear from the discussions that India has moved from a state-financed and managed higher education system to a state-funded but privately managed (aided sector) and further to a full cost recovery model of higher education development. In this new arrangement, private institutions play a dominant role in the provision of services and the households pay for it. The recent trends indicate that an increasing number of households are relying on student loans to support higher education of their children. The loan amount released exceeds that of the public expenditure on education indicating the dominant influence of market forces in higher education decision-making.

INDIA HIGHER EDUCATION REPORT (IHER) 2018: FINANCING OF HIGHER EDUCATION

As discussed in previous sections, Indian higher education system is experiencing reforms in recent years in many respects including, teaching learning, curriculum, quality enhancement, institutional ranking, financing and governance structure. However, within these changes and transitions there is a shift in financing of higher education sector from public to private financing. New methods and approaches are experimented to shift the burden of higher education financing from public to private (particularly, households) or student financing. Centre for Policy Research in Higher Education (CPRHE) conducted a study on 'Financing of Higher Education'. It explored the strategies adopted by public HEIs when there is a decline in public funding.

One of the important activities of the centre is to bring out an annual publication on higher education in India. The centre invites articles from renowned academics and experienced decision makers. The process involves peer review meeting of these authors to arrive at a common framework and understanding on the Report, while individual authors differ in their analysis and arguments. The present report, titled, IHER 2018: Financing, is fourth in the series and contains important contributions from several renowned authors and policy specialists in the area of higher education financing.

The report is organized into four major themes. They are: (a) state, market and financing of higher education, (b) responses to declining public funding, (c) student financing in higher education and (d) private higher education.

STATE, MARKET AND FINANCING OF HIGHER EDUCATION

The first theme on state, market and financing of higher education consist of four chapters dealing with state market dynamics in higher education, university–industry linkages, foreign aid and gender budgeting (GB).

The Chapter 2 on 'State Market Dynamics in Higher Education Financing' by Saumen Chattopadhyay deals with state market dynamics by giving a theoretical overview of several modes of public financing of higher education. The chapter introduces a brief discussion on possible conceptualization of higher education which is followed by a critical discussion on various modes of public funding. It also discusses about the new initiatives of the government to finance HEIs in India like HEFA, graded autonomy and funding of Institute of Eminence are critically analysed and discussed in the chapter.

Chapter 3 by M. M. Ansari on 'Towards Augmenting Resources: University–Industry Linkages' has addressed the requirements and significance of cooperation and collaboration between industry and HEIs in recent context as happening around the globe, as well as a step forward required for India. The chapter has reviewed the status of university–industry arrangements in the present context and emerging options, and the growing need to generate additional resources. Ansari has identified the major impediments in promoting interface between university–industry and the way forward to address those obstructions to meet the requirements for funding as well as enhancing quality. Finally, he has suggested ways and measures for taking appropriate actions by the government, industry and HEIs for operationalizing and strengthening university–industry linkages.

The Chapter 4 on 'Foreign Aid for Higher Education in India' by Sailabala Debi gives a critical overview of various dimensions of foreign aid for higher education. The chapter discusses the rationale for foreign aid in higher education, trends and patterns of foreign aid in higher education, and a critical assessment of the intra-sectoral distribution of aid for education in India. Various issues pertaining to the effectiveness and sustainability of foreign aid are also observed.

The Chapter 5 pertaining to first theme of the IHER 2018 on 'Gender Budgeting in Higher Education' by Mona Khare addresses a new aspect in higher education—a mapping of policies and practices of gender responsive budgeting (GRB) in Indian higher education system. The chapter has explored, initially, the policies and practices in GRB for higher education in India. Various conceptual aspects of GB as a tool for gender mainstreaming (GM) are discussed thoroughly with a description of the evolution and progress of GB in India. A detailed analysis of GB in the higher education sector in India, in last 10 years, is made and represented in the chapter which argues about the rationale and need for GB in Indian context.

RESPONSES TO DECLINING PUBLIC FUNDING

The second theme is on responses to declining public funding and it consists of three chapters focusing on strategies to declining funding, self-financing courses in public institutions and changing sources of funding of public HEIs.

The Chapter 6 by Jinusha Panigrahi on 'Institutional Strategies to Overcome Declining Public Funding in Higher Education' focuses on the implications of decline in public funding on HEIs and strategies adopted by them to meet the growing demand for higher education based on an empirical study. The chapter gives a brief overview of arguments for public financing of higher education followed by public expenditure on tertiary education in selected developed and developing countries, and the trends in the public funding of higher education. Based on the findings of a large scale empirical study, the chapter elaborates on the strategies adopted by public HEIs to address the issues of declining public funding.

The Chapter 7 by Subir Maitra on 'Self-financing Courses in Public Institutions' provides a review of self-financing courses offered by public institutions of higher education in India. It elaborates on the nature of self-financing courses and pricing of courses. The issues related to quality of programmes offered and teachers selected for teaching in self-financing courses, and regulations regarding self-financing courses maintaining quality of such courses are critically discussed in the chapter making way for certain policy suggestions.

A micro picture of changing sources of funding of a public university and efforts put therein to overcome financial difficulties for bearing the cost of day-to-day expenses of the institution is presented in Chapter 8 by Harvinder Kaur. Her chapter on 'Changing Sources of Funding: A Study of Punjabi University', based on an empirical study, analyses and discusses about the changing sources of funding of selected public HEIs and various challenges therein of the institution in the recent context of growing requirement of funding due to rising enrolment in the universities. It argues for enhancement of public funding as well as the necessity for mobilizing additional funding from non-government sources.

STUDENT FINANCING IN HIGHER EDUCATION

The third theme on student financing in higher education consists of three chapters dealing with scholarship schemes, student loans and fee reimbursement schemes (FRSs) for students in private institutions.

The Chapter 9 on 'Scholarship Schemes on Student Financing' by Narayana analyses the trends in the public expenditure on higher education scholarships. It also gives a description of the scholarship schemes for the higher education students and the characteristics of recipients of the scholarships by courses and the role of scholarships in private expenditure on higher education.

The Chapter 10 on 'Student Mortgage Loans vis-à-vis Income-Contingent Loans: Problems and Prospects' by Mausumi Das and Tridip Ray makes a comparison between traditional mortgage type of loan and income-contingent loan (ICL) in Indian context. It looks in detail the problems and prospects of implementing a viable student loan programme, with special focus on ICL examining the design and implementation of income-contingent student loan schemes in various developed as well as developing countries (e.g., Australia, South Africa, United Kingdom, Ghana and so on). The chapter articulates the relative merits and demerits of ICL scheme in comparison to other existing education financing schemes.

The Chapter 11 on 'Public Financing of Private Education: A Case Study of FRS in Andhra Pradesh' by Shiva Reddy and Anji Reddy gives an empirical analysis of a new method of intervention by government to encourage the students from poor socio-economic backgrounds to access private engineering colleges without being deterred by cost. The pros and cons of such a method of financing in addressing the very objective of the scheme is assessed and presented in the chapter. The chapter thoroughly elaborates the background behind the idea of FRS and the need for the introduction of such type of scheme in Andhra Pradesh. Various salient features of the scheme and its implementation design are discussed by the authors in the chapter. The implementation and coverage of FRS in engineering education in the state of Andhra Pradesh along with the admission procedure, fee structure and overall impact of the scheme on higher education are critically examined by the authors.

PRIVATE HIGHER EDUCATION

The fourth and final theme of the report on private higher education consists of two chapters focusing on the growth and expansion of private higher education and financing of private higher education sector.

The evolution and growth of private HEIs in India are discussed by M. Muzammil in Chapter 12 on 'Growth and Expansion of Private Higher Education'. The chapter also gives a critical assessment of the quality of private HEIs, their regulations and governance.

Chapter 13 on 'Financing of Private HEIs in India' by Sangeeta Angom gives an analysis of financing patterns of private HEIs. Based on an empirical study of selected private HEIs in India, the author discusses the nature of courses and enrolments in private HEIs of India followed by a discussion on the sources of financing and patterns of expenditure of private HEIs.

REFERENCES

Cemmell, J. (2002, October 17–18). *Public vs private higher education: Public good, equity access is higher education a public good?* (Paper presented at the First Global Forum on International Quality Assurance, Accreditation and the Recognition of Quality in Higher Education). Paris: UNESCO.

Clark, R. B. (1998). *Creating entrepreneurial universities: Organisational pathways of transformation*. Oxford: Pergamon (for IAU).

Coleman, J. S., & Court, D. (1993). *University development in the third world: The Rockfeller foundation experience*. Oxford: Pergamon.

Heaton, C. (1999). The equity implications of public subsidization of higher education: A study of Fijian case. *Education Economics, 7*(2), 153–166.

Johnstone, D. B., Arora, A., & Experton, W. (1998). *The financing and management of higher education: A status report on worldwide reforms*. Washington, DC: World Bank.

Marginson, S. (2011). Higher education and public good. *Higher Education Quarterly, 6*(4), 411–433.

MHRD. (2012). *All India survey of higher education (AISHE)*. New Delhi: Government of India.

Moyo, D. (2009). *Dead aid: Why aid is not working and how there is a better way for Africa*. New York, NY: Farrar, Straus and Giroux.

Musgrave, R. A. (1969). *Fiscal systems*. New Haven and London: Yale University Press.

Neave, G. (2000). Diversity, differentiation and the market: The debate we never had but we ought to have done. *Higher Education Policy, 13* (1), 7–21.

NUEPA (2005). *Report of the CABE Committee on financing of higher and technical education*. New Delhi: NUEPA.

OECD. (2017). *Education Spending (indicator)*. OECDiLibrary. doi: 10.1787/ca274bac-en.

Panigrahi, J. (2018). *Financing of higher education: Institutional responses to decline in public funding* (A research synthesis report). New Delhi: CPRHE–NIEPA.

Planning Commission. (2013). *Twelfth Five-Year Plan (2012–2017): Faster, more inclusive and sustainable growth*. New Delhi: Government of India.

Psacharopoulos, G. (1994). Returns to education: A global update. *World Development, 22*(9), 1325–1343.

Rani, P. G. (2017). Financing higher education and education loans in India: Trends and troubles. *Journal of Social Sciences, 12*(4), 182–200.

Samuelson, P. (1954). The pure theory of public expenditure. *Review of Economics and Statistics, 36*(4), 397–391.

Steer, L., & Smith, K. (2015). *Financing education: Opportunities for global action.* Washington, DC: Centre for Basic Education at Brookings.

Stiglitz, J. E. (1999). Knowledge as a global public good. In I. Kaul, I. Grunberg, & M. Stern (Eds.), *Global public goods: International cooperation in the 21st Century* (pp. 308–332). New York, NY: Oxford University Press.

Tilak, J. B. G. (2006). On allocating 6% of GDP to education. *Economic and Political Weekly, 41*(7), 613–618.

———. (2008). Higher education: A public good or a commodity for trade? Commitment to higher education or commitment of higher education to trade. *Prospects, 38,* 449–466.

———. (2016). A decade of ups and downs in public expenditure on higher education in India. In N. V. Varghese & G. Malik (Eds.), *India Higher Education Report 2015* (pp. 307–332). London and New Delhi: Routledge (Taylor & Francis Group).

Van de Walle, N. (2005). *Overcoming stagnation in aid-dependent countries.* Washington, DC: Centre for Global Development.

Varghese, N. V. (2001). *The limits to diversification of sources of funding in higher education.* Paris: IIEP.

———. (2004a). Incentives and institutional changes in higher education. *Higher Education Management and Policy, 16*(1), 27–40.

———. (Ed.). (2004b). *Private Higher Education: Country experiences.* Paris: IIEP.

———. (2010). Higher education aid: Setting priorities and improving effectiveness. *Journal of International Cooperation in Education, 13*(2), 173–187.

———. (2015). *Challenges of massification of higher education* (CPRHE Research Occasional Papers No. 1). New Delhi: CPRHE/NIEPA.

Varghese, N. V., & Panigrahi, J. (2017). *Report on the international seminar on innovations in financing of higher education.* New Delhi: National University of Educational Planning and Administration.

Williams, G. (1992). *Changing patterns of finance in higher education.* Buckingham: SRHE & Open University.

Woodhall, M. (1991). *Student loans in higher education:* Vol. 2. *Asia* (Report of an IIEP Educational Forum). Paris: IIEP.

World Bank. (1994). *Higher education: The lessons of experience.* Washington, DC: World Bank.

PART I

State, Market and Financing of Higher Education

Chapter 2

State–Market Dynamics in Higher Education Financing

Saumen Chattopadhyay

INTRODUCTION

Exploring new ways of financing higher education continues to be a major issue in higher education policymaking world. Perennial fiscal constraint coupled with the imperative of overcoming poor governance of the public-funded higher education institutions (HEIs) have led to a move in favour of private sector financing as well as reforming the mode of funding HEIs. Policy changes to facilitate this transition are bringing about changes in the state market dynamics in financing of higher education in India. The proposed changes are supposed to achieve efficiency in the use of resources in the delivery of education and conduct of research with the primary intention to achieve excellence. This chapter makes an attempt to provide a theoretical overview of the different modes of public funding of higher education and trace out their possible implications for access and equity, efficiency and quality in the delivery of education and conduct of research. Since, in general, there are several modes of funding higher education, there is a need to analyse them within a framework and classify them.

Since the issue of public funding of higher education is linked with the way how higher education is characterized in terms of whether it is a public or a private good or a blend of the two, we begin with a brief discussion on possible conceptualization of higher education. This is followed by a discussion on various modes of public funding in a framework as suggested by Jongbloed (2004). We end with a discussion on some of the recent measures related to education loans followed by an analysis of the Higher Education Funding Agency (HEFA), graded autonomy and funding of Institute of Eminence (IoE) mooted in 2016 has now become operational.

HIGHER EDUCATION AS A PUBLIC GOOD

Issues related to funding of higher education are to be analysed and understood with reference to the characterization of higher education as a public or a private good. One way of looking at the policy discourse in higher education would be to understand it in terms of a contestation of the nature and extent of public–private divide in funding of higher education. Higher education is mostly referred to as a public good which forms the basis for arguing in favour of public funding of higher education. However, dealing with the debate on public–private divide requires a deeper understanding of what a public good is from an economic perspective. Public good is defined in terms of two characteristics, non-rivalry in consumption and non-excludability (Samuelson, 1954). If consumption by one does not preclude others from consuming the same good and this is what non-rivalry in consumption is, it becomes difficult to exclude people from consumption. In a way, non-excludability follows from non-rivalry in consumption. If we go strictly by the definition of public good, higher education is not a pure public good. There is rivalry in consumption as the number of seats for admission in a HEI is given and the students seeking admission is indeed excludable. It is, therefore, best argued as a quasi-public good (Chattopadhyay, 2012; Marginson, 2007) as it combines the features of both a private and a public good. The outcome of education in the form of human capital (HC) formation is embodied in an individual who stands to gain in terms of higher stream of future earnings as a reward for higher productivity. However, higher education generates positive externalities of various kinds in terms of inculcation of moral and ethical values, sensitivity and concern for others, and fostering citizenship. The development of scientific literacy is essential for distribution of knowledge and promotion of arts and culture (Marginson, 2016). These are essential for the maintenance of social order and a vibrant democracy. Because of these externalities that higher education generates, higher education essentially becomes a mixed good or a quasi-public good which calls for public support in the form of subsidization of the HEIs to reap the enormous benefits higher education generates. Education is not a mere consumption good people can do without for their survival. It is essential for a dignified living and social mobility. This requires provisioning of equal access to higher education as there is a need to subsidize education for the people who cannot afford to bear the cost of pursuing higher studies. This is not only necessary to achieve participatory and inclusive development but also to gain from merit and cultivate talent to build up a knowledge-based competitive economy.

Therefore, the issue of extent of subsidization depends on how much importance is assigned by the policymakers to externalities that the nation gains from higher education and imperatives of upholding equity principle for building an inclusive socio-economic order. It is because of the externalities that the social demand curve lies above and to the right of the private demand curve. The argument that education should be treated as a merit good depends on the individual preferences which are not adequately matured, suffer from bounded rationality and myopic vision. This type of preference will result in inadequate demand for education resulting in sub-optimal provisioning of education. Generally, primary education is considered to be a merit good which warrants full public support for the schools as the Right to Education (RTE) exemplifies. Therefore, to provide equal access to all those who are willing to pursue higher education, meritorious or otherwise, and to reap the benefits of externalities higher education generates, arguments are given in favour of public support for higher education. It is also argued, charging tuition fees to recover costs has the potential to make the students responsible and serious towards studies. If fees are found to be unaffordable, the government may provide education loans in concessional terms and vouchers to make informed choice about so that access does not suffer.

FUNDING POLICIES FOR PUBLIC HEIs

There are basically three questions; one, how to overcome the overall resource constraint being faced by the government for higher education; two, in connection with the first, how to encourage the universities to mobilize more resources and explore alternative channels of financing; three, how to design the mode of funding by bringing in the elements of market to deal with some of the objectives the government has prioritized. This issue has two important dimensions: One, how does the state fund higher education and two, how would the state like to build a market for higher education to generate competition, promote sovereignty and achieve efficiency in the process of mediating the state resources towards the universities. Designing of funding mechanism should also ensure that institutional diversity in terms of institutional mission and types, and student diversity are promoted as both these dimensions of higher education are undermined in the wake of increasing private participation and marketization (Michael, 2005). The overall goal of reforming higher education funding would be to achieve the best possible allocations of limited resources at the level of the economy to meet the twin objectives of improved social efficiency and equity in the entire educational process (McMahon, 1982).

Funding and regulatory interventions are not two separate instruments of higher education policymaking. Mode of funding can be so designed, it can be used as a regulatory intervention in the form of generating incentives for the students and the teachers to change their behaviour to achieve the desired objective as after all, the teachers and the students are the crucial actors who determine the quality of education and research and help fulfil the mandate of the institutions.

In general, a publicly funded university does not face a market to recover the cost of delivery as long as funding is cost based. In absence of a market mechanism and weak accountability, the mode of funding can be so designed so as to simulate a market-like situation or even construct a market. This renders the HEIs accountable to the forces of the market. Since what all are produced by a university are not readily quantifiable, such as, teaching and research, it is often argued that there would generally be a lack of adequate effort on the part of teachers and the students to dedicate themselves wholeheartedly to deliver the best possible output. If funding is directed to output, measures of accountability would be linked to funding which provide for rewards to spur the stakeholders to act and deliver. Accordingly, there arise two main questions that need to be addressed in classification of the funding mechanism. These are: What is funded and how is it funded (Jongbloed, 2007).

In a university system, the inputs are the students, teachers and the physical infrastructure along with financial resources. Under input-based funding mechanism, public funding is generally meant for the teachers and the infrastructure. The quantum of funding would be determined by the policy decisions, the requirements of the system and negotiations between the institutions and the funding agency. In such a system, it is believed that the teachers and the students are trustworthy and they remain intrinsically motivated in their academic engagement. This is the system which provides utmost freedom to the students and the teachers to organize their academic activities. If, however, they lack motivation in absence of any accountability mechanism, funding can be linked to what they produce. Making funding contingent upon their performance will incentivize them and motivate them into action to deliver as they face the threat of not being remunerated or being denied of additional financial benefits. This has implications for their academic freedom as output-based funding requires valuation of output and weighting of various components of university output to arrive at a single measure.

We can classify the various modes of funding based on the two major dimensions, what is it that is funded and how is it funded. Based on this classification, there can be four modes of financing as 2×2 combinations of these dimensions (Jongbloed, 2004). On the left extreme of the horizontal axis it is entirely input-based funding and on the right, it is entirely output-based funding. The horizontal line shows the spectrum of various combinations of input- and output-based funding.

Along the vertical axis, the channelization of funds shows a transition from a system of centralized system of fund allocation to a system of decentralization. In case of a firm, as described in economic theory, revenue is mobilized by selling output, which pays for the cost of production and accommodation of profit. For an educational institute, because the tuitions fees are subsidized in varying degrees, there does not exist any market to garner revenue, practically speaking. It matters, therefore, how the public funding is channelized to the institutions because decentralized mode of channelization tantamount to market-based financing.

At the top of the vertical axis, it is when the funds are released directly to the universities by the funding agency, the University Grants Commission (UGC). At the bottom of the axis, the funding is channelized through the students when they reveal their demands for pursuit of their studies in the form of the courses they would like to choose and the institutions they would like to study from. The advocates of the market model would argue for freedom of expression in the market to reveal the choices of the students and the very empowerment of students which would infuse competition among the institutions to cater to the students, to respond to their demand and to recover the cost operation.

PERFORMANCE-BASED FUNDING

With revenue from research gaining steam, income from research has become a major source of income for some of the reputed universities in the West. We can also incorporate this additional source of revenue for the universities. The two dimensions of funding, as referred to previously, are relevant for research-based funding as well. For the universities higher up in the ranking, the proportion of research funding would be on the higher side. In Q3 (Table 2.1), which is a combination of output-based funding and channelization of funding resources through market means that the students would be funded to exercise their choices for the courses they prefer and the institutions based on the performances of the institutions. In Q4, though the fund allocation is decentralized but the extent of funding will be based on the cost of the inputs for the delivery of education. It can happen when the fees are cost determined and the students are supported by the government either through the vouchers or through the loans to pay for the fees.

Table 2.1 *Mode of Funding Higher Education: State versus Market*

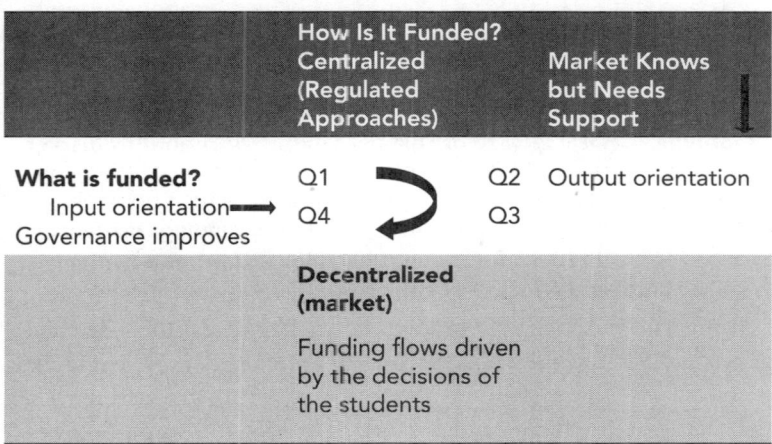

	How Is It Funded? Centralized (Regulated Approaches)		Market Knows but Needs Support
What is funded?	Q1	Q2	Output orientation
Input orientation⟶ Governance improves	Q4	Q3	
	Decentralized (market) Funding flows driven by the decisions of the students		

Source: Jongbloed (2007).

In Q3, since the students respond to the performances while making their choices, the possibility of making profit or generating surplus by the institutions is not entirely ruled out. The examples would be self-financing courses and online courses like massive open online courses (MOOCs).

Case 1 *(Q1): Input-Based Funding*

Input-based funding resembles the prevailing system of financing the most in which the HEIs are funded directly by the governments, the Centre and the states, and the extent of funding depends on the maintenance cost, primarily the salaries of the teaching and non-teaching staff and other infrastructural costs.

Concerns expressed for input-based funding have been mounting as the unstated underlying assumption of this type of funding is that the teachers and the students are trustworthy and they are intrinsically motivated to deliver the very best from their side in their academic engagement, teaching and learning, and doing research. The policymakers feel that this freedom bestowed on the students and the faculty has been abused and hence, there is a need to infuse some accountability measures in the university governance to alleviate the problem of lack of motivation.

There are two ways of doing this. One, is to continue with the input-based funding but the teachers and the students are to be regulated in a defined and well-specified manner. The present system of UGC Regulations (MHRD, 2016a) is an example of this. Since the recruitment of the teachers and career advancement scheme (CAS) are guided by the UGC Regulations which requires fulfilment of a set of criteria to become eligible for career advancement and faculty recruitment, input-based funding is apparently devoid of any consideration of output-based funding. However, the PBAS-API (UGC Regulations) (MHRD, 2016b) entails objectivity and fairness in the process of promotion and selection by quantifying the performances and guides and encourages the faculty to conform to the target set by the UGC. The other one is to effect a shift towards output-based funding which would install an accountability mechanism in a very strong and robust manner as the possible implications for non-compliance would be serious in terms of material and non-material. This move towards output-based funding is supposed to energize the entire university system by ruling out any tolerance for laziness and lackadaisical attitude.

Case 2 (Q2): Performance-Based Funding

In this system, the HEIs are funded based on their performances. This system of funding is likely to be effective in teasing out the efforts which are supposed to be put in by the teachers and the students by linking funding to the university performances which are merely the outcomes of performances of the teachers and the students. This system fixes accountability in a robust and explicit manner. By changing the accountability parameters, this funding mechanism can guide the university output towards a particular direction. For example, funding can be linked to performances measured in terms of National Assessment and Accreditation Council (NAAC) or National Institutional Ranking Framework (NIRF) or even in terms of the parameters used by the world university ranking agencies to construct the league table.

In addition to the input-based funding, the UGC rewards departments by giving them additional grants based on the performances of the universities through various schemes such as Departmental Research Support (DRS), Department of Special Assistance (DSA), CAS as well as at the university level like award under the scheme of University for Potential for Excellence (UPE) which is a reflection of the collective performance of the university. The departments and the universities are required to compete with others for the award of the grants. In addition, the UGC insists that the HEIs are to be accredited by the NAAC. The NAAC score and the NIRF ranking will increasingly be relied upon to assess the performance of the institutions and allocate funds among the universities. Students' performances and their employability are being given adequate importance by the NAAC. As we are moving towards the NIRF, the weightage given in the ranking exercise will gradually become the guiding principles in the realm of academic governance in aspiring for the colleges and the universities.

Case 3 (Q3): Market Construction with Public Funding

In Q3, the HEIs are funded by the government but through the market. This is one way of constructing the market as the market participants, particularly the students, are empowered financially to pay for their education. While the rationale for public funding is indisputable for higher education, the cons associated with public funding like apathetic university community are sought to be addressed by the voucher system. This was originally proposed by Milton Friedman (1962). It was argued that government failure is intrinsic to the functioning of a publicly funded institution which can be overcome by holding the institutions accountable to the articulation of students' demands through the market. The students' sovereignty will make the HEIs compete for funds to recover their cost of operations resulting in a thorough churning of the university governance. Further, it is argued that the market creation should lead to efficiency in the use of resources and the competitive pressure will eventually goad on the institutions to realise their potentials and achieve excellence.[1] Since the funding is not directed towards the institutions, fees would have to be raised to the levels of cost recovery and it is the uncertainty with respect to the demand and, therefore, cost recovery which will be a compelling force for the institutions to perform and deliver as

---

[1] The link between efficiency and excellence is somewhat nebulous and tenuous.

the institutions compete among themselves to carve out a share of the market and sustain their operations.[2]

This will, in the process, lead to a serious compromise with the academic autonomy in what the faculty and the institutions would seek to pursue as the concern for cost recovery would be hanging ominously on their thinking and planning. The hallmark of the universities and the higher education system, in general, is academic freedom which is so essential for creativity and path-breaking research. Research by its very nature is a venture in uncharted territories with looming uncertainty. While in a typical goods market, consumers are supreme and their sovereignty is highly desirable not only for their own sake but also for their competition; in case of an education market, it may not be so. Students' role in university governance has long been debated. Students are the co-producers of quality education and research and they need to put in effort to learn, and to do research. As it happens, for the best of the institutions, the best of the students who select best of the institutions to study from are generally serious and would put pressure on the institutions to deliver. For the middle and lower portion of the pyramid, students are more eager for credentials. This would lead to changes in the responses of the institutions to the competition generated by the students. Depending on the mix in the mode of funding, the institutional responses would vary. Further, the demand revealed by the students should not be the sole guiding factor for the HEIs to respond to as they suffer from information asymmetry, they may be myopic and can fail to anticipate the future demand for skill. Extreme market orientation in channelizing funding to the HEIs is, therefore, best avoided. Depending on the mandate of the university and its relative ranking, a judicious blend of input and output orientation is to be determined. A construction of a quasi-market for education is argued to be fostering necessary conditions for allocation in the sphere of the market and technical efficiency in the realm of the institutional functioning.

Two issues are raised by Jongbloed (2004). The first issue refers to the intrinsic problem of information asymmetry and, therefore, the ability of the students to make informed choices

---

[2] There arises an issue of prioritization of choice of courses vis-à-vis choice of institutions. Because of the eligibility criteria for seeking admission into the HEIs, the choice-making would neither be free nor should it be so (Chattopadhyay, 2012).

and the second issue is all about competition and its efficacy in case of education in improving quality. Though in today's age, the problem of information asymmetry in making choices is overcome to a large extent because of the increasing availabilities of Internet facilities and development in the information and communication technology, we need to be concerned about four kinds of constraints (Jongbloed, 2004). They are (a) the valuation of knowledge cannot be left to the market because of its imperfectness, particularly the students whose objective is primarily governed by their own interests. Subjects with less demand will, therefore, not be offered, (b) protection of institutions in specific regions is of importance because of the nstitutional and community linkages. With specific regional characteristic, (c) not all students need equal amount of support as the students from the challenged socio-economic background may need greater financial support and (d) ensuring good quality education is important as the delivery of quality is not inevitable in case of education. Since quality is jointly constructed in case of education, students who suffer from information asymmetry may not be the most reliable agencies in the Indian context to ensure quality education as education remains an experience good.

Though the voucher system is essentially meant for establishing an education market with the financial support from the government, essentially to end the problem of government failure, the problems associated with market failure are not to be discounted (West, 1995). Adam Smith (2003/1776), long ago argued in favour of full cost recovery from the students to defray the remuneration of the teachers so that the teachers are made to be accountable to the students and in the process they cease to be indolent.

EDUCATION LOANS

If higher education is more of a private investment, it makes sense that the students should borrow as investors to fund their higher studies. Education loans are particularly promoted to pay for the high fees of

---

[3] This argument is of course not tenable as the students are not typical consumers as they are required to be diligent and motivated to learn and facilitate formation of human capital. Fees are to be fixed at so high a level, access to education is bound to suffer unless the deserving students are financially supported.

the courses which are market-oriented. But the credit market for educational loans is riddled with the imperfection, particularly the absence of collateral as HC is embodied. The government should therefore provide education loans in concessional terms to support the students who need them.

Based on the argument that expenditure on education is akin to investment, as augmented cognitive capacity is rewarded with a certificate and arguably a job, the students will be able to earn their livelihood. To finance education, therefore, in the face of fiscal constraint, the government has been trying to promote education loans as a major means of financing education. Given higher private participation particularly in the professional education sector, education loans have been heavily relied upon by the students to pay for high fees. The question is, to what extent education loans would emerge as a solution to the funding constraint as fees are raised in all the streams of higher education applied and non-applied?[4] The cost for pursuing medical education is exorbitantly high particularly in the medical institutions.[5]

Education loans raise the cost of financing education, and, therefore, given the job prospects and capacity of the students, return from investment in higher education would fall (Becker, 1975/1964). However, the advocates argue, given the prospects of job, as long as returns remain high, education loans would not be a major deterrent for pursuing higher studies. It may be noted that higher education is not an investment option competing with other sectors for investment. It is a stage

---

[4] Outstanding loans have grown at a compound annual growth rate (CAGR) of almost 30 per cent since 2005 while education loan accounts have grown from 0.25 million to 3 million at a CAGR of 32 per cent during the same period. Education loans account for 11 per cent of total enrolment which was only 2 per cent in 2002–2003 (Re-imagining Higher Education in India, Yes Institute, 2016, website: http://www.yesinstitute.in)

[5] For example, one private university, located in the NCR, charges for BTech from ₹8 lakhs to ₹11 lakhs. For MBA ₹1.25 lakhs per annum to ₹6 lakhs per annum and for undergraduate programmes, ₹60,000, and ₹150,00 for postgraduate programmes, per annum. Those who score 93 per cent and above get 100 per cent scholarship and those with 90 per cent and above get 50 per cent scholarship. Hostel expenses, lodging and food are extra. There is a wide variation in the tuition fees from ₹35,000 to ₹350,000 if we consider the entire spectrum of private providers.

after secondary education (Majumdar, 1983). Hence, the possibility of higher cost of studies has the potential to distort choice-making in favour of higher studies and choice of courses made by the students, particularly from underprivileged socio-economic backgrounds.

Besides these, there are inherent imperfections in the credit market for education loans.[6] Job market uncertainty is a major issue. There could be discrimination in the process of sanctioning of loans in the form of gender, class and region. As mentioned earlier, the possibility that one has to take loans to study courses distorts the choices of the individuals at much earlier levels which can hamper social mobility. The coaching industry charges exorbitant fees for imparting training in engineering and medical studies. Since, choices made in education are irreversible, the underprivileged who can ill afford to pay high fees would suffer the most as they choose courses which are affordable and these are the courses that lack good job prospects in general. In order to overcome the uncertainty faced by the students in terms of getting a job and even the expected salary to be adequate enough to repay the loans, ICL are being now argued to be a better alternative.[7]

Case 4 (Q4): Market-Based Funding of Inputs

Under this category, it is input-based funding but the government support is to be channelized through the students in a decentralized manner. The university seeks to recover the cost of inputs engaged in teaching from charging tuition fees for the courses offered. This would, therefore, require the universities to respond to the market by offering self-financing courses, mostly applied courses which are in high demand. Since the assurance of sustained public funding ceases to exist, the public universities will be required to compete with the private ones for a larger share of the students to recover the cost of funding. What distinguishes

---

[6] Transaction costs such as the cost of information, screening and collection, and defaulting are high for educational loans. No possibility for collateral.

[7] Loans are required to be paid back in the form of interest and capital repayments if the income earned exceeds a certain limit. In case the students remain unemployed or start their career with low.

this system from the previous one is the fees is to be fixed at the level of cost of delivery. Under both the systems of decentralized funding, the universities will have a natural tendency to cut costs to keep the tuition fees at competitive levels. The variation in the tuition fees can be explained by the differences in the brand value of the HEIs and their concern about maintaining quality of the courses. The inevitable differentiation will be a marker of quality differentiation as well as costs and quality remain positively related.

The universities would apply for projects to the national and international funding agencies to recover the cost of doing research. It is natural that all universities will not be equally placed to compete for funds. The best ones will do better and outcompete the mediocre ones. This type of competition will lead to further differentiation within the university system.

The centralized funding agency can directly pay to the universities based on the number of students admitted. Based on some predetermined criteria to defray the cost of delivery of certain courses, the universities will claim reimbursement from the government. In the earlier case, the amount of vouchers would determine the extent of reimbursement. Students' needs and socio-economic backgrounds would determine the voucher amount. Onus would be on the universities to achieve efficiency and deliver quality to attract more students. Actually there is not much difference between Q3 and Q4. The relationship between competition, efficiency and quality is rather tenuous in case of higher education. Since with the best of the inputs, the students and the teachers tend to select best of the institutions, what is called selection-based efficiency (Winston, 1999), the hierarchy in the ranking of the HEIs acquires stability which limits the efficacy of competition to improve quality. This distinguishing feature of higher education market is attributable to non-replicability of the quality of HC embodied in the inputs.

Case 5: *Public Private Partnership (PPP)*

Promotion of PPPs takes the middle path between the two extremes of public funding and private funding or what is called a third way out. As discussed above, given the quasi-public good nature of higher education, privateness of higher education entails private funding by the students while publicness in the form of generation of externalities for the society, achieving equity and nurturing of merit requires public support. The neoliberal argument that the public-funded institutions suffer from poor governance adds to the arguments in favour of private sector funding and private sector management of public-funded institutions. While the costs of teaching and research can be supported by public funding, in order to gain from efficiency under private sector management, the policymakers tend to advocate PPP. Private participation for improvement in governance and achieving efficiency in the use of resources is expected to introduce innovative practices in teaching–learning, respond to the new developments in the fields of science and technology, and explore opportunities for establishing linkages between industry and the academia. In addition, it is also being felt that the private sector can be encouraged to invest in higher education to supplement inadequate public expenditure on higher education.

Several models of partnerships have been suggested by the government but each model depending on the nature of partnership would have different sets of implications (Chattopadhyay, 2015).

Different Models of PPP

There could be various ways in which the PPP in education can be envisaged. The government can think of a connection with the delivery of education, such as, (a) the investor in land and building to begin the operation, (b) an employer of the teachers, the main input in this service sector, (c) producer and the deliverer of services and having control over its delivery in terms of curriculum and pedagogy and, finally, (d) the buyer of services, that is, education. In case of (b) and (c), the private sector will be involved in the governance and most likely it will be designed in line with the new public management (NPM). For each of the models of PPP, therefore, the mode of public funding of private provider will vary with varying implications for governance (Chattopadhyay, 2015).

Some Possible Implications for PPP

In each model, costs of setting up the HEIs and operation and participation in the governance are shared between the public and private sector.
Some general observations are made below for PPP, the relevance of
which would vary model-wise.

Under PPP, the governance structure will be designed in line with
the principles of NPM which propounds installation of accounting and
audit culture, extensive use of written contracts and performance agree-
ments, economic rewards and sanctions to effect improvement in public
service delivery, institutional separation between different categories
of functions, advisory, delivery and regulatory functions, contracting
out of services, mainly non-core services and emphasis on contestable
provision, a larger space created in favour of commercial enterprises,
deregulation of market and privatization and so on.

In order to understand the possible implications of PPP on efficiency
in the use of resources or achieve technical efficiency and delivery
of quality education, the most important issue is to ascertain the real
motive behind private sector participation in higher education particularly when education is not for business. There can be two broad
categories of motives, for-profit and not-for-profit. If the purpose is
to make profit or generate reasonable surplus for reinvestment as per-
missible, then there will be pressure to recover cost by raising tuition
fees and/or increasing grants from the government, unless the costs
of operations are reduced. Reducing the cost of operations through
elimination of wastage is desirable but non-judicious reduction in costs
can hamper quality as costs and quality are positively related. In fact,
theoretically, achieving technical efficiency is only feasible if optimiza-
tion exercise is undertaken by the private entity. If profit maximization
cannot be the objective, as it is the case mostly, how can efficiency
be achieved remains an issue, unless there is some incentive in some
form being dangled in front of the private investor. Growing privatization of higher education in India is yet to contribute in a significant
manner towards quality as cost minimization is routinely resorted to
by the majority.

SOME RECENT POLICY INITIATIVES

Higher Education Funding Agency (HEFA)

In order to overcome the problem of inadequacy of resources being faced by the universities to improve their infrastructure and other academic facilities in some of the premier educational institutions, the Union Cabinet approved the establishment of a HEFA in the Union Budget for 2016–2017. The HEFA is authorized to leverage equity to raise up to ₹20,000 crores for funding projects for infrastructure and development of world class labs in the IITs/IIMs/NITs and such other institutions along with donations and corporate social responsibility (CSR) funds from public sector undertakings (PSUs) or corporates over and above the budgetary support.

The HEFA would extend a 10-year interest-free loan, the principal of which has to be repaid through the 'internal accruals' (earned through the fee receipts, research earnings and so on) by the institutions in receipt of the loans. The government pitches in with the offer to service the interest portion. This scheme is applicable for all the centrally funded HEIs who can become eligible members of the HEFA. What is important is that for joining as members, the institution should agree to escrow a specific amount from their internal accruals to HEFA for a period of 10 years. Now that the HEFA board, a not-for-profit organization, has been set up and has approved 27 projects of ₹2,067 crores for the IITs during the end of November 2017, it is worthwhile to examine the possible implications of such a funding mechanism.

Implications of HEFA for Quality and Governance

While the idea to constitute the HEFA is apparently novel in the Indian context, the challenge lies with linking repayment of principal amount of the loans to internal accruals that the institutions are required to generate. Implementation of the academic activities envisaged by the HEIs to be funded by the HEFA is unlikely to remain immune to the imperatives of ensuring internal accruals to pay for the loans. Binding the institute in receipt of such loans to commit to internal accruals, whether in the form of enhanced levels of fees or earnings, from doing research will entail compromise with the academic freedom desired to execute the envisaged academic programme. But not all HEIs are equally placed to borrow and repay loans albeit interest free. It will accentuate differentiation among the HEIs in their race to move ahead and compete globally. High fees may distort the choice of the students who are meritorious but cannot afford to bear the cost of education.

GRADED AUTONOMY AND IMPLICATIONS FOR FINANCING

In order to understand the role of funding, and in particular mode of funding in university reform, the salience of complying with regulations cannot be brushed aside. This comes out very clearly in the recent two policy initiatives by the government. One is the graded autonomy[8] and two is accord the status of IoEs to select 20 institutions for them to become world class within a decade. This approach to categorize institutions for differential treatment is already evident in many of the countries world over. As pointed out by Salmi (2009) and Marginson (2016, p. 75), we can discern two broad strategies being adopted by the governments for the purpose of enabling universities to become world class universities, to compete globally and feature in the list of world ranking of universities. One is 'rewarding quality' and the other is 'picking winners'. The first strategy is to rely on the ranking and accreditation score to generate competition with the purpose of creating differentiation among the universities followed by dedication of resources to the top few who have performed satisfactorily as assessed by the national level quality assurance agencies and accountability mechanisms. In the second category of strategy, the government decides to infuse resources to a select group of universities with potentials for becoming world class. The selection may involve competitive bidding.

---

[8] Approved by the UGC on 9 January 2018. The way categorization of the universities has been conceived of are as follows for the grant of graded autonomy. Category I: NAAC score of 3.5 and above or with ranking among the top 50 for two continuous years in the NIRF; Category II: NAAC score between 3.01 and 3.49 or with ranking among the top 51–100 for two continuous years in the NIRF; Category III: Neither I nor II as above.

On 9 January 2018, the UGC approved the plan for graded autonomy which seeks to classify universities based on their performances in terms of ranking in the NIRF and the NAAC score for differential treatment with regard to the autonomy and the extent of compliance with the regulatory interventions under the scheme of 'Graded autonomy'. The policy regarding graded autonomy resembles the first type of approach where reward comes in the form of liberation from compliance with UGC Regulations, apparently with no assurance for additional funding for the top category of institutions. The underlying idea is to enforce regulations (UGC Regulations) to achieve minimum standard and do well in terms of NAAC and NIRF.

However, exercise of academic autonomy will remain circumscribed in absence of additional financial support. For the category III particularly, it is expected that a strict compliance with the Regulations would ensure quality improvement as long as basic inputs are funded by the government.

But the major infusion of funds to the HEIs would be meant for the select IoEs. This policy approach adopted by the UGC seems to have veered towards the second one, 'picking winners'. The decision is to select 20 institutions, 10 from the public and 10 from the private for additional funding along with liberation from the Regulations to exercise academic freedom to chart out their courses of action to become world class within 10 years. The other option could have been building universities anew to be world class but it would have required a huge increase in the budgetary allocation for investment in building up of the new universities, the advantage is that the design of the new university would not remain encumbered by the history, culture and the mission of the select university. Since, setting the target to be world class rather than being at the top of the NIRF table requires liberation from NIRF and NAAC frameworks, a different governance structure outside the present framework is envisaged. It has remained debatable whether developing a higher education nationwide system would be better than concentrating resources for a select few to acquire the world class status at the expense of other HEIs (Palfreyman & Temple, 2017).

CONCLUDING REMARKS

Funding of higher education, both quantum of funding and mode of funding, is central to the higher education reform today. While inadequacy of budgetary resources for public higher education is identified to be one major reason for poor quality, absence of good governance is the other crucial factor which needs to be addressed. The issue is, therefore, how to address the resource crunch being faced by the HEIs while at the same time, the issue of poor governance problem is negotiated and tackled. Given the quasi–public good nature of higher education, the challenge is how to overcome the resource constraint faced by the HEIs and design mode of public funding to usher in changes in the governance mechanism to achieve efficiency and deliver quality.

Based on Jongbloed (2007), this chapter looks at the issue of mode of funding from two perspectives, what is it that is funded and how is it funded. While the first issue pertains to the funding of university inputs vis a vis university outputs, the second issue looks at how the funding is released to the universities, directly or through the market mechanism where the students assume the centre stage. This chapter takes forward the framework of 2 by 2 classification by bringing in the two distinct university outputs, related to students and research. This distinguishes between the two sources of funding in the context of the market, the students to finance their academic programme and the research funding agencies to fund research. A transition from input-based funding with no strings attached to performance-based funding may lead to some compromise with the university mission and academic freedom but it is expected to improve the university performances. The second aspect of mode of funding is to channelize resources in a decentralized manner mainly through the students in order to develop a market-based funding mechanism. The chapter discusses various interactions between the state and the market by giving examples of the self-financing courses and online courses like MOOCs, education loans, the voucher system, performance-based funding and the PPP in addition to the recently announced policy initiative by the government, the HEFA. As funding becomes a tool for regulation, the chapter touches upon two recent policy initiatives of the government, one is the graded autonomy and the other is to set up 20 IoEs. Categorization of universities for selective funding and efficacy of regulations in the wake of inadequate budgetary resources is debatable. The inherent conflict between the two policy thrusts, cost recovery and liberation from regulatory interventions needs to be judiciously negotiated otherwise both quality and inclusive expansion may suffer in the process. The emerging scenario in the state of funding HEIs entails a careful examination of the various sources of funding HEIs, the transition from input-based funding to performance-based funding and a construction of a quasi-market to channelize funds to the HEIs is set to usher in major changes in the Indian higher education system.

REFERENCES

Becker, G. S. (1975/1964). *Human capital: A theoretical and empirical analysis with special reference to education.* Chicago, IL: University of Chicago Press.

Chattopadhyay, S. (2012). *Education and economics: Disciplinary evolution and policy discourse.* New Delhi: Oxford University Press.

———. (2015). New modes of financing higher education: Cost recovery, private financing and education loans. In V. Varghese & G. Malik (Eds.), *India higher education report* (pp. 333–352). Abington: Routledge.

Friedman, M. (1962). *Capitalism and freedom.* Chicago, IL: Chicago University Press.

Jongbloed, B. (2004). Regulation and competition in higher education. In P. Teixeira, B. Jongbloed, D. Dill, & A. Amaral (Eds.), *Markets in higher education: Rhetoric and reality?* (pp. 87–111). Dordrecht: Kluwer Academic Publishers.

———. (2007). Creating public–private dynamics in higher education funding: A discussion of three options. In J. Enders & B. Jongbloed (Eds.), *Public–Private dynamics in higher education: Expectations, developments and outcomes* (pp. 113–138). New Brunswick, NJ Transcript, Transaction Publishers.

Majumdar, T. (1983). *Investments in education and social choice.* Cambridge: Cambridge University Press.

Marginson, S. (2007). Five somersaults in Enschede: Rethinking public/private in higher education for the global era. In J. Enders & B. Jongbloed (Eds.), *Public–Private dynamics in higher education: Expectations, developments and outcomes* (pp. 187–220). New Brunswick. NJ: Transcript, Transaction Publishers.

———. (2016). *Higher education and the common good.* Victoria: Melbourne University Publishing.

McMahon, W. (1982). Efficiency and equity criteria for educational budgeting and finance. In W. McMahon & G. Terry (Eds.), *Financing education: Overcoming efficiency and inequity* (pp. 1–35). Urbana, IL: University of Illinois Press.

MHRD, Government of India. (2016a, May 5). University Grants Commission (Minimum Standards and Procedure for Award of MPhil/PhD Degrees) Regulations, 2016. *The Gazette of India*, Extraordinary, Part III, Section 4. Retrieved from https://www.ugc.ac.in/pdfnews/4952604_UGC-(M.PHIL.-PH.D-DEGREES)-REGULATIONS,-2016.pdf

———. (2016b, July 11). University Grants Commission (Minimum Qualifications for Appointment of Teachers and other Academic Staff in Universities and Colleges and Measures for the Maintenance of Standards in Higher Education) (4th Amendment), Regulations, 2016. *The Gazette of India*, Extraordinary, Part II, Section 4. Retrieved from https://www.ugc.ac.in/pdfnews/3375714_API-4th-Amentment-Regulations-2016.pdf

Palfreyman, D., & Temple, P. (2017). *Universities and colleges: A very short introduction.* Oxford: Oxford University Press.

Michael, S. O. (2005). Financing higher education in a global market: A contextual background. In S. O. Michael & M. A. Kretovics (Eds.), *Financing higher education in a global market* (pp. 3–32). New York, NY: Algora Publishing.

Salmi, J. (2009). *The challenge of establishing world-class universities.* Washington DC: World Bank.

Samuelson, P. (1954). The pure theory of public expenditure. *Review of Economics and Statistics, 36*, 387–389.

Smith, A. (2003/1776). *An inquiry into the nature and causes of the wealth of nations.* New York, NY: Bantam Books.

West, E. G. (1995). The economics of higher education. In J. W. Sommer (Ed.), *The academy in crisis: The political economy of higher education* (pp. 135–169). New Brunswick, NJ: Transaction Publishers.

Winston, G. C. (1999). Subsidies, hierarchy and peers: The awkward economics of higher education. *The Journal of Economic Perspectives, 13*, 13–36.

Chapter 3

Towards Augmenting Resources
University–Industry Linkages

M. M. Ansari

The country faces a dissonance and disconnect between higher education and its relevance to industry, a demand–supply mismatch as the economy is in need of more 'skilled' workforce as also the managers and entrepreneurs than the country produces annually. This need can be fulfilled by creating and operating suitable collaborative arrangements between Higher Educational Institutions and industries.

—University Grants Commission (UGC, 2015)

INTRODUCTION

A well-educated pool of human resources is imperative for accelerating economic growth. Industry and business organizations require a highly skilled workforce to meet the demands of increasingly competitive and knowledge-based global economy. Improving quality and fostering excellence in our institutions of higher education are among the major challenges as most graduates who seek employment in the complex corporate world lack expertise and experience of business education which the companies need.

Higher education institutions (HEIs) must, therefore, reorient their degree programmes to blend the traditional economic and business courses with the practical experiences and operational challenges faced in the working world. The issue, therefore, is how to improve entrepreneurship education, training and skills. Entrepreneurs innovate, bring new products and concepts to the market, improve market efficiency and create new value for customers and shareholders in the market. They are the drivers of economic growth and employment generation.

The responsibility of regulating the higher education system for reaping the benefits of 'demographic dividend' is vested with the government, which must take appropriate policy measures to produce tangible results. In effect, the university graduates should not only be job seekers but must also be prepared for creating abundant job opportunities. Indeed, a university is expected to provide entrepreneurial solutions to the problems faced by the society and economy.

The HEIs would, therefore, require developing entrepreneurial skills for leadership, creativity, marketing, sales, financial management and a wide range of interpersonal skills. In the broadest sense, HEIs will have to take up research and innovative activities which lead to the creation and management of a new organization for augmenting economic and business opportunities. For success in this regard, HEIs will need financial help and professional support of the government and industry as well.

In this backdrop, an attempt is made to (a) underscore the significance of cooperation and collaboration between industry and HEIs, (b) review the status of university–industry arrangements, (c) identify the major impediments in promoting the interface between university–industry, (d) suggest ways and measures for appropriate actions to be taken by the government, industry and HEIs for operationalizing and strengthening university–industry linkages. Finally, the main conclusions are summarized.

SIGNIFICANCE OF UNIVERSITY–INDUSTRY LINKAGES

The interface between institutions and industry is critical for improving the productivity of each sector. While industry needs to utilize new knowledge and technology for ensuring its global competition, higher education requires coping with the daunting challenge on account of qualitative improvement and quantitative expansion for democratization of learning opportunities. Lack of required resources devoted to the institutions for attracting and retaining competent faculty, for providing research support and for improving governance has contributed to internal and external inefficiency of higher education system, which has made the institutions dysfunctional.

As a result, there are serious concerns for reducing the mismatch between education and jobs. A significant majority of university graduates, who seek employment in modern business and industrial sectors, are unemployable due to unacceptably low quality of relevant education, training, research and innovative activities. It is, therefore, not possible to reap the 'population dividend' and to expedite the process of national development.

With increased numbers of unemployed and underemployed youth, improving employability is a core issue for policymakers and other stakeholders, namely, teachers, researchers and the business community. In the globalized era, the requirements of the world of work have been changing. A college degree alone does not guarantee employment anymore. To better prepare and adapt the new generation for the labour market, the cooperation between universities, businesses and governments has to provide students with the necessary skills and competences.

The planners are, therefore, necessarily concerned with the question of how can HEIs better prepare and adapt the new generation for the labour market? It is critical to design strategies by which HEIs and industry would be able to provide students with the necessary skills and competences for the knowledge economy. Providing students with the necessary skills to help the youth adapt to the rapidly changing contemporary world is vital for higher education, fulfilling its mandate and commitments to the society and economy. But higher education requires resources to cope with the challenge of development of human capital (HC).

The conventional sources of funding for higher education, mainly the government, student fees, support from charitable and philanthropic organizations, have obvious limitations arising from general financial constraints. Industry and business organizations are direct beneficiaries of educational and training programmes and it can be argued that a significant amount of the profits they generate are attributable to subsidized educational inputs, mainly graduates' professional competence and research findings. They have a genuine self-interest in supporting educational programmes and the resources to do so.

But to mobilize this potential support from industry, an appropriate environment for cooperation needs to be created, because the corporate sector is a major stakeholder in promoting quality of higher education and research. And, therefore, it can play a pivotal role in improving the system as well as in meeting future aspirations. Corporations may collaborate with the academia in several ways, with varying funding commitment under various mutually acceptable programmes. The area and forms of cooperation between industry and HEIs are discussed further.

STATUS OF HEIS AND INDUSTRY COOPERATION: A REVIEW

The strategies for the emerging economy need to focus on strengthening HEIs to prepare each student to participate in a wide range of socio-economic and business activities, which may enable them to acquire different kinds of knowledge and skills to deal with multidisciplinary tasks. This is, however, not possible without strategic cooperation and coordination of various activities carried out by HEIs and industry. The reasons are as discussed in the following sections.

There is widespread recognition that there has been a qualitative shift in the way that economies and business activities are organized in almost all the countries.

In the knowledge economy, productivity growth and welfare gains are no longer purely explicable in terms of investments in land, labour and machinery. It is commonly understood that the improvements in living standards are driven by investments in knowledge capital, development of skills and competencies within workers, rather than purely their hard labour efforts. Growth is increasingly dependent on the capacities to innovate and drive change in productive ways. And this happens when knowledge is produced in HEIs and then taken up by industry to generate socio-economic benefits. At times, both those who are concerned with generating it, HEIs, and those who seek to exploit it, industry and business, produce knowledge interactively. In the process, knowledge achieves value by bringing societal improvements. It is, therefore, for the government to facilitate and regulate the activities of the concerned institutions responsible for shaping the knowledge processes towards socially productive ends.

In this context, the issue of cooperation between HEIs, industry and business is at the forefront of policy agenda. And the benefits that this brings back to the education sector as well as to the society justify university–business cooperation, particularly from the perspective of promoting teaching, research and innovations. The fact that universities and businesses are important stakeholders for each other, the most effective cooperation is delivered by identifying and building common platforms together where these areas of potential mutual benefit can be achieved.

The institutions, for instance, may garner additional resources from industry and business organizations in the form of philanthropic contributions from the public and private enterprises and trusts and non-resident Indians (NRIs); the industry may establish chairs in university departments; the industry may provide support for organizing knowledge parks, innovation centres and centres of excellence, and the expenses of these supports may be met from the budget of CSR funds. On this reckoning, institutions are encouraged by providing seed money support to establish units for promoting linkages between industry and institutions.

All India Council for Technical Education (AICTE) has launched the scheme of industry–institute partnership which is intended to promote industry–institute interaction. The main objective of this scheme is to establish institute–industry partnership cells (IIPCs) in AICTE-approved technical institutes/technical departments of universities, which will act as liaison centres between industries and various departments of the institutes for mutually beneficial activities. To start with, in the first year, the council provides financial assistance up to a maximum of ₹5 lakhs as one-time nonrecurring grant and ₹5 lakhs as recurring grant to create IIPCs in selected technical institutes. It is envisaged that after two years these cells will be self-supporting.

The major objectives of IIPC scheme are (a) maintenance, coordination and promotion of consultancy services, (b) establishment of proper links, coordination with departments and agencies, and taking necessary action for promotion of consultancy services, (c) encouraging internship programmes/students' fellowship programmes, (d) organizing industry study tour programmes and liaison with concerned industries/industrialists, (e) signing of memorandum of understanding on behalf of the institution, (f) generating funds from industry/other agencies for maintenance and development of the cell, (g) assisting industries in obtaining tax incentives from Government of India (GoI) by supporting research and development (R&D) programmes in the institution, (h) maintaining and distributing funds obtained from consultancy services, assisting weak departments in the institutes/universities with the funds generated through consultancy for strengthening of the university/institute/department, and (i) inviting experts from industry to participate in curriculum development and training from time to time in consultation with the department/institute/university.

During the period 2011–2012, the council has provided financial assistance to establish 14 new cells and an amount of ₹98.33 lakhs was released under the scheme.

The data on the total number of industry–institute cells established in the HEIs and the outcome of this initiative in terms of improvement in quality of teaching and research, and funding support from industry is, however, lacking. In view of large number of HEIs, the number of institutions having established such cells and financial assistance to them is indeed very small while the task of popularizing mutually beneficial activities is a major challenge before the government and other stakeholders.

Like AICTE, UGC too has recently, in October 2015, prepared and circulated guidelines for establishing university–industry centres for mutual help and cooperation to realize their mandatory objectives. The HEIs, which have been receiving UGC's financial support, namely, central and state universities, are eligible for financial assistance of ₹2 crores for creating start-up centres. The UGC, as on date, is in the process of scrutinizing applications submitted by the universities for establishing the centres for promoting industry and academia collaborations. The data on outcome of these exercises are lacking, as the process of such interaction has just begun.

There are, however, reasons to believe that several HEIs, mainly IITs/IIMs, and a few central universities effectively cooperate with industry in different areas and forms for promoting mutually beneficial programmes such as organization of seminars/conferences and short-term training courses. In particular, the following categories of the ongoing cooperation among the HEIs in India are identified (Ansari & Sharma, 1991, p. 146).

General research support is provided by industry for promoting excellence in teaching and research. And the support is extended in the forms of donations of laboratory equipment linked to sponsored research projects. Industrial endowments for establishment of chairs have been another source of support for research programmes.

Cooperative research support strengthens research ties between industry and HEIs which jointly conduct research in theoretical and applied areas. In this category, industry not only provides funding support for accomplishment of projects but also participates in curriculum design. Research fellowships are also provided, particularly in the subject areas which do not attract many researchers.

Knowledge transfer is facilitated through exchange of personnel between institutions and industry, mainly in the form of visiting professorships, assignments at institutions in the areas of mutual interest, consultancy, seminars, participation in workshops and lectures by industrial scientists and other professional leaders, mainly in the short-term specialized courses.

Technology transfer programmes are designed to capitalize on university research or to integrate technological results of research into private sector programmes or commercial products. Such programmes are designed (a) to address specific research problems in a company, (b) to provide technical assistance to companies in need of developing new products or new business, and (c) to help entrepreneurs start a new company in high technical and professional areas. A few technical institutions offer extension services for improving economic performance of smaller companies. This is done through organization of 'technology parks' or exhibitions for popularizing the application of new technology in new methods of production.

The feedback obtained from both the institutions and the companies revealed, as reported in the aforementioned study, that the interface between them has been at the low ebb for various reasons, a few of which are identified further. And generation of resources by the institutions from industry's sources is negligible as compared to the overall university budget. For an objective appraisal of the nature and extent of cooperation, a reputed research institution should take up a comprehensive survey study.

MAJOR IMPEDIMENTS IN HEI–INDUSTRY INTERACTION

As evident from the foregoing, it was only in 2015 when the UGC took a deliberate policy decision to encourage HEIs to promote university–industry linkages. AICTE did it in 2012. Obviously, the government's policy support has been lacking. However, our observations and interaction with the concerned officials from industry and academia point out the following major barriers in promotion of interface between HEIs and the companies.

First, there is lack of mutual trust, understanding and appreciation of respective fields of activities between academics and leaders of industry about complementary nature of activities, which if properly harnessed could herald a new era of industrial development. Such misgivings as these are major constraints in promoting cooperation between industry and HEIs.

Second, much of the research conducted at HEIs is in areas of knowledge, which are not relevant for promotion of industrial and business activities. This is attributable to both the low quality of teaching and research programmes as well as lack of relevance of research outputs to multinational corporations. What is needed, therefore, is the articulation of its needs by industry and toning up of academic programmes in applied areas to meet the requirements of the industrial sector.

Third, lack of relevance of teaching and research activities is chiefly responsible for the bulging size of 'unemployable graduates', who do not possess requisite technical and professional competence to be able to function in the globalized economic environment. HEIs do not design and implement curriculum or provide sufficient guidelines that may prepare entrepreneurs to enable the graduates to undertake industrial ventures. Fourth, most HEIs suffer due to shortage of competent faculty, mainly in science and technology disciplines. At least one-third of approved faculty positions are perpetually vacant for several years. And ad hoc staff that is lowly qualified and experienced, hired at a pittance, substitutes faculty requirements.

More importantly, the model of higher education and research, as pursued in India, is unsuited to carry out research and innovation programmes in HEIs. While HEIs, mainly universities and colleges, are largely engaged in teaching, the national laboratories under the aegis of Council for Scientific and Industrial Research, and Defence Research and Development Organisation are responsible for conducting research and innovative activities in various disciplines. In search of a better career and employment opportunities, researchers from HEIs move out to such organizations that offer superior employment opportunities. Since teaching and research are closely related, quality of education and training suffers. In effect, HEIs' outputs, graduates and quality of research findings, do not meet needs of globalized economy.

Fifth, inadequacy of funds for modernization of infrastructure, mainly workshops and laboratories for advanced training and research work in industrial fields, is a major impediment in promoting cooperation among HEIs, and institutions are unable to respond to the needs of commercial bodies that thrive on the basis of highly qualified and trained manpower who enable the companies to improve productivity of resources and effectively compete in the competitive economy.

Sixth, tax concessions and other fiscal incentives given to educational institutions are considered inadequate and unattractive for donors. Under the relevant provisions, donations given to institutions and other organizations that run and manage educational programmes attract tax benefits to the extent of 50–100 per cent for charitable institutions and 125 per cent for scientific research. The 50 per cent tax relief on donations applies to those given to specified educational institutions (charitable) only, subject to the specified limit of donor's income. The expenses incurred for educational institutions run by industry are not tax-deductible. Besides, it is contended that the fiscal concessions under the Income Tax Act are neutralized by paperwork, which has to be completed for submitting details of the expenditure.

Thus, the statutory provisions relating to tax concessions for companies running their own institutions or other donors are not only inadequate but also cumbersome and are in need of revision—with a view of broadening the concessions and streamlining the bureaucracy. Less constraining legislations would encourage a greater degree of industrial support for HEIs, which are expected to undertake industry-oriented education and research activities.

THE WAY FORWARD

Interface between HEIs and industry is critical for improving responsiveness of the university sector to the society and economy, which not only provides financial wherewithal for sustenance of institutions but also is the beneficiary of HEIs' outputs, the quality of which determines the pace of development. Economic performance and competitiveness of industry and business organizations that are profit-making entities heavily depend on quality of outputs of HEIs, mainly competence of graduates as well as research findings and innovations, which are utilised as inputs by commercial bodies. HEIs and industry are mutually required to share their resources, physical and financial, to improve their respective productivity.

HEIs need to equip its graduates with transferrable skills that maximize their applicability in the knowledge economy sectors. To enable the graduates to work with technology sectors, institutions need to introduce curricular elements that make students more entrepreneurial, creative or innovative. The graduates, in turn, may bring a range of different perspectives from a range of academic approaches in humanities, social sciences, engineering, natural sciences and life sciences to address the challenges of industry and business organizations. Specifically, the stakeholders may take the following measures for facilitating a closer cooperation between industry and institutions.

To promote interaction between the two sectors, it is essential that government, institutions and industry together create conditions that are conducive to effective cooperation. To achieve this, the following policy and strategic measures need to be taken.

Policy Interventions by Government

Ensure university autonomy to form partnership: The best people to decide a university's strategy are those who are directly responsible for its success, mainly various university authorities and faculty heads. In an educational marketplace, each actor must have a certain freedom of action to react quickly to the challenges and opportunities. They cannot forever be second-guessed by the officials of the government who control budget for education and research. The best performing universities of the world already operate with a fair degree of autonomy from political control. HEIs should be granted functional autonomy to set the university's strategy to improve its responsiveness to the societal needs.

And they must be held accountable for their decisions. They should, in consultation with stakeholders in government, industry, the local community, staff and students, specify a set of performance metrics by which they will be judged. And if they are failing, it must be easy to replace them or to modify the rules of the game.

Reward the collaborative universities: The government should reward those universities and companies that pursue partnerships successfully. For the universities, this can be a bonus in public funding and other incentives for innovation and knowledge sharing. For companies, it can be a specific tax incentive for collaboration.

In effect, a concerted effort should be made to get more universities and companies to try their hand at partnership. The record of university–industry collaboration is spotty across the country, having nearly 800 such universities.

For sustained success in innovation, strategic partnerships are essential between industry and academia. The role of government is to facilitate this natural tendency, which requires specific action in terms of the following: (a) Enlarge the scope of fiscal incentives for industrial support to education, especially for programmes in technical, managerial and professional education as well as R&D activities, which have significant bearing on industrial productivity; (b) Streamline and simplify the procedures for obtaining tax concessions and for granting recognition to industry-supported institutions; (c) Ensure that institutions are not penalized for generating income from external sources; (d) Allow institutions to market courses of high economic value on a full-cost basis; (e) Involve industry in the decision-making process for educational development. To ensure this, statutory provisions should be created for the representation of industry on the planning and management boards of institutions; (f) Exert pressure on various industrial and educational associations to promote cooperation, particularly in such areas as course design, R&D programmes and the sharing of facilities; (g) Remove any administrative and legal barriers to encourage faculty and industrial managers to share their experiences and expertise through participation in teaching, research and short-term courses including seminars and conferences; (h) Provide funding commensurate with what is needed for the creation and strengthening of basic facilities for teaching and research, so that HEIs, especially technical, professional and management institutes, are able to offer research and consultancy services of an acceptable standard; (i) Encourage and support the organization of events with a view of promoting mutual understanding between industry and educational institutions; (j) Create an agency to monitor the progress of industry education linkages and to provide feedback for effective policy intervention; (k) Reward those institutions that engage in contracts with industry and establish awards for firms that support and promote education.

Strategic Planning by HEIs

In pursuance of the guidelines of UGC and AICTE for establishing start-ups, HEIs must strive to operationalize collaborative arrangements. Specifically, the following strategic action needs to be taken.

Evolve mechanisms to promote industry education linkages with a view to realise a key objective of HEIs—the development of an enlightened and prosperous society. Modify the rules of employment and the accountability criteria for faculty members to encourage academics to participate effectively in collaborative programmes, such as industry-funded research projects, short-term courses and so on. Carry out surveys to identify and establish action-oriented programmes with the aim to upgrade and widen the knowledge base, skills and technical know-how, particularly in the institution's local region. Make arrangements for the regular exchange of staff between the institution and firms for specialized services and for the organization of programmes for knowledge and technology transfer. Provide extension services to disseminate knowledge and ensure effective application of new technology. Design user-oriented courses and offer them to industry on a cost-sharing basis. Improve internal efficiency through more effective utilization of resources and greater relevance of programmes to workforce requirements. Adopt an entrepreneurial approach and develop basic managerial skills in staff. Evolve objective criteria for sharing income/profits among staff, faculty and the institution.

Concerted Efforts by Industry

The university outputs, mainly graduates and research findings, are used as critical inputs for improving productivity of the economic sector, mainly industry and business organizations. Industry must, therefore, be associated with HEIs' activities, particularly in respect of the following.

(1) Make budgetary provisions on a regular basis, at a minimum of one per cent of gross profits, for providing direct support to teaching, research, and training programmes in educational institutions.

(2) Be prepared to provide substantial support for the development of educational infrastructure, so as to help raise the standard of education and maintain it at a high level.

(3) Adopt institutions and/or sponsor specific programmes with funding and technical support.

(4) Provide opportunities to faculty and students for greater exposure to the operational aspects of industry and business.

(5) Participate in surveys, in association with institutions, (a) to identify the needs for technical and professional training of industrial workers/managers; (b) to investigate various aspects of the promotion and diversification of products; and (c) to explore ways and means of minimizing adverse effects of industrial activities, such as environmental degradation.

(6) Articulate the needs for various types and levels of educated workers and systematically exploit scientific research and new technologies. (Ansari, 1999, p. 321)

A committee constituted by the Kerala State Higher Education Council has made a detailed recommendation. This may be seen in the Appendix.

CONCLUDING REMARKS

Evolve mechanism for collaboration: The industrial and educational sectors need to function in close collaboration, which may require them to evolve a mechanism to facilitate and encourage linkages between them. In this context, industry should be involved in the decision-making process at all stages of educational development. This would not only guarantee a high level of industrial involvement in education but would also ensure the quality of relevant educational and training programmes, as required by industry. In this context, the central and state governments must work towards creating and facilitating alliances for research and linking university departments with research institutions and industry to accelerate the process of knowledge development. HEIs must, therefore, be given full autonomy to engage with industry for promoting mutually beneficial R&D programmes.

Establish incubator centres: To realize the vision of 'Make in India', it is incumbent upon the HEIs to actively promote the establishment of 'start-up incubators' in various university departments for training and preparation of entrepreneurs in such areas as manufacturing, sales/marketing and financial services. Necessary financial wherewithal and administrative support should be extended to HEIs, wherever needed. The guidelines issued by UGC and AICTE duly support such ventures.

As the economy is plagued by high levels of graduate unemployment, HEIs should help students to launch their own businesses. HEIs should, therefore, work in partnership with students who aspire to be entrepreneurs to conduct market research and to obtain finances for creating viable businesses. And industry should provide the necessary technical and financial support for successful execution of programmes.

Sharing of facilities: In both the sectors, very substantial resources have been deployed for the creation of facilities for learning and for carrying out productive activities. Industry and HEIs can benefit mutually from the sharing of such facilities as labs, libraries, workshops and from an associated exchange of staff.

Incentivize collaborative arrangements: The need for broadening the scope of fiscal concessions for support provided to education is clearly a priority from the point of view of industry. In view of the resource crunch faced by the government and its inability to fulfil its oft-repeated commitment to raise educational expenditure from the prevailing 3.5 per cent to 6 per cent of gross domestic product (GDP), the fiscal incentives for educational funding need to be extensively reviewed and revised so that they respond to the financial needs of institutions. HEIs' share may thus be gradually increased from less than 1 per cent to 2 per cent of GDP for promoting excellence in teaching, research and innovation.

Transparent cost recovery policy: A significant proportion of educational services, mainly technical and professional programmes, has considerable economic and commercial value in its potential to enhance industrial productivity. Industry and business look at these programmes from a commercial perspective and are, therefore, willing to pay a reasonable price provided, of course, that the costs and financial aspects of education are transparent. It is necessary, therefore, to design a suitable and transparent pricing policy for different types and levels of education.

There is, moreover, another reason for rationalizing the financial aspects of education. The current policy of indiscriminate subsidization of education has generally favoured the better-off section of Indian society and so has perpetuated socio-economic disparities. The mechanisms for funding education need to be rationalized, focusing on who pays, who benefits and with what consequences. It should then be possible not only to increase private sector participation but also to recover the costs of education on valid grounds.

Finally, institutions should reorient their programmes such that the training needs of companies, especially those in their local region, could be effectively provided for. In fact, to be able to attract adequate funds from industry and business organizations, educational institutions must improve their performance and credibility by offering the educational and training programmes required to improve productivity in their region. These programmes have direct benefits for the local community in that they are an important part of socio-economic development.

APPENDIX

The following sections have been taken from the *Report of the Committee on Industry–Academia Linkages* (the Kerala State Higher Education Council, 2012).

1. Recommendations for Enhancing Industry-Academia Linkages

One of the endemic problems faced by research universities and research labs is that some of their inventions languish on the shelf, because those who might be able to commercialize them are simply unaware of the invention itself. A recent effort to increase what is called in the literature 'open innovation' has been the creation of mechanisms to link up inventors with potential users. 'Lead-user research' is one such initiative.

A newer initiative, which in essence is the opposite of the X-prize type mechanism, is a website named Marblar, where new inventions are posted, with a challenge to users to come up with potential new uses.

1.1 Incentivizing Faculty

- Provide consulting incentive such as % of consulting fee.
- Possibly additional matching grants from government (open to both public and private colleges), or from the institutions themselves.
- Incentives for publishing in listed journals (national and international) as well as for textbooks, also from the institutions.
- Establishment of sponsored chairs.
- Training in leadership and management from industry.
- New programmes and facilities.

1.2 Rotating Industry People into Academia

- Relaxing existing regulations to allow sabbaticals of 1 year for industry people to spend time in academic institutions.
- Creating more part-time Master's and Doctoral studies programmes such as PGSEM at IIM Bangalore.
- Bringing in retired industry people into academia for a second career in teaching.

1.3 Rotating Faculty into Industry on Sabbaticals

- Paid sabbaticals for faculty in industry to pursue PhDs.
- Post-doctoral programmes in industry.

1.4 Industry Outreach Programmes

1.4.1 Strategies

The Working Group on Technical Education for the XII Plan constituted a Sub-Group on Skills and Employability. Some of these suggested strategies, which can be adopted by Kerala State could be considered for implementation on a pilot basis by a few government/ government aided/private institutions. These pilots can be scaled up as regular programmes if positive outcomes have yielded.

Industry Institute Student Training Support

Objectives:

- To connect industry directly with students through training programmes.
- Such initiatives to operate in specific specializations
- Training to be imparted in every District Headquarters on regular and need based pattern.

Industry Institute Continuous Interaction Scheme (Student-Centric and Faculty Centric)

Objectives:

- To support 4–5 industrial interaction per month (one per week).
- Industrial expert spends two full days of activity in an institutional environment alongside faculty and students.

Intensive Interaction—Train the Teachers (Faculty Centric)

Objectives:

- To make faculty learn about the needs and environment of industry by spending a month in industry during summer vacation time.
- 5% of the staff encouraged and incentivized to take it up every year.
- Incentivizes could be honorarium and living expenditure.
- Periodic refresher courses or workshops to familiarize with changing needs.

1.4.2 Other General Suggestions that Could be Adopted by All Institutions

Industry representation in Governing Councils and Board of studies:

- Industry inputs in curriculum designing
- Student mentoring
- Making regular college visits, a part of industry initiative (e.g., as per CII proposal)
- Non-summer student projects so that specific tasks can be handed off to them by industry (undergraduate and graduate)
- Designation of industry clusters and nodal academic institutions to spearhead contacts with these cluster representatives
- Regular programme of inviting industry people to academic institutions as guest faculty (also as per CII proposal)

1.5 Regional Incubation Centers

- Technology parks to twin with institutions for incubation (e.g., Techno park and its existing incubation mechanism)
- Top institutions to provide facilities for technology parks (as has been done, for instance, by IIT Madras and Stanford University)

1.6 New Knowledge Clusters

- Knowledge City in Trivandrum, Kochi, Kozhikode, Malappuram: knowledge ecosystem, urban scale and services, socio-cultural climate, faculty relocation preference.

The Narayana Murthy Committee Report has suggested clusters at various levels:

- National level: Bangalore, Chennai, Delhi, Hyderabad, Mumbai, Pune.
- Secondary: Ahmedabad, Chandigarh, Coimbatore, Gurgaon, Jaipur, Kolkata, Mysore, Raipur and Dehradun-Roorkee.

Along the same lines, Regional Hubs can be set up in various places, for instance in Trivandrum with Indian Institute of Science Education and Research, Indian Institute of Space Science and Technology, CET, University College and the Regional Cancer Center, the Sree Chitra Thirunal Institute of Medical Sciences & Technology, the Rajiv Gandhi Center for Biotechnology, and other research institutions.

2. Technological Solutions Investment

The year 2012 has seen a boom in the area of Massively Open Online Courses (MOOC), where a globally distributed audience of 10,000 or even 150,000 might take a course offered by an eminent faculty. Using this mechanism it is possible to dramatically improve the availability of teaching material and to leverage the work of eminent faculty in a way that does not require additional investments by industry.

Using recorded materials, students can learn at their own pace. It is also possible to create simulcast lectures with the possibility of interaction between the faculty and students, but this model has been proven expensive (high bandwidth requirements), unsatisfying (to both teachers and students, as compared to a face-to-face lecture) and too rigid (everyone has to learn at the same pace, by definition).

On the other hand, it will be possible to deliver high-quality teaching material to a wide audience with little difficulty and at low cost, essentially only the cost of bandwidth using basic tools such as YouTube. The student can also consume material on relatively inexpensive smart phones. Since smartphones are predicted to be ubiquitous, they become a good delivery mechanism.

In addition, under the NMEICT mission, there is a proposal to provide Aakash tablets to every student, and also for teachers to be given adequate technical training. However, the primary interest we have here will be in the ability of the tablet (or smart phone) to deliver content. Further, IIT Bombay's 'A-view software' can be leveraged by institutions for undertaking capacity building programmes for faculty.

Educational institutions may create studio facilities to beam training sessions conducted by IIT Bombay for the training of faculty.

Industry experts can be identified to create detailed content for students that will enable them to come to industry with a fair grasp of the things they will need to be familiar with. Localized content is another possibility—with experts providing information in Malayalam, or with specific local context (e.g., in tourism and hospitality, the way in which knowledge of history and culture may be a major value-add in offering a 'glocalized' product that appeals to high-value tourists).

2.1 Leveraging Digital Content

There is much material already available free of charge on the internet. But some of the new entities are likely to charge.

- Using the vast amount of material available from various online 'Universities' like Udacity, Coursera, edX, Minerva, Khan Academy as well as IGNOU.
- A co-certification mechanism may be provided to give credit for classes taken under this mechanism (but this will require new ways of grading exams for remote students, with the attendant problems of plagiarism).

Higher Education institutions to submit proposals under the NMEICT Mission of GOI.

2.2 Bridging the Digital Divide

How can students without Internet access use this material? Based on smart phone and tablet availability (e.g., the Aakash 2 experiment by the Indian government) many students will be able to download video content. By providing facilities to view content in classrooms using projection systems, the entire class may be able to watch the course together.

REFERENCES

AICTE. (2012). *Annual report*. New Delhi: All India Council for Technical Education.

Ansari, M. M. (1999). The education–industry interface in India: Assessing industry's involvement in education. *Industry and Higher Education, 13*(5), 316–322.

Ansari, M. M., & Sharma, T. C. (1991). Industry and universities in India: Is the collaborative effort succeeding? *Industry and Higher Education, 5*(3), 143–154.

The Kerala State Higher Education Council. (2012). *Report of the committee on industry–academia linkages*. Kerala: The Kerala State Higher Education Council.

UGC. (2015). *UGC guidelines for establishing university–industry inter-linkage centers in universities*. New Delhi: University Grants Commission.

Chapter 4

Foreign Aid for Higher Education in India

Sailabala Debi

INTRODUCTION

The economies have become competitive and knowledge-based in the context of globalization. A vibrant higher education system is one of the necessary conditions to meet such challenges as it provides the knowledge base and skilled and specialized human capital (HC) to garner the gains of globalization. However, the funding for higher education has not kept pace with these aspirations and funding is quite inadequate to provide quality higher education in many countries. Public funding and share of public institutions in enrolments in countries such as India are declining. Many countries rely on foreign funding to meet the financial requirements of the sector. This chapter makes an attempt to analyse various dimensions of foreign aid for higher education in India.

The data on foreign aid to higher education in India is either not readily available or very sporadic. The present study relied on the data on foreign aid to education and higher education from United Nations Educational, Scientific and Cultural Organization (UNESCO) Statistics, World Bank Report, Global Education Monitoring Report (GEMR) by UNESCO, Human Development Report and world development indicators. The budgetary data is collected from the budget of Department of Higher Education, Ministry of Human Resource Development (MHRD). External assistance to India from different sources is taken from Economic Survey, Government of India (GoI), and others.

The chapter is organized as follows. The following second section discusses the rationale of foreign aid for higher education. The third section explains the development of foreign aid for higher education in India. The analysis of the trend and pattern of aid flows to education in India is presented in the fourth section. The intra-sectoral distribution of aid for education in India is discussed in the fifth section. The aid and development of higher education are discussed in the sixth section. The issues relating to effectiveness and sustainability of foreign aid are presented in seventh section. The last section recapitulates the main findings along with concluding observations.

RATIONALE FOR FOREIGN AID

The crucial role of education in economic growth was well recognized with the revolutionary work of Schultz (1961). The recent emphasis on education to achieve the sustainable development goals (SDG) by 2030 has further reinforced the role of education in development. Studies have also found that there is a significant relationship between socio-economic indicators of development (HDI, GDI, LEB, IMR, TFR and poverty) and higher education (Tilak, 2003).

The gross enrolment ratio (GER) in higher education in India is 24 (2014) which is lower than China (39) and high-income countries (74). India is expected to become the most populous nation by 2030 reaching 1.46 billion, with the highest youngest populations in the world, with a median age of 32 years, as compared to 35 in Brazil, 39 in the United States, 42 in the United Kingdom, 43 in China and 52 in Japan. The faster growth of middle-class population in the country enhances the demand for higher education. The budget for education of middle-class families has increased from 7 per cent of the total household expenditure in 2008 to 13 per cent in 2013 resulting in more spending in higher education (FICCI, 2013). Thus, it is very clear that the importance of higher education in India in contributing to its process of growth is inevitable. But the resources allocated to higher education are negligible as they are less than 1 per cent (0.69%

in 2013–2014) of gross domestic product (GDP) and over the years remain more or less constant.

After five decades of Kothari Commission recommendation, we are far away from the target of allocating 6 per cent of GDP to education. Punnayya Committee also suggested the same and rightly stated that 'Higher Education determines its (India's) economic and technological progress. Government funding must continue to be an essential and mandatory requirement for support to higher education. The Government/State must continue to accept the major responsibility for funding…' (Punnayya, 1993). The outlay on education should be raised to at least 6 per cent of GDP without further loss of time suggested by Subramanian (2016).

In view of the upsurge in demand for higher education in India, finance seems to be one of the main constraints to meet the growing demand. The government is trying its best to tap various sources of funding for its higher education sector and foreign assistance is one of the important sources of funding to add/supplement to the government funding for higher education. In addition to augmenting the domestic resources, foreign aid would 'best be an interim contribution to meet the resource gap' in education (GoI, 1993).

FOREIGN AID FOR HIGHER EDUCATION IN INDIA

The public expenditure on education in India increased substantially over the years, but the share of higher education in GDP is extremely low (less than 1%). The higher education sector in India has received external funding from multilateral, bilateral and private non-profit sources since Independence. The list of countries and agencies providing foreign aid in detail is provided in Table 4A.1.

The foreign aid for higher education to India started in the early 1950s when India received international aid for food security under Peace Law 480 (PL 480) from the United States and was ultimately given this money as grant for higher education which was used to set up some of the IITs in India. External funding in the form of scholarships to the teachers and students of India is also provided by the developed countries such as the United States, United Kingdom, Germany, Soviet Union to cover the full or partial cost to pursue higher education in their countries. Several such scholarship schemes are available to Indian scholars from developed countries for higher education and research that are monitored by University Grants Commission (UGC) and also directly by some of the international organizations in India such as USIS and Ford Foundation.

Another form of external aid is the cultural exchange programmes under which Indian scholars visit some of the countries such as France, Canada, Germany and Soviet Union for short periods, mainly monitored by Indian Council of Social Science Research (ICSSR) and MHRD (GoI). These types of external funding do not yield any financial return to the donor country. It helps the recipients in gaining skills and advanced knowledge and in exchange of ideas in respect of sociocultural dimensions of both the countries.

During the 1960s and 1970s, a large part (about 80%) of the World Bank aid was given to secondary and higher education (World Bank, 1980). From 1980 onwards, the external funding for higher education started declining, mainly because in the early 1990s the priority of donors shifted from higher education to primary education after the World Conference on Education for All (EFA) in 1990 at Jomtien. In order to achieve EFA, India was hard-pressed to accept foreign aid for its primary education as large numbers of children (about 30–40 million) remained out of school. During this period with structural adjustment programme (SAP), the country was facing serious economic crisis to finance its education sector. For the first time, the World Bank and quite a good number of international aid-giving organizations entered into the primary education sector in India and many programmes to achieve the goal of EFA and Universal Elementary Education were undertaken. The first such programme was District Primary Education Programme and the ongoing programme is Sarva Shiksha Abhiyan (SSA) that is still ongoing successfully in the country. During this period, the government also reduced the budgetary support to higher education and introduced some of the policy reforms such as introduction of cost recovery mechanism, student loan and privatization of higher education. Afterwards, the aid for higher education started to take an upturn and again in 2007–2008, world economic crisis affected the aid of some of the donor countries.

India was not very receptive to aid for its higher education sector, largely due to (a) the conditionality put by the aid agencies from time to time and their intervention; (b) most of the aid was in the form of concessional loans which increases financial burden on the country; (c) there was also a fear of losing the cultural traditions and (d) encroachment of its autonomy and brain drain and so on. The government also tried to raise its domestic resources not only by increasing the budgetary resources but also through the introduction of taxes in the form of education cess of 2 per cent and 1 per cent respectively to finance the basic and secondary/higher education.

India is also a donor and provides funds to scholars of other developing countries under Colombo Plan for higher education and research since long. In recent years, Indian aid has not only increased in its volume but also expanded in its coverage. Indian aid mainly provides support to technical education, training, tertiary education and IT education. India's foreign aid was around $1.6 billion in 2015–2016 accounting for 0.2 per cent of its GDP (Varghese, 2016).

ANALYSIS OF TRENDS AND PATTERNS OF FOREIGN AID

Foreign Aid: The International Commitment

There is a long-standing target that aid of the donors needs to be 0.7 per cent of their GDP/gross national income (GNI) which was reaffirmed in Addis Ababa Conference on financing of development in 2015. Contrary to this, it is found that the total official development assistance (ODA) by all countries together constituted less than 0.5 per cent of their GNI (0.3%) in 2014 and it remained more or less constant over the years since 2002–2003. Only six countries have fulfilled the international commitment of aid as enlisted in Table 4.1.

Foreign Aid by Different Types of Countries

The main objective of developed countries giving aid to the low-income countries is to provide financial help, but in practice, only one-fifth of the aid goes to these categories of countries. The aid for each category of country has declined The distribution of aid shows that the allocation of aid is distorted as more than 50 per cent of the total aid goes to middle-income countries. This type of trend, if continues,

Table 4.1 *List of Donor Countries Aid ≥ 0.7% of Their GNI*

Countries	Aid as % of GNI			
	2002–2003	2013	2014	2015*
Denmark	0.9	0.85	0.86	0.85
Luxemburg	0.82	1	1.06	0.93
Netherlands	0.8	–	–	0.76
Norway	0.9	1.07	1	1.05
Sweden	0.82	1.01	1.09	1.4
United Arab Emirates*	–	1.34	1.26	1.09

Source: GEMR (2016).

Note: * Preliminary.

is likely to widen the gap between the developed and the less developed countries. The main reasons for the donors to reduce their aid to low–income countries are (a) lack of good policy for full utilization of the aid money, (b) low absorption capacity of the aid, (c) lack of leadership/governance for proper management of the aid and so on. Table 4.2 shows the aid by different category of countries.

Table 4.2 *Percentage Share of Aid in Total Aid by Different Category of Countries*

Country Category	% of Aid for Each Category of Country	
	2002–2003	2014
Total aid (both bilateral and multilateral)		
Low-income countries	25.6	21.5
Lower middle-income countries	37.3	35.7
Upper middle-income countries	19.5	14.5
High-income countries	1.1	0.5
Unallocated income countries	16.5	27.7

Source: GEMR (2016).

Foreign Aid in India

Share of Aid in GDP of India

The contribution of foreign aid can be examined through the ratio of external assistance to the GDP of India. The external assistance constitutes both grants and loans. In India, the grant component of external aid is constantly declining and the loan component is increasing over the years. The loan component is 90–95 per cent which implies that it would tend to increase the external debt burden of the country. This may be confirmed from the rapid increase in debt–service ratio which was just double in 2016 (8.8%) as compared to 2009 (4.4%). The repayment of principal with interest by the GoI began to exceed the value of new aid receipts 1997 onwards. The gap between the growth of GDP of India and total external assistance received is very high. During the period from 1991–1992 to 2016–2017, the annual compound growth rate of external assistance is 5.6 per cent per annum which is less than half of GDP growth during the same period (i.e., 12.7%). The relationship between external assistance and GDP shows that external assistance was only 1.7 per cent of GDP in 1991–1992 and it has declined to 0.3 per cent in recent years, and over the last five years it remained flat (0.3% of GDP). Figure 4.1 reflects the GDP and external assistance relationship. Table 4.3 presents the details of total external assistance to India.

1. Replace hyphen with en-dash.
2. Do not truncate the numbers, for example, instead of 2008–09 use 2008–2009.
3. Change '% of aid' to '% of Aid'.

It would be interesting to examine the statistical relationship between foreign aid and GDP. Table 4.4 contains the results of regression. The coefficient of external assistance has a positive and statistically significant effect on GDP. Since the coefficient is more than 1 and close to 2, it may be interpreted as elastic. In other words, it implies that GDP is quite responsive to changes in external assistance to India.

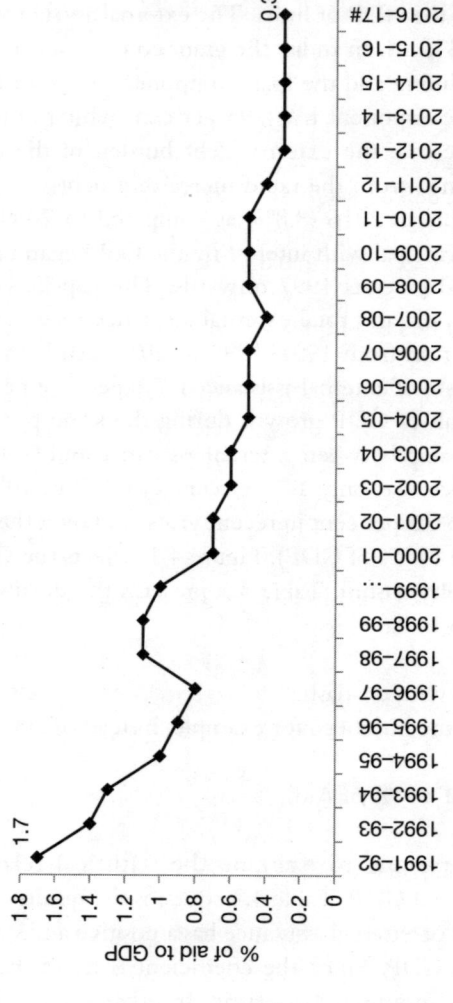

Figure 4.1 Percentage of External Aid to GDP in India

Source: GEMR (2016).

Table 4.3 *External Assistance from All Sources to India (₹ in Crores) at Current Prices*

Year	Loan	Grant	Total	Loan (%)	Grant (%)	External Assistance as % to GDP
1991–1992	10,695.9	919.1	11,615	92.1	7.9	1.7
1992–1993	10,102.2	879.6	10,981.8	92	8	1.4
1993–1994	10,895.4	885.6	11,781	92.5	7.5	1.3
1994–1995	9,964.5	916	10,880.5	91.6	8.4	1
1995–1996	9,958.6	1,063.6	11,022.2	90.4	9.6	0.9
1996–1997	10,892.9	1,085.6	11,978.5	90.9	9.1	0.8
1997–1998	10,823.4	921.3	11,744.7	92.2	7.8	1.1
1998–1999	12,343.4	895.5	13,238.9	93.2	6.8	1.1
1999–2000	13,330.7	1,073.9	14,404.6	92.5	7.5	1
2000–2001	13,527.2	727.2	14,254.4	94.9	5.1	0.7
2001–2002	16,111.7	1,447.6	17,559.3	91.8	8.2	0.7
2002–2003	13,898.3	1,835.8	15,734.1	88.3	11.7	0.6
2003–2004	15,271	2,073.4	17,344.4	88	12	0.6
2004–2005	14,660.9	2,490.7	17,151.6	85.5	14.5	0.5
2005–2006	16,097.8	2,790.6	18,888.4	85.2	14.8	0.5

(Continued)

Table 4.3 (Continued)

Year	Loan	Grant	Total	Loan (%)	Grant (%)	External Assistance as % to GDP
2006–2007	16,890.6	2,528.4	19,419	87	13	0.5
2007–2008	17,177.7	2,673.7	19,851.4	86.5	13.5	0.4
2008–2009	24,089.9	2,803.8	26,893.7	89.6	10.4	0.5
2009–2010	27,617.8	3,121.2	30,739	89.8	10.2	0.5
2010–2011	35,116.1	2,789.5	37,905.6	92.6	7.4	0.5
2011–2012	29,349.4	2,926.2	32,275.6	90.9	9.1	0.4
2012–2013	25,494.1	2,373.6	27,867.7	91.5	8.5	0.3
2013–2014	31,772.4	3,415.8	35,187.5	90.3	9.7	0.3
2014–2015	35,257.3	1,491.7	36,749	95.9	4.1	0.3
2015–2016	40,146.2	2,196.5	42,342.7	94.8	5.2	0.3
2016–2017*	47,313.1	985.2	48,298.3	98	2	0.3
Annual compound growth rate (%)			5.6			12.7

Source: GoI (2017, Table No. A128).
Note: *Provisional.

Total Aid and Per Capita Aid for India

Of the total aid (ODA) to different countries, India received only 4 per cent of the total aid in 2002–2003 and after more than a decade (2014), its aid receipts declined by 1 per cent (equal to 3%).

Table 4.4 *Regression Estimates of Relationship between Foreign Aid and GDP, 1991–2016*

Dependent Variable: Log(GDP)			
Explanatory variables	Coefficients	t values	Adj R-square
Constant	–2.009	–4.39	0.932
Log (external assistance)	1.984*	18.618	
F-ratio		346.62	
Durbin–Watson statistics		0.992	
N	26		

Source: Author.

Notes: The Breusch–Pagan/Cook–Weisberg test of heteroscedasticity confirms that there is no heteroscedasticity and D-W shows no auto correlation.

* Significant at 1 per cent level.

In respect of per capita aid, it is found that during the 1990s its aid receipts averaged only around $2 per person per year and in 2014 it slightly increased to $4 per person per year which is one-fifth less of the group of lower middle-income countries (average lower middle-income countries: $21). India's per capita aid is not only lower than lower middle-income countries but also lower than upper middle-income countries ($10) and high-income countries ($6) (Table 4.5). But it may be a matter of complacency that India's per capita aid was higher than China ($1 in 2014). The per capita aid for Brazil and South Africa in 2014 was $6 and $25, respectively, higher than India.

It is very clear from the foregoing discussion that with respect to the total aid, per capita aid and aid share in GDP, India may be considered as grossly under-aided. This was also observed by Colclough and De (2010).

Aid for Education/Higher Education

Aid for Education by Type of Countries and India

The percentage share of education aid in total aid has either remained constant or declined for all the types of countries during 2002–2003

Table 4.5 *Per Capita Aid (in US$) for Different Category of Countries and India*

Category of Countries	2002–2003	2014
Per capita aid in US$		
Low-income countries	48	59
Lower middle-income countries	13	21
Upper middle-income countries	8	10
High-income countries	8	6
Unallocated income countries	–	–
All countries total	17	28
Per capita aid of India in US$	3	4
India's share in total aid (%)	4.1	3

Source: GEMR (2016).

to 2014 except India. The decline in education aid is largely due to the change in priority of aid by the donor countries, more in favour of health and infrastructure than education as the share of health, since 2002, has risen from 15 per cent to 18 per cent and infrastructure from 24 per cent to 31 per cent (Education Commission, 2016, p. 110).

It is interesting to note that the share of aid for education in high–income countries is the highest among all categories of countries. It may be noted here that despite the higher level of educational development in these countries, the share of education aid in total ODA is very high. This shows the distortion in the allocation of aid for education. Table 4.6 presents the total aid and the share of education aid received by different category of countries.

Share of Aid for Higher Education by type of Countries and India

Not only the aid for education declined for all types of countries over the decade but also the share for higher education aid in total education

Table 4.6 *Percentage Share of Education Aid in Total Aid for Different Type of Countries and India*

Country Category/India	% of Education Aid in Total Aid	
	2002–2003	2014
Aid to education (% to total aid)		
Low-income countries	8	8
Lower middle-income countries	10	9
Upper middle-income countries	10	11
High-income countries	36	19
Unallocated income countries	5	4
All countries total	9	8
Aid for education in India	11	16

Source: GEMR (2016).

aid declined, with the exception of high-income countries. The aid distribution is supposed to be more in favour of low-income countries. In contrast to this, the aid for upper middle-income countries is found to be the highest and that for low-income countries, the lowest. It is very interesting to notice that the foreign aid for higher education for high-income countries increased from 16 per cent of the total aid for education in 2002–2003 to 29 per cent in 2014 (Table 4.7). This clearly indicates that more aid for higher education goes in favour of the countries which already have a developed higher education system. The aid for India is lower than the lower middle-income category of countries (India is included under this category) and it remained constant over the decade. This was also observed by Varghese (2010) as he stated that 'higher education aid either remains concentrated in selected countries with expanded higher education systems, or is fragmented and spread too thinly mostly in countries with less expanded higher education systems'. This pattern of aid distribution would increase the gap between the developed and less developed countries in the higher education system.

Table 4.7 *Percentage Share of Foreign Aid for Higher Education in Total Aid for Education by Different Category of Countries*

Category of Countries	2002–2003	2014
Low-income countries	20	15
Lower middle-income countries	40	27
Upper middle-income countries	68	58
High-income countries	16	29
Unallocated income countries	64	35
All countries total	44	32
India	19	19

Source: GEMR (2016).

Share of Foreign aid in Higher Education Expenditure in India

In India, the budget for education is so high that the proportion of foreign aid to expenditure on education in general and higher education in particular seems to be quite insufficient as well as inadequate. The proportion of education aid to expenditure on education was 4 per cent in 2002–2003 and it declined to 0.4 per cent in 2014 (Table 4.8).

The proportion of foreign aid for higher education to the total expenditure on higher education was 7.4 per cent in 2002–2003 and after more than a decade (2014), it has despondently declined to 0.5 per cent. This indicates that the external aid to education does not seem to supplement the domestic spending on education. The GoI has initiated an effort to raise its domestic resources for education to meet the vast requirement of resources of education in general and higher education in particular. The government had introduced education cess for higher education to be spent exclusively for education. In this background, the government would not like to withdraw from financing its education sector in general and higher education sector in particular. The reason behind this decline in aid for higher education needs to be empirically verified through the projects either completed or ongoing. International experiences also show that aid has not shown any significant effect in

Table 4.8 *Percentage Share of Education/Higher Education Aid in Total Expenditure on Education/Higher Education in India*

Year	% of Aid for Education to Total Expenditure on Education	% of Aid for Higher Education to Total Expenditure on Higher Education
2002–2003	3.7	7.4
2006	0.7	1.2
2007	1.0	0.6
2008	1.0	0.9
2009	1.2	1.1
2010	0.6	0.4
2011	0.6	0.4
2012	0.2	0.6
2013	0.2	0.4
2014	0.4	0.5

Source: Author.

Notes:
1. The aid values given in $ are converted into INR for respective years.
2. Both aid and expenditure are deflated at 2007 prices.

small countries of Africa and Latin America where the flow of foreign aid to education is very high.

INTRA-SECTORAL DISTRIBUTION OF AID FOR EDUCATION

Among the bilateral donors, Germany was the highest donor to education ($1,815 million) followed by France ($1,477 million) in 2014. The other important contributors to education include United States of America and United Kingdom. These four countries together contribute more than 60 per cent of the total bilateral aid to education. Similarly, The World Bank and European Union (EU) institutions contribute more than 70 per cent of the total multilateral aid to education.

Bilateral aid was influenced by historical and political circumstances. Multilateral aid is less likely to be politically driven and more likely to be channelled to the recipient countries on the basis of need than that of bilateral donors (Riddell, 2007).

While examining the relative priority accorded by each source of aid to different categories of education, it is found that bilateral donors give more priority to higher levels of education and multilateral donors give higher priority to basic and secondary levels of education. In 2002–2003, more than half (52%) of the aid was given to higher education by bilateral sources and it declined to 39 per cent in 2014. About 55 per cent of the multilateral aid was given to basic education and it declined by 18 per cent in 2014 but the share for secondary education increased in 2014. Basic and secondary education, together, get about 60 per cent of the total multilateral aid. Table 4.9 reflects the distribution of aid for different levels of education and by source.

Intra-sectoral Distribution of Aid for Education in India

Intra-sectoral distribution of aid for different years is presented in Table 4.10. There is a decline in aid for all levels of education except secondary level over the years. In 2002–2003, one-fifth of the total aid

Table 4.9 Aid from Bilateral and Multilateral Sources (%) by Levels of Education

	Bilateral		Multilateral	
Level of Education	2002–2003	2014	2002–2003	2014
Aid to basic education	21.9	24.3	54.8	36.9
Aid to secondary education	7.0	11.9	8.8	22.6
Aid to post-secondary education	52.3	38.7	12.1	14.7
Aid to education level unspecified	18.8	25.2	24.3	25.7
Total	100	100	100	100

Source: Calculated by the author using data from GEMR (2016).

Table 4.10 *Intra-sectoral Distribution of Foreign Aid in India (in %)*

Level of Education	2002–2003	2006	2007	2008	2009	2010	2011	2012	2013	2014
Basic	70	32	5	57	70	58	63	35	2	31
Secondary	4	3	76	14	5	9	6	6	59	44
Post-secondary	20	33	15	20	9	16	10	51	29	19
Level unspecified	6	32	4	9	16	17	20	9	10	5
Total	100	100	100	100	100	100	100	100	100	100

Source: The author.

Note: All years' data were converted into 2007 base in order to compare between different years.

was given to higher education and it declined by 1 per cent in 2014. There is no consistent pattern in the aid flow to education over the years. It is found that basic and secondary education together get the highest share of aid with the exception of the year 2012 when higher education got a greater share.

Intra-sectoral Aid for Education: India and China

It would be interesting to compare India and China in respect of their foreign aid to the education sector in general and higher education in particular (Table 4.11). The total aid to India rose dramatically between 2013 and 2014 and it was about five times more than that of China. The total aid to China during this period had declined, but the share of aid for education in the total aid for China is more than double that of India. Across different levels of education, India's share of aid to basic and secondary education together is the highest while China's share of aid for higher education is the highest. Interestingly, China's share for higher education is about five times more than that for India. This may be the reason for China producing highly-skilled and technical manpower with most advanced technological development by utilizing the aid money properly. From this finding, one may infer that more aid to higher education might have a significant effect on the technological development of the recipient country.

FOREIGN AID AND DEVELOPMENT OF HIGHER EDUCATION

Aid and Development of Higher Education by Type of Countries

It would be interesting to analyse the distribution of aid in different regions as per their development in higher education. The educational development is taken in terms of the GER (proxy for educational development). Table 4.12 shows that the GER is the highest in high-income countries but the share of aid for higher education is the lowest in these countries. The GER is the lowest in low-income category of countries and the share of aid in these countries is much higher than the high-income category of countries. It clearly shows that aid for higher education does not necessarily influence the access in terms of

Table 4.11 *Intra-sectoral Aid for Education in India and China (in 2014; US$ in Million)*

Aid to Education	India			China		
	2002–2003	2013	2014	2002–2003	2013	2014
Total aid	3,384	4,515	5,185	2,500	1,713	1,389
Aid to education	376	384	806	364	518	490
% Share of education aid to total aid	11	9	16	15	30	35
Direct aid to education	355	384	806	364	518	490
Direct aid to basic education	257	9	247	10	4	4
% Share of basic education	72.4	2.3	30.6	2.7	0.8	0.8
Direct aid to secondary education	13	227	356	20	21	35
% Share of secondary education	3.7	59.1	44.2	5.5	4.1	7.1
Direct aid to post-secondary education	66	111	157	320	443	416
% Share of post-secondary education	18.6	28.9	19.5	87.9	85.5	84.9
Aid to education level unspecified	19	37	44	13	51	35
% Share of education level unspecified	5.4	9.6	5.5	3.6	9.8	7.1

Source: GEMR (2016).

enrolment in higher education because the aid for higher education is mostly given in terms of scholarship, institution building, capacity building for skill enhancement and so on. The public expenditure per pupil for higher education in high-income countries is the highest while the same is the lowest in low-income countries. Hence, it is most likely that the domestic government expenditure on higher education influences the GER rather than aid per se for higher education.

Table 4.12 *Aid, Public Expenditure and GER in Higher Education by Different Categories of Countries*

Country Category	% of Aid for Higher Education to Total Aid for Education	Public Expenditure per Student for Higher Education (in Constant 2013 PPP$)	GER in Higher Education
Low income	9.6	1,615	8
Lower-middle income	36.2	–	22
Upper-middle income	36.5	–	41
High income	1.1	9,614	74
Unallocated income	16.6	–	–

Source: GEMR (2016).

Aid and Development of Higher Education in India

The share of aid for higher education in expenditure on higher education was 7.4 per cent in 2002–2003 and it declined constantly to 0.5 per cent in 2014. In view of the vast expenditure in higher education, the share of aid is too low to contribute to the higher education sector of India. The share of expenditure on higher education in total expenditure on education increased till 2008 and after that it declined and remained constant during recent years. The expenditure on higher education as percentage of GDP does not show any change over the period. The GER is increasing constantly during this period as it was 12 in 2002–2003 and became double (24.3) in 2014. This indicates that the GER does not seem to be influenced much by aid because despite the decline in foreign aid, there is an increase in the GER. It is again reaffirmed that the GER over the period is more likely to be influenced by domestic government expenditure than by aid for higher education. Table 4.13 presents the details of share of aid, expenditure and GDP in India.

Table 4.13 Percentage Share of Foreign Aid, Expenditure and GDP for Higher Education in India

Year	GER	% of Aid for Higher Education to Total Expenditure on Higher Education	% of Expenditure on Higher Education to Total Expenditure on Education	% of Higher Education Expenditure (Both General and Technical) to GDP
2002–2003	12.0	7.4	9.9	0.5
2006	12.4	1.2	19.3	1.1
2007	13.1	0.6	24.5	1.1
2008	13.8	0.9	24.3	1.2
2009	15.0	1.1	10.0	1.3
2010	19.4	0.4	21.3	1.3
2011	20.8	0.4	16.1	1.1
2012	21.1	0.6	17.0	1.2
2013	23.0	0.4	17.9	1.2
2014	24.3	0.5	16.2	1.2

Source: Estimated by the author using data from GEMR and Analysis of Budgeted Expenditure, GoI (various years).

Aid and Quality Improvement Initiatives in India

During the 1970s and 1980s, much of the education aid focused on improving school enrolment emphasizing on supply side policies such as the construction of school building and the provision of equipment (Coombs, 1985; Tilak, 1988). Aid for education can improve quality of education if it focuses on both supply side and demand side interventions (Masino & Niño-Zarazúa, 2016). Some of the quality improvement initiatives for higher education are ongoing in India with the assistance of external finance. Two such programmes are briefly discussed here.

Technical Education Quality Improvement Programme (TEQIP)

The attempt by World Bank is initiated through TEQIP in India to improve the quality of technical education in India (Box 4.1).

Box 4.1 *TEQIP: World Bank—GoI Initiative Focusing on Quality and Equity*

In pursuance of the National Policy on Education 1986 (revised in 1992) with a goal to upscale and improve the quality of technical education and enhance the existing capacities of the technical education system with special focus on quality, TEQIP was conceived in collaboration with World Bank. It was a long-term programme of 10–12 years in three phases to support excellence and transformation in technical education in the country and the first phase was launched in December 2002 by the MHRD. It became effective in March 2003 and was completed on 31st March 2009 with a total cost of ₹1,389 crore. The Phase 1 of TEQIP was implemented in 13 States and covered 127 institutions including 18 centrally-funded institutions. TEQIP Phase 2 was started as a centrally sponsored scheme (CSS with the assistance of the World Bank at a total cost of ₹2,430 crore for a duration of four years covering about 200 institutions based on competitive funding. The programme was implemented in 2010–2011 and supported more than 250 engineering institutes and thousands of faculty members and made a considerable impact on the quality of education by implementing institutional and policy reforms focusing on institutional autonomy and accountability. TEQIP Phase 3 was approved by The World Bank Board with financial assistance of US$ 201.50 million to enhance the quality and equity of engineering education across several focus states in India (World Bank, 2017).

UK-India Education and Research Initiative (UKIERI)

The improvement in quality of higher education is not concentrated to technical higher education but to general higher education and research, which is very poor in quality in India. For this, United Kingdom and GoI have taken the initiative under the programme

UKIERI, laying emphasis on improvement of the quality of research. A brief description is given in Box 4.2.

Box 4.2 *UKIERI: UK-INDIA Research Initiative*

The Newton Fund in India known as Newton-Bhabha Fund was initially launched in 2014 as a £375million fund over five years and was subsequently extended and expanded to a £735 million fund until 2021, with matched resources from the partner countries. Under this, United Kingdom and India worked together to build a capacity of researcher capacity, develop new research collaborations and translate this knowledge into tangible benefits.

This programme builds its foundations laid by UKIERI. It was launched in April 2006 to enhance educational links between India and the UK, with the potential to deliver substantial, long-term prosperity benefits for both countries. UKIERI seeks to strengthen relations between the two countries and has successfully facilitated over 1,000 UK–India partnerships in education and research so far in the first two phases. UKIERI Phase 3 (2016–2021) was launched in April 2016 and will work on the key priorities as identified by the two governments. The overarching aim for UKIERI Phase 3 is to build on the achievements of the previous two phases through a focused and targeted approach in order to maximize its impact. UKIERI Phase 3 is looking forward to scale up research, collaborate on key research themes and create a second tier of researchers to take it forward.

EFFECTIVENESS AND SUSTAINABILITY OF AID

Effectiveness of Foreign Aid

The significant and positive effects of aid depend on the composition of aid (Asiedu & Nandwa, 2007; Mavrotas, 2002), marginal reforms in the aid mechanism, level of development of the countries, better policy regimes (Collier & Dollar, 2004) and aid absorption capacity (Lewis, 2009) of the developing countries. Varghese (2010) suggested that the effect of aid on higher education is positive if efforts are made to revitalize both institutions and the higher education system strategically by making the aid more flexible. Burnside and Dollar (2000) claim that aid might work but only under favourable political and institutional conditions in the recipient country. Actually, the contribution of aid and its effectiveness can be verified with some empirical evidence and there has been surprisingly little empirical work on various facets of aid (Krueger, 1986).

The aid is effective if there is no fungibility of aid money. For instance, if the aid money meant for education is diverted to other sectors, this may create the fungibility of education aid. This is one of the constraints of aid effectiveness in less developing countries. In order to avoid this, the recipient country needs to focus on the outcome of education aid and the government should neither shift nor reduce its budgetary support for education. The effectiveness of aid depends on better service delivery at the institutional level. It is possible if the recipient country as well as the donor country have good governance and a favourable policy regime. The aid is more effective if it is need-based, and the flow of aid needs to be channelled to regions which are least exposed to higher education. But the present analysis shows that aid is given to the regions which are already having a well-developed system of higher education.

It is difficult to assess the effectiveness of aid for education. Projects such as roads, buildings and borewells can be easily assessed as they have a definite budget and visible outcomes at the end. But in the case of education, the gestation period is too long to assess the immediate or short-term impact of aid on educational outcome, specifically on quality improvements. Most of the donors concentrate on the short-term impact of aid, undermining its long-term impact. If some baseline survey is conducted before the aid disbursement of a particular project, at the end it may be possible to assess some impact of aid in terms of its effectiveness.

Sustainability of Foreign Aid

Sustainability is related to the continuation of a project once the support of the donors is discontinued. In the context of India, a question may be raised: Is there any policy and legislation in place which are judged to be able to guarantee the continuation of the particular aided project when the support of the donor countries has been phased out? Is it possible to continue the project with domestic resources without aid money?

As discussed earlier, most of the donors are not only behind their target of 0.7 per cent of GNI but also cut their budgets of aid which may be a threat to sustainability of aid. For instance, recently United Kingdom has made a major cut in their budgets for police, health, higher education, welfare, social housing and local government sectors. Most often there is also delay in release of aid fund and the released amount is less than the committed amount which is one of the barriers to operating a project in time. All these are likely to raise doubts about the sustainability of aid. In fact, the sustainability of a particular project can be judged with some empirical evidence in terms of long-term effects of aid of a particular project. The policy for making the aid sustainable requires reform in the policy, but reform in any policy in India takes a long time. In view of this, sustainability of aid for higher education seems to be a distant dream.

CONCLUDING OBSERVATIONS

Not only has the aid in general declined but also the target of donating 0.7 per cent of their gross national product is yet to be fulfilled by all the donors as only six countries have reached this target. India is considered as grossly under-aided, as total external assistance to India as proportion of GDP is not only negligible (0.3%) but also declining constantly over time. The loan component of aid is more than the grant component and is increasing over the years. The per capita aid for India is much less than the lower middle-, upper middle- and even the high-income countries. The proportion of aid is supposed to be more for low-income countries but in practice more aid is flowing to the middle-income countries. The share of aid for education in high-income countries is the highest despite the higher level of educational development in these countries resulting in distortion in the allocation of aid for education. The percentage of total aid for education to public expenditure on education declined from 3.4 per cent in 2002–2003 to

0.4 per cent in 2014. The share of aid for higher education in the total expenditure on higher education has also declined constantly and it is too negligible to add or supplement the budget of higher education. Intra-sectoral distribution of aid shows that the aid share to higher education as compared to other levels over the years has declined. It is observed from the analysis that it is not higher aid per se but the domestic government expenditure for higher education that has a positive effect on higher GER. The effectiveness and sustainability of aid is found to be inconclusive as more exhaustive analysis with detailed time series data on aid and educational outcome is necessary to arrive at any conclusion which is lacking in the papers.

To conclude, however, researchers of education are of the opinion that it is difficult to assess the contribution of aid to education as not only are the problems of education multifaceted, and many times invisible, but also the gestation period of education is long to feel the immediate effect of aid. The distribution of aid needs to be in favour of the countries with low level of higher educational development. Moreover, the impact of aid on education is significant when it is channelled through the framework of budget and expenditure and part of national policies. The aid needs to concentrate on both the supply side and demand side interventions to achieve balanced development in higher education. The grant component of aid should be more than the loans. The government should raise more resources from its own sources in order to make the education project sustain after the aid money is phased out. The aid may be more effective if the objectives of aid are in unison with the policies of the recipient country.

APPENDIX

Table 4A.1 Sources and Types of Foreign Aid for Higher Education

Sources (Grant and Loan)		
Bilateral	Multilateral	Private Non-Profit Sector
Australia	African Development Bank	Charitable Foundations
Austria	African Development Fund	Voluntary organisations
Belgium	Arab Fund for Economic and Social development	Ford Foundation
Canada	Asian Development Bank Special funds	Rock Feller Foundation
Czech Republic*	Asian Development Fund**	and such other organisations
Denmark	BADEA (The Arab Bank for Economic Development in Africa)	
Finland	Climate Investment Funds (CIF)	
France	EU Institutions	
Germany	World Bank (IDA)	
Greece	Inter-American Development	
Iceland*	Bank Special Fund	
Ireland	International Monetary Fund	
Italy	(Concessional Trust Funds)	
Japan	OPEC Fund for International	
Kuwait*	Development	
Luxembourg	UNDP	
Netherlands	UNICEF	
New Zealand	UN Peacebuilding Fund	
Norway	UN Relief and Works Agency	
Poland*	for Palestine Refugees	

(Continued)

Table 4A.1 (Continued)

| | Sources (Grant and Loan) | |
Bilateral	Multilateral	Private Non-Profit Sector
Portugal	World Food Programme	
Republic of Koreay		
Slovak Republic*		
Slovenia*		
Spain		
Sweden		
Switzerland		
United Arab Emirates		
United Kingdom		
United States		
Estonia		
Hungary		
Kazakhstan		
Lithuania		
Romania		

Source: The author.

Note: *Preliminary.

REFERENCES

Asiedu, E., & Nandwa, B. (2007). On the impact of foreign aid in education on growth: How relevant is the heterogeneity of aid flows and the heterogeneity of aid recipients? *Review of World Economics*, *143*(4), 631–649.

Burnside, C., & Dollar, D. (2000). Aid, policies, and growth. *American Economic Review*, *90*(4), 847–868.

Colclough, C., & De, A. (2010). *The impact of aid on education policy in India* (RECOUP Working Paper No. 27). Cambridge: University of Cambridge.

Collier, P., & Dollar, D. (2004). Development effectiveness: What have we learnt? *Economic Journal, 114*(496), F244–F271.

Coombs, P. H. (1985). *The world crisis in education: The view from the eighties.* Oxford: Oxford University Press.

Education Commission. (2016). *The learning generation: Investing in education for a changing world* (A report by International Commission on Financing Global Education Opportunity). Retrieved from http://report.educationcommission.org/

FICCI. (2013). *Higher education in India: Vision 2030* (FICCI Higher Education Summit). New Delhi: FICCI.

GEMR. (2016). *National launch of 2016 global education monitoring report.* Paris: UNESCO.

GoI. (2017). *Economic survey (2016–2017).* New Delhi: Planning Commission.

———. (1993). *Education for All: The Indian scene.* New Delhi: Ministry of Human Resource Development.

Krueger, A. O. (1986). Aid in development process. *The World Bank Research Observer, 1*(1), 57–58.

Lewis, S. (2009, March 11). Funding for higher education: Facts and figures. *Science and Development Network.* Retrieved from https://www.scidev.net/global/migration/feature/funding-for-higher-education-facts-and-figures.html

Masino, S., & Niño-Zarazúa, M. (2016). What works to improve the quality of student learning in developing countries? *International Journal of Educational Development, 48,* 53–65.

Mavrotas, G. (2002). Aid and growth in India: Some evidence from disaggregated aid data. *South Asian Economic Journal, 3*(1), 19–48.

Punnayya, K. (1993). *Report of Justice Dr K. Punnayya Committee on UGC funding of institutions of higher education.* New Delhi: UGC.

Riddell, R. (2007). *Does foreign aid really work?* Oxford: Oxford University Press.

Schultz, T. W. (1961). Investment in human capital. *American Economic Review, 51*(1), 1–15.

Subramanian, T. S. R. (2016, May 7). *Report of the committee for evolution of the new education policy (NEP)* (Submitted its report to MHRD). New Delhi: GoI.

Tilak, J. B. G. (1988). Foreign aid for education. *International Review of Education, 34*(3), 313–335.

———. (2003). Higher education and development in Asia. *Journal of Educational Planning and Administration, 17*(2), 151–174.

Varghese, N. V. (2010). Higher education aid: Setting priorities and improving effectiveness. *Journal of International Cooperation in Education, 13*(2), 173–187.

———. (2016, December). The SDG for India and for Indian aid to tertiary education and training overseas? *Norrag News 54.*

World Bank. (1980). *World development report.* New York, NY: Oxford University Press.

———. (2017). *World development indicators.* Washington, DC: The World Bank.

Chapter 5

Gender Budgeting in Higher Education

Mona Khare

INTRODUCTION

Right to education (RTE) is a basic human right. Efforts by international agencies and national governments have contributed to the progress towards improving educational opportunities. Gender equality is one of the core elements and commitments outlined in all global and national efforts. The recently formulated sustainable development goals (SDGs) also reinforce the importance of gender equality.

Data suggest that despite several efforts, a large number of girls are still unable to enrol and/or complete schooling, the gross enrolment ratio (GER) of girls is dropping down sharply from primary through secondary to tertiary education. The 10 year review of the implementation of the Beijing Platform for Action pointed that out of the 104 million children of school going age who are out of school, 75 per cent are in Africa and 57 per cent are girls. Not very long ago, UN had proclaimed that after poverty, gender is the most influential factor to keep people out of reach with regard to education (United Nations,

2013). Gender inequalities in the education sector are concentrated in more vulnerable communities, being significantly higher in urban slums, rural areas, in poverty-stricken communities, among excluded groups (castes, ethnic and linguistic minorities, and the disabled), in conflict and fragile regions.

Although, it is reported that women enrolments are rising fast and the gender gaps are narrowing down but women participation continues to be lower in science and technology, and high status disciplines, in prestigious institutions globally as well as in India (Bebbington, 2002; Becher, 2006; Beede et al., 2011; Chanana, 2012; Dyhouse, 2003; Equality Challenge Unit, 2011; MHRD, 2015–2016; Morley, 2006; Morley & Lugg, 2009; UNESCO, 2010). Women are concentrated in subject areas associated with low-wage sectors of the economy (World Bank, 2002). There are disparities in mathematics and language learning, gendered curricula and subject choices (EIU, 2014; Morley, 2006, 2012; Ramachandran, 2010), gender insensitive pedagogy (Welch, 2006). Moving forward from the students to the domain of staff and faculty, studies point at under-representation of women in positions of power and decision-making, opportunities of work and career progression (British Council, 2015; Chanana, 2013; Khare, 2016; Knight & Richards, 2003; Morley, 2013; Pritchard, 2010) as well as wages (Kingdon, 2007). Also, opportunities and freedoms gained through education remain unequally distributed. Despite gravity of such a sensitive issue of promoting gender balance in higher education (HE), countries are not likely to invest much in tackling it. A recent British Council report (2015) points at deficient supply of good initiatives to promote GB in HE and the problem of sustainable funding in cases where they do exist.

The Commission of the Status of Women (CSW) reports to the UN Secretary General and the agreed recommendations of the 55th session of the CSW in 2011 reiterated this concern by urging countries to adopt gender-responsive budgeting/gender budgeting (GB) to ensure that public resources in education, science, technology, research and development (R&D) benefit women and men equally, and contribute to the empowerment of women. Thus, both resource allocation and utilization become extremely important for gender mainstreaming (GM) in HE. As a result, gender analysis of public budgets is emerging as an important tool for determining the differential impact of expenditures on women and men to help ensure the equitable use of existing resources.

This chapter tries to explore the policies and practices in Gender Responsive Budgeting (GRB) for HE in India. The first section deals with the conceptual aspects of GB as a tool for GM and provides a description of the evolution and progress of GB in India followed by an analysis of GB in HE sector in India in the past 10 years, thereby emphasizing the rationale and need for GB in Indian HE. Next section attempts at a spatial mapping of Indian states for taking the exercise forward in India followed by the conclusion.

GB AS A CONCEPT: WHAT ARE GENDER RESPONSIVE BUDGETS

A gender responsive budget is a budget that acknowledges the gender patterns in society and allocates money to implement policies and programmes that will change these patterns in a way that moves towards a more gender equal society. Gender Budget initiatives are known by a range of different names. They have, for example, also been referred to as 'women's budgets, 'gender-sensitive budgets', and applied gender budget analysis. (Ministry of Women and Child Development, 2015)

The need for GB arises from the very fact that budgets don't impact men and women alike. Given the differences in needs, GB is a more complex process to look at every part of the government budget and assess how it will address the different needs of male and female. It is not about simply dividing government money 50–50 between men and women or boys and girls. The overall aim is to ensure that every part of the government budget takes gender differences into account. GB is, therefore, a rather technical exercise as will become more evident from the five step framework (Box 5.1).

Box 5.1 *The Five Step Framework for GB*

Step 1: Situational Analysis: An analysis of the situation for women and men, and girls and boys (and the different subgroups) in a given sector.

Step 2: Gendered Policy Analysis: An assessment of the extent to which the sector's policy addresses the gender issues and gaps described in the first step. This step should include an assessment of the relevant legislation policies, programmes and schemes. It includes an analysis of both the written policy and the implicit policy reflected in government activities. It should examine the extent to which the above meets the socio-economic and other rights of women.

Step 3: Gendered Budgetary Analysis: An assessment of the adequacy of budget allocations to implement the gender-sensitive policies and programmes identified in Step 2 above.

Step 4: Assessment and Monitoring: Monitoring whether the money was spent as planned. What was delivered and to whom. This involves checking both financial performance and the physical deliverables (disaggregated by sex).

Step 5: Outcome analysis: An assessment of the impact of the policy/programme/scheme and the extent to which the situation described in Step 1 has been changed in the direction of greater gender equality.

(GB rather ideally should happen at all five steps)

Source: Budlender, Elson, Hewitt. & Mukhopadhyay (2002); Sharp (2003); UNIFEM–UNFPA (2018).

EFFICACY OF EDUCATION GB (EGB)

Theoretically, EGB is an approach designed to mainstream the education-related gender dimensions into all stages of the budget cycle from planning to execution to review. It has a three-pronged objective.

Adequacy objective: It is not necessarily about whether an equal amount is spent on women and men but whether the spending is adequate to women and men (pupils and teachers), needed in education.

Responsive objective: Assesses the extent to which the national education budget responds to the needs of boys, girls, men and women, female and male (pupils and teachers) at all levels of the education system.

Impact objective: Consider the impact of any form of public expenditure or method of raising revenues on women and girls, as compared to men and boys; whether it reduces disparities, increases disparities, promotes discrimination and so on?

EVOLUTION OF GB IN INDIAN PLANS

Gender perspective on public expenditure made inroads in India as early as 1974 with the publication of the report of the committee on the status of women. The Sixth Five-Year Plan focused on health, education and employment of women and the following Seventh Plan initiated the monitoring of 27 beneficiary-oriented schemes to establish the impact of these schemes on women. The Eighth Plan (1992–1997) emphasized that 'special programmes on women should complement the general development programmes' in order to ensure a definite flow of funds to women. The Ninth Five-Year Plan (1997–2002) adopted Women Component Plan as one of its major strategies. Directions were given to both central and state governments to ensure a minimum of 30 per cent of the funds/benefits to be earmarked in all the women's related sectors and be especially vigilant in monitoring them.

The National Policy for the Empowerment of Women was adopted by the Ministry of Women and Child Development (WCD) in 2001. A subgroup on GB by the Ministry of Finance in India was formed in 2003 to develop an institutional framework and matrix to capture financial data of budgetary allocations from the gender perspective. The tenth plan (2002–2007) considered component plan and GB as complementary tools. In the budget speech 2005–2006 (Para-25), the finance minister for the first time introduced a gender budget statement (GBS) with growing concern to provide money specifically for women and announced that 'in course of time, all Departments will be required to present gender budgets as well as make benefit incidence analyses'.

Every year the ministries/departments are requested through the Annual Budget Circular to highlight the quantum of public expenditure earmarked in the budget for women. The eleventh plan (2007–2012) added gender outcome assessment to GB across board, initiating creation of separate GB cells in all ministries and departments to undertake the task of collating relevant data on a regular basis for more evidence-based budgeting and greater transparency by making it available in the public domain. The Twelfth Plan noted, that 'Mainstreaming gender through Gender Budgeting' is imperative for furthering gender equity and hence its reach needs to be extended to all ministries, departments and state governments.

STRUCTURE AND INSTITUTIONAL MECHANISM

The structure of GB in India borrows from Rhonda Sharp's three-way categorization of expenditure (Sharp, 2003): (a) gender-targeted expenditure; gender-specific expenditure targeting women and girls (e.g., women's literacy projects, women scholarships), (b) equal opportunity expenditure; expenditures promoting equal opportunities in the public sector (e.g., evaluation of job descriptions to promote equitable hiring of faculty) and (c) mainstream expenditure (the rest); budget expenditures not included under the two previous points.

The GBS in India, however, categorizes it only in two parts and has a purely quantitative format where allocations are disaggregated by sex to be reported in the GBS. Part A details schemes in which 100 per cent allocations are for women and Part B reflects schemes where allocations for women constitute at least 30 per cent of the provisions.

The institutional mechanism comprises of GB cells in the ministries/departments which are envisaged as focal points with the Ministry of WCD as the nodal agency for supporting the process of GRB. The Ministry of WCD has taken several initiatives and even facilitated for engendering the schemes and programmes for better planning and resource prioritization. Over the years, several states too have introduced GB with considerable success (Table 5.1) although many still remain to do so.

Table 5.1 GB in the States—Year of Adoption

Early Adopters	Subsequent Adopters	Recent Adopters
Odisha 2004–2005	Madhya Pradesh 2007–2008	Andaman and Nicobar Islands
Tripura 2005–2006	J&K 2007–2008	(November 2012)
Uttar Pradesh 2005	Arunachal Pradesh 2007–2008	Rajasthan (August 2011)
Karnataka 2006–2007	Chhattisgarh 2007–2008	Maharashtra (January 2013)
Gujarat 2006	Uttarakhand 2007–2008	Dadra Nagar Haveli 2011–2012
	Himachal Pradesh 2008	
	Bihar 2008–2009	
	Kerala 2008–2009	
	Nagaland 2009	

Source: Ministry of Women and Child Development (2015).

States such as Karnataka, Kerala, Gujarat, Rajasthan, Madhya Pradesh, Chhattisgarh and so on have taken significant steps such as identification of a nodal department for GB, constitution of GB cells, formulation of a state policy for gender, setting up committees for over sight, creating a gender data bank, making checklists, including a gender statement in the state budget, capacity building, preparation of a brochure and handbook and conducting performance audit and linkages with the Results Framework Document (RFD) in order to institutionalize GB by using a range of mechanisms.

PROGRESS OF GB IN INDIA

As a result of such concerted and continuous efforts, the number of ministries reflecting such allocation has increased over the years as is evident from Table 5.2.

While the number of ministries adopting GB has grown consistently from 9 to 35 in the past 10 years and the number of demands too has

Table 5.2 *Gender Budget of Ministries/Departments at a Glance*

Year	No. of Ministries/ Departments (No. of Demands)	Total Magnitude of Gender Budget (BE) (in crores)	Percentage of Gender Budget to Total Budget
2005–2006	9(10)	14,378.68	2.79
2006–2007	18(24)	28,736.53	5.09
2007–2008	27(33)	31,177.96	4.50
2008–2009	27(33)	27,661.67	3.68
2009–2010	28(33)	56,857.61	5.57
2010–2011	28(33)	67,749.80	6.11
2011–2012	29(34)	78,251.02	6.22
2012–2013	29(34)	88,142.80	5.91
2013–2014	30(35)	97,133.70	5.83
2014–2015	36(39)	98,029.84	5.46
2015–2016	35(35)	79,257.87	4.46

Source: Expenditure Budget Vol. I (various years).

risen almost at the same rate, the magnitude of gender budget as percentage to total budget started declining from the year 2011–2012 such that even the absolute budget declined in the year 2015–2016. Does this in any way mean that the need for specific allocations to improve gender gaps no longer exists? It is a question that needs greater probe and shall be attempted little later in the chapter.

GB IN EDUCATION: AN ANALYSIS OF UNION BUDGETS

Although GB in education started in the year 2004–2005, GB cell, department of higher education was set up only in 2012 in the Ministry of Human Resource Development (MHRD). While an inter-sectoral comparison of GB in India reveals that the overall share of GB in education sector budget is much more than that of the share of consolidated GB in total Union Budget, this too has witnessed a drop in recent years. While the education sector gender budget is more than one-third of the total education budget (Table 5.3), the percentage of GB to total budget has hovered around 5 per cent since the last decade (Table 5.1). But, the share of GB on both fronts has declined and forces one to ask questions.

Sub-sectoral Shares of GB in Education

GB in education that grew sharply between 2008–2009 and 2013–2014 has witnessed a drop thereafter (Figure 5.1) including that in school education. But the amount in absolute terms has grown for HE sector since 2011–2012.

However, it is the school education and literacy that has a reasonably high share of gender component, this percentage being more than 40 per cent always (Table 5.4). While the percentage share of gender budget in HE is not even a double digit (Table 5.5), although the

Table 5.3 Percentage of Gender Budget on Education by Total Expenditure on Education (in Crore)

S. No.	Year	Total Gender Budget on Education	Total Expenditure on Education	% (2 in 3)
	1	2	3	4
1	2005–2006	7,227.31	17,823.16	40.55
2	2006–2007	9,272.62	23,873.47	38.84
3	2007–2008	2,822.49	26,769.75	10.54
4	2008–2009	3,948.25	34,435.67	11.47
5	2009–2010	14,374.48	39,941.69	35.99
6	2010–2011	17,796.41	51,905.38	34.29
7	2011–2012	24,048.6	60,260.80	39.91
8	2012–2013 (RE)	28,675.82	66,818.97	42.92
9	2013–2014 (BE)	30,113.84	78,701.04	38.26

Source: Planning Commission (2005–2006 to 2013–2014).

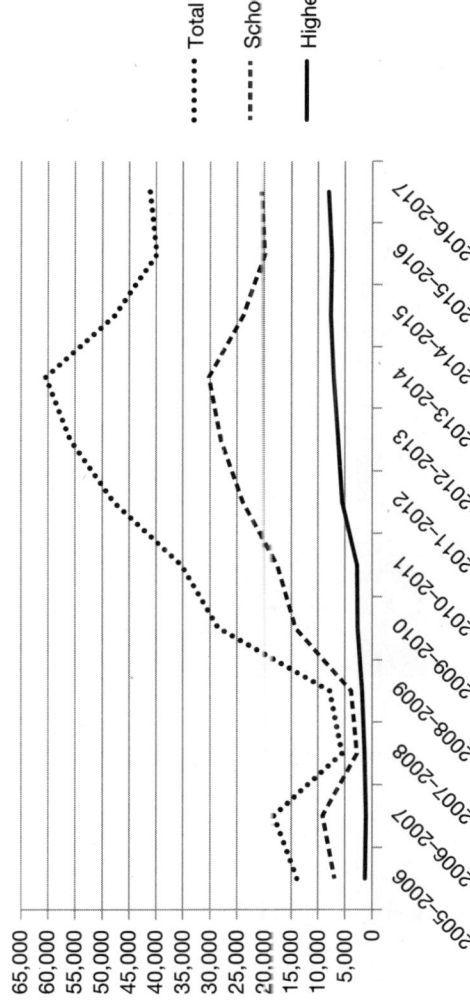

Figure 5.1 *Gender Budget in Education in Crores*

Source: Gender Budget and Analysis of Budgeted Expenditure on Education (Various years).

Table 5.4 Percentage of Gender Budget into Education Expenditure (Sub-sectoral Levels)

Year	2005–2006	2006–2007	2007–2008	2008–2009	2009–2010	2010–2011	2011–2012	2012–2013 (RE)	2013–2014 (BE)
School and literacy	42.18	42.63	6.99	8.89	45.13	41.1	45.71	48.06	44.38
Higher education	7.13	4.84	5.12	5.4	6.68	5.45	9.28	9.46	9.08

Source: Gender Budget and Analysis of Budget Expenditure on Education (various year).

Table 5.5 Gender Budget by Category—School Education and HE

Year	Total Education Gender Budget		School Education Gender Budget		Higher Education Gender Budget	
	Category A (%)	Category B (%)	Category A (%)	Category B (%)	Category A (%)	Category B (%)
2005–2006	3.62	96.38	4.29	95.71	0.05	99.50
2006–2007	1.77	98.23	1.95	98.05	0.55	99.45
2007–2008	1.20	98.80	2.34	97.66	0.00	100.00
2008–2009	0.96	99.04	1.82	98.18	0.00	100.00
2009–2010	0.96	99.04	0.33	99.67	3.62	96.38
2010–2011	0.93	99.07	0.31	99.69	4.07	95.93
2011–2012	1.93	98.07	1.87	98.13	2.12	97.88
2012–2013	2.48	97.52	2.74	97.26	1.56	98.44
2013–2014	1.98	98.02	2.57	97.43	0.00	100.00

Source: Expenditure Budget Vol. 1, Statement-20 (various years).

Note: The 00.00 per cent figures as reflected in the table are likely to be erroneous data reporting an anomaly often found in the records.

gender disparities are more pronounced in this sector. The increase in the share of EGB for HE in recent years may be considered as a realization to this need. In the year 2014–2015, school education had a total of 22 schemes under GB and HE had been provided for 23 line items under GB. In 2015–2016, 24 schemes amounting to ₹7,446.34 crore have been reflected in Part B of the HE GBS while the spending of union government on girls' school education has declined by 8.36 per cent.

The interesting point here is that the decline was mainly witnessed in the major flagship programmes, namely, Sarva Shiksha Abhiyan (SSA), Rashtriya Madhyamik Shiksha Abhiyan and National Programme of Nutritional Support to Primary Education (midday meal scheme). For instance, the spending on SSA declined around 9 per cent during 2014–2015 and 2015–2016.

Contrarily to school education, the spending on HE for girls has increased from the year 2014–2015 to 2016–2017. In this period, the sanction to UGC has increased from ₹2,959.61 crores to ₹3,113.54 crores. It can thus be seen that the gender component of budget has been increasing at the HE level in the past few years vis-à-vis school education although it is the latter that still gets a greater share of EGB (Figure 5.2). The increasing share of higher education in EGB is reflective of the government's rising attention towards its policy of inclusive education by promoting girls participation in HE.

Ironically, today, there are a large number of schemes and scholarships that have been earmarked for women in both school and HE sector but the special focus on gender equity is more clearly reflected in the programmes for education of girls at elementary level and to some extent at secondary levels, but it is rather vague at HE level. At the school level, there are specific schemes that aim to reduce gender gap, increase access through girls' hostels, provide life skill education and additional incentive of school uniforms (National Programme for Education of Girls at Elementary Level). Schemes like Kasturba Gandhi Balika Vidyalayas are residential schools which cover hard-to-reach girls, especially the deprived ones belonging to the SC, ST, OBC community and minority groups. At the HE level, although

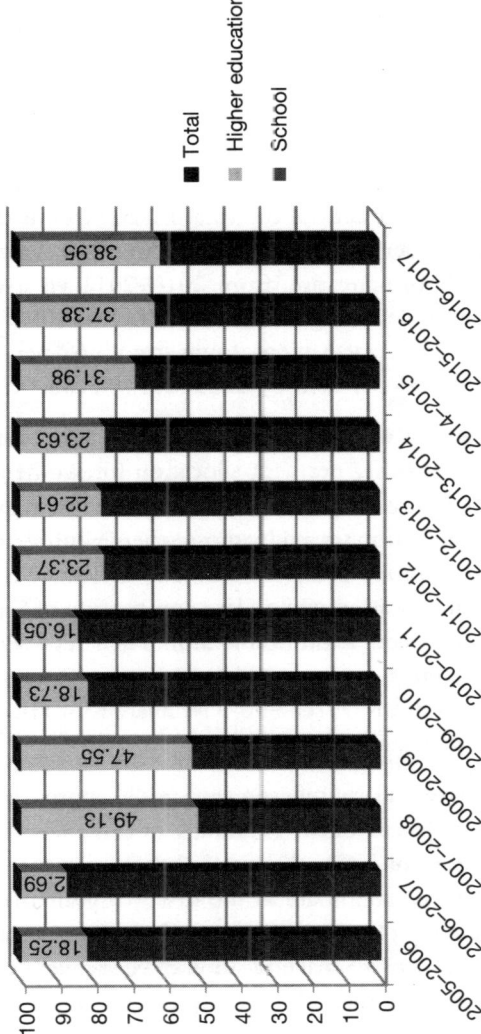

Figure 5.2 *Proportion of Gender Budget on Education by Level (%)*

Source: Expenditure Budget Vol. 1, Statement-20 (various years).

the GB is increasing, there is lack of clarity on the interventions other than the scholarship for college and university students that rose from ₹110 crores to ₹135 crores. A list of all schemes meant for girls under Category A (100% funding for women) as well as Category B (30% of funding meant for women in both school and HE sector) are placed as appendix to support the above statement.

A break-up of category-wise EGB also reveals that commitment towards 100 per cent women EB is declining. As is clear from Table 5.5, it is Category B (at least 30% allocation for women) that comprises more than 95 per cent of the total EGB. Same is true for both school and HE gender budget. A marginal increase can be seen in Category A for school education from 2010–2011 vis-à-vis HE where it is continuously declining. In fact, the share of 100 per cent women's schemes in Category A went down from 3.62 per cent in 2005–2006 to a mere 1.98 per cent by 2013–2014 (Table 5.5).

Most of the Category B expenditure in the EGB does not categorically ensure a minimum of 30 per cent allocation for women but is just assumed to be so. Many a times, women do not even comprise 30 per cent of the total population served by those schemes/programmes/ courses. For example, women comprise only 27 per cent of the total enrolment in technical education while a large proportion of Category B EGB goes to technical education (Table 5.6). Their representation in the elite IITs is a mere 8 per cent and even these institutes figure in the Category B allocations. A scheme-wise analysis of HE gender budget further substantiates the above observation.

The first two columns clearly reflect a shift in the approach to GB in HE in the very first decade of the beginning of this exercise at the national level. The share of UGC that caters largely to general education had a very high average share in the first five years that went down drastically in the next five years by more than 40 per cent while that of the technical and professional education category went up from not even 2 per cent to more than 40 per cent. Recent years continue to reflect this changing trend. Ironically, much of this allocation is for setting up of new IITs, IIMs or other technical institutes and their upgradation, which does not justify to be counted under Category B

Table 5.6 *Gender Budget in HE—Scheme-Wise (% Share)*

Category A 100%	2005–2010 (Average)	2010–2015 (Average)	2015–2016	2016–2017
1 Access and equity	0.21	0.00	0.00	0.00
2 Women's hostel in polytechnics	0.75	1.60	0.00	0.00
Category B (30%)				
1 UGC	85.43	53.95	41.81	39.13
2 Distance education and ICT	2.05	2.94	1.31	1.13
3 Polytechnics	2.78	4.05	0.00	0.00
4 Language and promotion	1.22	1.31	0.00	1.25
5 Technical and professional	1.50	30.24	39.48	43.77
6 Loans and fund	0.00	3.18	8.58	7.30
7 Scholarship for college and university students	0.41	1.95	1.81	1.68
8 RUSA and consortium for higher education electronic resources	0.00	1.91	5.56	5.74
9 Total HE GB	100.00	100.00	100.00	100.00

Source: Gender Budget in India Statement-20 (various years).

Note: Description to each item mentioned in Table 5 6 is given in Appendix.

schemes where a minimum of 30 per cent is to be ensured for women/ girls if the proportion of girls enrolled in such institutions is much lesser. Yet another component that makes its presence visible in later years is loans and funds comprising of interest subsidy with little guarantee that at least 30 per cent of the allocation under this head is being utilized for girl's education. The interest subsidy gets covered by way of a concession that is provided to girl students and also to economically poor students through a central government subsidy scheme announced by the government in 2009–2010. This scheme allows for an interest subsidy on education loans to students from economically disadvantaged sections (family income less than INR 450,000 a year) pursuing technical or professional studies in India. It will be interesting to see what percentage of girl students from this category of population are taking benefit of this scheme for this allocation to qualify under Category B, as needless to say that their proportion in technical education is certainly not going to be more than the overall per cent of girls enrolment in such programmes. However, such an analysis is outside the purview of this chapter. But some indications of lesser participation of women in educational loan schemes and also there being higher percentage of female education loan defaulters can be found in other studies in India (Bandyopadhyay, 2016). Similar questions can be asked with respect to distance education and information and communication technology (ICT), polytechnic education and so on particularly when there is high focus on skill development and vocational education in recent years. Such a situation leaves one wondering if decline in allocations (now being reported as zero) for improving access and equity is justified or not? Also, if gender is to be understood in its right perspective and not as a synonym to women, should medical education also not find some place in gender budget in order to promote male participation? There, certainly is a case for redistribution of the gender budget earmarked under Category A for access and equity within the HE sector but completely doing away with it is not yet called for. However, given the fact that there are several purely women's schemes under implementation (Box 5.2), zero reporting under Category A in the past few years seems to be a reporting error unless the allocations for these schemes are merged in the UGC, technical education or scholarship heads under Category B allocations. Such anomalies call for serious corrections in the gender budget reporting as also the importance of increasing the share of 100 per cent women targeted schemes to improve participation of women in specific courses other than just scholarships or interest concession on loans. Such observations call for serious gap analysis in gender budget reporting as is evidenced by few

Box 5.2 *100% Women's Scheme*

> **UGC Schemes:**
> Swami Vivekananda Single Grl Child Scholarship for Research in Social Sciences.
>
> Post Graduate Indira Gandhi Scholarship for single girl child applicable to single girl child students up to the age of 30 years for non-professional courses only at postgraduate (PG) level.
>
> Post-Doctoral Fellowship to the unemployed women candidates holding PhD degree (aim to accelerate the talented instincts of the women candidates to carry out the advanced studies and research).
>
> 100 per cent funding for construction of hostels for women and other related infrastructural facilities in colleges.
>
> Day care centres for married scholars/students in universities and colleges (Day care facility on demand basis for children of three months to six years of age)
>
> **AICTE:**
> PRAGATI (Providing Assistance for Girls' Advancement in Technical Education Initiative) envisages selection of one girl per family where family income is less than six lakh per annum on merit at the qualifying examination to pursue technical education

Source: Author.

examples of select schemes that qualify to be reported under Part A and are identified in Box 5.2.

Of the three categories of expenditures that form a part of GB, such schemes (Box 5.2) should have been reflected in Category A, which certainly exist and would have qualified for a good amount of share in the HE gender budget, if reported properly. It is difficult to say whether several of the Category B allocations should have qualified for equal opportunity expenditure or mainstream expenditure. Like the ones on IITs, IIMs, upgradation and setting up of new schools, and so on—neither does the policy nor does the practice prove a minimum of 30 per cent of women participation in this category of institutions. Until and unless the policy provides for such reservations for women, these should be treated as mainstream expenditure and not reported under Category B. Categorizing the expenditure into the theoretical connotations, following inferences may be drawn with respect to HE gender budget in India:

Gender-targeted expenditure: Gender-specific expenditure targeting women and girls (e.g., women's literacy projects, women scholarships) exists but is not correctly reported.

Equal opportunity expenditure: Expenditures promoting equal opportunities in the public sector (e.g., evaluation of job descriptions to promote equitable hiring of faculty) are lacking and need to be strengthened. There may be several ways of doing it. For example, allocations for improving women's employability and research capacity, academic growth, job potential, internship opportunities, jobs in science/technology labs, research and innovation centres and so on, more meaningful and rewarding PhDs, providing and creating awareness towards opportunities to improve economic participation rather than just perform non-economic activities.

Mainstream expenditure (the rest): Budget expenditures not included under the previous two categories. It comprises a major chunk and requires to be assessed for its gender differential impact, which is a rather technical and time-consuming exercise. Availability of sex-disaggregated data and technically trained personnel to undertake such work are the two major challenges towards any such analysis.

It can thus be seen that GB in HE falls short of its first two objectives, that is, the adequacy objective and second is the responsive objective (assessment of the third objective, that is, impact objective to consider the impact of any form of public expenditure or method of raising revenues on women, is beyond the scope of this paper). Firstly, the adequacy objective much needs to be done to improve and shift the participation of women as well as men in order to achieve greater gender balance in several disciplines and courses, institutions and regions. Secondly, the responsive objective several needs of women (pupils and teachers), in particular still need to be addressed both for the students and faculty in the HE system, some of which have been identified under the equal opportunity expenditure in the above paragraph.

CONTINUED NEED AND RATIONALE FOR GB IN HE

It is suggested that effectiveness of education financing campaigns can be measured on how far they promote participation of boys and girls and reduce disparities between men and women (adequacy objective), promote fair conditions for both male and female (pupils and teachers), address school related gender-based violence and discrimination, and empower men and women in employment and development. Let us try to briefly examine some of the above aspects in order to see why GB in HE is still justified and try to identify few important intervention areas. A story that begins with gender disparity in participation in HE gets translated into participation and promotion both in HE and in the labour market.

Gender Disparity in HE Participation

According to the latest census estimates, although, the literacy rate has risen to 73 per cent in 2011, the gender gap has narrowed only slightly, with women literacy levels 16 per cent below men (Ministry of Home Affairs, Office of the Registrar General & Census Commissioner, 2011). The story that begins with adverse female graduate ratio, the gap between male and female HE graduates' share in population being almost a quarter per cent. Barring the state of Kerala where the female share in graduate population outnumbers male by 10 per cent, points that this ratio favours men in all other states of the country, the gap being as high as 52 per cent in favour of men in the state of Bihar followed by Jharkhand, Rajasthan and Arunachal Pradesh. Further, a continuing adverse Gender Parity Index (GPI) in HE proves that GER for girls at higher education is still lower than men (MHRD, 2015–2016). In fact, GPI is favourable for women (greater than one) in only six of the major Indian states in the country and the gap is much higher for Scheduled Tribe (ST) and Scheduled Caste (SC) being 10 and 4, respectively. Several disciplines continue to remain male bastions, more importantly the ones that are job-oriented.

Females constitute more than half of the student enrolment in arts and social sciences but their representation is lesser even in pure science and commerce disciplines (Table 5.7). The gendered biases are more distinct in technical and professional courses where their representation is barely above one-fourth and one-third respectively. It needs to be stressed here that graduates from the latter disciplines have a higher probability of being in demand by the employers (Khare, 2014). As such, women's capacity to actively participate and contribute economically gets stifled at an early stage.

Gender Disparity in Labour Market Participation

Data prove that women's transition from HE to labour market as well as career advancement is highly skewed in favour of men as is evident from an adverse graduate employment ratio. As against 69 per cent of male main graduate workers, there are merely 27 per cent female main graduate workers. However, for the non-worker category, this share is almost reverse with female graduates comprising 67 per cent as non-workers as against male graduates (Ministry of Home Affairs, Office of the Registrar General & Census Commissioner, 2011). The situation is no different for even the technically or professionally qualified. Not only is the ratio of male-to-female engineers, which is 1.96, but also current ratio of females to males employed in IT industry is lower than that of the engineering population (Peoplestrong, CII, & Wheebox, 2014). Available literature says that women engineers not only face difficulty in getting jobs as employers are reluctant but also they get less promotions and less salaries as compared to men which eventually leads to less professional recognition. Similarly, only 3 per cent of legislative, management and senior official positions are quoted to be held by women (Nandy, 2014). Under-representation of women in senior roles is something that is brought to fore time and again by several authors (ASSOCHAM, 2012; ECU, 2011; Jha, 2008; Morley, 2011, 2012; UNESCO, 2012; World Economic Forum, 2009, 2010).

Table 5.7 *Male–Female Ratio in Enrolments at UG Level in Major Disciplines*

Year	Arts and Social Science	Science and IT/ Computer	Engineering and Technology Total	Commerce	Medical Science	Professional Education	Library and Information Science	Others	Grand Total
2010–2011	1	1.7	2.4	1.4	0.9	2	1.2	0.3	1.3
2015–2016	0.9	1.1	2.6	1.2	0.6	1.9	NA	0.8	1.1

Source: MHRD (2015–2016).

Gender Disparity in HE Employment

Ironically, a place that should foster and correct adversities in the gender participation, doing by example is itself best with inherent biases in fair treatment to their female employees reflected in adverse faculty ratio. The point is proven by the fact that there are merely 64 female teachers per 100 male teachers in India with their percentage being lower in all the states of the country (MHRD, 2015–2016). Furthermore, there is not a single state in the country where the male–female faculty ratio has improved/inched towards becoming in favour of female from the level of assistant professor to that of professor. Rather this ratio at the professor's level gets much more skewed in favour of males. What is even more depressing is the fact that in the past five years, only five states have shown some marginal improvement in the ratio of female faculty at both professor and assistant professor's level (Table 5.8). In fact, over the years, the situation instead of improving in favour of women faculty has deteriorated vis-à-vis men in most states.

Representation of women in R&D, faculty positions in HE, leadership, management and decision-making positions is critically low (Chanana, 2000, 2012; UNESCO, 2010). The reasons quoted are not because most women are refusing, resisting or dismissing senior leadership and making strategic decisions to not to apply, but are discriminatory recruitment, selection and promotion procedures, gendered career pathways or exclusionary networks and practices in women-unfriendly institutions so that gender remains a strong determinant of many educational inequities, and better presence of women in HE has a limited impact on the labour market (UNESCO, 2010; Chanana, 2013).

Logically, as women's participation in HE grows, their labour market participation should also improve. However, across the globe it is found that such transformation is not happening.

So whilst it is true that there are far more students nowadays and the majority are women this does not mean that there is more than formal equality in terms of 'the numbers game'. This is controversial as the 'numbers game' is a mask for continuing power plays whereby the 'rules of the game' remain misogynistic. (David, 2015)

Table 5.8 *Ratio of Male/Female Faculty (2015–2016)*

State	Gujarat	Karnataka	Odisha	UP	Arunachal Pradesh	Bihar	Chhattisgarh
Professor	2.7	2.79	4.02	3.18	8.58	4.79	2.42
Assistant professor	1.84	1.31	2.16	2.21	1.65	4.52	1.33
	J&K	Kerala	Madhya Pradesh	Himachal Pradesh	Uttarakhand	Maharashtra	Rajasthan	All India
	2.71	1.62	2.17	3.44	4.51	2.96	2.85	2.87
	1.27	0.66	1.58	1.32	1.82	1.62	1.9	1.54

Source: MHRD (2015–2016).

India slipped by 21 positions from 2016 to be ranked 108 among 144 countries according Global Gender Gap Index 2017 as per the World Economic Forum (*Hindu*, 2017).

Studies also suggest several enablers to break these multidimensional social, cultural, economic and institutional barriers to women in HE and leadership. These include structured interventions and investments in training and development, support and mentorship, career advice, international networks and mobility (British Council, 2015), pro-women organizational culture and facilities (Karup, Maithreyi, Kantharaju, & Godbolle, 2010). According to the 2016 report by the International Monetary Fund, gender budget is positive and significant for primary school enrolment equality and can potentially improve gender equality in primary education, and thus has an important role to play in doing so in HE. As rightly put by Morley and Crossouard (2015), policies on gender equality and GM need to be developed and accompanied by strategic action plans, resource allocation and reporting mechanisms. These should include timelines, goal/performance indicators and effective evaluation procedures all of which are intrinsic part of the five step gender budget framework described in earlier pages. Thus, the need for gender budget in Indian HE in order to strengthen several visible and invisible trends in favour of women is not unjustified.

SPATIAL MAPPING OF SHIFTS IN GENDER PARITY IN HE

It is indeed worrisome to note that over the past five years, the gender parity in several states has either deteriorated or remained almost stagnant, showing only marginal improvement. States showing a deterioration in GPI over the past five years include 14 states in all (Figure 5.3), some of which are also those that have adopted gender budget. Does this mean gender budget does not help? Studies have shown that gender budget does have a positive impact on reducing gender inequalities and, therefore, serves as a motivation for countries to adopt GB (Chakraborty 2016; Kolovich & Shibuya, 2016; Sharp & Elson, 2008; Stotsky, 2016). Chakraborty (2018) in the study on Asia Pacific countries proves, 'Gender budgeting has significant effect on increasing Gender Development Index (GDI) and small but significant

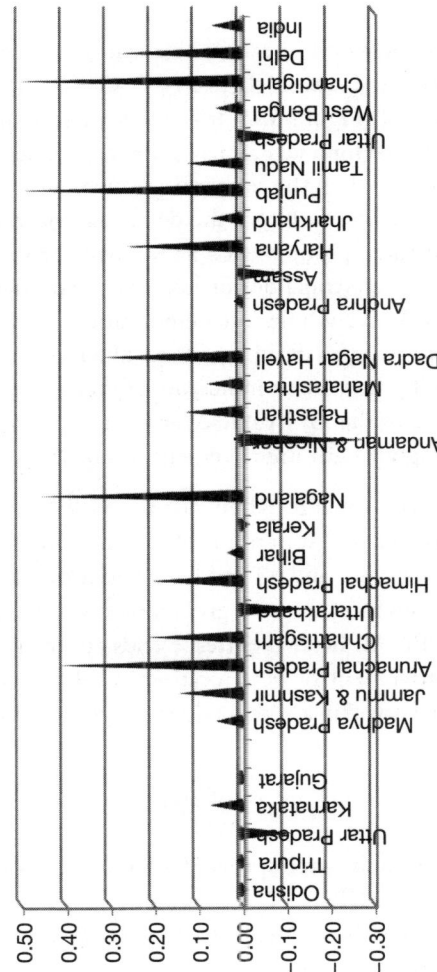

Figure 5.3 *Change in GPI between 2010–2011 and 2015–2016*

Source: Author.

potential to reduce GII. These results strengthen the rationale for employing GB to promote inclusive development'. Not only does this justify for taking gender budget in HE more seriously but also making deeper analysis into what works and where does the implementation/ programmatic gaps lie.

There are several states where the GPI as a whole might not be giving alarming signs but if the same is checked for SC/ST students, the situation might be different (Figure 5.4). It is not necessary that if the GPI as a whole has improved for a state, it has improved for all category of students. These are cases when the higher improvement in the GPI of general category students camouflages the deterioration in the GPI for the socially disadvantaged group of SC/ST students or vice-versa. States like Jharkhand, that are tribal dominated, have experienced an improvement in the GPI as a whole but deterioration for the tribal community. Infact, there are even developed states like Kerala that have a proven track record of pro-women indicators of literacy and GERs have witnessed a decline in the GPI value over the period as a whole and also for the SC category with improvement in only ST category.

Several such indications emerge when just a simple spatial mapping of the states is undertaken just in terms of the direction of shift in GPI for all students and by SC and ST students between 2010–2011 and 2015–2016. Superimposing the two gives nine distinct combinations of variations in GPI. At the two extreme ends are the states that have experienced improvement or deterioration in GPI for all three groups of students. In between are several other permutations and combinations.

These nine categories of states are as follows:

1. All three categories have shown improvement: Comprises 11 states, maximum have adopted GB.
2. All three categories have shown deterioration: Three states including Uttar Pradesh, the most populous.
3. Improvement as a whole but drop for SC/ST: Bihar, one of the poor performing states, falls in this category. It is clear that socially disadvantaged groups deserve more focus in the state.

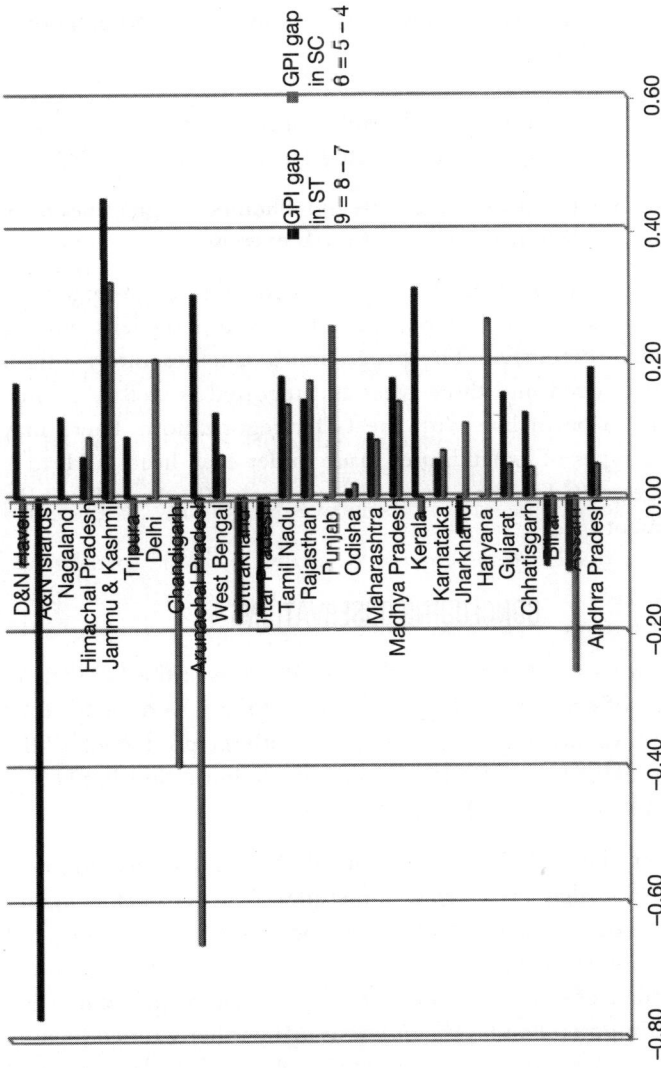

Figure 5.4 Change in GPI for SC and ST (2010–2011 to 2015–2016)

Source: Calculated by the Author.

4. Deterioration as a whole but improvement for SC/ST: The only state that qualifies to be in this category is Odisha. The state, thus, possibly needs to look at the drop in the GPI for general and other category of students that must be significant enough to pull down the overall GPI.

Similar observations can be made with respect to other states (Table 5.9) and specific groups may be targeted for improving the GPI.

More such detailed analysis of HE and schemes/programmes from a gendered lens shall help improve the GB exercise.

In order to improve gender sensitivity in schemes/programmes, Table 5.10 gives a frame for looking at schemes from the lens of being more gender responsive. The programmes/schemes/interventions may be categorized into three types and reported as well as assessed accordingly to be in line with the GB categorization. There may be all three types of expenditures made under each head as Head I: gender targeted (GT), Head II: equal opportunity (EO) and Head III: empowerment (Em).

CONCLUDING OBSERVATIONS

It is needless to say that prior to the introduction of the GBS, there was no way of even estimating how much of the government's total expenditure was flowing to women. Now with the production of the GBS as part of the Union Budget documents, an institutionalized effort is being made to answer this basic question.

However, the GBS does not capture all the women focused inter-ventions. Anomalies are several. Sometimes, 100 per cent women's schemes are not reported under that category while those that may not qualify to be in the Category B are placed. This is not to undermine the importance of smaller amounts, that is, less than 30 per cent. They are equally important and relevant just as many other women focused interventions where the allocations in themselves may be lesser than 30 per cent of the total budgets. Unfortunately, they do not get captured by the GBS. Although they remain a part of the mainstream budget,

Table 5.9 *Classification of States by Direction of Shift in GPI (2010–2011 to 2015–2016)*

All Three +ve	All +ve SC/ST -ve	ALL -ve SC/ST +ve	Only ST +ve	Only SC +ve	Only ST -ve	Only SC -ve	All Three -ve	No Change (cat)
Andhra	Bihar	Odisha	Kerala	Uttarakhand	Jharkhand	Arunachal	Assam	Gujarat (all)
Arunachal						Chandigarh	Uttar Pradesh	Haryana (ST)
Chhattisgarh						Tripura	Andaman and Nicobar	Punjab (ST)
Karnataka						D&N Haveli		Delhi (ST)
Maharashtra								Nagaland (SC)
Rajasthan								
Tamil Nadu								
Madhya Pradesh								
West Bengal								
J&K								
Himachal Pradesh								

Source: Compiled by the author (MHRD, 2015–2016).

Note: +ve means improvement in GPI; –ve means drop in GPI; All refers to all category of students; SC: Scheduled Class, ST: Scheduled Tribe.

Table 5.10 *Framework to Improve Gender Sensitivity in Schemes/ Programmes*

Scheme and Challenge	Aim and Interventions	Scope of Work to Improve Gender Responsiveness
Head I: Improve girls enrolment and retention	Nationwide, identified subjects/disciplines/districts/communities Special focus on girls' participation in technical education, aiming to target the 'hardest to reach' girls through residential facilities/transport facilities/and other.	Increasing number of women teachers, especially in rural areas, providing special concessions/guidance and so on from school level itself.
Head II: Improve participation and learning	Improve girls' attendance Interventions: Gender-sensitive pedagogy, separate toilets/restrooms for girls, bridge course, recruitment of 50% women teachers, medical/dispensary facilities and an innovation fund for need-based interventions at different places.	Providing/enabling learning conditions/environment for women Hostel facilities and scholarships for girls including skill-based training as part of the overall curriculum Assessment and provision of safety in schools for young girls.
Head III: Improve confidence and empowerment	Provide opportunities of cognitive as well as non-cognitive learning	Career guidance and counselling Provide space within the education programme for increasing awareness about women's rights, Family counselling Knowledge about key legal instruments and laws and information on how to negotiate the justice chain

such expenditures too can certainly go a long way in addressing the gender-based challenges of women in HE; but impact analysis of this portion of budget on its gender relevance is a tough task that requires special expertise and good data, both of which are lacking. Sex disaggregated data are still not available on several schemes. Assumptions behind reporting any specific proportion of funds and benefits accruing to women in various development schemes are not clear in the GBS.

Even for the specifically earmarked funds for women, inconsistencies in GBS can be noticed. While there are schemes currently under implementation and reflected in the outcome budgets, they are not listed in Part A and at times schemes reported in Category B may show more than 100 per cent allocations against them. In the case of some of the educational/scholarship-based programmes, loans, professional and technical education and so on allocations are reported under Part B of the statement without any clear justification (by way of data on enrolments/number of scholarships provided).

A good GB relies heavily on data, so that policies, programmes and budgets can be evidence-based rather than based on myths or assumptions. Data are needed at all five stages of the budgeting process and required to be used to take informed decisions. Even simple spatial analysis with sex-disaggregated data can provide insights into the real need and problem. Only then can money flow to the right people at the right places. Several states in the country can be seen to be performing poorly on several fronts in attaining gender equality in HE, for example, Bihar. While there are many others that may show a good gender balance on one front but not on the other. Even socially developed states like Kerala that have many indicators favouring women's participation in HE is found to be unfavourable to them on certain counts. What is most frustrating is the fact that in all states of the country, the economic participation of female HE graduates is much low. Corrective actions need to be taken within the HE sector for them to get translated outside and become cumulative by triggering a virtuous cycle. The relevance of GB in HE can thus be re-emphasized. As a gender neutral or gender blind national budget ignores the different, socially determined roles and responsibilities of men and women and is bound to reach and benefit the men more than the women unless concerted efforts are made to correct gender-based discrimination (Das

& Mishra, 2006). Situation in the Indian HE is more complex given its rising numbers and increasing diversities on campus, sociocultural, regional connotations to the existing biases. Region-specific interventions through spatial mapping at subnational level broken further down to district level may be more helpful.

The major challenges faced in the implementation of GB may be identified as lack of gender disaggregated data, budgetary constraints, need for political support, attitudes, knowledge and capacity, continuity and institutionalization, coordination, technical expertise, identifying GS line budget items (bifurcation on expenditures and outcomes, GS training programme for men/women teachers).

Although, the HE sector in India is massifying at a pace as never before, with girls enrolments outnumbering boys in many courses (medical education being an important one) but still there are several visible and invisible dimensions of gender discrimination that hinder women's progression in job and constraints them to perform economic activities, thereby contributing in economic growth. As a result, even many of those states that have implemented gender budget are falling back on GPI. This calls for taking up the gender budget exercise in right earnest with data-based evidential guidance. There can be no hesitation in saying that even after 10 years of gender budget, many states need to adopt practicing it, GB in HE has a long way to go to achieve its adequacy and responsive objective. In fact, there is immense scope and need to continue with gender-targeted, equal opportunity as well as empowerment expenditure all of which should have clear cut deliverables marked and measured.

APPENDIX
Gender Budget 2015–2016 (India)

Table 5A.1 List of Schemes/Institutions Receiving Gender-Specific Budgets in India

Department of HE			
Demand No. 60			
1	UGC
2	IGNOU
3	National Institute of Technical Teacher's Training and Research
4	Scholarship for College and University Students
5	Education Loan Interest Subsidy
6	National Mission in Education through ICT
7	Indian Institutes of Technology
8	Indian Institutes of Management
9	Indian Institute of Science, Bengaluru
10	National Institute for Industrial Engineering, Mumbai
11	National Institute of Foundry and Forge Technology, Ranchi
12	Indian School of Mines, Dhanbad
13	National Institutes of Technology
14	Schools of Planning and Architecture
15	Grants for promotion of Indian languages
16	Support for the Polytechnics in the States
17	Support to Indian Institute of Science (IISC) and Indian Institute(s) of Science Education & Research (IISER)
18	Interest Subsidy and contribution for guarantee fund
19	Assistance to other institutes including SLIET, NERIST Ranchi, CIT Kokrajhar
20	New SPA
21	Rashtriya Uchcha Shiksha Abhiyan (RUSA)
22	Consortium for Higher Education Electronic Resources
23	National Initiative for Excellence in Humanities and Social Science
24	Setting up of IITs/IIMs including upgrading five IITs/IIMs

Notes

1. Access means the needs of women in the areas like health, education and employment and so on.
2. Equity means fairness of treatment for women and men according to their respective needs. This may include equal treatment or treatment that is different but which is considered equivalent in terms of rights, benefits, obligations and opportunities.
3. Distance Education = IGNOU.
4. Polytechnics = Community Polytechnics + UpGradation of Existing/Setting up of New Polytechnics.
5. Language & Promotion = National Council for Promotion of Urdu Language + Rashtriya Sanskrit Sansthan + Central Institute of Indian Language+ Kendriya Hindi Sansthan + Central Hindi Directorate + Grant for Promotion of Indian Languages.
6. Technical & Professional = Sant Longowal Institute of Engineering & Technology (SLIET) + National Institute of Technical Teachers Training and Research (NITTTR) + North Eastern Regional Institute of Science and Technology, Itanagar + Central Institute of Technology, Kokrajhar + Indian Institute of Technology + Indian Institute of Science Bengaluru + Indian Institute of Information Technology (Design & Manufacturing) Kanchipuram + National Institute for Industrial Engineering, Mumbai + National Institute of Foundry and Forge Technology, Ranchi + Indian Institute of Information Technology + Indian Instittue of Science for Education and Research + National Institutes of Technology + Indian Institute of Management + Indian School of Mines, Dhanbad + School of Planning and Architecture + Indian Institute of Information Technology (Design & Manufacturing) Kanchipuram + Support to Indian Institute of Science (IISC) and Indian Institute(s) of Science Education & Research IISER + New Schools of Planning and Architecture (new SPAs) + National Initiative for Excellence in Humanities and Social Science + Setting Up of IITs/IIMs including upgrading five IITs/IIMs + Assistance to other institute including SLIET NERIST Ranchi CIT Kokrajhar.

   Loans and Fund = Education Loan Interest Subsidy + Interest Subsidy and Contribution for Guarantee Fund.

REFERENCES

ASSOCHAM. (2012, April 21). In financial services top job generator in tier II, III cities (ASSOCHAM Report). Retrieved from http://www.business-standard. com/article/companies/fin-services-top-job-generator-in-tier-ii-iii-cities-112042100037_1.html

Bandyopadhyay, A. (2016). Studying borrower level risk characteristics of education loan in India. IIMB Management Review, 28, 126–135.

Bebbington, D. (2002). Women in science, engineering and technology: A review of the issues. Higher Education Quarterly, 56(4), 360–375.

Becher, T. (2006). The significance of disciplinary differences. Studies in Higher Education, 19(2), 151–161. New Delhi: SAGE Publication.

Beede D., Tiffany J., Langdon D., McKittrick G., Khan B., & Doms M. (2011). Women in STEM: A gender gap to innovation. Washington, DC: Springer.

British Council. (2015). Defined by absence: Women and research in South Asia. Retrieved from https://www.britishcouncil.org/sites/default/files/women_researchers_jan15_print.pdf

Budlender, D., Elson, D., Hewitt, G., & Mukhopadhyay, T. (2002). Gender budgets make cents: Understanding gender-responsive budgets. London: Commonwealth Secretariat.

Chakraborty, L. (2016). Asia: A survey of gender budgeting (Working Paper No. 16/150). Washington, DC: IMF.

———. (2018, June). Gender budgeting as accountability initiative: Public expenditure effectiveness on fiscal space and gender equality. Austaxpolicy: Tax and Transfer Policy Blog. Retrieved from https://www.nipfp.org.in/media/medialibrary/2018/06/Gender_Budgeting_as_Accountability_Initiative_Public_Expenditure_Effectiveness.pdf

Chanana, K. (2000). Treading the hallowed halls: Women in higher education in India. Economic and Political Weekly, 35(12), 1012–1022.

———. (2012). Higher education and gender issues in the knowledge economy: Who studies what, why and where? In D. Neubauer (ed.), The emergent knowledge society and the future of higher education: Asian perspectives (pp. 177–193). Oxfordshire: Routledge.

———. (2013). Leadership for women's equality and empowerment in higher education. India International Centre Quarterly, 39(3/4), 81–94.

Das S., & Mishra Y. (2006). Gender budgeting statement: Misleading and patriarchal assumptions. Economic and Political Weekly, XLI(30), 3285–3288.

David, M. E. (2015). Women and gender equality in higher education? Education Sciences, 5(1), 10–25.

Dyhouse C. (2003). Troubled identities: Gender and Status in the history of the mixed college in English universities since 1945. Women History Review, 12(2), 169–194. Retrieved from https://doi.org/10.1080/09612020300200354

EIU. (2014[2012]). *Where are the women? Analysing trends in higher education management in Afghanistan, Bangladesh, India, Nepal, Pakistan and Sri Lanka* (A Report for the British Council). London: EIU, European Commission.

Equality Challenge Unit. (2011, December). *Equality in higher education: Statistical report 2011 Part 2: Students.* London: Equality Challenge Unit. Retrieved from http://www.ecu.ac.uk

Jha, S. (2008, January 2). Women on top in exams, not promotions. *Hindustan Times.* Retrieved from http://www.hindustantimes.com/india/women-on-top-in-exams-not-promotions/story-ugU91DFTPbnbsVX8lVOcBJ.htm

Karup, A., Maithreyi, R., Kantharaju, B., & Godbolle, R. (2010). *Trained scientific women power: How much are we losing and why?* Bangalore: Indian Academy of Sciences and National Institute of Advanced Studies.

Khare, M. (2014). Employment, employability and higher education in India: The missing links. *Higher Education for the Future, 1*(1), 39–62.

———. (2016). Higher education/university: Taking the skills march forward in India—transitioning to the world of work. In Matthias Pilz (ed.), *India: Preparation for the world of work* (pp. 103–139). Berlin: Springer.

Kingdon, G. G. (2007). The progress of school education in India. *Oxford Review of Economic Policy, 23*(2), 168–195.

Knight, D., & Richards W. (2003). Sex discrimination in UK academia. *Gender, Work & Organization, 10*(2), 213–238. Retrieved from https://doi.org/10.1111/1468-0432.t01-1-00012

Kolovich, L., & Shibuya, S. (2016). *Middle East and Central Asia: A survey of gender budgeting efforts* (Working Paper No. 16/151). Washington, DC: IMF.

Morley, L. (2006). *Gender equity in selected commonwealth universities* (Research Report No. 65). London: Department of International Development.

———. (2011, December). Cycles of domination of top roles by men must be broken. *Times Higher Education, 6, 29.* Retrieved from https://www.timeshighereducation.com/news/cycle-of-domination-of-top-roles-by-men-must-be-broken/422031.article

———. (2012). Cycles of domination of top roles by men must be broken. Times Higher Education, 6 December 2012, p. 29. https://www.timeshighereducation.com/news/cycle-of-domination-of-top-roles-by-men-must-be-broken/422031.article

———. (2013). *Women and higher education leadership: Absences and aspirations* (Stimulus Paper). London: Leadership Foundation for Higher Education.

Ministry of Women and Child Development. (2015, October). *Gender budgeting handbook.* New Delhi: GoI.

Ministry of Home Affairs, Office of the Registrar General & Census Commissioner. (2011). *Census of India.* New Delhi: GoI. Retrieved from http://censusindia.gov.in/.

MHRD. (2010–2011). *All India survey of higher education (AISHE) (2010–2011).* New Delhi: GoI. Retrieved from http://aishe.nic.in/aishe/reports;jsessionid.

————. (2015–2016). *All India survey of higher education (AISHE) (2015–2016)*. New Delhi: GoI. Retrieved from http://aishe.nic.in/aishe/reports;jsessionid

Morley, L., & Crossouard, B. (2015). *Women in higher education leadership in South Asia: Rejection, refusal, reluctance, revisioning* (British Council Report). New Delhi: Centre for Higher Education & Equity Research, University of Sussex.

Morley, L., & Lugg, R. (2009). Mapping meritocracy: Intersecting gender, poverty and higher educational opportunity structures. *Higher Education Policy*, *22*(1), 37–60.

Nandy, S. A. B. (2014). Corporate glass ceiling: An impact on Indian women employees. *International Journal of Management and International Business Studies*, *4*(2), 135–140.

Peoplestrong, CII, & Wheebox. (2014). *India Skills Report 2014*. Retrieved from https://wheebox.com/wheebox/resources/IndiaSkillsReport.pdf

Peppen, V., & Rossie. (2016). *Gender equality and education in the sustainable development goals*. UNESCO Digital Library. Retrieved from http://unesdoc.unesco.org/images/0024/002455/245574E.pdf

Planning Commission. (2005–06 to 2013–14). GOI. *Gender Budget in India Statement-20*. New Delhi: Government of India.

————. (Various years). *Five-year plans*. New Delhi: GoI.

Pritchard, R. (2010). Gender inequalities among staff in British and German universities: A qualitative study. *Compare: A Journal of Comparative and International Education*, *40*(4), 515–532.

Ramachandran, V. (2010). *Gender issues in higher education: Advocacy brief*. Paris: UNESCO.

Sharp, R. (2003). *Budgeting for equity: Gender budget initiatives within a framework of performance oriented budgeting*. New York, NY: UNIFEM. Retrieved from http://www.genderbudgets.org/uploads/user-S/10099456961R.Sharppaper.pdf

Sharp, R., & Elson, D. (2008). *Improving budgets: A framework for assessing gender responsive budget initiatives*. Adelaide: Hawke Research Institute for Sustainable Societies, University of South Australia.

Stotsky, J. G. (2016). *Gender budgeting: Fiscal context and overview of current outcomes* (Working Paper No. 16/149). Washington, DC: International Monetary Fund.

The Hindu. (2017). India slips 21 slots on WEF gender gap index. Retrieved from https://www.thehindu.com/news/national/india-slips-21-slots-occupy-108th-rank-on-wef-gender-gap-index-2017/article19966394.ece

UNESCO. (2010, September 9–11). *Gender equality: The missing link? Rethinking the internationally agreed development goals beyond 2015*. Athens: UNESCO Future Forum on Gender Equality.

————. (2012). *World atlas of gender equality in education*. New York, NY: UNESCO.

UNIFEM–UNFPA. (2018). *Gender responsive budgeting and women's reproductive rights: A resource pack*. Retrieved from https://www.unfpa.org/sites/default/files/pub-pdf/gender_responsive_eng.pdf

United Nations. (2013). *The MDG Report.* Retrieved from http://www.un.org/millenniumgoals/pdf/report-2013/mdg-report-2013-english.pdf

Welch, P. (2006). Feminist Pedagogy Revisited. Learning and Teaching in the Social Sciences, 3(3), 171–199.

World Economic Forum. (2009). *The global gender gap report 2009.* Retrieved from http://www3.weforum.org/docs/WEF_GenderGap_Report_2009.pdf

World Bank. (2002). *Constructing knowledge societies: New challenges for tertiary education.* Washington, DC: World Bank.

———. (2010). *The corporate gender gap report 2010.* Retrieved from http://www.alba.acg.edu/media/2492/coporategendergap_report.pdf

PART II

Responses to Declining Public Funding

Chapter 6

Institutional Strategies to Overcome Declining Public Funding in Higher Education

Jinusha Panigrahi

INTRODUCTION

The contribution of higher education in the emancipation of knowledge has always got a favour to remain under the purview of the government. Theoretically, starting from human capital (HC) theory to the endogenous growth theories, the role of education and particularly higher education has been argued to contribute to the growth and development of any economy of the world. In line with the importance realized for higher education like other countries, traditionally, Indian higher education system has been funded by the government. But due to the adoption of Structural Adjustment Programmes (SAP) in 1980s, many developing countries experienced a shift in funding policies in their higher education systems. The adoption of new public management regimes compelled many countries to adopt cost recovery measures in higher education. The measures to share the cost of education with the students/parents (e.g., student fee, student loans) or employers (e.g., graduate tax method) became common. Similarly, facing a decline in public funding, public higher education institutions (HEIs) experimented these cost-sharing measures along with certain income-generating activities to mobilize additional resources to meet the day-to-day expenses.

The challenges faced by the HEIs in India, due to decline in public funding, vary from institution to institution. The state-funded universities receiving very little nonrecurring/development grants from the Centre receive different percentage of recurring grants from their respective state governments which hardly cover recurring expenditures. The central universities receiving majority of their funding from the central government are better placed even to explore various income-generating activities to generate additional resources. However, majority of the HEIs are compelled to restructure their day-to-day expenses adjusting with the changing requirements of resources.

This chapter attempts to examine the ways in which public institutions responded to a decline in public funding. The empirical evidence of this chapter is based on a study conducted by the Centre for Policy Research in Higher Education (CPRHE) in five provinces of India.[1] The first section gives a brief description of the role of higher education and arguments for the requirements of public financing of higher education. In the second section, the public expenditure on tertiary education by selected countries of the world is discussed. Public expenditure on higher education in Indian context by central and provincial government and changing policy initiatives are discussed in the third section. The alternative sources of financing of higher education explored by India are discussed briefly in the fourth section. The fifth section depicts the findings of the study regarding institutional responses to decline in public funding in Indian context. The sixth section is about concluding observations and the way forward.

ARGUMENTS FOR PUBLIC FUNDING OF HIGHER EDUCATION

Higher education plays an important role in economic growth and development. Education contributes to economic growth through its

---

[1] The CPRHE/NIEPA research study on 'Financing of Higher Education: Institutional Responses to Decline in Public Funding' was implemented in five provinces of India representing several zones of the country and coordinated by the author.

role in improved productivity and increased national product (as opined by HC theory). In the knowledge economies, the contribution of higher education has become far more important due to its role in knowledge production through various research and development (R&D) activities and in the production of knowledge-based goods.

The HC theory argues for investment in education to enhance productivity and earnings of an individual which ultimately leads to a higher level of economic growth of a nation (Becker, 1964; Schultz, 1961). Along with investment, the theory equally argues for the significance of various physical capabilities such as ability, motivation or intensity of work and the earnings that impact morale and aspirations of the individuals (Becker, 1975). The HC theory was also identified with the endogenous growth models where the concept of knowledge and innovations, and hence the role of R&D, was given more emphasis in the argument for investment in education (Lucas, 1988; Romer, 1989).

The role of the state in financing of higher education is also identified with the nature of higher education as a good. Higher education can be characterized as a public good when it is non-rivalrous (R. A. Musgrave & Musgrave, 1989) in the publicly funded HEIs (but excluding the possibility of congestion due to higher demand for it) and the positive externalities associated with it not only benefit its ultimate consumer (i.e., the student), but also benefit the society at large in terms of social cohesion, ethical values, morality and many such related moral aspects. Therefore, it is argued that the non-market benefits or the spillover social benefits of investment in HC such as the patriotic feelings, maintenance of the democratic values and compliance with the cultural norms are difficult to measure as the market is missing to value such externalities (Dreze & Sen, 1996; McMahon, 2006). Due to such market imperfections, the burden of financing of higher education is argued to be taken care of by the government (Lleras, 2004). The efficiency and equity argument in a market-driven economy necessitates public financing of education. To correct market failure in the instances of imperfect market and asymmetric information and for equitable income redistribution, public intervention gets significant value (R. A. Musgrave & Musgrave, 1989).

PUBLIC EXPENDITURE ON TERTIARY EDUCATION

Looking at the status of public expenditure on tertiary education across different countries from various regions shows an increase on higher level of public expenditure except selected few.

Table 6.1 shows a gradual increase in public expenditure on tertiary education as a percentage of gross domestic product (GDP) except countries such as India, Finland, Ukraine and China, Macao special administrative region. The expansion in enrolment has also raised the expenditure by the government too. A detailed discussion on public expenditure on university or higher education is done in the next section.

Public Expenditure in India

India reached a stage of massification in higher education with gross enrolment ratio (GER) of 15 per cent in 2009–2010 and within eight years, higher education enrolment has increased, and reached a level of 25.8 per cent GER in 2017–2018 (Table 6.2). With this rapid expansion in enrolment, the HEIs, particularly private universities and deemed to be universities, have also expanded to meet the growing aspirations of higher education. Earlier, the twelfth plan document also pointed out how the massive expansion is driven by private HEIs (GoI, 2013) and how India's massification is due to larger participation of private universities (Varghese, 2015).

However, such expansion in higher education has not commensurate with the public funding of higher education by both the central and state government. India showed a decline in GDP per capita due to massification of higher education as the expenditure on tertiary education fell short of the rapid expansion in enrolment (Panigrahi, 2018a).

As shown in Table 6.3, the share of public expenditure of both central government and provincial governments (state/union territories [UTs]) taken together is 4.04 per cent of GDP by 2014–2015. There has been no significant increase in the share of public expenditure on education to GDP in recent years when compared to 2010–2011. Comparing the share of public expenditure to GDP at different levels

Table 6.1 *Expenditure on Tertiary Education from Government Sources in Selected Countries as a Percentage of GDP*

Country	2010	2011	2012	2013	2014
Argentina	1.00	1.03	1.07	1.10	1.09
Australia	1.24	1.18	1.16	1.36	1.38
Austria	1.58	1.5	1.83	1.79	1.77
Barbados	1.98	–	1.59	1.89	2.45
Bolivia (Plurinational State of Bolivia)	2.27	1.98	1.61	1.69	1.91
Brazil	0.93	0.96	1.01	1.09	1.15
Burundi	1.23	1.05	1.2	1.31	–
China, Hong Kong special administrative region	0.98	0.98	1.15	1.46	1.04
China, Macao special administrative region	1.27	1.6	2.27	0.92	0.87
Finland	2.08	2.08	2.05	2.01	2.00
India	1.24	1.33	1.24	1.10	–
Indonesia	0.45	–	0.59	0.55	0.49
Malaysia	1.71	2.13	1.63	1.67	–
South Africa	0.68	0.7	0.76	0.75	0.74
Spain	1.13	1.14	0.99	0.97	0.96
Sweden	1.92	1.89	1.94	1.96	1.94
Ukraine	–	2.12	2.17	2.13	1.85
United Kingdom of Great Britain and Northern Ireland	0.95	1.25	1.35*	1.35	1.39
United States of America	1.39	1.36	1.48	1.35	1.37

Source: UIS (2018).

Note: * Data of 2013.

of education shows that the share of university and higher education is not only comparatively lower than elementary and secondary education but also faced a decline in share in 2014–2015. Irrespective of massive expansion in enrolments in higher education, particularly at state-level universities and colleges, there is a decline in public expenditure on

Table 6.2 Expansion of HEIs and Enrolments in India

Year	Central Universities	State Universities	Deemed to be Universities	Institutes of National Importance	Private Universities	Total	Colleges	Enrolments (in Millions)	GER %
2005–2006	18	205	95	18	7	343	17,625	11.6	11.6
2009–2010	40	227	105	41	23	436	25,938	20.7	15
2014–2015	44	329	122	75	182	752	38,498	34.2	24.3
2017–2018	46	365	123	101	263	898	39,050	36.6	25.8

Source: MHRD (2011a, 2016a, 2018) and NUEPA (2005).

Table 6.3 *Share of Public Expenditure on Education by Levels in 2010–2011 and 2014–2015*

Sector	Expenditure as % of GDP					
	State/UTs		Centre		Total	
	2010–2011 (A)	2014–2015 (EE)	2010–2011 (A)	2014–2015 (BE)	2010–2011 (A)	2014–2015 (BE)
Elementary education	1.27	1.42	0.43	0.40	1.70	1.82
Secondary education	0.89	0.87	0.10	0.11	0.99	0.98
University and higher education	0.53	0.44	0.33	0.22	0.86	0.66
Adult education	0	0.01	0.01	0	0.01	0.01
Technical education	0.24	0.32	0.24	0.25	0.48	0.57
Total (education)	**2.94**	**3.06**	**1.11**	**0.99**	**4.04**	**4.04**

Source: MHRD (2011b, 2016b).

university and higher education both by the central government and the provincial governments.

This is the repercussion of the neoliberal principles and SAP which India adopted in 1980s. To reach out the level of global standard and self-reliance, India initiated the establishment of eminent HEIs such as Indian Institute of Technology for engineering courses, Indian Institute of Management for management courses and All India Institute of Medical Sciences for medical courses in 1950s and 1960s. These were completely funded by the government along with other public universities and colleges as well as private colleges. But SAP and principle of new public management in lieu of greater cost efficiency persuaded a market-oriented management of public sector. This was reflected through a policy revolution in Indian higher education system that moved towards privatization of public HEIs and encouraged the private sector to meet the growing demand for technical and professional courses.

Many committees and commissions set up by the government gave suggestions for various cost-sharing measures to share the cost of higher education and, therefore, reducing the financial burden of public exchequer. While Punnaya Committee (UGC, 1993) suggested recovery of cost and hence generation of income to a level of 15–25 per cent of annual recurrent expenditure of the university concerned, the Swaminathan Committee (AICTE, 1994) suggested for cost recovery from students of HEIs and introduction of education cess from industries set up in India. From time to time various committees and commissions have emphasized on alternative sources of financing in addition to public financing such as Ambani-Birla Committee Report in the year 2000 (emphasizing on academia–industry linkages and public private partnership [PPPs]), CABE committee Report in the year 2005 (allocation and utilization of resources and generation through research collaboration activities), National Knowledge Commission in 2006 (GoI, 2007; suggestions for improved management of HEIs and promotion of intellectual property rights), Yashpal Committee Report in 2009 (encouraging fundraising through philanthropy, alumni and other non-governmental sources and foreign university participation) and N. R. Narayana Murthy Committee Report in 2012 (corporate sector participation in higher education to further the market participation for improving efficiency and autonomy) (Panigrahi, 2018a).

The impact of such recommendations, and thereby policy changes, has been reflected in terms of changing or relative decline in financing of higher education both at the central and state level as shown in Table 6.3. Even states with higher public expenditure on university or higher education compared to others have not commensurate with growing demand for higher education and rising enrolments of students in their respective HEIs (Panigrahi, 2017). Similarly, the nonrecurring or development grants by the central government funding agencies to provincial level HEIs are very little for their growth and development. It has been pointed out by the twelfth plan document (GoI, 2013) that while state system enrols more than 15 times of central institutions, they received only one-third of grants in eleventh plan and half of the central funds went to central institutions.

The separate policies of the central and provincial governments to finance higher education creates a 'Great Institutional Divide' between central universities and institutions (with ample funds) and expanding body of affiliated colleges (with ceaseless struggle for their existence surviving with scarce funds received from government and specialized agencies) which force the latter type of institutions to fall in the trap of underdevelopment and therefore suffer in all fronts such as quality, equity and excellence in higher education (Azad, 1985). It can't be ignored that the funding of a university must have a direct relationship to its objectives and should be designed to promote quality, efficiency, autonomy, accountability and relevance (UGC, 1993).

ALTERNATIVE SOURCES OF FINANCING HIGHER EDUCATION AND RESOURCE MOBILIZATION IN INDIA

The decline in public funding as a result of fiscal constraints of government post SAP and several policy reforms have encouraged various cost-recovery or cost-sharing measures, and exploration of income-generating activities by HEIs to cope with the scarcity of funds at their disposal.

Cost-Sharing Measures

Student fee has got most of the attention for sharing of cost of higher education with the argument that students are more benefitted out of higher education. Cost recovery, particularly in terms of student fees, has become an important source of income in public institutions in many countries including India (Varghese & Panigrahi, 2015). The High Power Committee (AICTE, 1994) recommended fee enhancement in higher education for admission, examination and examination-related expenses, laboratory and library, sports and extra-curricular activities, hostel and consumables such as electricity and water. The twelfth plan document also suggested for increasing the fees to reasonable and sustainable levels by provincial universities and colleges.

Educational loan is another popular method to share the cost of higher education with students/parents. India initiated educational loan scheme in 1963 by implementing a scheme of interest-free national scheme with the objective of improving access to higher education for deserving students without getting deterred by its cost. It was revised in 2001 as new educational loan scheme and subsequently revised in 2004–2005. The current scheme is the loan guarantee authority covering bank loans for accredited universities of India and abroad (NUEPA, 2008). Apart from the defaulter, problems that are there are the inherent difficulties in implementation of student loans in India such as poor recovery rate, access to loan, coverage of total educational expenses (Tilak, 2007), students from general category coming from middle- or high-income families getting access to educational loan due to their capacity to repay loan (collateral security unofficially demanded), delay in disbursement of loans, partial coverage of study expenses, emphasis on ranking of HEI, attitudes of banking personnel (Panigrahi, 2010).

Other methods of cost-sharing such as graduate tax method, HC contract and voucher system are not much emphasized or implemented in Indian context.

Resource Mobilization by HEIs

As an impact of privatization policy, new courses and programmes, and short-term courses are started in many public HEIs in self-financing mode to generate some income.

As per recommendations mentioned before by committees at policy level, various research programmes and consultancy activities are undertaken serving departments of central and state governments, public and private sectors, industries and other bodies which cover the expenses of staffs involved and required infrastructure.

Renting out of institutional infrastructure is practiced as a method of resource mobilization by selective HEIs. But such resource generation was at the expense of maintenance grants received from government (AICTE, 1994). However, with the recommendation of the High Power Committee, a mechanism of matching grant was given by UGC to provide an incentive grant that encourages universities to explore and mobilize additional resources.

Role of alumni association, corpus fund and philanthropic contributions or generation of endowments from individuals and corporate sector are also methods as per some of the recommendations adopted by certain universities but confined basically to central level HEIs.

The High Powered Committee (AICTE, 1994) recommended that the resources generated by the universities should constitute at least 15 per cent of the total recurring expenditure at the end of the first 5 years and at least 25 per cent at the end of 10 years.

However, the CABE Committee Report (NUEPA, 2005) suggested for delicate balancing between mobilization of resources to safeguard the virtues of social equity, economic efficiency, and educational excellence.

Most recently a new initiative has been geared up by the GoI to complement its financing of HEIs with borrowing from financial markets by the HEIs. The central government rolled a new initiative called Higher Education Finance Agency (HEFA) with the objective to leverage funds from the market and supplement them with donations and corporate social responsibility (CSR) funds. As per Union Budget, 2016–2017 these funds will be used to finance quality infrastructure such as buildings, state-of-the-art research labs and other infrastructure in topmost educational institutions of India such as IITs, NITs, IIITs and IISERs and central universities (GoI, 2016). The debts would be serviced through market borrowings; CSR funds from public sector undertakings, donations received from the CSR funds and escrowed student fee accounts.

While the impact of such an initiative is yet to be analysed, an overview of such scheme gives a glimpse of uncertainty with respect to well-established HEIs due to underdeveloped and vulnerable financial markets and the huge debt burden the debtor HEIs would face might deteriorate their financial autonomy if they fail to generate funds through the suggested options as mentioned above. By any means, HEFA can't be an alternative arrangement of provincial universities and colleges who have never been independent from political interference in their governance structure and financial management.

EMPIRICAL FINDINGS ON INSTITUTIONAL RESPONSES TO DECLINE IN PUBLIC FUNDING[2]

As discussed in previous section, there is a relative decline in central government funding at a juncture where there is a rapid expansion of higher education system. With the growing enrolment in HEIs, particularly at the provincial level, the government funding is expected to play an important role to meet the rising demand for resources by HEIs in provinces. Nine HEIs from five provinces representing different zones of the country are selected for the study.

Institutional Responses to Declining Public Funding

Over the years, the establishment expenses of selected universities have grown, particularly the salary expenses of both teaching and non-teaching staff of most of the universities. Very little amount is left for other components of establishment expenses such as staff welfare, fees and honorarium, employees retirement and terminal benefits, and pension fund such as contingency and other developmental purposes. The academic expenses such as expenditure on field/research activities, examination, participation in conferences/seminars/workshops conducted in the university, payment to guest faculty, student welfare, scholarships/stipends to students, printing, library and other academic expenses, administrative expenses such as expenses on infrastructure, communication, advertisement and publicity, legal expenses and miscellaneous expenses, and finally expenses of repairs and maintenance of the university gets very less revenue to be spent on. Strategies adopted by selected HEIs to decline in public funding are summarized in Figure 6.1.

a. Cost-Sharing Measures

As an immediate response to declining public funding, the cost-sharing measures came to the rescue of HEIs in India (like many HEIs in

---

[2] The findings are based on CPRHE–NIEPA research study on 'Financing of Higher Education: Institutional Responses to Decline in Public Funding' completed by the author and submitted as a Research Synthesis Report in June 2018 (Panigrahi, 2018b).

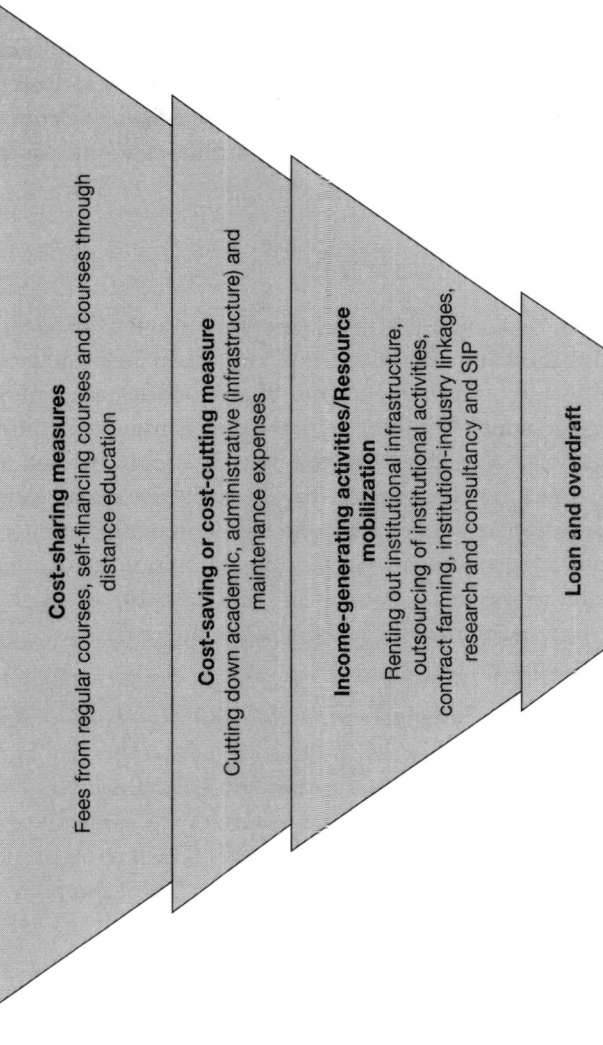

Cost-sharing measures
Fees from regular courses, self-financing courses and courses through distance education

Cost-saving or cost-cutting measure
Cutting down academic, administrative (infrastructure) and maintenance expenses

Income-generating activities/Resource mobilization
Renting out institutional infrastructure, outsourcing of institutional activities, contract farming, institution–industry linkages, research and consultancy and SIP

Loan and overdraft

Figure 6.1 *Institutional Responses to Decline in Public Funding*
Source: Author.

developed and developing countries). This type of measure became an obvious method after the policy orientation of Indian higher education system towards new public management and privatization of public HEIs. Therefore, based on importance or dependency on alternative methods of funding of Indian HEIs the cost-sharing measures stand out to be in the top of a reverse pyramid. Looking at the declining grants from central and state government, universities, particularly at the state level, and their affiliated colleges resort to various self-financing courses which ensures higher tuition and other fees contributing to the existing resources of the institution concerned.

Student Fees

The contribution of student fees to the income source of state-level universities and their respective affiliated colleges is large in many instances. Tuition fee is an integral part of any course/programme. However, regular course fee hike is protested, particularly tuition fee, and it is exempted for deprived groups such as girls, SC and ST students with respect to policy measures by the respective state government. Hence, with increasing expenditure requirements of state-level universities and colleges with growing enrolment, tuition fee does not contribute much to the total resources in many instances of selected institutions despite variations in the amount of tuition fee charged across selected HEIs (Figure 6.2).

Nonetheless, various other fees which are paid by students irrespective of their social and economic status, happens to be very high. Among all other types of fees, examination and assignments fees, and development fees contributes a lot to the total resources under fee category. Again there are variations among selected HEIs in terms of such fees. During focused group discussions with students, it is also pointed out that the students from deprived groups such as SC, ST and OBC pay more in lieu of examination fee as they appear for back papers. If the exam fee is higher, it is burdensome for students from deprived groups.

Similarly, other fees too add to the income sources of the aided colleges and autonomous college which cover development fee, sports fee, library fee, seminar fee and so on.

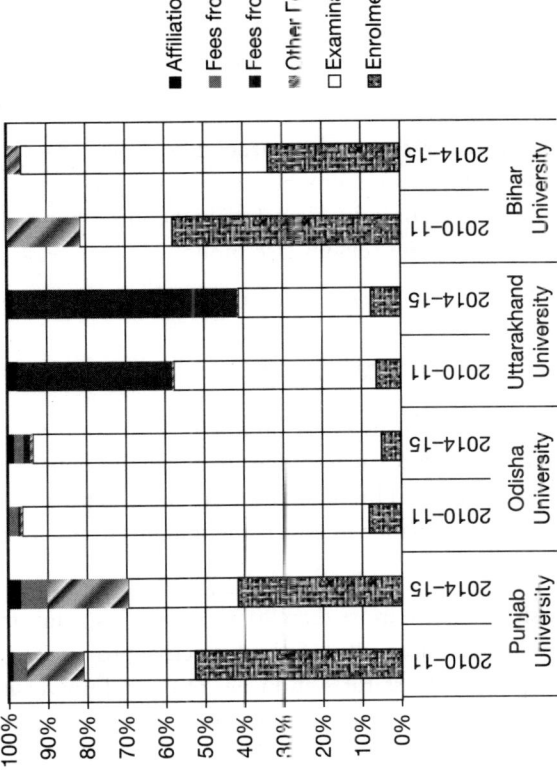

Figure 6.2 *Revenue from Fees*

Source: Author's compilations from finance data of selected institutions.

Note: Receipts from self-financing courses of Bihar University is merged with enrolment and tuition fee.

Provincial universities, in response to the decline in public funding, have also responded with an increase in the number of self-financing courses and distance education courses.

Self-financing Courses

Apart from fees, the easiest route has been charging very high amount of fees through self-financing courses. While self-financing courses in state-level universities are offered in few selective courses such as management and natural sciences, and very few courses in social sciences, the contribution in lieu of tuition fees, examination fees, development and other fees varies across selected institutions. There is a growing reliance on self-financing courses particularly by autonomous and government aided colleges.

So, self-financing courses are encouraged to compensate the resource crunch of provincial government and resource gap in resource starved colleges mostly in technical and professional courses but courses offered in social sciences under self-finance mode is also increasing in private aided colleges.

Distance Education

Distance education is emerging as a new option for many of provincial universities to generate additional resources to meet the deficits due to decline in public funding. This adjusts the resource gap to certain extent due to decline or stagnancy in government grants to universities at the provinces.

Central universities receive more than 90 per cent of its grants from central government and welfare grants from respective provincial government. With respect to the statutes and rules of central universities, it does not have self-financing courses per se but course fee in regular engineering, medical, nursing and other such technical and professional courses is higher than general courses. Similarly, fees collected under distance mode also add up to their resources.

Overall, the contribution from self-financing courses for the colleges and distance education in case of universities has contributed substantially to the internal sources of income of universities and colleges.

b. Resource Mobilization through Income-Generating Activities

Provincial universities in their present capacity are unable to generate or mobilize resources from various alternative sources. Various popular income-generating measures such as contribution from alumni, research and consultancy activities, initiation of short-term courses and programmes, university–industry linkages and so on are rare for such institutions compared to their counterparts in established central universities/institutions who have such contributions from different individuals or bodies. The instances of renting out of university infrastructure such as guest house, auditorium, playground, seminar hall and so on are evident but generate lesser amount of resources.

Alumni Contributions

Contributions from alumni are negligible in case of provincial universities compared to well-established central universities who have eminent alumni group who can contribute towards the growth and development of their alma mater, the institutions from where they graduate. One of the selected provincial universities, being one of the oldest universities, has created eminent alumnus but very few of them have contributed from time to time in an irregular basis for the development of selective infrastructure in the university campus such as auditorium and library. Provincial level affiliated colleges barely have received any contributions under this head.

Consultancy, Research Projects and Short-Term Courses

Income under new collaborative research projects, consultancy activities and short-term courses are barely being initiated by many departments of universities and colleges at the provinces. Few exceptions could be in case of physical and life sciences, that too for any particular point of time related to research projects. But these are not consistent source of internal resources like the selected central university which has the capacity and capability to attract collaborative research, consultancy activities or offer new short-term courses which will attract students to get enrolled for a degree valued in the market.

Colleges are alien to such kind of idea, looking at their stance in terms of infrastructure and quality faculty members who are having PhD degrees or oriented towards research.

University–Industry Linkages

HEIs at the provinces located in an industrial region take advantage of their location to opt for academic and industry linkages. However, the contribution from this source is not much to the total income source of the institution. On the other hand, central universities can afford to have such collaborations and industrial sector would be ready to absorb its students after graduating from this university. An earlier study (Tilak & Rani, 2003) also argued for growing imbalance between various disciplines due to consultancy activities and university–industry linkages.

Renting out Institutional Infrastructure and Outsourcing Institutional Activities

Any kind of such activities for generation of income are negligible in government aided colleges who have shortages of infrastructure facilities such as seminar halls and auditorium, and are struggling to accommodate the growing number of enrolments in different courses. But autonomous colleges having their own infrastructure or generation of some infrastructure facilities through the operation of self-financing courses are able to mobilize some resources even though the amount is not quite significant. Outsourcing of university activities such as mess, security, transport, bank, post office, shops and so on contribute somehow but insignificantly in many instances.

Interest Deposits/Sale of Royalty/Publications

Some miscellaneous activities such as sale of publications, royalty, recovery of loans, interest bearing investments are also a part of resource mobilization but contribute less in case of few provincial universities.

In order to adjust inadequate public funding, government aided colleges have explored with earning interest from bank deposits (receipts fluctuating), water and electricity charges and usage of college transport.

Mobilizing Resources through Other Region-Specific Initiatives

Contract farming is found to be one significant contributor as an income generation source to provincial university located in hilly region. Such type of university with other constraints in expansion of infrastructure facilities (to start new courses or accommodate rising enrolment) by respective Hill Development Authority of the state, rent out the available unused land of it for farming purposes. It contributes around 30 per cent of its income from internal sources.

Students from Abroad

Well-established central universities have created an environment through appropriate infrastructure facilities for foreign students. This contributes little to the university. It needs to be explored further in terms of new courses and programmes. Such kind of initiative requires huge investment for which the resource scarce provincial universities and colleges can't put their foot forward to create a world class campus.

PPPs

Selected central university has taken up some initiatives for PPPs. These could be important sources of funding to compensate with decline in public funding. However, selected provincial universities and colleges are yet not out of this Pandora box where they can get associated with private bodies to generate some resources for their respective institutions.

c. Cost-Saving or Cost-Cutting Measures

Adjustments among Departments

The larger departments get a larger share of contingency fund compared to the smaller departments which barely solves their purpose for managing some of the activities as well as development of basic amenities. Though National Assessment and Accreditation Council sets research as a criterion for funding of HEIs, over the years the resource crunch of the provincial universities has pushed down the expenditure on research by many of the state universities with few exceptions. The expenses on conferences, seminars, workshops and so on have gone down unless it has been sponsored by the organizers outside the university. The institution does not give much emphasis to such activities except few initiatives by HODs of science departments who organize international seminars and conferences too.

Except salary income, the other benefits such as medical, child education, LTC, insurance policies, pensions and so on have been reduced substantially across universities and colleges which is meant for both regular academic and non-academic staff.

Except autonomous colleges, the government aided colleges also fail to fulfil many of the requirements of several departments. This is somehow a lack of initiative too at the level of departments due to lack of autonomy of HODs to take decisions in many financial issues of their respective departments, which is with the principal of their respective colleges. They merely remain a head on paper only.

Temporary Appointment of Teaching and Non-teaching Staff

To adjust the resource gap and growing expenditure of the institution, the university resorts to manage with guest, ad hoc and reemployed faculty, and contractual staff instead of making permanent employment which is also dependent upon the provincial government policy. No sanctioned positions are filled once they are vacant both in case of teaching and non-teaching staff.

The shortages of teaching and non-teaching staffs is adjusted with multitasking of staffs, employing temporary staff both in teaching and non-teaching, ad hoc or guest teachers or reemployed teachers. Otherwise, some of the university activities are outsourced through private bodies. There are instances of appointment of part-time non-teaching staffs too in Bihar offering very indecent amount of salary.

There are instances of adjustment with contractual faculty with a very non-acceptable salary of less than rupees 10,000 per month that too without issuing any appointment letter to the respective teacher concerned. This indirectly impacts the quality of teaching–learning as well as creates an uncertainty in the availability of teachers for different courses in the college. Such types of arrangements are basically in private aided colleges where majority of courses are under self-financing mode. These are not necessary for the technical and professional courses rather liberal arts, science and commerce courses. This also shows loose regulations in terms of offering of self-financing courses in the name of encouraging privatization of public institutions.

Adjustment by Cutting Down Expenditures on Infrastructure and Maintenance

The infrastructure development and maintenance activities are reduced to a greater extent. The renovations of the buildings, rooms, labs, toilets, student common rooms, staff rooms and so on are affected with little amount of money left for such activities. The expenditure on repair and maintenance is very low in provincial universities even though with few exceptions. Similarly, government colleges have almost a scanty amount for maintenance but autonomous colleges have stagnant expenditure and aided colleges somehow take some initiative to increase spending on maintenance of available infrastructure facilities. This has long-run repercussions on the growth and development of the institution.

Similarly, there is a decline in investment on books, journals and periodicals in the library, chemical materials, and equipment in the laboratories and other infrastructure like computers are shared by students and faculty members.

d. Loans from Financial Agencies and Overdraft

After exploring various alternative measures such as cost-sharing measures, cost-cutting or cost-saving measures and various income-generating activities to finance the institution due to shortage of resources, the universities and colleges at the provincial level many a times get dragged into extreme steps like borrowings of loans from the bank to adjust the deficits.

Such borrowings are basically for establishment of new infrastructure or completion of incomplete buildings due to insufficient development grants from government or delay in receipt of grants due to multiple reasons. The inflationary rise in prices are not taken into account in the development grants for new infrastructure. This adds up to the deficit of the institution which compels them to seek bank loans to rule out possible future financial loss. The delay in receipt of grants is due to delay in disbursement of instalments from the higher education authority or respective funding agencies.

State universities also resort to overdrafts to meet some part of day-to-day recurring expenditure which is compensated later with other sources received in subsequent financial years. There are overdrafts in case of autonomous college too to improve its infrastructure facilities for self-financing courses.

In an earlier study, it was observed that the delay of funds receipt is compensated with other alternatives such as overdraft, supplementary grants, curtailing of expenditure, postponing expenditure, transferring funds from one account to other (Mridula, 1985).

CONCLUSION

The National Education Policy of 1986 had pointed out the need of larger assistance that the provinces due to the expansion of the higher education system. According to the Punnaya Committee Report (UGC, 1993), the input-based funding that India follows, promotes cost consciousness, autonomy and accountability but impacts the quality because it limits research, innovations and diversification. The Central Advisory Board of Education (CABE) committee (NUEPA, 2005) suggested for an appropriate mix of block grants, maintenance grants, matching grants and development grants to meet all the important needs of higher education such as promote excellence in research, innovative teaching, achieve equity and efficiency (due to performance-based grants).

The twelfth plan advocates a paradigm shift in funding from demand-based grants and input-based funding to entitlement based grants or outcome based funding through the flagship programme Rashtriya Uchchatar Siksha Abhiyan (RUSA) with the objective of norm-based funding and future grants to be outcome based. RUSA states that mandatory accreditation in India's higher education sector would enable it to become a part of the global quality assurance system.

The declining public funding results in deep repercussions for the provincial universities and colleges. As the study finds, under such circumstances, the major cost-sharing measure for the state universities are resorting to self-financing courses and distance learning courses. Apart from that, there has been no new recruitment rather manage with ad hoc or guest faculty or reemployed faculty. Apart from salaries, the other benefits given to the faculty members are cut down or shared. As income-generating activities, there are instances of contract farming, particularly in hilly areas, institution and industry linkages, and interests generated from bank deposits. There are barely any research overheads, alumni funds and short-term courses to generate additional resources for state-level institutions. The plight of the affiliated colleges of such state universities is very pathetic when compared with the state universities. The initiatives by the central universities for sharing of costs and generation of additional resources are such as charging for the usage of labs, library, computer, Wi-Fi and so on by the projects undertaken at the university, reducing the subscription of print journal (many of them are unused) and shift to online journals, charging for water and electricity connections, renting out playgrounds, guest house, auditorium, vehicles and so on and outsourcing many of the university activities.

All these affect the growth and development of these universities and colleges despite meeting the majority of higher education demand at the state level. The well-established central universities have a better scope to mobilize resources from different sources such as consultancy, projects from national and international agencies, renting out their available infrastructure such as markets, shops, auditorium, vehicles, seminar halls and so on and outsourcing various services like securities, canteen, hostel mess and so on. But for state universities mobilizing resources in case of shortages in public funding or delay in receipts make them resort to fees. In some instances, the tuition fee is higher with large number of students. Fees collected as examination fee also contributes a larger share within fees components.

Though self-financing course does not contribute to state universities but aided colleges get a larger proportion of income from running self-financing courses. The scope for any other income-generating sources is limited with few instances of contract farming, investments income from bank deposits and renting out minimum facilities of the institutions particularly by aided colleges.

The mounting expenditures of these institutions resort to various cost-saving measures which indirectly impacts the growth and development of these institutions and fulfilling the purpose of provision of higher education. There is the need of policy interventions for these struggling HEIs where grants for development purposes would make these institutions to improve their quality in an era of global rankings and higher competitions. The major area to be intervened would be to filling out vacant posts and providing adequate resources to run the overburdened salary expenses. Similarly, there is the need of extending development grants to state universities and colleges according to the requirement to reach a level of competitiveness to improve quality of teaching–learning as well as to get equipped with basic infrastructure to cater the growing enrolment of students in such institutions.

REFERENCES

AICTE. (1994). *Report of the high-power committee for mobilization of additional resources for technical education* (Swaminathan Committee Report). New Delhi: AICTE.

Azad, J. L. (1985). *Financing of higher education in Indian states: A case study of Andhra Pradesh, Gujarat, Haryana, and Orissa.* New Delhi: NIEPA.

Becker, G. S. (1964). *Human capital: A theoretical and empirical analysis with special reference to education.* New York, NY: Columbia University Press.

———, G. S. (1975). *Human capital: A theoretical and empirical analysis with special reference to education.* New York, NY: Columbia University Press.

Dreze, J., & A. Sen. (1996). *Indian economic development and social opportunity.* Delhi: Oxford University Press.

GoI. (2007). *Report to the nation 2006.* New Delhi: National Knowledge Commission.

GOI. (2013). *Rashtriya Uchchatar Shiksha Abhiyan (RUSA)*. New Delhi: MHRD in association with TISS, Mumbai.

———. (2016). *Union Budget 2016–2017*. New Delhi: GoI.

Lleras, M. P. (2004). *Investing in human capital: A capital markets approach to student funding*. Cambridge: Cambridge University Press.

Lucas, R. E. Jr. (1988). On the mechanics of economic development. *Journal of Monetary Economics, 22*(1), 3–42.

McMahon, W. W. (2006). Education finance policy: Financing the non-market and social benefits. *Journal of Education Finance, 32*(2), 264–284.

MHRD (2011a). *Statistics of Higher and Technical Education*. New Delhi: MHRD. GoI.

MHRD (2011b). *Analysis of budgeted expenditure on education 2007–2008 to 2009–2010*. New Delhi: Bureau of Planning, Monitoring and Statistics, Department of Higher Education, GoI.

———. (2012). *Analysis of budgeted expenditure on education 2008–2009 to 2010–2011*. New Delhi: Bureau of Planning, Monitoring and Statistics, Department of Higher Education, GoI.

———. (2014). *Analysis of budgeted expenditure on education 2010–2011 to 2012–2013*. New Delhi: Bureau of Planning, Monitoring and Statistics, Department of Higher Education, GoI.

———. (2015). *Analysis of budgeted expenditure on education 2011–2012 to 2013–2014*. New Delhi: Bureau of Planning, Monitoring and Statistics, Department of Higher Education, GoI.

———. MHRD (2016a). *All India Survey of Higher Education 2014–15*. New Delhi: MHRD. GoI.

———. (2016b). *Analysis of budgeted expenditure on education 2013–2014 to 2014–2015*. New Delhi: Bureau of Planning, Monitoring and Statistics, Department of Higher Education, GoI.

———. MHRD (2018). *All India Survey of Higher Education 2017–2018*. New Delhi: MHRD. GoI.

Mridula. (1985). *State funding of universities: A Study of maintenance grants to universities*. New Delhi: Association of Indian Universities.

Musgrave, R. A., & Musgrave, P. (1989). *Public finance in theory & practice* (5th ed., p. 627). New Delhi: McGraw-Hill Book Company.

NUEPA. (2005). *Report of the CABE Committee on financing of higher and technical education*. New Delhi: NUEPA.

NUEPA. (2008). *Background paper on 11th Five Year Plan in higher education strategies for effective implementation*. New Delhi: NUEPA.

Panigrahi, J. (2010). Determinants of educational loan by commercial banks in India: Evidence and implications based on a sample survey. *Journal of Educational Planning and Administration, 24*(4), 379–400.

———. (2017). *Resource allocation and innovative methods of financing higher education in India* (CPRHE Research Paper No. 6). New Delhi: NUEPA.

————. (2018a). Innovative financing of higher education: Changing options and implications. *Higher Education for the Future, 5*(1), 61–74.

————. (2018b). *Financing of higher education: institutional responses to decline in public funding* (A Research Synthesis Report). New Delhi: CPRHE–NIEPA.

Romer, P. M. (1989). Capital accumulation in the theory of long run growth. In Robert Barro (ed.), *Modern business cycle theory* (pp. 51–127). Cambridge: Harvard University Press.

Schultz, T. W. (1961). Investment in human capital. *The American Economic Review, 51*(1), 1–17.

Tilak, J. B. G. (2007). Student loans and financing of higher education in India. *Journal of Educational Planning and Administration, 21*(3): 231–256.

Tilak, J. B. G., & Rani, G. P. (2003). Changing pattern of university finances in India. *Journal of Services Research, 2*(2), 5–46.

University Grants Commission (UGC). (1993). *Report of Justice Punnayya Committee on UGC Funding of institutions of higher education.* New Delhi: UGC.

UNESCO Institute of Statistics (UIS). (2018). Education: Government Expenditure on Tertiary Education as a percentage of GDP (%). Retrieved from http://data.uis.unesco.org/index.aspx?

Varghese, N. V. (2015). *Challenges of massification of higher education in India* (CPRHE Research Papers 1). New Delhi: National University of Educational Planning and Administration.

Varghese, N. V., & Panigrahi, J. (2015, July). *Report on the international seminar on massification of higher education in large academic systems.* New Delhi: National University of Educational Planning and Administration.

Chapter 7

Self-financing Courses in Public Institutions

Subir Maitra

INTRODUCTION

In a knowledge-driven globalized society, higher education plays an important role in supplying high-quality labour and fostering faster growth. Higher education is expected to improve functional ability and competence of an individual, making an individual more employable. Adequate provision of state finance is arguably the best option for developing the higher education sector. But given the size of fund requirement for expansion of higher education, it is most unlikely that a state would be able to meet the financial requirements of the fast-expanding sector. Therefore, the non-government sources of funding become important. The introduction of cost recovery and income-generating activities in the public institutions of higher education are examples of this trend. Among the measures adopted to generate additional income, offering self-financing courses is common in many universities and colleges.

This chapter provides a review of self-financing courses offered by public institutions of higher education in India. The next section discusses higher education expansion followed by an introduction to the nature of self-financing courses in the second and third sections. The fourth and sixth sections elaborate on the nature of self-financing courses and their pricing. The subsequent sections discuss issues related to quality of programmes offered and teachers selected for teaching in self-financing courses, and regulations regarding self-financing courses maintaining quality of such courses. The last section concludes this chapter by way of making some policy suggestions.

PUBLIC HIGHER EDUCATION INSTITUTIONS (HEIs) IN INDIA

The higher education sector in India is characterized by the existence of a variety of institutions. At present, the main categories of university/university-level institutions are: central universities, state universities, private universities, deemed-to-be universities and university-level institutions, Institutions of National Importance, institutions under State Legislature Act, colleges/institutions maintained/affiliated with university and stand-alone institutions not affiliated/recognized with university (Table 7.1).

On the basis of funding, these HEIs can broadly be classified into two categories: public and private institutions. Public institutions include both government institutions and aided institutions such as universities and affiliated colleges, and other institutes, whose major source of fund is the government, both the central and the state. Therefore, all central and state universities, Institutions of National Importance and institutions under State Legislature Act are known as public institutions. Those deemed-to-be universities, such as Dayalbagh Educational Institute, Agra; Gandhigram Rural Institute, Gandhigram, Dindigul; and Tata Institute of Social Sciences (TISS), Mumbai, and stand-alone institutions which receive plan and non-plan grants from the government also fall in the category of public institutions. In this chapter, we shall refer to this category of public (higher education) institutions.

Private unaided institutions, however, sustain primarily on the fees charged from their students. Private universities such as Amity University, ICFAI University, Adamas University and Techno India University, and private self-financing engineering, medical and general degree colleges are known as private unaided institutions. These institutions are all 'not-for-profit' institutions.

Table 7.1 *HEIs in India*

Category of Institution	Details
Central university	A university established or incorporated by a Central Act.
State university	A university established or incorporated by a Provincial Act or by a State Act.
Private university	A university established through a State/Central Act by a sponsoring body, namely, a society registered under the Societies Registration Act 1860, or any other corresponding law for the time being in force in a state or a public trust or a company registered under Section 25 of the Companies Act, 1956.
Deemed-to-be university	An institution deemed-to-be university, commonly known as deemed university, refers to a high-performing institution which has been so declared by central government under Section 3 of the University Grants Commission (UGC) Act, 1956.
Institution of National Importance	An institution established by Act of Parliament and declared as an Institution of National Importance such as Indian Institute of Technology (IIT), National Institute of Technology (NIT), Indian Institute of Information Technology (IIIT) and Indian Institute of Science Education and Research (IISER).
Institution under State Legislature Act	An institution established or incorporated by a State Legislature Act such as Nizam's Institute of Medical Sciences, Hyderabad; Sri Venkateswara Institute of Medical Sciences, Tirupati; Sher-i-Kashmir Institute of Medical Sciences, Srinagar; Indira Gandhi Institute of Medical Sciences, Patna; Sanjay Gandhi Postgraduate Institute of Medical Sciences, Lucknow.
Colleges/Institutions maintained/affiliated with university	These are institutions which can run degree programmes but are not empowered to provide degrees on their own and have to necessarily be attached with some university/university-level institution for the purpose of awarding a degree. Colleges can be of two types: (a) university/constituent college—a college maintained by the university and (b) affiliated

(Continued)

Table 7.1 (Contiuned)

Category of Institution	Details
	college—a college affiliated to a university. Some colleges are given autonomous status. The UGC provides financial assistance to eligible colleges which are included under Section 2(f) and declared fit to receive central assistance (UGC grant) under Section 12(B) of UGC Act, 1956 as per the approved pattern of assistance under various schemes.
Stand-alone institutions not affiliated/recognized with university	There are several institutions which are outside the purview of a university and college. These institutions generally run diploma/ postgraduate (PG) diploma level programmes for which they require recognition from one or other statutory bodies. Such institutions are known as stand-alone institutions. Such institutions mainly fall under following categories:
	—Indian Institute of Management (IIM) awarding PG diploma in management of two years duration whose entry qualification is graduate.
	—Diploma awarding institutions under the control of All India Council for Technical Education (AICTE), for example, Lal Bahadur Shastri Institute of Management awarding PG diplomas in management for two years' duration, whose entry qualification is graduate.
	—Diploma awarding institutions under the control of Indian Nursing Council (INC).
	—Government or government-recognized institutions to conduct teachers training courses whose entry qualification is 10 + 2, for example, District Institute of Educational and Training (DIET) or similar institutes.
	—Polytechnics.
	—Company Secretary, charted accountancy, actuarial science and the likes.

Source: http://mhrd.gov.in/sites/upload_files/mhrd/files/ebook/ebook_files/annexures/Annexure-2.pdf

SELF-FINANCING COURSES

Self-financing courses in public institutions refer to certain career-oriented courses being conducted by the government aided universities/colleges/institutions without the financial support of the government. The recurring expenditure to run these courses is met by students' fees and the likes (MHRD, 2012).

Self-financing courses were launched in the public institutions (universities and colleges) during the Tenth Plan with a view of equipping students through an add-on course with some practical knowledge along with the regular bachelor's degree course. Later, professional degree level courses were launched under self-financing mode, based on the principle of recovery of cost of the course. Many of these courses were interdisciplinary in nature.

Initially, public institutions had some reluctance and reservation against the introduction of self-financed courses. But with the passage of time, these institutions could come out of their reservations and reluctance and soon a variety of self-financed courses covering various disciplines, subjects and skills were introduced. These courses ranged from certificate to diploma, graduate to PG courses, short-term to long-term courses and totally knowledge-based to completely skill-oriented courses. Even courses of preparatory nature for facilitating entry of students to higher level courses as well as jobs were also introduced.

Initially, the UGC provided funds to run vocational courses in the colleges. But in view of growing demand of these courses amongst students on account of their employment potential and students' willingness to pay, these courses began to be offered by the public HEIs on self-financing mode.

NECESSITY OF SELF-FINANCING COURSES IN INDIA

According to the human capital (HC) theory, expenditure on education primarily is an investment which earns a net positive rate of return for the investor (student) in terms of a future stream of higher earnings than what would have been otherwise possible, over and above the costs of education comprising explicit as well as implicit costs. Based on this, it is argued that higher education should be primarily funded by the investor as the private rate of return exceeds the social rate of return narrowly defined (Psacharopoulos & Patrinos, 2004). Employment-oriented courses which are in high demand can, therefore, be offered through self-financing mode, as the students are willing to pay for these courses in view of employment prospects. This is precisely the theoretical rationale behind launching self-financing courses in India.

In India, the growth of student enrolment in higher education has been quite phenomenal during the last four decades with student enrolment growing by 78.96 per cent between 1980–1981 and 1990–1991, 70.54 per cent between 1990–1991 and 2000–2001, 102.10 per cent between 2000–2001 and 2010–2011 (UGC, 2011).

Gross Enrolment Ratio (GER) in higher education has also been on the rise from 4.3 per cent in 1990–1991 to 8.1 per cent in 2001–2002, 19.4 per cent in 2010–2011 (MHRD, 2012) and further to 24.5 per cent in 2015–2016 (MHRD, 2016). The GoI has, however, set a target of 30 per cent for GER in higher education to be achieved by 2020.

Twelfth Five-Year Plan sought to achieve this target by expanding the institutional base of higher education (including technical, professional and vocational education) by creating additional capacity in existing institutions, establishing new institutions and incentivizing state governments. This requires a huge public investment on behalf of the central as well as the state governments. But with the central government expenditure as a percentage of gross domestic product remaining more or less stagnant at around 1.25 per cent, it is most unlikely that new capacity would be created. Hence, to accommodate more students in higher education, self-financing courses in regular as well as distance mode may be launched by the existing higher education institutes.

With the advancement of science and technology, trade and commerce, and a boom in the service sector, new professions are emerging. The rising demand of this 'new' labour in the market encouraged the universities and colleges to introduce new curricula with technology and management orientation, focusing primarily on the need of the service sector. These courses are in high demand and students completing these courses also get immediate employment. Such courses may be offered on self-financing mode by the public higher education institutes. All universities and colleges should have the autonomy to start self-financing courses, particularly in new and emerging areas where job opportunities exist, subject to the overall framework provided by their funding and regulatory bodies.[1]

Our current higher education curriculum is founded on the creation of knowledge stocks and then pushing these stocks to students and industry. However, our future education should be founded to curate the knowledge flows, where knowledge and insights are pulled from industry experts. For the sake of churning out employable graduates, it becomes pertinent for industry experts to collaborate with higher education institutes. There is a need to grant autonomy to individual institutions for designing curriculum. Universities may provide a broad framework within which individual faculty members, both within the university and in the colleges, should be encouraged to innovate and experiment to transform teaching and learning into a fascinating and rewarding experience. The universities and colleges should focus equally on academic and job-oriented programmes while planning for new programmes to make higher education relevant for the world of work.[2] Since, presently, industry spends money on training of newly recruited graduates, curriculum in the higher education institutes may be so customized as to suit the requirements of the industry. Such courses may partly be financed by the industry and partly by the students.

SELF-FINANCING COURSES BEING OFFERED BY THE PUBLIC INSTITUTIONS IN INDIA

Self-financing courses came to be introduced in the public higher education institutes in India during the mid-1990s either as an offshoot or

---

[1] *Report of the Central Advisory Board of Education (CABE) Committee on Autonomy of Higher Education Institutions*, 2005 (NIEPA, 2005).
[2] ibid.

as continuation of the vocational courses that were introduced in these institutes at the undergraduate (UG) level. These courses were mostly interdisciplinary in nature, involving different departments such as general science, social science, library science, law, management, computer science, information technology (IT), home science, travel and tourism, mass media and journalism, and so on (Rao & Singh, 2002). The courses were introduced at all three levels: degree, diploma and certificate. Degree courses were of varied duration from one year to five years. The duration of diploma courses varied between six months to two years. Certificate courses were of two months to one year duration. Students are admitted to these courses through different methods. For some courses which are in high demand, students are admitted through admission tests. For other courses, students having the required qualification are asked to apply and then a merit list is prepared, based on which admission of students takes place. For those courses that are not in much demand, admission is done on the first come, first served basis. A list of all such courses is given in Table 7.2.

IITs, for quite some time, have been offering MTech and PhD courses with some seats reserved for self-financed and sponsored candidates. IITs are charging higher fees ranging between 90 per cent and more than 300 per cent of regular fees for self-financed and sponsored candidates. IIMs also offer popular management development programmes and customized executive programmes for different organizations including corporates, government, public sector undertakings, educational institutions, regulatory bodies and so on. All these programmes are of self-financed variety.

Many central universities also have self-financed courses. For example, Jamia Millia Islamia of New Delhi has as many as 10 PG, 9 UG, 6 PG diplomas, 1 advanced diploma, 8 diplomas and 6 certificate courses, all under self-financing mode. Tezpur University has a provision for admission under Self Supported Scheme (SSS). The waitlisted candidates on merit basis are eligible for admission under SSS with additional fees. Maulana Azad National Urdu University of Hyderabad offers self-financed paramedical certificate and diploma courses, certificate courses in TV and media industry disciplines.

Table 7.2 Self-financed Degree/Diploma/Certificate Courses Offered by Different Universities/Colleges

Duration	
In Years	Title of Courses
1 year	BLib/MLib and Information Science, LLB (Professional) MSc Computer Cognition Technology, MTech, BEd.
2 years	MBL, MBA, MFC, MHRM, HRDEM, MFAM, MIM, MFC (Finance and Control), MIB, MFA, MTA, MSc (Holistic Psychological Counselling, Software System, Advanced Computer Communication, Finance and Computer Communication, Computer Science, IT, Biotechnology, Energy Science, Industrial Bio-Tech, Bio-informatics, Micro Biology, Home Science), MSc (MMTL).
	MA (Counselling Psychology, Educational Commission, DS, Criminology and Forensic Science), Masters in Multimedia Development, MPhil, MTech, MPhil, MSW, MA/MSc Mathematics, Masters in Global Business Management, LLM;
	MA in English, Hindi, Sanskrit, History, Political Science, Economics, Public Administration.
	Partly Self-Financed Courses in Sociology, Political Science, History Performing Arts (DDM), Social Work, Kannada English, Zoology, Applied Genetics, Electronic Science, Statistics, Bio-Technology, Geography, Psychology, Library & Information Science, Sericulture, Chemistry, Bio-Chemistry, Mathematics, M Com. MBA, MCA, MS Communication, LLM-Law.
3 years	MBA (Executive/Evening), BBA, BBM (Bachelor in Bank Management), BCS (Corporate Secretaryship), BTTM, BIBF (International Business and Finance), BSc Bio-Technology/Bio-Chemistry/Micro Biology, BSc Costume Designing and Fashion Art, BSc Computer Maintenance, Industrial Fish and Fishery, BSc Space Designing and Draftsmanship, BA/BSc Photography, Industry, Fishers, BSc Family and Community science and Fashion Designing, BSc IT, BSc Costume Designing and Fashion Art.

(Continued)

Table 7.2 *(Continued)*

Duration	
In Years	**Title of Courses**
	BA/BSc, BCom (Evening), BHA (Hospital Administration), Bachelor of Lab Technology, TDC.Com (Evening).
	BEd with Options in English, Malyalam, Hindi, Arabic, Commerce, Maths, Physical Science Natural Science Home Science and Social Science.
4 years	BSc Tourism and Management, BTech (Chemical, Paints, Plastics, Food, Oil Fats and Waxes), BPharma.
5 years	BA LLB

Diploma	
Duration	**Title of Courses**
6 months	PGD Course in Preservation and Conservation of Medical and Aromatic Plant
1 year	PG Diploma in Human Rights and Duties Education, Diploma in Criminology, Diploma in Taxation Laws, Labour Law, Labour Welfare and Personal Management, Co-operative Law, PGDMLE, PGDEL, PGDHRL, PGDMM, DMLT, DNYS, DNYS, PGD in Counselling and Psychology Diploma in Company Secretaryship, PGDTHM, PGD in Tour and Guiding, Tourism.
	PGD Marketing, Business Management/IRPM/HRD/ CCP, PGD Fashion Designing/Nutrition Dietetics/ Interior Designing and Environment, DIB, PGDCA, Office Management, PGD Geographic Information System (GIS)/Remote Sensing, Diploma in Glass, PGD in Mass Media and Creative Writing, (Hindi)/TV Journalism/ Hindustani, Journalism, Diploma in Public Administration and Local Self Government, Diploma in Yoga, Music and Dance, PGD in Pharmaceutical Marketing, Advanced PGD in Computer Application, IT.
1 year 6 months	Home Science Diploma for Women
	PGD in Medical Technology
2 years	PGD in Fashion Technology PGDCA

Certificate	
Duration	Title of Courses
2 months	Computer Automation in Office Management
2 months	Basic Course in French, Basic Course in German, Advanced Course in French, Computer Foundation Course
4 months	Computer Education, Web Designing, Computer Education, C++ and Oracle8
6 months	Computer Education and Panting
9 months	Hindi
1 year	Sanskrit, Professional Lab Chemistry, Advanced Computer Application Course, Fine Arts

Source: Rao and Singh (2002).

State universities are also offering self-financed courses. Utkal University, for example, has 17 self-financing courses such as two-year executive MBA, MBA (financial management), five-year integrated MBA, 5 year integrated MCA, MSc applied micro-biology, MSc environmental science, BPharma, master of journalism and mass communication, PG diploma in remote sensing and GIS. The Maharaja Sayajirao University of Baroda, in fact, has a huge bouquet of self-financed courses involving almost all faculties. This university is presently offering 71 higher payment/self-financing courses of all varieties such as PG, graduate, PG diploma, diploma and certificate. Some of their courses are quite unique such as MA in Russian (military aviation), MA in Russian (philology), BSc fashion communication, MSc in medical biotechnology and MSc in petroleum geology. The University of Mysore has a few self-financed courses such as MCom (financial services), PG diploma in banking and insurance management, PG diploma in research methodology and quantitative techniques for data analysis, certificate course in Indian economic policy analysis and so on. University of Madras offers self-supportive programmes such as MSc in biotechnology and molecular biology, MSc in actuarial science, MSc HRD psychology, MJ online media, MA Bharatanatyam, MSc neuroscience and MA yoga theory and practice.

A variety of self-financed courses are also being offered by the affiliated colleges, particularly autonomous colleges all over the country. Over time, some of these courses have been discontinued or partially modified according to the demand of the market. For example, IT-related courses have been withdrawn because of lack of demand and new courses have been introduced. Some institutions have been quite innovative in designing their courses. Taking advantage of its autonomous status, Christ College of Kerala has started offering courses such as BSc computer science with computer graphics and web design as an elective subject, Bachelor of Arts (BA) Malayalam with cyber Malayalam as an elective subject and BA social work with social work with elderly as an elective subject.[3] Kongunadu Arts and Science College of Coimbatore, affiliated to Bharathiar University, is offering innovative courses such as Bachelor of Commerce (BCom) professional accounting, BSc costume design and fashion, PG courses in customer relationship management, Tally 9.0 practical and investment management, and vermitechnology.[4] Madras Christian College also has self-financing courses in geography, tourism and travel management, visual communication, social work and so on. St. Xavier's College in Kolkata offers UG courses in mass communication, microbiology, film studies, computer science and so on and PG courses in computer science, microbiology, biotechnology and multimedia, all under self-financing mode. St. Xavier's College also offers PG diploma courses in a variety of subjects such as logistics and supply-chain management, human resource management, integrated marketing communication, certified accounts professional, NSE certified capital market professional, and foreign trade practices and management.[5]

Non-autonomous colleges, however, are not so much innovative in introducing self-financing courses for obvious reasons. For example, Rastraguru Surendranath College, Barrackpore, affiliated to the West Bengal State University offers PG courses in computer science, microbiology, geography, food and nutrition, accounts, finance and

---

[3] http://christcollegeijk.edu.in/showcontent?cid=17&title=Degree+Programmes

[4] http://www.kongunaducollege.ac.in/courses.php

[5] http://www.sxccal.edu

control. Fakir Chand College, Diamond Harbour, affiliated to the University of Calcutta, has self-financing master degree courses in Bengali, history, education, commerce and mathematics. Indraprastha College for Women affiliated to the Delhi University offers BA honours degree course in multimedia and mass communication. Atma Ram Sanatan Dharma College affiliated to the same university offers only BSc (honours) computer science course under self-financing mode.

PRICING OF SELF-FINANCED COURSES

So far as the charging of fees for self-financed courses is concerned, UGC does not provide any guideline. Since public institutions had ready infrastructure (hence no fixed cost as such), they could charge user fees only to recover the recurring expenditure (i.e., variable cost). Still the fee structures for self-financing courses have been found to vary from institution to institution and from course to course. The fee structure of courses has been found to depend ordinarily on (a) category of the course (degree/diploma/certificate and so on), (b) the duration of the course, (c) the demand for the course, (d) the name and reputation of the institute offering the course, and (e) market value of the course. Factors (d) and (e) are linked with the quality of the course and collectively they influence the demand for the course.

Of all the self-financed courses in India, probably IIMs charge the highest fees for their management courses. For example, IIM Ahmedabad charges ₹200,000 for its executive programme in business finance, a weekly programme of six months duration. IIM Kolkata's executive programme in applied finance comprising 270 hours of live online classes, and three campus visits spanning nine days cost ₹244,000 per student. IITs also charge a substantially higher fees to sponsored/self-financed students in MTech/MSc/PhD programmes. IIT Guwahati charges ₹51,545 per semester to sponsored/self-financed students staying at the hostel.

Affiliation aided colleges also have a different fee structure for self-financed courses which is significantly higher compared to the aided courses. Atma Ram Sanatan Dharma College of Delhi charges about ₹11,000 for first year admissions to aided BSc (honours) course but charges ₹45,000 for admission to self-financed BSc (honours) computer science course.[6] In Gurudas College of Kolkata, the first year fees for admission to self-financed BSc with honours in computer science/microbiology/BSc chemistry course aggregates to about ₹35,000 and that for admission to BA with honours in journalism and mass communication is about ₹28,000. In comparison to this, the admission fee for regular aided BSc (honours) course is only ₹4,105 and for BA (honours) course is only ₹3,295, for the first year in the same college.[7] St. Xavier's College (autonomous) in Kolkata charges ₹35,200 for admission to first year aided BSc (honours) course in physics/chemistry and ₹85,000 for admission to first year self-financed BSc (honours) course in computer science and microbiology. For BSc multimedia course, the first year course fee comes to about ₹117,000 in the same college.

ISSUES RELATING TO QUALITY OF SELF-FINANCING COURSES

The quality of self-financing courses reportedly varies from institution to institution. In higher education, cost and quality are positively related, as good quality education requires better infrastructure and better teachers. This implies that the value attached to a self-financed degree or certificate should depend on how much the student had to pay for the education. Higher the fees, better is the expected quality of the course. But self-financing course being an experience good/service, that is, good or service for which quality is observed by the buyer only after purchase, the problem of asymmetric information could well be present here. In that case, fees may not reflect the actual quality of the course.

Some self-financed courses offered by the universities and colleges have been quite popular among the students. In Maharashtra, courses such as Bachelor of Mass Media (BMM), Bachelor of Management Studies (BMS), Bachelor of Accounting and Finance (BAF) and Bachelor of Banking and Insurance (BBI), introduced in 2000 in some colleges affiliated to the Mumbai University, have been in high

---

[6] http://arsdcollege.ac.in/fee.aspx?id=217

[7] http://gurudascollege.edu.in/fees

demand among students as these courses, being tailor-made to meet the career needs of students, have an edge over the standard BA or BCom courses.[8] The curriculum of self-financed courses is better linked to the industry compared to regular courses. It includes several practical programmes. Specialized courses tend to have better employment opportunities, with banking firms preferring BBI graduates and angle broking firms hiring BAF students. As the number of students in a class for self-financed course is limited to 60 pupils, unlike 120 in regular UG classrooms, students normally get more attention from their teachers. Given the smaller size of class, teachers can also experiment several teaching methodologies such as role plays and seminars.

Questions are also being raised about the quality of self-financing courses. The students opting for self-financed courses suffer due to lack of competent teachers, poor infrastructure in colleges and shortcomings of the curriculum. Many self-financed courses involve project-based learning. However, many colleges don't have information and communication technology and other resources in place. So they run these courses just like other regular courses. Again, in self-financed courses, most of the teachers are appointed on temporary basis. They have little industry exposure and, as a result, the curriculum lacks sufficient practical aspects. Due to this, many students don't get jobs in their respective areas of expertise.

There has been quite a phenomenal increase in the number of public institutions in India since the mid-1990s, offering a bouquet of self-financing courses in engineering, medicine, pharmacy, architecture, management, law, media, fashion, journalism, tourism and others. The self-financing courses in management and business administration have boomed, so have courses in microbiology, biochemistry, biotechnology, computer science, IT, multimedia, social work and so on. This rather unusual growth in self-financing courses raises several .questions about its propriety. In India, where education is a not-for-profit sector, the proliferation of such courses in public universities and colleges is quite intriguing. Among the public institutions, the maximum proliferation has taken place in the aided private autonomous

---

[8] http://www.hindustantimes.com/education/how-useful-are-self-financed-courses/story-oNmMT0TynuucSuGwbNZWK.html

colleges. Since the fees charged by the colleges for self-financing courses are substantially higher in comparison to regular aided courses, questions can be raised about the motives of at least some of these institutions. There are reports that some institutions are generating surpluses out of these self-financing courses. Thus, they are 'not-for-profit' de jure, but 'for-profit' de facto. These institutes, sometimes, use these surplus funds for other purposes not related to the self-financed courses. This has a damaging impact on the quality of courses. As employability is linked with the quality of most of the self-financed courses, the employability of students graduating from these institutions suffers due to this.

The presence of 'informational asymmetry' makes it more difficult to ascertain quality. This informational asymmetry also acts as a boon to some institutions, which may like to generate huge surpluses at the cost of quality. Due to the presence of asymmetric information, a prospective student often makes wrong decisions about the course and institute. Some public institutions can also take advantage of the asymmetric information and provide their students with education of such quality which is much poorer than what they promised to deliver. If they resort to costcutting exercises in order to realize a larger surplus, that would definitely affect quality of education. The majority of graduates from these institutes will come out as 'unemployable' and their so-called 'degrees' just won't have the right fundamental education behind them. Generally, the institutes which are more concerned about their reputation would not enter into such malpractices.

SELF-FINANCING COURSES AND TEACHER RECRUITMENT

Although the students of self-financed courses in public institutions are charged substantially higher fees, it is quite doubtful whether they are being properly trained or not, as the teachers teaching them may not be competent enough. This is quite a common feature for many aided colleges affiliated to different universities. There are very few permanent faculty and the courses are being run with underpaid, overworked ad hoc teachers. In most cases, teachers are paid by the hour. Teachers need to engage themselves in other vocations or private tuitions to make out a living. University rules on qualifications and appointments are often flouted and underqualified teachers are employed. Some institutions employ underqualified teachers to keep costs low. Reservation policies are frequently ignored.

The peripatetic life of ad hoc teachers in self-financed courses is a major concern in higher public education. In self-financed course, the teachers will have jobs for as long as these courses can attract enough students willing to pay the high fees. This chronic insecurity allows exploitation and affects quality. They do not get paid leave or dearness allowances and their services are frequently terminated despite possessing the same qualifications, teaching the same syllabus as aided courses and sharing the burden of examination related work.[9]

REGULATION OF SELF-FINANCING COURSES

The regulatory framework of higher education in India is bewilderingly complex as a result of both the federal structure and the legacies of the country's colonial past. There are multiple regulating agencies and a complex web of rules and regulations. The state governments, the professional councils at the national level such as AICTE, Council of Architects and Pharmacy Council of India, and professional councils at the state level, the state councils and affiliating universities, are stakeholders in the regulatory system.

As per the Indian Constitution, education is a joint responsibility of state and central governments. The central government was assigned the exclusive power to coordinate and determine the standards through Entry 66 of the Union List of the Constitution of India. However, the power to 'maintain' standard was explicitly vested neither on central government nor on state governments. But realizing that neither coordination nor determination is possible without having some control, the role to maintain standard has been assumed by the central government in the course of evolution of higher education system in India

---

[9] https://timesofindia.indiatimes.com/city/mumbai/Students-make-a-beeline-for-self-financed-courses/articleshow/52284607.cms

(Singh, 2004). The central government discharges its responsibilities primarily through the MHRD. In addition, there are at least 15 other ministries/departments in the GoI that either establish, finance or regulate HEIs. The central government has also set up various statutory bodies for this purpose.

As regards self-financing courses, the central universities and UGC maintained that deemed-to-be universities must seek prior approval of the UGC for introduction of new courses. They may also ensure that the degree proposed to be awarded is one among the specified degrees duly approved by the UGC (2006).

The colleges affiliated to the state universities are required to apply to the university along with a 'No Objection Certificate' of the state government, requisite fee and an undertaking that the college authority shall bear all the expenditure for running the said self-financing course. Consequent to this, an inspection committee is appointed by the university. The inspection report is considered by the university and, if satisfied, the university allows/grants affiliation to the college for the said self-financing course. No college can start any self-financing course without prior permission of the university. Affiliated colleges can offer only university-approved courses in self-financing mode. Once affiliated, the university makes no distinction between a college offering a course in self-financing mode and another college offering the same course in regular (aided) mode in respect of syllabus, conduct of examination and declaration of results.

Autonomous colleges under state universities need to take permission from the state government but they can design their own courses to be offered under self-financing mode. They enjoy freedom in framing a course as per demand in the market. They have their own board of studies, which can rope in industry experts and professionals to develop their own courses and their syllabi. They also have their own evaluation system.

Apart from giving permission and affiliation, the regulating agencies also have some other roles to play. Promotion of competition and offering incentives in some form may improve the quality of self-financing courses and, at the same time, may reduce fees charged by the institutions for these courses. The regulator should also have some control over the fees charged by the institutions offering self-financing courses so that the fees do not become exorbitant. Given the salient role of education in ensuring social mobility and social cohesiveness, allowing such market-determined price of education to be charged to the students would surely deprive a section of the students who cannot afford the fees. This would not only relegate talent and erode India's edge in knowledge economy but also pave the way for social disaster.

The terms and conditions for the recruitment of both academic and other staff also require attention of the regulator. However, the regulator will face both adverse selection and moral hazards problems while dealing with such courses. A layer of asymmetric information seems also to exist between the institute and its regulators, due to which regulators often fail to realize the true quality of education.

CONCLUSION

Globally, there has occurred an ideological shift towards the market as a coordinating mechanism in higher education. Today, in many countries, including India, higher education increasingly functions in quasi-markets, where governments (through some regulators) play an important guiding and facilitating role. The state as a 'market engineer' is central to the notion of market governance (de Boer, Jongbloed, Enders, & File, 2008). This concept refers to the use of the market mechanism of supply and demand in governance processes. In this governance mode, government interventions are focused on the shaping of a level playing field, which facilitates self-regulation (de Boer et al., 2008; Jongbloed, 2003). Devising an appropriate incentive scheme for qualitative development of higher education is of vital importance in this system. Although quality is observable for an experience good (service) like higher education, it is not verifiable. If the quality is verifiable, its level can be described ex ante in a contract and ascertained ex post by a court. When quality is unverifiable, the regulator must recreate the incentives of an unregulated institution to provide quality on the basis of output. In case of an experience good like higher education, incentives to supply quality and those to reduce cost are inherently in conflict, at least in the short run.

Such incentive schemes may not, however, work if higher education institutes have little interest in maximizing their reputation or prestige. If a higher education institute prefers to stay at low level equilibrium with the sole objective of maximizing its surplus, market-based regulation system with focus on incentive and quality may not work at all. Regulators will face both adverse selection and moral hazard problems while dealing with such institutes. By developing a ranking system of institutes, the regulators may be partly successful in sensitizing some institutes, but majority of institutes may remain neutral. Some of them may prefer exiting to going through the elaborate process of evaluation and ranking.

REFERENCES

de Boer, H., Jongbloed, B., Enders, J., & File, J. (2008). *Progress in higher education reform across Europe. Governance reform:* Vol. 1. *Executive Summary Main Report.* Sydney/Germany: CHEPS/International Centre for Higher Education Research Kassel. Retrieved from http://novebojeznanja.hr/UserDocsImages/ Dokumenti%20i%20publikacije/Dokumenti%20i%20publikacije%20 referirani%20u%20SOZT-u%20(popis%201)/109b%20Progress%20in%20 higher%20education%20reform%20across%20Europe,%20Governance%20 Reform,%20Vol.%201.pdf

Jongbloed, B. (2003). Marketisation in higher education, Clark's triangle and the essential ingredients of markets. *Higher Education Quarterly, 57*(2), 110–135. Retrieved from https://doi.org/10.1111/1468-2273.00238

Ministry of Human Resource Development (MHRD). (2012). *All India survey on higher education, 2011–2012.* New Delhi: Ministry of Human Resources Development, GoI.

———. (2016). *All India survey on higher education, 2015–2016.* New Delhi: Ministry of Human Resources Development, GoI.

NUEPA. (2005). *Report of the CABE committee on financing of higher and technical education.* New Delhi: National University of Educational Planning and Administration.

Psacharopoulos, G., & Patrinos, H. A. (2004). Human capital and rates of return. In G. Johnes & J. Johnes (Eds.), *International Handbook on the Economics of Education* (pp. 1–57), Cheltenham: Edward Elgar Publishing.

Rao K. S., & Singh, M. (2002). *Self-financed courses in the universities and colleges.* New Delhi: NUEPA. Retrieved from http://www.nuepa.org/libdoc/e-library/articles/2002ksr&mks.pdf

Singh, A. (2004). Challenges in higher education. *Economic and Political Weekly*, *39*(21), 2155–2158.

UGC. (2006). *Annual report 2005–2006.* New Delhi: University Grants Commission.

———. (2011). *Annual report 2010–2011.* New Delhi: University Grants Commission.

Chapter 8

Changing Sources of Funding
A Study of Punjabi University[1]

Harvinder Kaur

INTRODUCTION

The higher education system has experienced several transformations all over the world during the past three to four decades. One of the important changes, especially since the 1980s, is a move from state funding to market-oriented strategies for higher education development. This change has led to the introduction of cost-sharing and revenue-generating activities in institutions of higher education. Many countries introduced tuition fees, student loans and shifted the burden of pursuing higher education to the households. It also needs to be noted that student support systems also were on the rise in these decades. For example, student aid in the US is mainly in the form

[1] This chapter is based on the data collected through a well-structured questionnaire by 3rd semester students of five courses for the Session 2015–2016 in Punjabi University, Patiala, for CPRHE/NIEPA's research project on 'Financing of Higher Education: Institutional Responses to Decline in Public Funding'. The author would like to thank Dr Jinusha Panigrahi, Co-ordinator of the CPRHE/NIEPA's Research Project. The author also thanks Professor N. V. Varghese, Vice-Chancellor, NIEPA, and all participants of two peer review meetings on the 'IHER 2018' held at NIEPA for their useful comments, observations and suggestions.

of Need Based Pell Grants (Mumper, 2003) but it includes income-contingent loans (Greenway & Hayens, 2003), subsidized loans (Dur, Coen, & Thijs, 2004), merit-based scholarships (Stanley & French, 2009) and so on in different countries.

The introduction of economic reforms in the 1990s and the recommendations of the Ambani Group Report 2001 (Garg, 2015), The National Knowledge Commission (NKC) in 2006 and the N. R. Narayana Murthy Committee on Corporate Participation in Higher Education 2012 (Mathew, 2015) have oriented Indian higher education towards market-oriented policies. Consequently, the nation has not only opened up the higher education sector but has also embarked on the path towards privatization of public higher educational institutions. Till the 1990s, higher education was mainly a state-funded sector with (Tilak, 1993) about three-quarters of the total expenditure being borne by the government. In the post-1990s, the government support to the sector has been on the decline consequently; many states and universities in India moved from a system of free higher education to introduction of reform measures aimed at cost-sharing, cost-recovery and cost-saving strategies. Public higher education institutions (HEIs) have also been exploring new innovative methods to generate resources on their own.

Punjab, like many other states of India, has also experienced a declining trend in public funding of higher education. The declining role of the state government towards funding of education in general and higher education in particular has put this sector under too much pressure and experimentation. Although Punjab is better placed as compared to other states of India in terms of general economic and social development, the higher education sector was poorly placed due to lack of adequate public funding by the state universities, government colleges and aided colleges that have been confronted with the situation of financial adversity. These are exploring alternative sources to generate revenue at their own and struggling to reduce expenses. Besides, the opening up of this sector has not only promoted the commercialization and commoditization of higher education but has also commenced a challenge for public HEIs to compete with the private sector and to maintain standard.

Presently, there are 360 state universities in India and out of these, 9 universities are in Punjab (UGC, 2017). Among these, 3 are 'general' universities and all the three—Punjabi University, Patiala; Panjab University, Chandigarh; and Guru Nanak Dev University, Amritsar— are in financial difficulties. This chapter is based on a study of Punjabi University, Patiala, and will focus on the financial crisis faced by the university and leasers adopted by the university to overcome the financial difficulties.

Punjabi University was established before 1966 when the state was reorganized. Since the establishment of Punjabi University, Patiala, a huge and steady expansion in terms of institutional area, students, teachers, non-teaching staff, courses, off campuses has been taking place in the university. The state government has played a significant role in funding the university and almost three-fourths of the expenses were met by the state funds provided in the form of maintenance grant/ grant-in-aid for a long time. But now the situation is different and the university has been facing a condition of serious resource crunch for the last few years.

The first section gives an overview of higher education in Punjab. A brief profile of Punjabi University is given in the second section. Various sources of funding of the university are explored in the third section. The overall physical condition of the university is observed in the fourth section. The subsequent section is about implications of cost-sharing and cost-saving strategies. The last section deals with conclusion and policy implications.

AN OVERVIEW OF HIGHER EDUCATION IN PUNJAB

Punjab holds a dominant place in the Indian economy as it takes pride in being the largest contributor to food granary of India despite being one of the smaller states of India in terms of area (1.53%) and population (2.29%) of the country (Government of Punjabi University, 2015). Known for its brave, energetic and hardworking people, the state has been making many endeavours to strengthen an appropriate education system to enhance human development but lacks in structuring any sound education policy. No doubt, its position regarding literacy rate and level of education has been progressing, but the share of sub-sector higher education in all terms such as institutions, enrolment and teachers is comparatively very less in different levels of education. However, the narrowness of the apex of the pyramid of students' enrolment, number of institutions and teachers from primary to secondary and from secondary to tertiary level has slightly broadened.

Higher education has never endured the priority in the state; however, a few efforts have regularly been made to increase its access, equity and quality, and now it has been promulgated up for the private sector too. Since the reorganization of the state in 1966, the number of universities in the state has increased from 3 to 27 and among these a large share is of the private universities which have been opened recently (UGC, 2017). Also, the total number of colleges, teachers and students along with the share of female teachers and female students in higher educational institutes has tremendously increased. In 1980, there were only 188 colleges, 91,254 total students with only 40 per cent girl students and 6,535 teachers with only 31 per cent female teachers in the state (Statistical Abstract of Punjab, 2017). Presently, there are 1,080 colleges, 753798 students with 51 per cent girls University Grants Commission (UGC, 2016) and 46,284 total teachers with 59 per cent female teachers (GoI, 2017).

A large number of colleges/institutions have been opened up in the rural areas to bridge the gap in rural–urban differences in access to higher education. Inter-group inequalities in access to higher education are also gradually narrowing down in the state but the lower proportion of Scheduled Caste (SC) students in each successive stage of higher education is a cause of concern. For example, the share of SC students in total students enrolled under BA, MA, MPhil, and PhD courses was less than 10 per cent in 1980. No doubt, this share in these courses improved to the level of more than 20 per cent but their share was 25.11 per cent in BA, 16.8 per cent in MA, and 12 per cent in MPhil and PhD in 2015 (Government of Punjab, 2016). The situation of UG bloom and research gloom prevailing in the state conforms to the national one. It is a positive manifestation that the position of Punjab in maintaining Gender Parity Index in higher education is encouraging with females outnumbering males. Regardless of these developments, as per the data given in All India Survey of Higher Education Report (GoI, 2017), the state holds the position lower than 12 to 20 states in most of the higher education indicators such as the number of universities, state universities, colleges, colleges per population, average enrolment per college, gross enrolment ratio of various social groups and so on, and a large gap exists in the value when compared to the topper state with respect to each indicator. The public funding in the education sector is unsubstantial in Punjab. For instance, the ratio of expenditure on total education and on higher education to the aggregate expenditure on revenue account of the state budget (18.3% and 1.35%, respectively) and to gross state domestic product (GSDP) (2.45% and 0.18%, respectively) in 2014–2015 budget estimate (BE) was also very less in Punjab (GoI, 2015) .

BRIEF PROFILE OF PUNJABI UNIVERSITY, PATIALA

A premier institution of higher education in north India, Punjabi University, Patiala, was established on 30 April 1962 under the Punjab Act No. 35 of 1961. This is the second university in the world named after a language, the first being Hebrew University of Israel (Punjabi University, 2015). The university is recognized by the UGC under Section 2 (f) and 12 (b) of UGC Act 1956. The university has a modern well-planned campus situated on the Patiala–Chandigarh road at a short distance from the main city of Patiala in semi-urban area and is spread over 635 acres of land (312 acres main campus and 323 acres area of 13 satellite campuses). It is a teaching-cum-research university.

Presently, it has been covering disciplines such as humanities, arts, sciences, engineering, languages, fine arts, biotechnology, forensic science, space science and many more. Its 1,500+ teachers (more than 500 at the campus) are imparting instructions and guidance to around 50,000 students (14,000+ regular students at the main campus) in 70+ teaching and research departments/chairs on its campus, 27 regional centres/neighbourhood campuses/constituent colleges, and Department of Distance Education (DDE) covering the disciplines of 11 faculties. DDE is managing more than 40 multi-faculty courses and on an average, 20,000 students attain higher education through distance mode in this university.

This university assumes great significance in Punjab. It covers mainly the Malwa region of the state and caters to the educational needs of nine districts of Punjab, especially the rural ones. The university offers a variety of study programmes such as postgraduation, integrated masters, MPhil, PhD, certificate courses, diploma, PG diploma and UG courses. Majority of the programmes are of the level of postgraduation and above. A large number of colleges (278) are affiliated to it, which cater to the needs of more than two and half lakh students. NAAC has awarded the university 'five star' grade in the first cycle (2002–2007) and 'A' grade in second and the third cycles. The admission to the university is preferred in the region because of its comparatively nominal fee structure for most of the study programmes as compared to other government and private universities in the state. For example, the tuition fee ranged from ₹1,800 to ₹103,310 per semester for various programmes covering regular and professional degrees and all other charges (except examination and assignment fee) were in the range of ₹7,615 to ₹50,045 per annum for most of the courses during 2014–2015.

The largest share of students is in engineering and social sciences streams. More than 50 per cent of the students in the main campus are girls. A majority of the teachers are permanently employed. However, almost one-fifth of the total sanctioned posts of teachers are lying vacant. Due to financial constraints, the university has avoided formal and regular appointments of teachers to the vacant positions. Most of the teachers recruited are on a temporary basis.

The proportion of female faculty members is less than male faculty members in the university. Student–teacher ratio also varies in various streams in the university. It is much higher in the courses under social sciences, management and engineering faculties and specifically in computer science, physics, commerce, statistics and civil engineering departments. So, there is a need to recruit regular faculty in these courses at the earliest. Furthermore, as a cost-saving strategy, the university has employed and re-employed (retired) faculty and recently has started employing guest faculty in all the departments in the case of a shortage of faculty.

SOURCES OF FUNDING OF THE UNIVERSITY

Before the 1990s, the state universities had been getting a major share of their funding from their respective state governments. From the early 1990s, along with the process of privatization of higher education, many states were not in a position to support higher education and in many instances the state universities were asked to generate their own resources. In this process, several alternatives including student fees, student loan and graduate tax (Tilak, 1995) were emphasized to increase funds for public higher education. Varghese and Panigrahi (2015) have also noted that cost recovery, mainly through student fees, has become an important source of income in public institutions. Nowadays, in the case of state universities, resources flow from three streams. In the words of Oak (2015), 'The first stream comprises grants from the government, the second is the tuition fees from students and the third from donations and philanthropy'.

So far as Punjabi University, Patiala, is concerned, Figure 8.1 throws light on the amount of total receipts of the university and its growth during the decade of 2008–2009 to 2017–2018. It reveals that the total amount of receipts was ₹155.32 crores in 2008–2009 which increased to ₹440.58 crores in 2016–2017 with compound annual growth rate (CAGR) of 15.32 per cent per annum during the period of 2008–2009 to 2016–2017.

Figure 8.2 shows the share of receipts from different sources in the university. Earlier the state government had been contributing the major share but with the decline in state's share, the university started exploring alternative sources to generate its own revenue. It has started professional courses with higher fee structures and has applied differential fee structure in order to generate revenue to meet ever-growing expenses. Resources in the university flow mainly from fees, grant-in-aid from the state government and funds under UGC and non-UGC schemes. However, the major share is of fees, while grant-in-aid from the state government occupies the second place and the share of all other sources such as rent receipts, alumni contribution, income from consultancy and so on is very less. The gravity of the fiscal imbalance is such that recently the university has been resorting

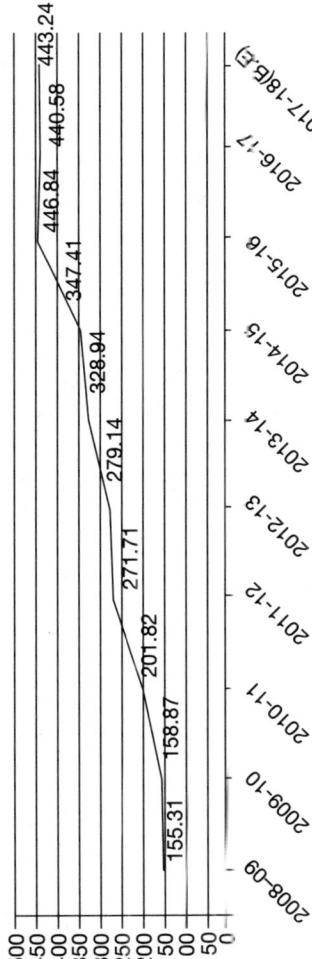

Figure 8.1 *Total Amount of Receipts of the University (₹Crore; CAGR* 15.32%)*

Source: Punjabi University, Budget Estimates, Financial Year from (2011–2012 to 2017–2018).

Notes: Figures for 2017–18 are Budgeted Estimates.

*CAGR has been calculated by using the Semi-Log Model.

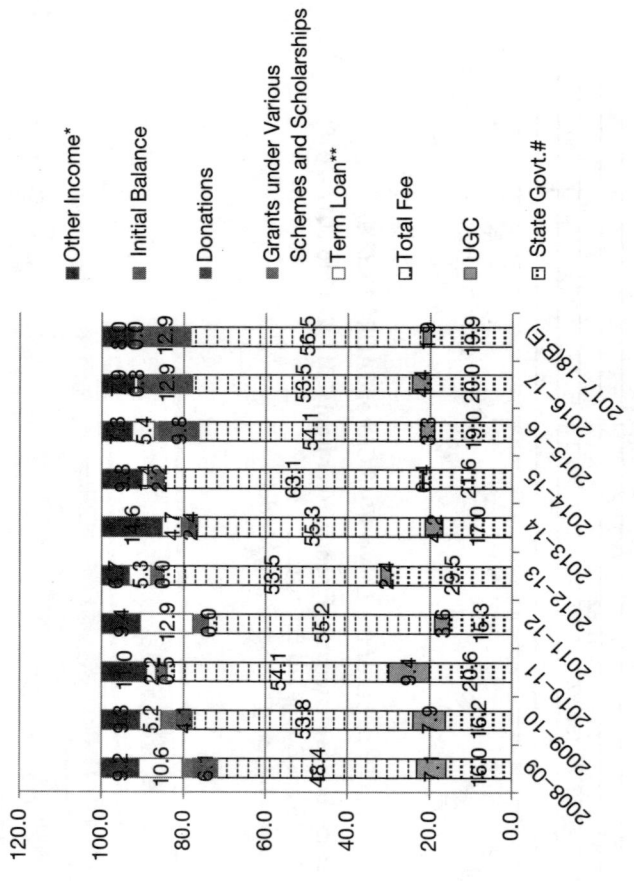

Figure 8.2 *Share of Different Sources in the Total Receipts of the University*

Source: Author's calculations based on BEs for various years, published documents, Punjabi University, Patiala.

Notes: [a]Other income includes sale of admission and other forms, syllabus and prospectus; youth welfare fund; rent, revenue from bus service and various units such as test lab, X-rays, physiotherapy and homeopathy units in health centre, Punjabi development fund; college development fee; receipts of employees loans and so on.

[b]For some years, the amount of loan and for some amount of overdrafts.

[c]The share for the year 2012–2013 is the highest as in addition to the amount of maintenance grant, the university received an

to borrowing from banks for construction purposes and using method of overdrafts to meet even the growing recurrent expenses.

State Grants

It is the department of higher education of the Punjab state that provides maintenance grant in the form of grant-in-aid to the university. Every year, the university sends a request to the state government for grant during the months of October to December or we can say almost four to six months before the forthcoming financial year. The amount requested comprises mainly the amount of non-planned grant almost equal to the amount allocated to the university under the budgetary provision during the current year's state budget (subsistence grant), estimated additional burden for the payment of two instalments of Dearness Allowance and additional amount required for annual increments (including gratuity, leave encashment and so on), ₹1.5 crore per year for the newly opened constituent colleges and some amount of funds for infrastructural development of the university colleges. The request also includes the revised estimates for the grant for the current year. However, the state allocates only as per the budgetary provision, so the university gets lesser amount as compared to the requested amount every year. The share of state grants is stagnant and barely constitutes one-fifth or less than one-fifth of the total receipts, whereas earlier more than three-fourths expenses of the university could be met by these grants. Therefore, the reduction in the share of grant from the state government has led the university towards critical fiscal period. The main issue is that there is no proper criterion of the state government on the basis of which it allocates the resources to the universities. Tilak (1995) revealed that in order to improve such ad hoc system of grants, the UGC Committee in the 1990s recommended unit-cost formula based grants mechanism to the universities, according to which most of the state grants will be related to enrolments. Despite recommendation of the formula, the suggestions are not effectuated.

Exhibiting the causes of declining state funding in Punjab, Singh (2017) has also rightly mentioned,

[T]he paradigm shift from education as a public good to a private good does not happen at one stroke but as a gradual process of different turns and twists in which parts of a publicly funded university are privatized bit by bit along with opening of fully privatized institutions as competitors to the publicly funded university. The aspect highlighting the pressure towards partial privatization of publicly funded universities is the gradual withdrawal of the state from funding the universities.

Such pressure has hit the financial position of the state universities, and similar is the case with this university of Punjab.

Funds from Central Government Agencies

The central government agencies which provide grants under various schemes and research projects to this university are mainly the UGC, Department of Science and Technology, All India Council for Technical Education, Indian Council of Social Science Research, Indian Council of Historical Research, ISRO and the Ministry of Tourism. The largest share among all other agencies is of the UGC. It provides general development assistance to the university and has been providing financial assistance for the research projects of the faculty in the university. The amount which the university gets from UGC is very less, has no uniformity in the trend and has been observing a declining trend. Similarly, the amount of non-UGC grants under various schemes and projects has declined. The amount which the university gets under various research projects from UGC varies and is very less. It sticks around ₹3–4 crores annually.

Fee Revenue

In line with many other countries, since the early years of the 1990s, various committees in India too have been suggesting resource generation through cost recovering measures, specifically the revision of fees and fee income as a major source of financing higher education. The Punnaya Committee (1993) and National Knowledge Commission Report to the Nation (2006) also suggested an upward revision in the fee structure (Chattopadhyay, 2007). In many other countries, tuition fee in higher education has unprecedentedly risen faster albeit in varying degrees. All the more, in order to restrain them, the need to cap increase in tuition fee has arisen in many countries. For example, in South Korea in 2010, the government capped annual tuition fee increase for both private and public institutions. In India, in the 1990s, the cost recovery and self-financing of public institutions increased with the proliferation of self-financing HEIs in the private sector (Varghese & Malik, 2016).

Many state universities for many years have also been generating major share of revenue from fees. Madras University collected 50.4 per cent or more of its operating budget, while in the Bangalore University, the corresponding percentage was 63.7 per cent and in Punjab University, Chandigarh, it was 50.4 per cent (Agarwal, 2015 quoted in Ghosh, 2015) even one decade ago. Punjabi University has also been yielding more than half of its expenses through cost-recovery measures like various types of fees. On the part of fee revenue, an amount of ₹75.16 crores was generated in 2008–2009 which registered a very high rate of growth of 16.72 per cent per annum and generated ₹235.69 crores in 2016–2017 and it is expected that the university will attain ₹250 crores in 2017–2018. The largest share of receipts is generated from fees. It was 48 per cent in 2008–2009, which thereafter increased by 5–7 percentage points and hovered between 53 per cent and 55 per cent. The university has undertaken differential fee structure and fees for various courses vary. Tuition fee and other charges are much higher in the case of courses in physiotherapy, engineering, medical and management as compared to the courses under social sciences, languages and science faculties for which tuition fee is lesser and for long has not been revised. The ratio of total course fees for various streams is in the range 1:10. It is less for traditional courses, while much high for professional courses. However, quite a significant amount is garnered through other funds and charges.

Undoubtedly, the university generates huge part of its receipts from the total fees of students. Furthermore, the share of various types of fees and funds such as tuition fee, examination fee, registration fee,

fee from distance education students and other funds in the total fee revenue of the university is demonstrated in Figure 8.3. It is discerned that examination fee, tuition fee and other fee and funds are the major constituents of fee revenue. The share of examination fee has been increasing as a result of proliferating number of students in the main campus, other campuses and in its affiliated colleges. A facility to appear as private candidates provided to girl students also contributes. The share of other fees and funds is also contributing significantly since 2010–2011. Tuition fee constitutes less than one-third of the total course fee in the case of most of the courses under social sciences, languages and sciences faculties, so its share has declined. Hence, it is notified that in order to meet the needs of growing expenses and to generate its own resources to cover up the gap created by the declining share of state funding, the university, by exercising the cost-sharing method—specifically by adopting differential fee structure and by raising other fees, funds and charges, has put the major burden on its students and their households.

Donations

The university had been getting some amount as donations (however, these were negligible) till 2012–2013, but thereafter, there has been no contribution of donations.

Term Loan and Overdrafts

With the denial of the adequate state support, the gravity of the fiscal crisis has reached to the extent that the university has been borrowing for construction purposes for long and resorting to the method of over-drafts to meet even the recurring expenses such as payment of wages and salaries. The university had overdraft of ₹44 crores and ₹57 crores in 2015–2016 and 2016–2017, respectively. In the university, there used to be a corpus fund called the 'sink fund', which continued till June 2012. But this is no more maintained now because of the scarcity of funds.

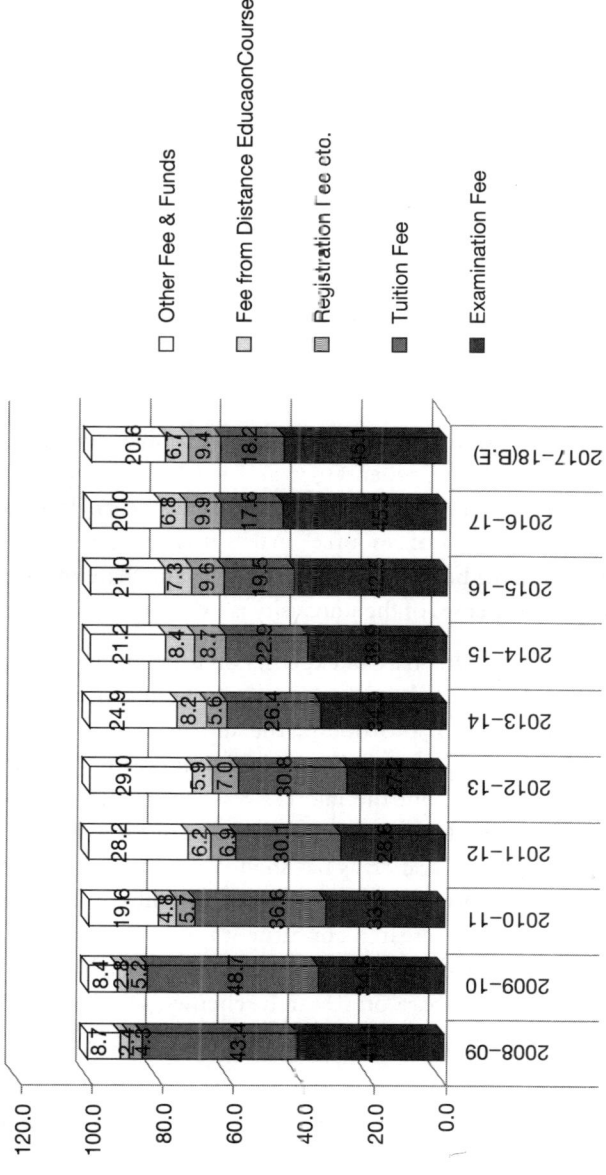

Figure 8.3 *Share of Various Types of Fees and Funds in the Total Fee Receipts of the University*

Source: Author's calculations based on BEs for various years, published documents, Punjabi University, Patiala.

Pattern of Utilization of Resources

The university has been advancing since its establishment. It has flourished in terms of number of students, courses, buildings, faculty and staff in the main as well as the old and new off campuses established during the last two decades. Accordingly, the needs of expenditure of the university have also grown. In Figure 8.4, the total amount of expenditure of the university during the period of 10 years is manifested. The total expenditure of the university was ₹101.25 crores in 2008–2009 and recording a very high compound annual growth rate of 22.09 per cent per annum. The amount of expenditure reached to ₹500.32 crores in 2016–2017. Further, the amount is expected to cross ₹540 crores during 2017–2018.

To redress the situation of fiscal imbalance, the university has been trying its best to curtail the expenditure and has been using various cost-saving and cost-reducing measures for the last few years. The study of the pattern of utilization of resources makes it clear how and what type of adjustments have been made. To explore it, the share of various constituents of total expenses of the university is exhibited in Figure 8.5.

It is good to note that the share of expenses on teaching and research departments is the largest and growing at a very high growth rate of 21.43 per cent per annum. No doubt, the university has managed to reduce the share of expenses on general administration from 21.4 per cent to 13.4 per cent, but the rate (15.8% per annum) at which it has grown is also quite large. The expenses on constituent colleges have also been growing. Fiscal crisis has shed its repercussions on the library and research aspects as the expenses on the library are fewer and the share disbursed on research constituent is not only less but has rather declined during the study period. Particularly since 2014–2015, the amount as well as the share on research schemes, scholarships and stipends has declined.

The data for three years 2014–2015 to 2016–2017 (Punjabi University) reveals the picture about capital expenses and operational/revenue account expenses. Capital expenses include expenses on library, new equipment for laboratories, engineering workshops, studios, other expenditure on creation of capital assets (excluding expenditure on land and buildings).

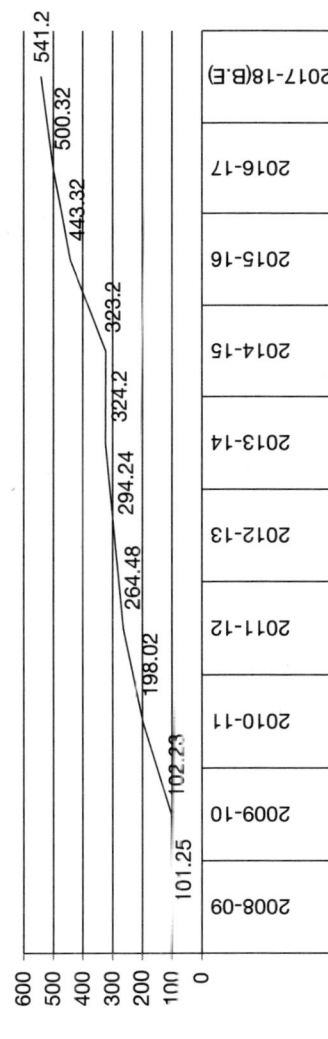

Figure 8.4 *Expenditure of the University (₹ Crore; CAGR 22.09%)*

Source: Author's calculations based on the BEs for various years, published documents, Punjabi University, Patiala.

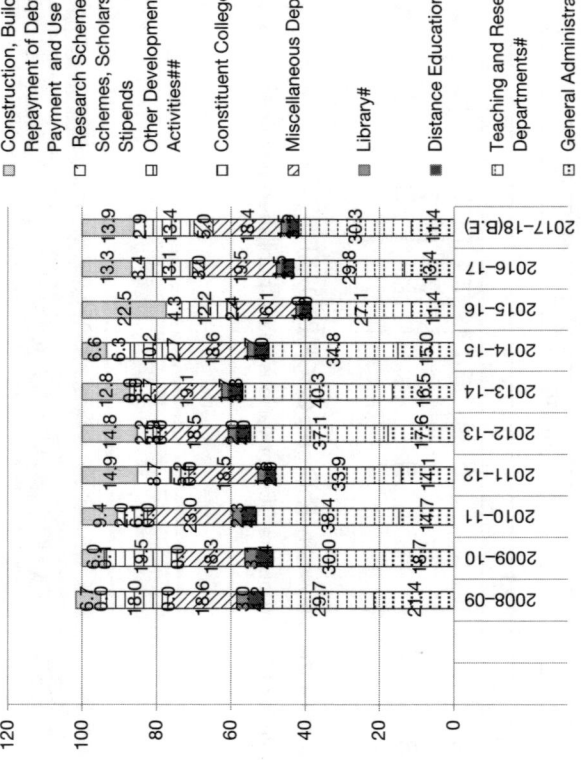

Figure 8.5 *Share of Various Components of Expenditure in the University*

Source: Author's calculations based on the BEs for various years, published documents, Punjabi University, Patiala.

Notes:

aIncludes expenses on university scholarships, conferences, seminars and so on, translation, computer centre, development of Punjabi language, pension fund and so on.

bTotal expenses including wages and salaries, and other expenses.

cExpenses on wages, salaries and other components of offices of Vice Chancellor, Registrar, DPM, Dean Academic Affairs, Dean Students Welfare, examination and so on.

Annual operational expenditure includes expenses on salaries (teaching and non-teaching staff), maintenance of academic infrastructure or consumables, other running expenditures and so on (excluding maintenance of hostels and allied services), seminars/conferences/workshops and so on. The university thus itself proclaims that an overwhelming share is spent on operational/revenue expenses and minuscule is left for capital expenses. So a very less and declined share of research schemes, scholarships and stipends and library in the total expenditure reveals that as a result of adjustments made to curtail the expenditure, the university had to compromise with many important affairs and has given even lesser importance to the issue of student support and to the construction of new buildings.

OVERALL FISCAL CONDITION OF THE UNIVERSITY

Fiscal condition is pretty uncomfortable in the university. During the study period of 10 years from 2008–2009 to 2017–2018, the amount of receipts expanded at a smaller rate of 15.32 per cent per annum, while expenditure accrued comparatively at a very high rate of 22.09 per cent per annum in the university. The outcome, thus, is the fiscal crunch. In order to explore how much the university has adjusted with such an unfavourable fiscal scenario, an analysis of BEs and actual position with regard to deficit/surplus for 10 years' time period has been portrayed in Table 8.1. Budgeted estimates of receipts for all the years have remained less than actual revenue, while the budgeted estimates of expenditure have remained much larger than the actual expenses for most of the years. So far as the extent of the deficit is concerned, budgeted estimates have been showing an ever-growing deficit in the university but actually the university has managed the resources in such a manner by using various cost-sharing, cost-saving and revenue-generating methods that there remained surplus in 7 years out of 10 years' time period. In the budgeted estimates, salaries of all sanctioned posts either filled or vacant were added to the budget till 2016–2017. Estimated expenditure of the vacant posts is also included in the budget since these may be filled up during the financial year for which the budget is prepared (however, that practice has been abolished in the

Table 8.1 Budgeted and Actual Surplus/Deficit Condition of Punjabi University, Patiala (₹ Lakh)

	Budgetary Surplus/Deficit	Actual Surplus/Deficit*
2008–2009	–386.01	5406.6
2009–2010	–479.91	5,663.14
2010–2011	–972.36	380.0179
2011–2012	–2,602.29	722.3644
2012–2013	–4,826.61	–1,509.86
2013–2014	–9,376.16	474.6142
2014–2015	–15,736.4	2,420.58
2015–2016	–20,814	352.56
2016–2017	–13,059.8	–5,974.41
2017–2018(BE)	–9,796.01	

Source: BEs for various years, published documents, Punjabi University, Patiala.
Notes: During 2008–2009 and 2009–2010, the receipts from UGC, donations, loan, revenue from tuition fee of engineering colleges and grants under various schemes were kept under different accounts, so these were not part of the main budget. But, thereafter they have been added in the receipts, and since 2013–2014, these have become part of the main budget. So, in order to make the data uniform for the period under study, calculations in actual and budgetary income for the years 2008–2009 and 2009–2010 have been made and income from UGC, donations and so on have been added, and such additions in figures of BE for 2010–2011 and 2011–2012 have been made.
* Includes initial balance.

budget 2017–2018). On account of mainly this reason, estimated budget usually proclaimed huge deficits. Hence, for most of the years, the amount of actual expenses has remained less than the estimated budgeted expenditure. Despite these efforts, the university has been actually facing huge fiscal crisis. Actual fiscal imbalance troubled during 2012–2013 for the first time. Since 2016–2017, the university has been confronting a grave fiscal crisis and the deficit has surged to the level of almost ₹100 crore.

IMPLICATIONS OF COST-SHARING AND COST-SAVING STRATEGIES

To escape from the divergence from the objectives of access, equity and affordability in access to higher education as a result of the present mode of financing, especially the declining share of state funding to institutions, the gap is tried to be filled by the state with the direct public student support in the form of scholarships, free-ships, student loan and so on in most of the countries. But, in India, decline in the share of the state support to institutions is compensated with limited support to students directly from the government. Thus, with the adoption of cost-sharing measures, whether we are approaching or moving away from the objectives is a crucial question. Punjab has also been continuously slipping down on the economic front and is gripped in problems such as fiscal crisis, unemployment and so on. Since the Punjabi University under study has exercised differential fee structure for various courses and has tuition as well as other fees and funds of quite a higher range as compared to many other state universities—even more than that of the economically backward states—therefore, the implications of the cost-sharing strategy in terms of access, equity and affordability are studied. During the last decade, as per the data given in the SSR reports of 2008 and 2015 of the University, the number of students increased from around 17,000 and 80,000 in 2006–2007 to 40,000+ and 2.5 lakhs+ in 2014–2015 in the main campus and the total students catered by the university in the off campuses, respectively. The share of male, female and total students from other states increased from 3.8 per cent, 2.47 per cent and 2.81 per cent in 2006–2007 to 4.74 per cent, 5.94 per cent and 5.38 per cent, respectively, in 2014–2015. The share of girl students has also increased from 46.73 per cent to 50 per cent from 2006–2007 to 2014–2015, respectively. It reveals that the accessibility of this institution of higher education for total as well as various social groups has increased during the last decade. However, the objective of equity is not adequately satisfied as the share of SC students undoubtedly increased from 10.27 per cent to 14.01 per cent (Punjabi University, 2008, 2015), but the class is under-represented in the university as compared to its share in the total population of the state.

Implications on affordability and how people of the state, with lower GSDP per capita of ₹151,624 and positioned 16th among all

Table 8.2 Sources of Fee Payment by Students

Semester Fee (₹) (1)	No. of Students (2)	No. of those who paid fee from Parental Income (3)	% of students in the respective group whose Fees Paid by Parents (4)	Fee Paid through Scholarships (5)
Nil	41(16.87)	0	0	Covered under PMS scheme
5,583	70 (28.81)	67	95.71429	4 (100%) 1 (52%)
8,435	44 (18.11)	39	88.63636	4 (100%)
8,548	28 (11.52)	28	100	0
26,845	60 (24.69)	57	95	2 (100%) 1 (46.56%)
Total	243 (100)	191	78.60082	

Source: Kaur et al. (2017).

states and UTs of India, manage for the payment of fee for higher education of their wards are further explored on the basis of sources of fee payment by students. The data in Table 8.2 reveals that majority of the students (88% to cent per cent) from various groups had been paying fee from their parental income. Further, economic condition of students' households is examined on the basis of their father's as well as mother's monthly income and the data is shown in Table 8.3. The cost of higher education is mainly borne by the households, especially male members as mothers of only 12 per cent students are economically active. In Punjab, otherwise, female 'work participation rate' (13.9%) is very low (Census of India, 2011). The earnings of the fathers of one-third students are less than ₹10,000 per month. One-fourth of the total respondents belong to the category of ₹10,000 to ₹25,000, while less than one-third (only 31%) are such whose fathers have been earning above ₹25,000 per month. The percentage of students belonging to high-income category is very less. People belonging to even lower economic category are managing by their own for their ward's higher

Table 8.3 *Distribution of Student Respondents on the Basis of Monthly Income of Mother and Father (₹)*

	Mother		Father	
	Frequency	%	Frequency	%
Not earning	210	86.4	1	0.4
Less than or equal to 5,000	3	1.2	21	8.6
5,001–10,000	5	2.1	65	26.7
10,001–25,000	3	1.2	63	25.9
25,001–50,000	14	5.8	58	23.9
50,001 and Above	4	1.6	18	7.4
No reply/Without mother or father	4	1.6	17	7.0
Total	243	100	243	100

Source: Kaur et al. (2017).

education. In such a situation, state support either to the institution or directly to the weaker students is a must.

The examination of the implications of cost-reducing measures is also paramount. Since the large amount (more than 60%) is spent on wages and salaries, so a small part is left for other developmental and research activities. In order to arrest expenses, various cost-reducing measures are also exercised, such as quite a large proportion of teaching as well as non-teaching sanctioned posts are not deliberately filled and most of the new appointments on the vacant posts are made on temporary basis with fixed salary. More than one-third of the teaching sanctioned posts (36%) and more than one-fourth of the non-teaching posts are lying vacant. In order to manage with the limited resources, other important expenses such as those on contingency, research and library have also declined. The university has imposed a cut of 20 per cent on all expenses other than salary, pension and other committed expenditure. So, the university has been actually spending less than needed. All these have repercussions on the overall functioning of the university.

At present, the gravity of the fiscal crisis is such that the payment of monthly salaries to temporary, part-time and permanent staff, both teaching as well as non-teaching, is delayed. But, mostly the sufferers are the pensioners as the payment of pensions to the retired employees is often delayed. The retiral benefits are often not paid timely. The university resorts to the method of borrowing from banks for capital expenses like construction of new buildings. Now the condition is such that the university has been resorting to the method of overdrafts even to meet the current expenses and it has become a common feature in the university. The autonomy of the university is also affected due to the crisis as the state government has allotted additional amount of ₹50 crores to ease the fiscal crisis on certain conditions. These include stopping the re-employment of retired professors and non-teaching staff and no overtime payment to employees. Resultantly, the university has started appointing guest faculty where there is a shortage of faculty.

CONCLUSION AND POLICY IMPLICATIONS

Financial crisis has become a major issue with the state universities of Punjab and similar is the case with the Punjabi University, Patiala. The main financial resources of the university are grants-in-aid/maintenance grants, funds for research projects and general development assistance received from the central government agencies, mainly UGC, and its own receipts comprise tuition, other funds charges, examination fee, registration fee/migration fee and so on. Fiscal crunch driven state government has been shrinking its hands in providing funds to public higher educational institutions. The contribution of central government is negligible and the share of central government agencies such as UGC and non-UGC in the financing of the university is very less. The university has adopted cost-sharing measures and is generating huge revenue from fees. No doubt, the university is reluctant to increase tuition fee, but it has been generating huge revenue from other funds and charges and mainly due to the adoption of differential fee structure. As an overwhelming majority of students has been paying fee from their parental income, the burden of bearing the cost of higher education on economically weaker households has increased. The share of other alternative sources is negligible and uncertain. Since a large number of students come from rural areas and low economic background, so the alumni participation in financial matters is very less. Since most of the consultancy work is done either free or at nominal rates, the amount thus generated is minuscule. Around 60 per cent of the expenses going towards salaries, the university is left with very limited funds to bring out major academic and administrative changes. The university does not have sufficient funds to make adequate budgetary provisions for research and library facilities. An overwhelming share being spent on operational activities, minuscule is left for capital account expenses. Diverse prudency measures such as common pool of resources, reduction in examination expenses and appointing guest faculty have recently been taken. However, resorting to borrowing for construction purposes and to the method of overdraft to meet the growing expenses, even the current expenses of salary payments due to increasing number of faculty and staff in the main and off campuses have become a common practice.

In the end, it is suggested that state universities require adequate funds and especially state support to meet objectives such as access, equity, affordability and quality of higher education. If a university caters to mainly rural and weaker sections, then it cannot generate more resources on its own, as it has to offer lower tuition costs. So, the need of state support is rather more. However, it is also necessary that the university should explore more alternative sources of revenue. It can open new courses of international importance, increase the number of seats of the courses where demand ratio is high, improve funded research and consultancy and resort to many more such options.

REFERENCES

Census of India. (2011). *Census of India.* New Delhi: Ministry of Home Affairs, Government of India (GoI) office of the Registrar General and Census Commissioner. Retrieved from http://censusindia.gov.in/.

Chattopadhyay, S. (2007, October 20). Exploring alternative sources of financing higher education. *Economic and Political Weekly, 42*(42), 4251–4259.

Dur, R., Coen, T., & Thijs, V. R. (2004). Should higher education subsidies depend on parental income? *Oxford Review of Economic Policy, 20*(2), 284–297.

Kaur, H., Singh, B., & Kumari, N. (2017). Financing of Public Higher Education Institution in Punjab: A Study of Flow of Funds and their Utilisation in Selected Institutions. Report submitted, New Delhi: CPRHE/NIEPA.

Garg, S. (2015, December). Repositioning Indian higher education: Role of leadership in managing change. *University News, 52*(49), 28–34.

Ghosh, D. K. (2015). Rising costs for higher education: An analysis and a search for a workable mode. *University News, 53*(49), 53–56.

GoI. (2015). *Analysis of budgeted expenditure on education, 2012–2013 to 2014–2015.* New Delhi: Ministry of Human Resource Development, Department of Higher Education.

———. (2017). *All India survey on higher education 2016–2017.* New Delhi: Ministry of Human Resource Development, Department of Higher Education.

Government of Punjab. (2015). *A report of the task force on elimination of poverty.* Punjab: Department of Planning.

———. (2017). *Statistical abstract of Punjab 2016.* Punjab: Economic Advisor to Government of Punjab.

Greenway, D., & Hayens, M. (2003). Funding higher education in UK: The role of fees and loans. *The Economic Journal, 113*(485), 150–160. Retrieved from http://www.punjabiuniversity.ac.in/Download/NIRF/FinancialResource.pdf

Mathew, A. (2015). Commissions and committees on higher education in India— Perspectives and recommendations on major issues. In N. V. Varghese & G. Malik (Eds.), *India higher education report 2015* (pp. 41–62). Abingdon: Routledge.

Mumper, M. (2003). The future of college access: The declining role of public higher education in promoting equal opportunity. *The Annals of American Academy of Political and Social Science, 585,* 97–117.

Oak, S. (2015, May). Financing higher education for excellence. *University News, 53*(20), 18–24.

Punjabi University. (2008). *Self Study Report, Part I.* Patiala: Punjabi University

———. (2015), July. *Self Study Report (SSR), Part 1.* Patiala: Punjabi University.

Punjabi University, *Budget Estimates,* Financial Year from (2011–12 to 2017–18), Patiala.

Singh, P. (2017, April 21). Neo-liberal roots of PU crisis. *The Tribune.* Retrieved from http://www.tribuneindia.com/news/comment/neo-liberal-roots-of-pu-crises/395017.html

Stanley, R. E., & French, P. E. (2009). Evaluating increased enrolment levels in institutions of higher education: A look at merit based scholarship programs. *Public Administration Quarterly, 33*(1), 4–36.

Tilak, J. B. G. 1993. Financing higher education in India: Principles, practices and policy issues, perspectives on higher education in India. *Higher Education, 26*(1), 43–67.

———. 1995. Funding higher education in India. *Economic and Political Weekly, 30*(9), 426–429.

University Grants Commission (UGC). 2016. Annual report 2015–2016. New Delhi: University Grants Commission

———. 2017. *Annual report 2016–2017.* New Delhi: University Grants Commission.

Varghese, N. V., & Malik G. (Eds.). 2016. *India higher education report 2015.* Abingdon: Routledge.

Varghese, N. V., & Pangrahi, J. (2015). *Massification of higher education in large academic systems* (Report on the International Seminar jointly organized by CPRHE, NUEPA & British Council). New Delhi: NEUPA.

PART III

Student Financing in Higher Education

Chapter 9

Scholarship Schemes for Student Financing

M. R. Narayana

INTRODUCTION

Student-based financing of higher education (or post-secondary education) is composed of scholarship schemes, student loans, fee reimbursement schemes (FRSs), special schemes for disadvantaged and financial assistance to minorities. Scholarship is a merit-based and means-tested financial incentive for currently enrolled students in the higher education system. The scholarship schemes aim at recognizing, rewarding and encouraging the outstanding academic performers in prescribed examinations and offer financial support to eligible individual students to pursue higher education in and outside the country. Utilization of a scholarship amount is fungible between instructional and non-instructional purposes (e.g., out-of-pocket expenditure). Thus, scholarship schemes are distinguishable elements in the student support system and important instruments to move from institution-based to student-based funding of higher education.

Scholarships are important for analysis of the nature and extent of financing the higher education from the supply/production side and demand/consumption side. On the production side, scholarships add to a part of the total current expenditure on the provisioning of higher education services by institutions.[1] On the consumption side, scholarships reduce a part of the total private consumption expenditure on access to and utilization of the higher education services by students.

Few studies on financing of higher education in India make a reference to scholarships (Prakash, 2007; Rani, 2002, 2014). To our knowledge, a detailed and focused study on student scholarships as student-based financing of India's higher education is a new research issue. This chapter aims to seek answers to the following questions: (a) What are aggregate trends in nature and magnitude of public expenditure on the scholarships by the union government, state governments and Union Territories (UTs)? (b) How are the public-funded scholarship schemes designed? (c) What are the databases on scholarships for analysis of scheme-wise public expenditure and coverage of students? (d) Are there disparities in the allocation of public expenditure on the scholarships and public expenditure priority to scholarships across states and UTs and over time? If yes, which of the states and years show higher concentration of public expenditure and expenditure priority on scholarships? Are such disparities higher for general higher education than technical education? (e) Are there nationally representative sample survey data to estimate the recipients of scholarships by courses? If yes, will that data be useful to estimate the receipt of scholarship amount per student and coverage of students on scholarship by courses? (f) What is the extent to which such scholarships finance private expenditure on higher education by courses and management of institutions? (g) What are policy implications of the above analyses on the current and future roles of the scholarships in student financing of India's higher education?

To answer these research questions, this chapter (a) presents a detailed analysis of aggregate public expenditure on the scholarships

---

[1] Most recently, expenditure on scholarships is considered as one of the performance indicators for ranking of universities in Karnataka. For instance, Karnataka State Universities Ranking Framework (Government of Karnataka, 2016) includes the average annual expenditure during past 5 years on financial support for the economically weaker and scholarships for the academically qualified as social impact performance indicators of universities.

(loan and merit) at national level and its disaggregation at states/UTs over the period 2003–2004 to 2014–2015; (b) describes major types of scholarships by schemes and their related public expenditures; (c) analyses the nature and extent of financing of private expenditure on education by scholarships; and (d) draws implications on the scholarships as an instrument of financing of Indian students' higher education on the production and consumption sides. Throughout, the methodology is positive and descriptive, and based on secondary and published data. Three key databases used are (a) analysis of budgeted expenditure on education by the Union Ministry of Human Resource Development (MHRD) (b) Annual Report of the University Grants Commission (UGC) and (c) National Sample Survey (NSS) 71st Round (2014–2015) on social consumption (education) in India by the National Sample Survey Organization of the Government of India.[2]

This chapter is organized as follows. The first section analyses the trends in the public expenditure on higher education and scholarships. The second section gives a description of the scholarship schemes for the higher education and their related public expenditure. The fourth section focuses on the micro-level aspects of the scholarships for higher education by characteristics of recipients of the scholarships by courses and role of scholarships in private expenditure on higher education. Major conclusions and implications are given in the fifth section.

PUBLIC EXPENDITURE ON HIGHER EDUCATION AND SCHOLARSHIPS

Public and private sectors coexist in higher education in India. The government (comprising union government, state governments and UTs) finances public universities, government colleges and grants-in-aid to private higher educational institutions. We analyse

---

[2] The National Scholarship Portal (Government of India, 2017a) gives important information for applicants of the select pre- and post-matric scholarship schemes by the Central Schemes, UGC Schemes, All India Council of Technical Education (AICTE) schemes and state schemes. The portal does not include the public expenditure details on the scholarships in general and scheme-wise scholarships in particular.

further the trends in the public expenditure on higher education in India with reference to budgetary expenditure on the scholarships. Throughout, all expenditures refer to the revenue expenditure at current prices because scholarships are a part of the annual revenue expenditure on provisioning of educational services.[3]

Public Expenditure on Education

Aggregate public education expenditure on revenue account is equal to the sum of expenditures by the education and other departments of the union government, state governments and UTs. Other departments' expenditures are on training and higher education (e.g., medical education by the Ministry of Health and Family Welfare, agricultural education by Ministry of Agriculture and Farmers Welfare, and science and technology education by Ministry of Science and Technology). In total, 44 ministries/departments accounted for the public education expenditure, outside the education department, in 2014–2015.

Table 9.1 shows the trends in the aggregate public education expenditure from 2003–2004 through 2014–2015. Over these years, the size of aggregate expenditure increased from ₹89,079 crores in 2003–2004 to ₹244,687 crores in 2009–2010 and ₹502,929 crore in 2014–2015. The annual growth rate was positive but varied from 8.55 per cent in 2004–2005 to 29.42 per cent in 2009–2010 and 15.98 per cent in 2014–2015. A big rise in expenditure is evident around 2009–2010 for the pay revisions and payment of arrears to the university and college teachers with effect from 2006–2007. Of the aggregate expenditure, throughout, the share of the Education Department comprised about 80 per cent and the Government of India (GoI) about 27 per cent or less. These trends signify the public expenditure by the education department and the dominant role of the state governments in these expenditures. It is important to note that the expenditure share of the GoI is relatively less in the total expenditure

---

[3] All India Survey of Higher Education (AISHE) does not cover the finances (i.e., revenue and expenditure) and students' support system in higher education at university or collegiate level. This is evident, for instance, in AISHE 2015–2016 (Government of India, 2016).

Table 9.1 *Aggregate Public Expenditure on Education, India: 2003–2004 to 2014–2015*

	Aggregate Public Expenditure on Education by General Government				GoI's Share in	
	Aggregate Expenditure on Education (₹ crore)	Expenditure by the Education Department as a Percentage of (2)	Expenditure by the GoI as a Percentage of (2)	Expenditure by the GoI as a Percentage of (2)	Expenditure by the Education Department	Expenditure by Other Departments
Year	2	3	4	4	5	6
1	2	3	4		5	6
2003–2004	89,079.25	82.00		19.20	13.93	43.18
2004–2005	96,694.10 (8.55)	84.06		18.96	16.13	31.89
2005–2006	113,228.71 (17.10)	83.45		20.50	18.86	28.74
2006–2007	137,384.00 (21.33)	80.32		24.92	21.64	38.32
2007–2008	155,797.27 (13.40)	80.48		25.62	21.35	43.23
2008–2009	189,068.84 (21.36)	80.83		25.38	22.53	37.36
2009–2010	244,687.09 (29.42)	79.11		26.31	20.82	47.11
2010–2011	293,478.24 (19.94)	79.57		27.48	22.23	47.95

(Continued)

Table 9.1 (Continued)

Year	Aggregate Public Expenditure on Education by General Government				GoI's Share in	
	Aggregate Expenditure on Education (₹ crore)	Expenditure by the Education Department as a Percentage of (2)	Expenditure by the GoI as a Percentage of (2)	Expenditure by the Education Department	Expenditure by Other Departments
1	2	3	4	5	6
2011–2012	333,930.39 (13.78)	80.88	25.78	22.31	40.44
2012–2013	368,132.81 (10.24)	81.28	24.38	22.09	34.34
2013–2014 (RE)	433,640.59 (17.79)	81.04	23.43	21.25	32.74
2014–2015 (BE)	502,929.34 (15.98)	80.45	24.36	20.46	40.39

Source: Author's calculation using basic data in the GoI's *Analysis of Budgeted Expenditure on Education* (various issues).
Notes:
1. Figures in parentheses are simple annual growth rates (%).
2. General government comprises the union, state and UT governments.

by the education department than by the other departments. This is evident in columns 5 and 6 in Table 9.1.

Table 9.2 shows the trends in the general government's total expenditure on the general higher education (i.e., university and higher education) and technical education. The size of total expenditure increased although the annual growth rate has fluctuated over the years. For instance, the size increased from ₹11,893 crore in 2003–2004 to ₹32,065 crore in 2009–2010 and to ₹70,225 crore in 2014–2015. The highest annual growth rate (36.39%) is recorded for 2008–2009 which is a remarkable rise of 22 percentage points over the previous year (2007–2008). Throughout, the share of general (or technical) higher education is more than 70 (or less than 30) per cent. Further, the share of general (or technical) higher education in the total expenditure of the education department (i.e., sum of expenditure on elementary education, secondary education, university and higher education, technical education and language development) has been less than 14 (or 6) per cent. This implies that the share of the total expenditure on higher education has been less than 20 per cent of total expenditure of the education department. However, within the total expenditure on higher education, the share of the GoI is relatively higher for technical education than for the general higher education. This is evident in columns 6 and 7 in Table 9.2. For instance, GoI's share in general (or technical) higher education was 19.44 (or 49.42) in 2003–2004, 32.40 (or 60.16) in 2008–2009 and 26.88 (or 53.46) in 2014–2015. Thus, GoI's (or state governments') expenditure matters much for the technical (or general higher) education in India.

Public Expenditure on Scholarships in Higher Education

Public expenditure on the scholarships/fellowships are provided for the undergraduate (UG) and postgraduate (PG) studies and fellowships are awarded for the MPhil, PhD and post-doctoral studies.

Expenditure on Scholarships by Union Government

Trends in size and relative share of public expenditure on the scholarships by the union government are given in Table 9.3.

Table 9.2 *Total Public Expenditure by Education Department on Higher Education, India: 2003–2004 to 2014–2015*

Year	Total Expenditure on Higher Education by the Education Department (₹ crore)	Expenditure on Higher Education by the Education Department of the General Government			Expenditure by GoI as Percentage of (2)	
		Expenditure on General Higher Education as a Percentage of (2)	Expenditure on General Higher Education as a Percentage of Total Expenditure of the Education Department	Expenditure on Technical Education as a Percentage of the Total Expenditure of the Education Department (%)	General Higher Education	Technical Education
1	2	3	4	5	6	7
2003–2004	11,893.22	76.18	12.40	3.88	19.44	49.42
2004–2005	12,649.43 (6.36)	75.13	11.69	3.87	22.09	45.82
2005–2006	14,670.34 (15.98)	75.07	11.66	3.87	20.89	41.67
2006–2007	16,582.84 (13.04)	75.63	11.37	3.66	22.75	43.48
2007–2008	18,968.84 (14.39)	75.45	11.41	3.71	26.74	44.70
2008–2009	25,871.48 (36.39)	71.91	12.17	4.75	32.40	60.16

Year						
2009–2010	32,064.84 (23.94)	70.91	11.75	4.82	33.70	58.44
2010–2011	39,842.73 (24.26)	73.21	12.49	4.57	29.01	55.94
2011–2012	46,695.52 (17.20)	70.74	12.23	5.06	31.99	58.35
2012–2013	52,872.00 (13.23)	71.26	12.59	5.08	26.48	56.00
2013–2014 (RE)	66,260.29 (25.32)	73.55	13.87	4.99	25.46	52.75
2014–2015 (BE)	70224.58 (5.98)	72.79	12.63	4.72	26.88	53.46

Source: Author's calculation using basic data in the GoI's *Analysis of Budgeted Expenditure on Education* (various issues).

Notes:
1. Figures in parentheses are simple annual growth rates (%).
2. General government comprises the union, state and UT governments.

Table 9.3 Expenditure on Scholarships by Union Government, India: 2003–2004 to 2014–2015

Year	Total Expenditure on Scholarships by Union Government (₹ crore)	Aggregate (or Sum of Union, State and UT governments) Expenditure on Scholarships (₹ crore)	Union Government's Expenditure on Scholarships as a Percentage of (3)
1	2	3	4
2003–2004	0.76	25.5651	2.97
2004–2005	1.92	23.8367	8.05
2005–2006	9.94	59.0508	16.83
2006–2007	7.94	49.8399	15.94
2007–2008	1.28	111.1618	1.15
2008–2009	30.95	169.1932	18.29
2009–2010	59.10	276.501	21.37
2010–2011	107.75	365.9866	29.44
2011–2012	163.88	558.8746	29.32
2012–2013	1,115.93	1,542.05	72.37
2013–2014 (RE)	1,953.19	2,529.586	77.21
2014–2015 (BE)	2,327.00	2,908.433	80.01

Source: Author's calculation using basic data in the GoI's *Analysis of Budgeted Expenditure on Education* (various issues).

Expenditure includes scholarships for the general higher education and technical education. All the expenditures refer to merit scholarships and interest subsidy on education loans availed by students (since 2009).[4]

---

[4] Way back in 1963, the National Loan Scholarship Scheme was implemented for students in India's higher education. The scheme was funded by the Government of India and administered by the state governments. The eligibility

Interestingly, the trends in size of the scholarship expenditure of the GoI and its share in aggregate public expenditure on the scholarships (i.e., sum of scholarship expenditure by the union, state and UT governments) on higher education show a remarkable rise over the years: ₹0.76 crore in 2003–2004, ₹30.95 crore in 2008–2009 and ₹23.27 crore in 2014–2015. As a share in the aggregate public expenditure on the scholarships by the government, the expenditure of the central government increased from 2.97 per cent in 2003–2004 to 18.29 per cent in 2008–2009 and to 80.01 per cent in 2014–2015. These trends imply the growing importance of the public expenditure on the national scholarships, funded by the GoI, in higher education.

Aggregate Expenditure on Scholarship by States and UTs

Table 9.4 shows the trends in expenditure by the education department of the state governments and UTs on the scholarships. First, public expenditure on the scholarships in the education department is provided for students in elementary education, secondary education, university and higher education, technical and others. Total expenditure on the scholarships in the education department increased from ₹120 crore in 2003–2004 to ₹356 crore in 2008–2009 to ₹3,203 crore in 2014–2015. As compared to 2003–2004, expenditure on scholarships was about 17 times more in 2013–2014 or about 27 times more in 2014–2015. However, annual growth rates show wide fluctuations. The growth rates were negative in 2005–2006 and 2008–2009 and positive for the rest of years. Of the years of positive growth rates, the highest growth rate is evident for 2007–2008 (146.08%) and the lowest for 2006–2007 (1.48%).

---

conditions for the scholarship included both merit and limits on parental income. Before 1991, the amount of loan scholarship ranged from ₹720 per annum for undergraduate students to ₹1,750 per annum for doctoral or postdoctoral studies. The scheme was closed in 1991 for reasons including poor recovery, and limited amount and number of scholarship. A critical review of this scheme is given in Tilak (1992). Public expenditure on this National Loan Scholarship Scheme is not analysed in this chapter because it was closed before the start of the study period of this chapter (2003–2004).

Table 9.4 Expenditure on Scholarships by State and UT Governments, India: 2003–2004 to 2014–2015

Year	Total Expenditure on Scholarships by the Education Department (₹ crore)	Expenditure on Scholarships by State and UT Governments					Expenditure on Scholarships in Higher Education	
		Expenditure on Scholarship in Elementary Education as a Percentage of (2)	Expenditure on Scholarship in Secondary Education as a Percentage of (2)	Expenditure on Scholarship in General Higher Education as a Percentage of (2)	Expenditure on Scholarship in Technical Education as a Percentage of (2)	Expenditure on Scholarship in other General Education as a Percentage of (2)	Total Expenditure (₹ crore)	Expenditure on Scholarship in General Higher Education as a Percentage of (8)
1	2	3	4	5	6	7	8	9
2003–2004	120.07	33.77	29.02	15.36	5.30	16.55	24.81	74.33
2004–2005	170.94 (42.37)	43.95	35.78	9.01	3.81	7.44	21.92 (–11.64)	70.28
2005–2006	152.09 (–11.03)	27.97	27.34	26.77	5.52	12.40	49.11 (124.08)	82.91
2006–2007	154.34 (1.48)	31.60	29.24	23.76	3.39	12.01	41.90 (–14.69)	87.52

Year							
2007–2008	379.79 (146.08))	42.14	19.78	15.54	13.39	9.15	109.88 (162.27)	53.71
2008–2009	356.19 (–6.21)	32.34	18.70	23.54	15.27	10.14	138.24 (25.81)	60.64
2009–2010	613.17 (72.14)	29.63	29.67	12.72	22.74	5.25	217.40 (57.26)	35.87
2010–2011	1,293.60 (110.97)	56.33	20.03	7.62	12.34	3.68	258.24 (18.78)	38.19
2011–2012	1,880.72 (45.39)	42.31	32.34	7.08	13.92	4.35	395.00 (52.96)	33.70
2012–2013	2,040.50 (8.50)	31.59	42.61	8.17	12.71	4.92	426.12 (7.88)	39.13
2013–2014 (RE)	3,149.66 (54.36)	33.58	40.81	9.21	9.09	7.31	576.40 (35.26)	50.31
2014–2015 (BE)	3,203.20 (1.70)	35.61	38.95	8.93	9.23	7.29	581.43 (0.87)	49.17

Source: Author's calculation using basic data in the GoI's *Analysis of Budgeted Expenditure on Education* (various issues).

Notes:
1. Figures in parentheses are simple annual growth rates (%).
2. General government comprises the union, state and UT governments.

Further, a higher expenditure share of the scholarships is received by students in elementary and secondary education. In particular, their combined share is about 74 per cent since 2010–2011. Share of higher education (i.e., combined share of general and technical higher education) is less than 40 per cent with the highest share in 2008–2009 (38.81%) and lowest in 2004–2005 (12.82%). In addition, share of the scholarships' expenditure on the general higher education (or technical) has declined since 2008–2009 (or 2009–2010).

Columns 8 and 9 in Table 9.4 show the size of total scholarship expenditure on higher education and the share of general higher education in this total. The size of the expenditure has increased since 2007–2008 with a remarkable variation in the annual growth rates. For instance, the size of scholarships expenditure in 2003–2004 increased by 23 times in 2014–2015. Annual growth rates were negative in 2004–2005 and 2006–2007. Of the years with a positive growth rate, the highest annual growth is evident for 2007–2008 (162.27%) and lowest in 2014–2015 (0.87%). Further, within higher education, the share of expenditure on the scholarships to general higher education is highest up to 2008–2009 and to the technical education since 2009–2010.

Thus, the expenditure on the scholarships by the state governments and UTs from 2003–2004 to 2014–2015 is marked by distinct trends and patterns over time and across levels (within general education) and types of education (i.e., general higher and technical education).

Disaggregation of Expenditure on Higher Education Scholarships by States and UTs

Disaggregate analysis of public expenditure on scholarship by the states and UTs is useful to understand the (a) concentration or dispersion of expenditure across by the states and UTs and (b) relative priority given by the states and UTs to the scholarship expenditure.

Table 9.5 shows the trends in national share of individual states and combined share of all UTs in public expenditure on the scholarships in general higher education or university and higher education by states and UTs. Apparently, the share of states has been higher

Table 9.5 *Public Expenditure on Scholarships in University and Higher Education by States and UTs: 2003–2004 to 2014–2015*

States and All UTs	National Share of Public Expenditure on Scholarships in University and Higher Education (%)											
	2003–2004	2004–2005	2005–2006	2006–2007	2007–2008	2008–2009	2009–2010	2010–2011	2011–2012	2012–2013	2013–2014 (RE)	2014–2015 (BE)
Andhra Pradesh	19.13	5.75	14.99	8.70	5.41	36.68	0.00	0.55	0.30	0.15	0.59	0.35
Arunachal Pradesh	11.88	18.56	6.88	8.83	6.32	5.28	5.63	6.57	0.05	0.00	3.50	3.55
Assam	0.73	0.30	0.24	0.05	0.24	0.74	0.06	0.00	0.00	0.04	0.20	0.21
Bihar	0.00	0.00	0.00	0.00	0.00	0.00	0.00	0.00	28.34	16.48	16.24	13.15
Chhattisgarh	0.22	0.22	0.61	1.70	1.57	0.84	1.05	2.98	2.13	2.33	1.40	1.60
Goa	0.00	0.00	0.00	0.00	0.00	0.00	0.00	0.00	0.00	0.00	0.00	0.00
Gujarat	0.00	0.00	0.00	0.00	0.00	0.00	0.00	0.00	0.00	0.00	0.00	0.00
Haryana	2.68	2.81	3.11	3.08	32.74	1.98	2.00	1.70	1.18	1.06	0.71	0.67
Himachal Pradesh	0.00	0.00	0.00	0.24	0.00	0.00	0.00	0.00	0.00	0.00	0.00	0.00
J&K	0.48	0.58	0.24	0.28	0.21	0.14	0.09	0.07	0.02	0.05	0.03	0.03
Jharkhand	0.00	0.00	0.00	0.00	0.00	0.00	0.00	0.00	0.00	0.00	0.00	0.00
Karnataka	3.60	4.33	2.67	3.97	4.01	2.47	3.15	2.69	2.34	2.08	1.11	1.28
Kerala	4.87	4.65	4.09	3.59	5.49	11.50	33.39	25.95	21.41	22.74	11.71	13.83
Madhya Pradesh	0.61	1.01	0.45	0.41	0.96	0.17	0.98	0.66	1.42	3.97	2.97	3.46
Maharashtra	2.28	3.80	1.20	2.67	0.97	3.20	8.25	16.68	0.32	25.83	24.82	25.38

(Continued)

Table 9.5 (Continued)

	National Share of Public Expenditure on Scholarships in University and Higher Education (%)											
States and All UTs	2003–2004	2004–2005	2005–2006	2006–2007	2007–2008	2008–2009	2009–2010	2010–2011	2011–2012	2012–2013	2013–2014 (RE)	2014–2015 (BE)
Manipur	0.32	0.34	0.31	0.52	0.29	0.18	0.23	0.25	0.31	0.28	0.15	0.15
Meghalaya	8.34	3.41	31.29	5.20	0.44	2.19	0.66	0.52	0.39	0.35	0.80	0.85
Mizoram	1.82	2.18	0.91	1.09	0.73	0.57	1.12	1.95	0.66	3.06	2.99	2.98
Nagaland	9.06	7.11	4.65	5.17	2.90	2.24	3.34	3.41	3.16	1.33	1.33	1.35
Orissa	2.68	3.14	1.21	1.09	1.14	2.73	4.33	8.24	11.07	4.87	8.80	9.10
Punjab	1.73	0.26	1.45	0.83	0.24	0.21	0.21	0.18	0.22	0.19	0.13	0.13
Rajasthan	1.62	2.14	0.79	0.78	0.72	0.74	0.99	0.50	0.33	7.81	6.87	9.56
Sikkim	0.00	0.00	0.00	0.00	0.00	0.00	0.00	0.00	0.00	0.00	0.00	0.00
Tamil Nadu	12.82	16.50	14.02	6.63	5.76	8.14	9.02	9.83	12.20	1.02	0.64	0.65
Tripura	4.25	5.06	1.50	1.32	0.95	0.76	0.40	0.71	0.58	0.29	0.23	0.26
Uttarakhand	0.00	0.02	0.17	0.17	0.10	0.06	0.00	0.00	0.00	0.00	0.02	0.00
Uttar Pradesh	0.32	0.33	1.55	0.00	1.07	0.00	0.00	0.00	0.00	0.00	0.00	0.00
West Bengal	0.33	0.00	1.04	0.01	0.00	0.00	0.00	0.02	0.00	0.00	0.00	0.00
Telangana	0.00	0.00	0.00	0.00	0.00	0.00	0.00	0.00	0.00	0.00	0.00	0.03
All states	89.76	82.50	93.37	56.32	72.23	80.81	74.91	83.47	86.45	93.95	85.27	88.56
All UTs	10.24	17.50	6.63	43.68	27.77	19.19	25.09	16.53	13.55	6.05	14.73	11.44
All states and UTs	100.00	100.00	100.00	100.00	100.00	100.00	100.00	100.00	100.00	100.00	100.00	100.00

Source: Author's calculation using basic data in the GoI's Analysis of Budgeted Expenditure on Education (various issues).

than 70 per cent except for 2006–2007. Of the states, the shares of Arunachal Pradesh, Kerala, Maharashtra, Meghalaya, Mizoram and Tamil Nadu are relatively higher than the other states. The combined share of these six states varied from 49.26 per cent in 2003–2004 to 60.29 in 2009–2010, 51.27 per cent in 2003–2004 and to 46.60 in 2014–2015. Of these six states, three states (Arunachal Pradesh, Meghalaya and Mizoram) belong to the Special Category States (SCS) and the rest to Non-Special Category States (NSCS). The combined share of the NSCS has been relatively higher than the SCS. For instance, the combined share of the NSCS was equal to 19.98 per cent in 2003–2004, 50.66 in 2009–2010, 49.60 per cent in 2003–2004 and 39.86 in 2014–2015.

Table 9.6 shows the trends in the share of scholarship expenditure of individual states and all UTs in total expenditure on university and higher education by states and all UTs. Throughout, the expenditure on the scholarships has been higher for the UTs (about 2% or more) than the states (less than 1%). The SCS, such as, Arunachal Pradesh, Mizoram, Nagaland and Tripura, show a remarkable share of scholarship expenditure in their total expenditure on university and higher education. Of these states, the share of Arunachal Pradesh is prominent (in terms of being higher than average for all states) except in 2012–2013. Of the NSCS, the share is relatively higher for Kerala since 2006–2007, Maharashtra since 2012–2013, Tamil Nadu up to 2011–2012 and Orissa since 2010–2011.

Table 9.7 shows the trends in the national share of individual states and all UTs in the total public expenditure on scholarships in technical education by states and UTs. The trends are remarkably different from the university and higher education in Table 9.5. For instance, throughout, the expenditure share on the scholarships for states remained above 92 per cent and close to 100 per cent since 2008–2009. Of the states, five NSCS (Andhra Pradesh, Karnataka, Kerala, Maharashtra and Tamil Nadu) accounted for a higher share of expenditure on scholarship. The combined share of these states has increased from 87.06 per cent in 2003–2004 to 97.51 per cent in 2010–2011 and to 98.35 per cent in 2014–2015. Interestingly, these five states show marked diversities in their trends. For instance, Maharashtra's share has

Table 9.6 *Public Expenditure on Scholarships in Total Expenditure on University and Higher Education by States and UTs: 2003–2004 to 2014–2015*

States and All UTs	Public Expenditure on Scholarships as a Percentage of Total Expenditure on University and Higher Education in Each State/UT											
	2003–2004	2004–2005	2005–2006	2006–2007	2007–2008	2008–2009	2009–2010	2010–2011	2011–2012	2012–2013	2013–2014 (RE)	2014–2015 (BE)
Andhra Pradesh	0.41	0.15	0.66	0.3	0.3	2.76	0	0.03	0.02	0.01	0.06	0.05
Arunachal Pradesh	13.59	15.16	14.03	14.84	24.22	21.01	13.36	20.65	0.24	0	21.65	14.8
Assam	0.06	0.02	0.04	0.01	0.04	0.13	0.01	0	0	0.01	0.04	0.03
Bihar	0	0	0	0	0	0	0	0	2.12	1.07	1.37	1.02
Chhattisgarh	0.04	0.03	0.16	0.5	0.68	0.53	0.52	0.8	0.92	1.16	0.76	1.5
Goa	0	0	0	0	0	0	0	0	0	0	0	0
Gujarat	0	0	0	0	0	0	0	0	0	0	0	0
Haryana	0.24	0.22	0.6	0.44	4.16	0.38	0.25	0.24	0.2	0.21	0.21	0.17
Himachal Pradesh	0	0	0	0.11	0	0	0	0	0	0	0	0
J&K	0.1	0.1	0.19	0.09	0.09	0.09	0.04	0.03	0.01	0.02	0.02	0.02
Jharkhand	0	0	0	0	0	0	0	0	0	0	0	0
Karnataka	0.14	0.13	0.21	0.27	0.39	0.3	0.33	0.18	0.19	0.19	0.13	0.14
Kerala	18	0.14	0.32	0.24	0.54	1.3	3.33	2.54	2.22	2.46	1.81	1.73
Madhya Pradesh	0.04	0.05	0.05	0.05	0.15	0.03	0.17	0.12	0.26	0.76	0.76	0.82

State/UT												
Maharashtra	0.05	0.06	0.04	0.07	0.04	0.18	0.39	0.62	0.02	1.13	1.34	1.75
Manipur	0.11	0.07	0.11	0.3	0.28	0.25	0.26	0.32	0.31	0.34	0.3	0.28
Meghalaya	5.84	2.22	32.91	4.27	0.66	3.27	1.1	0.89	0.6	0.68	2.12	2.01
Mizoram	1.63	1.63	1.54	1.43	1.32	1.25	2	3.67	1.18	4.69	7.87	9.05
Nagaland	10.63	5.5	8.69	8.75	7.37	7.52	7.33	7.51	8.04	3.37	4.22	4.06
Orissa	0.19	0.16	0.14	0.09	0.13	0.39	0.37	0.62	1.29	0.76	1.15	1.52
Punjab	0.13	0.02	0.26	0.16	0.05	0.04	0.03	0.05	0.08	0.04	0.06	0.06
Rajasthan	0.11	0.12	0.11	0.1	0.15	0.18	0.14	0.08	0.07	1.46	1.83	2.57
Sikkim	0	0	0	0	0	0	0	0	0	0	0	0
Tamil Nadu	0.51	0.5	1.05	0.41	0.53	0.81	0.67	0.67	1.08	0.12	0.1	0.09
Tripura	3.58	3.25	2.58	2.09	2.5	2.42	0.77	1.7	1.64	0.81	0.81	0.84
Uttarakhand	0	0	0.08	0.05	0.04	0.04	0	0	0	0	0.02	0
Uttar Pradesh	0.01	0.01	0.1	0.08	0.08		0	0	0	0	0	0
West Bengal	0.01	0	0.07	0	0	0	0	0	0	0	0	0
Telangana	0	0	0	0	0	0	0	0	0	0	0	0.01
All States	0.23	0.17	0.44	0.22	0.42	0.57	0.41	0.42	0.54	0.61	0.73	0.75
All UTs	1.59	2.18	1.97	9.49	8.65	6.89	5.05	3.4	5.19	2.9	10.39	7.09
All states and UTs	0.25	0.21	0.47	0.38	0.57	0.69	0.53	0.49	0.61	0.64	0.85	0.83

Source: Author's calculation using basic data in the GoI's *Analysis of Budgeted Expenditure on Education* (various issues).

Note: Zero values are due to the absence of expenditure on scholarships or computed values are zero at two decimal.

Table 9.7 *Public Expenditure on Scholarships in Technical Education by States and UTs: 2003–2004 to 2014–2015*

State and UTs	National Share of Public Expenditure on Scholarships in Technical Education											
	2003–2004	2004–2005	2005–2006	2006–2007	2007–2008	2008–2009	2009–2010	2010–2011	2011–2012	2012–2013	2013–2014 (RE)	2014–2015 (BE)
Andhra Pradesh	78.87	80.54	60.06	50.14	5.16	2.89	0.58	0.44	0.25	0.03	0.52	0.26
Arunachal Pradesh	0.00	0.00	0.00	0.00	0.00	0.00	0.00	0.00	0.00	0.00	0.00	0.00
Assam	2.56	2.86	1.65	2.81	0.41	1.16	0.12	0.09	0.08	0.09	0.16	0.19
Bihar	0.00	0.00	0.00	0.00	0.00	0.00	0.00	0.00	0.00	0.00	0.00	0.00
Chhattisgarh	0.18	0.16	0.20	0.31	0.04	0.06	0.02	0.03	0.01	0.02	0.02	0.04
Goa	0.00	0.00	0.00	0.00	0.00	0.00	0.00	0.00	0.00	0.00	0.00	0.00
Gujarat	0.00	0.00	0.00	0.00	0.00	0.00	0.00	0.00	0.00	0.00	0.00	0.00
Haryana	0.36	0.31	0.19	0.49	1.20	0.83	0.67	0.87	0.58	0.44	0.45	0.51
Himachal Pradesh	0.00	0.00	0.00	0.00	0.00	0.00	0.00	0.00	0.00	0.00	0.00	0.00
J&K	0.00	0.00	0.00	0.00	0.00	0.00	0.00	0.00	0.00	0.00	0.00	0.00
Jharkhand	0.07	0.07	0.05	0.00	0.00	0.00	0.00	0.00	0.00	0.00	0.00	0.00
Karnataka	7.94	8.61	6.84	12.34	24.72	12.25	3.35	17.24	4.90	5.73	20.02	6.71
Kerala	0.01	0.15	0.06	0.01	0.00	0.00	3.71	4.93	0.00	7.71	8.73	16.92
Madhya Pradesh	0.41	0.64	0.53	0.67	0.06	0.07	0.02	0.01	0.01	0.01	0.02	0.02
Maharashtra	0.24	0.24	0.25	0.29	61.00	71.96	77.55	71.29	91.16	84.82	69.13	74.45

Manipur	0.19	0.27	0.29	0.07	0.01	0.00	0.01	0.00	0.00	0.00	0.01	0.01
Meghalaya	0.54	0.81	0.51	2.00	0.56	0.23	0.24	0.23	0.14	0.13	0.26	0.25
Mizoram	0.00	0.00	0.00	0.00	0.00	0.00	0.00	0.00	0.00	0.00	0.00	0.00
Nagaland	0.00	0.77	5.36	10.32	2.24	3.67	9.54	1.00	0.60	0.97	0.61	0.56
Orissa	0.04	0.00	0.03	0.00	0.00	0.00	0.00	0.00	0.00	0.00	0.00	0.00
Punjab	0.00	0.02	0.10	0.07	0.01	0.00	0.00	0.00	0.00	0.00	0.00	0.00
Rajasthan	0.00	0.00	0.00	0.00	0.00	0.34	0.00	0.00	0.00	0.00	0.00	0.00
Sikkim	0.00	0.00	0.00	0.00	0.00	0.00	0.00	0.00	0.00	0.00	0.00	0.00
Tamil Nadu	0.00	0.03	23.51	20.00	4.53	6.43	4.16	3.62	2.24	0.00	0.05	0.00
Tripura	0.26	0.40	0.31	0.20	0.05	0.07	0.03	0.02	0.03	0.04	0.00	0.06
Uttarakhand	0.00	0.00	0.00	0.00	0.00	0.00	0.00	0.00	0.00	0.00	0.00	0.00
Uttar Pradesh	0.00	0.00	0.00	0.00	0.00	0.00	0.00	0.00	0.00	0.00	0.00	0.00
West Bengal	0.02	0.00	0.00	0.00	0.00	0.02	0.00	0.25	0.00	0.00	0.00	0.00
Telangana	0.00	0.00	0.00	0.00	0.00	0.00	0.00	0.00	0.00	0.00	0.00	0.01
All states	91.67	95.90	99.93	99.71	99.99	99.99	100.00	100.00	100.00	100.00	100.00	100.00
All UTs	8.33	4.10	0.07	0.29	0.01	0.01	0.00	0.00	0.00	0.00	0.00	0.00
Total	100.00	100.00	100.00	100.00	100.00	100.00	100.00	100.00	100.00	100.00	100.00	100.00

Source: Author's calculation using basic data in the GoI's *Analysis of Budgeted Expenditure on Education* (various issues).

Note: Zero values are due to the absence of expenditure on scholarships or computed values are zero at two decimal.

been higher than 60 per cent since 2007–2008 and Andhra Pradesh, Karnataka and Tamil Nadu had a remarkable share before 2007–2008.

Table 9.8 shows the trends in share of scholarship expenditure in total expenditure on technical education by states and all UTs. The trends are in contrast with the university and higher education in Table 9.6. Throughout, the expenditure on scholarship has been higher for states (less than 5%) than UTs (less than 0.3%). Most importantly, the expenditure share on scholarship for UTs has been negligible and closer to zero since 2007–2008. Nagaland has a prominent share since 2005–2006, Maharashtra since 2008–2009 and Karnataka since 2007–2008.

These analyses show the wide disparities in national share and public expenditure priority on scholarship across the states and UTs. In addition, remarkable interstate disparities are evident by levels of education within the general education and between general higher education and technical education.

PUBLIC EXPENDITURE ON SCHOLARSHIP SCHEMES

National-Level Scholarship Schemes by the GoI

Schemes by the MHRD

The GoI offers merit-based national scholarships.[5] They are (a) Central Sector Scheme of Scholarship for College and University Students, (b) special scholarship scheme for students from J&K and (c) scholarship to students from non-Hindi-speaking states for post-matric studies in Hindi. The eligibility conditions, amount of scholarship and the number of the mentioned scholarships are summarized in Table 9.9.

---

[5] In addition, the MHRD facilitates the nomination process for the external scholarships offered by various countries, to meritorious and eligible Indian students. The external scholarships include the Commonwealth Scholarships for United Kingdom and New Zealand; scholarships offered by China, South Korea, Israel, Japan, Italy, Mexico and Sri Lanka; and Agatha Harrison Memorial Fellowship. Unlike the national scholarships, these external scholarships are not funded by public expenditure by the education or other departments and, hence, are not elaborated here.

Table 9.8 *Public Expenditure on Scholarships in Technical Education by States and UTs: 2003–2004 to 2014–2015*

States and All UTs	National Share of Public Expenditure on Scholarships as a Percentage of Total Expenditure on Technical Education in Each State/UT											
	2003–2004	2004–2005	2005–2006	2006–2007	2007–2008	2008–2009	2009–2010	2010–2011	2011–2012	2012–2013	2013–2014 (RE)	2014–2015 (BE)
Andhra Pradesh	4.85	3.68	3.14	1.3	1.3	0.92	0.18	0.11	0.09	0.01	0.14	0.13
Arunachal Pradesh	0	0	0	0	0	0	0	0	0	0	0	0
Assam	0.69	0.78	0.59	0.58	0.46	1.18	0.35	0.15	0.2	0.25	0.27	0.41
Bihar	0	0	0	0	0	0	0	0	0	0	0	0
Chhattisgarh	0.06	0.05	0.07	0.08	0.08	0.12	0.09	0.1	0.06	0.12	0.07	0.08
Goa	0	0	0	0	0	0	0	0	0	0	0	0
Gujarat	0	0	0	0	0	0	0	0	0	0	0	0
Haryana	0.05	0.04	0.02	0.03	0.54	0.19	0.19	0.71	0.59	0.4	0.35	0.31
Himachal Pradesh	0	0	0	0	0	0	0	0	0	0	0	0
J&K	0	0	0	0	0	0	0	0	0	0	0	0
Jharkhand	0.02	0.01	0	0	0	0	0	0	0	0	0	0
Karnataka	0.73	0.58	0.34	0.4	7.77	4.58	2.66	10.05	3.22	3.07	8.59	2.75
Kerala	0	0.01	0	0	0	0	1.88	2.45	0	3.55	3.99	6
Madhya Pradesh	0.03	0.05	0.06	0.04	0.04	0	0.02	0.01	0.01	0.01	0.03	0.03
Maharashtra	0.01	0	0	0	6.57	0.04	14.33	12.59	21	16.05	12.78	13.22
Manipur	0.33	0.44	0.62	0.13	0.16	6.74	0.28	0.01	0	0	0.37	0.36

(Continued)

Table 9.8 (Continued)

	National Share of Public Expenditure on Scholarships as a Percentage of Total Expenditure on Technical Education in Each State/UT											
States and All UTs	2003–2004	2004–2005	2005–2006	2006–2007	2007–2008	2008–2009	2009–2010	2010–2011	2011–2012	2012–2013	2013–2014 (RE)	2014–2015 (BE)
Meghalaya	0.28	0.22	0.3	2.34	7.72	0	6.22	5.58	2.86	3.95	5.47	5.2
Mizoram	0	0	0	0	0	0	0	0	0	0	0	0
Nagaland	0	0.43	2.76	8.26	15.38	0	72.19	21.51	17.2	21.82	16.85	14.43
Orissa	0.01	0	0.01	0.01	0.01	34.99	0	0	0	0	0	0
Punjab	0	0	0.03	0.01	0	0	0.01	0	0	0	0	0
Rajasthan	0	0	0	0	0	0	0	0	0	0	0	0
Sikkim	0	0	0	0	0	0.34	0	0	0	0	0	0
Tamil Nadu	0	0	1.18	0.6	1.38	0	2.7	1.09	0.86	0	0	0
Tripura	0.43	0.7	0.67	0.41	0.73	1.73	0.69	0.35	1.18	1.37	0.87	1.07
Uttarakhand	0	0	0	0	0	0	0	0	0	0	0	0
Uttar Pradesh	0	0	0	0	0	0	0	0	0	0	0	0
West Bengal	0	0	0	0	0	0.01	0	0.14	0	0	0	0
Telangana	0	0	0	0	0	0	0	0	0	0	0	0.01
All states	0.44	0.39	0.41	0.24	2.13	2.01	3.81	3.61	4.83	4.07	3.61	3.51
All UTs	0.54	0.27	0.01	0.01	0	0	0	0	0	0	0	0
Total	0.44	0.38	0.39	0.23	1.98	1.88	3.6	3.39	4.6	3.88	3.46	3.32

Source: Author's calculation using basic data in the GoI's *Analysis of Budgeted Expenditure on Education* (various issues).

Note: Zero values are due to the absence of expenditure on scholarships or computed values are zero at two decimal.

Table 9.9 GoI's National-Level Scholarship Schemes for Higher Education: 2014–2015

Scheme	Eligibility	Amount	No. of Scholarships
1. Central Sector Scheme of Scholarship for College and University Students	1. Secured above 80th percentile in the relevant stream from a particular board of examination in class XII and pursuing regular course. 2. Not availing benefit of any other scholarships. 3. Belongs to a family with income of less than ₹6 lakh per annum	1. ₹1,000 per month for graduation level for first three years of college and university courses and ₹2,000 per month for PG level. 2. ₹2,000 per month in the 4th and 5th years. 3. Duration of scholarship is 10 months in an academic year.	82,000 per year with the following reservation: 50% for girls, 15% for SC, 7.5% for ST, 27% for OBC students and 3% for students with disability. The total number of scholarships is divided amongst the state boards based on the state's population in the age group of 18–25 years, after segregating share of the Central Board of Secondary Education and Indian Certificate of Secondary Education on the basis of the number of students passing out from various boards in the country. The number of scholarships allotted to a state board is distributed amongst pass-outs of the science, commerce and humanities streams of the state board in the ratio of 3:2:1

(Continued)

Table 9.9 (Continued)

Scheme	Eligibility	Amount	No. of Scholarships
2. Special Scholarship Scheme for J&K	1. The students of J&K whose family income is less than ₹6.0 lakh per annum. 2. Passed class XII from the state and secured admission outside the state in institutions which are approved under Section 12 B of the UGC Act or recognized by AICTE or respective regulatory body.	1. Tuition fee (per annum) of ₹30,000 for general degree courses; ₹1.25 lakh for engineering courses; and ₹ 3 lakh for medical studies 2. Fixed maintenance allowance of ₹1 lakh per year to all students under the scheme.	About 5,000 fresh scholarships every year
3. Scholarship to students in non-Hindi-speaking states for post-matric studies in Hindi	Mother tongue is not Hindi and belongs to any of the non-Hindi-speaking states/UTs* At least 60% marks in the qualifying examination.	₹55 per month for BA/BSc/BCom (pass or Honours) or an equivalent examination ₹1,000 per month for MA, MLitt and equivalent courses and Hindi Teachers Training Course/PhD month	About 2,500 scholarships per year as per the quota of each non-Hindi-speaking state/UT

Source: Author's compilation from GoI (2017a, 2017b).

Note: *Non-Hindi-speaking states/UT are Andhra Pradesh, Assam, J&K, Karnataka, Kerala, Manipur, Meghalaya, Nagaland, Orissa, Punjab, Sikkim, Tamil Nadu, Tripura, West Bengal, Andaman and Nicobar Islands, Arunachal Pradesh, Chandigarh, Lakshadweep, Dadra and Nagar Haveli, Daman and Diu, Mizoram and Pondicherry.

In addition, scholarships are offered under the Special Component Plan for Scheduled Castes (SCs) and Tribal Area Sub-Plan.

Table 9.10 gives the expenditure on the national-level scholarship schemes by the MHRD from 2003–2004 to 2015–2016. Expenditure on National Merit Scholarship refers to Central Sector Scheme of Scholarship for University and College Students. Expenditure on the scholarship to students in the non-Hindi-speaking states for post-matric studies in Hindi is not reported for all years and no expenditure is reported on the special scholarship scheme for J&K. Size of expenditure on National Merit Scholarship increased from ₹19.83 crores in 2003–2004 to ₹63 crores in 2009–2010 and to ₹217.13 crores in 2015–2016. This growth is not characterized by a positive annual growth rate every year. On the other hand, throughout, annual expenditure on the scholarship for students in the non-Hindi-speaking states has remained less than ₹3 crores. Further, expenditure has been less than ₹4 lakh per year under the Special Component Plan for SC students and less than ₹2 lakh under Tribal Sub-Plan. However, the share of mentioned expenditure in the total scholarship expenditure on higher education has remained very small. For instance, the total expenditure on GoI's scholarships in Table 9.10 was about 10.39 per cent of the total expenditure on scholarships for higher education (Table 9.3) in 2012–2013.

In addition, since 2009–2010, the GoI has started a new scheme for student's financial aid in the form of interest subsidy and contribution for guarantee fund. The scheme aims at providing the interest subsidy during the moratorium period on educational loans taken by students with family income of less than ₹4.5 lakh per annum. A student loan guarantee corpus is proposed to be created under the management of a credit guarantee trust to guarantee against default in repayment of student loans. This is intended to protect the lending institutions from student default and, thereby, encourage them to make more student loans. In addition, the government guarantee is expected to reduce the rate of interest on student loans.[6]

---

[6] Most recently, the Union Government has established the Higher Education Financing Agency (HEFA) in 2016–2017 as a not-for-profit organization to

Table 9.10 *Expenditure on GoI's Scholarship by Schemes: 2003–2004 to 2015–2016*

Year	Central Sector Scheme of Scholarship for College and University Students or National Merit Scholarship (INR crore)	Scholarship to Students in Non-Hindi-Speaking States for Post-Matric Studies in Hindi (INR crore)
2003–2004	19.83	NR
2004–05	12.08	NR
2005–2006	24.04	NR
2006–2007	11.70	2.51
2007–2008	12.60	2.61
2008–2009	30.00	2.42
2009–2010	108.00	2.41
2010–2011	107.42	0.38
2011–2012	163.12	0.75
2012–2013	115.47	0.46
2013–2014	194.30	0.75
2014–2015	NR	NR
2015–2016	217.13	NR

Source: Author's compilation from the Expenditure Budget, Vol. II (MHRD), Union Budget Papers (various years).

Notes: Figures from 2003–2004 to 2008–2009 refer to revised estimate and from 2009–2010 to 2015–2016 to actual. NR refers to not reported.

The budgetary expenditure on the scheme is reported in the Union Budget since 2013–2014. Over the years, the expenditure has remained less than ₹2,000 crores. For instance, the expenditure was ₹1,524.27 crores (actual) in 2013–2014, ₹1,581 crores (revised estimate) in

leverage funds from the market and supplement them with donations and CSR funds. These funds are to be spent for improvement in infrastructure in the top higher education institutions (e.g., world class universities) and serviced through internal accruals. However, no fund in the HEFA is meant for spending on the scholarships and fellowships.

2014–2015, ₹1,960 crores (actual) in 2015–2016, ₹1,850 crores (revised estimate) in 2016–2017 and ₹1,950 crores (BE) in 2017–2018.[7]

Schemes by UGC

The UGC has different schemes for promotion of the teaching-learning process and research in India's higher education. The schemes may be broadly classified under (a) faculty-based schemes, (b) institution-based schemes and (c) student-based schemes. Faculty-based schemes include (a) major and minor research projects for teachers, (b) research awards to teachers with doctorate degree, (c) emeritus fellowship, (d) incentivization of teachers, subject/discipline based association for organization of various academic and research activities, (e) research scientists to attract meritorious scientists of Indian origin, (f) operation faculty recharge, (g) UGC-BSR (Basic Science Research) Faculty Fellowship Scheme, (h) one-time grant to teachers under BSR Programme and (i) start-up grant for newly recruited faculty. Institution-based schemes include (a) basic scientific research in universities (development grant for strengthening of infrastructure in colleges and universities science departments) and (b) networking research centres: summer–winter school. No details of these faculty- and institution-based schemes are given here as they are well documented and made available in public domain (UGC, 2016, 2017).

Our focus here is on the student-based schemes which include the merit scholarship and fellowship schemes to the students in general, technical and professional education. In total, the UGC has 17 schemes in 2015–2016 which are provided for the post-doctoral, doctoral and MPhil research and for PG and UG studies. In general, the fellowships/scholarship schemes are different by their years of inception, eligibility conditions, amount and duration, and number of fellowships/scholarships. Table 9.10 gives a summary of these differences in 2015–2016.[8]

---

[7] These figures are compiled from the Expenditure Budget, Vol. II (Ministry of Human Resource Development), Union Budget Papers since 2013–2014.

[8] The following list excludes the Junior Research Fellowship and Research Associateship for the foreign nationals. In general, the eligibility conditions, fellowship amount and number of fellowship for the foreign nationals are different

The differences highlight the key and special features of UGC's design of these scholarships and fellowships. First, the design is comprehensive in coverage by including (a) post-doctoral, doctoral, PG and UG education and students; and (b) general education, technical education and professional education courses. Second, the inception of the scholarships and fellowships is unique by schemes. The JRF was the earliest to be introduced in 1957–1958. After a gap of 40 years, the Post-doctoral Fellowship for Women was introduced in 1998. Interestingly, all the remaining 15 scholarships/fellowships were introduced in 2005–2006 and later. Third, the scholarships and fellowships are designed to reward the merit of the students with explicit consideration for gender (i.e., preference for girl students), social justice (dedicated schemes for students belonging to the SC, ST and OBC), physically challenged including blind students (additional amount of scholarships or fellowships for escort/reader services) and spatial inequality (special scholarship for students in Northeastern Region). Fourth, all scholarships and fellowships are restricted to students in regular but not distance mode of education. Fifth, there is uniformity across schemes in the amount of fellowships for MPhil and PhD. In contrast, considerable differences are observed in the amount of post-doctoral fellowships and PG scholarships due to diversity in eligibility conditions. Sixth, the number of scholarships and fellowships is different by schemes. This number is a policy decision by the UGC.

Varghese, Malik and Gautam (2017) have analysed the student-level data on those who applied, appeared and qualified for the UGC-NET/JRF test from January 2010 through January 2014. The analysis gives insights on, among others, the gender and social composition of the JRF-qualified candidates. For instance, of the total applicants (718,727 students) for the UGC-NET/JRF in January 2014, about 75 per cent (or 539,051 students) appeared for the test. Of this, about 0.69 per cent (3,717 students) qualified for the JRF and 4.92 per cent (26,512 students) for the NET. Of the total students that qualified for the JRF (or NET/JRF), 34.89 (or 37.63) per cent were female students. Of the social categories, 33.01 (or 28.01) per cent of JRF

---

from the Indian nationals. Details of fellowships for the foreign nationals are given in UGC (2016).

Scholarship or Fellowship Scheme (Year of Inception)	Eligibility Conditions	Scholarship/Fellowship Amount (INR) Per Student	No. of Scholarships or Fellowships Per Annum

I. Post-doctoral Fellowships

Scholarship or Fellowship Scheme (Year of Inception)	Eligibility Conditions	Scholarship/Fellowship Amount (INR) Per Student	No. of Scholarships or Fellowships Per Annum
1. Post-doctoral Fellowships for SC/ST (2006–2007)	(a) Obtained PhD and have published works (b) Belongs to SC/ST (c) Duration: 5 years	(a) ₹38,800 per month for first two years and ₹46,500 per month for third year onwards (b) Annual contingency of ₹50,000 for five years (c) ₹2,000 per month for escort/reader in case of physically disabled/blind candidates (d) House rent allowance as per the university rules	100
2. Post-doctoral Fellowship for Women (1998)	(a) Unemployed women having PhD degree and intend to pursue post-doctoral research (b) 55% marks at the UG level and 60% marks at the PG level in the case of general/open category and 50% marks at UG level and 55% marks at PG level for reserved categories (SC/ST/OBC/PH) (c) Upper age limit: 55 years for general category and 60 years for SC/ST/OBC/PH (d) Duration: 5 years	Same as in (1)	100

(Continued)

Table 9.11 (Continued)

Scholarship or Fellowship Scheme (Year of Inception)	Eligibility Conditions	Scholarship/Fellowship Amount (INR) Per Student	No. of Scholarships or Fellowships Per Annum
3. Dr S. Radhakrishnan Post-doctoral Fellowship in Humanities and Social Sciences (including languages) (2014–2015)	(a) Advanced studies and research in humanities and social sciences including languages in Indian universities and colleges recognized under Section 2(f) and 12B of the UGC Act, 1956, and institutes of national importance established by the central/state government (b) Doctorate degree in a relevant subject (c) 55% marks at the UG level and 60% marks at the PG level in the case of general/open category and 50% marks at UG level and 55% marks at PG level for reserved categories (SC/ST/OBC/PH) (d) Upper age limit: 35 years for general category and 40 years for SC/ST/OBC/PH/women candidates (e) Duration: 3 years	(a) ₹38,800 per month for first year; ₹40,300 per month for second year and ₹41,900 per month for third year (b) ₹50,000 per annum forcontingency for three years (c) ₹2,000 per month for escort/reader in the case of physically disabled and blind candidates (d) House rent allowance as per the GoI norms	200
4. Dr D. S. Kothari Post-doctoral Fellowship (2008–2009)	(a) Candidates who have either received a PhD degree or submitted their PhD thesis on research fellowship and to pursue post-doctoral research in basic sciences/medical/engineering and technology (b) Duration: 3 years	(a) Bridging fellowship: ₹34,100 per month for all three years (b) Post-doctoral fellowship: ₹43,400 per month for first year, ₹45,000 for second year and ₹46,500 for third year (c) Higher post-doctoral fellowship: ₹46,500 per month for all three years	500

II. Research Fellowships for MPhil and PhD

5 Junior Research Fellowship (JRF) for Indian nationals in sciences, humanities and social sciences (1957–1958)	(a) Qualified in National Eligibility Testing (NET/JRF) of the UGC or the UGC-CSIR joint test (b) Studies and research leading to MPhil/PhD degrees in sciences, humanities and social sciences, including languages (c) Duration: 5 years (2 years of JRF and three years of Senior Research Fellowship [SRF])	(a) ₹25,000 per month for JRF and ₹28,000 per month for SRF (b) Contingency: ₹10,000 per annum for JRF and ₹20,500 per annum for SRF in humanities and social sciences; and ₹12,000 per annum and ₹25,000 per annum in sciences (c) ₹2,000 per month for escort/reader in case of physically disabled/blind candidates (d) ₹3,000 per annum per student to the host institution for providing infrastructure (e) House rent allowance as per the GoI norms	8,800
6. Rajiv Gandhi National Fellowship for SC Candidates (2005–2006)	(a) Candidates belonging to the SC category to undertake advanced studies and research leading to MPhil/PhD degrees in sciences, humanities and social sciences, including languages, and engineering and technology (b) Duration: 5 years	Same as in (5) including contingency for science students extended to engineering and technology	2,000
7. National Fellowship for Higher Education of ST Students or Rajiv Gandhi National Fellowship for ST Candidates (2005–2006)	(a) Candidates belonging to the ST category to undertake advanced studies and research leading to MPhil/PhD degrees in sciences, humanities and social sciences, including languages, and engineering and technology (b) Duration: 5 years	Same as in (5) including contingency for science students extended to engineering and technology	750

(Continued)

Table 9.11 *(Continued)*

Scholarship or Fellowship Scheme (Year of Inception)	Eligibility Conditions	Scholarship/Fellowship Amount (INR) Per Student	No. of Scholarships or Fellowships Per Annum
8. Maulana Azad National Fellowships for Minority Students (2009–2010)	(a) Students belonging to the minority communities as notified by the central government, i.e., (i) Muslim, (ii) Sikh, (iii) Christian, (iv) Buddhist, (v) Parsi and (vi) Jain (b) To undertake advanced studies and research leading to MPhil/PhD degrees in sciences, humanities and social sciences, including languages, and engineering and technology (c) Duration: 5 years	Same as in (5)	756
9. National Fellowship for Students of OBCs (2014–2015)	(a) Candidates who belong to OBCs and wish to pursue higher studies such as regular and full-time MPhil and PhD degrees in sciences, humanities, social sciences and engineering and technology (b) 3% reservation of number of fellowships to research scholars from disabled category who belongs to OBC category (c) Duration: 5 years	Same as in (5) including contingency for science students extended to engineering and technology	300

10. Rajiv Gandhi National Fellowship for Students with Disabilities (2012–2013)	(a) Students with disabilities for pursuing higher education leading to degrees such as MPhil and PhD degree in universities, research institutions and scientific institutions (b) Reservation of fellowships: 15% for SCs and 7½% for STs(c) Duration: 5 years	Same as in (5) including contingency for science students extended to engineering and technology	200
11. Swami Vivekananda Single Girl Child Fellowship for Research in Social Sciences (2014–2015)	(a) Candidates belonging to a single girl child family (b) Admitted in regular, full-time PhD programmes in social sciences in universities/institutes (c) Age: Up to 40 years (d) Duration: 5 years	Same as in (5)	300
12. BSR Fellowship or Research Fellowship in Science for Meritorious Students (2006–2007)	(a) Candidates selected for registering to the PhD programme in sciences in Universities with Potential for Excellence/Centres with Potential for Excellence/Centres of Advance Studies and Departments of Special Assistance identified by UGC (b) Duration: 5 years	(a) For non-GATE qualified students: (i) ₹21,700 per month for the first two years with annual contingency of ₹12,000 (ii) ₹24,800 per month for the next three years with annual contingency of ₹25,000 (b) For GATE qualified students: (i) ₹24,800 per month for the first two years with annual contingency of ₹12,000 (ii) ₹27,900 per month for the next three years with annual contingency of ₹25,000. In addition, all students are given HRA as per the university rules.	1,500

(Continued)

Table 9.11 (Continued)

Scholarship or Fellowship Scheme (Year of Inception)	Eligibility Conditions	Scholarship/Fellowship Amount (INR) Per Student	No. of Scholarships or Fellowships Per Annum
III. PG Scholarships			
13. Postgraduate Scholarships for SC/ST Students in Professional Courses (2006–2007)	(a) Candidates belonging to SC/ST to pursue PG-level courses in professional education (b) Duration: 2/3 years depending on the degree course	(a) MTech students: ₹7,800 per month with annual contingency of ₹15,000 (b) Other courses: ₹4,700 per month with annual contingency amount of ₹10,000	1,000
14. Indira Gandhi Postgraduate Scholarships Scheme for Single Girl Child (2005–2006)	(a) A girl who is the only single girl child of her parents and obtained admission in regular, full-time first-year Master's degree course (non-professional course) in any recognized university or a PG college (b) Age limit: Up to 30 years (c) Duration: 2 years	(a) ₹3,100 per month for two years (20 months) (b) Tuition fee waiver by the institutions for first year of the course	No limit
15. Postgraduate Merit Scholarships for University Rank Holders at Undergraduate Level (2005–2006)	(a) The first and second rank holders at UG level with a minimum of 60% marks (b) Rank holders should be from the affiliating universities with at least 100 students or deemed universities/autonomous/non-affiliated colleges with at least 25 students have appeared in the examination at the UG level (c) Age limit: Up to 30 years (d) Duration: 2 years	₹3,100 per month for two years (20 months)	3,000

16. Postgraduate Scholarship for GATE/ GPAT Qualified Students of ME/MTech/ MPharma (not reported)	(a) GATE/GPAT qualified students and admitted to ME/MTech/MPharma courses and integrated dual degree programmes in technical education and HEIs (b) Duration: 2/3 years	(a) ₹12,000 per month with annual contingency of ₹5,000 for students who secured above 60% marks in GATE/ GPAT (b) ₹1,000 per month with annual contingency of ₹5,000 for students who secured below 60% marks in GATE/ GPAT	1,400

IV. UG Scholarships

17. "ISHAN UDAY" Special Scholarship Scheme for Northeastern Region (2014–2015)	(a) Students admitted to the UG courses in the general, technical and professional education (b) Duration: Full duration of the course	(a) ₹5,400 per month for general degree courses (b) ₹7,800 per month for technical programme and professional courses (including medical and paramedical courses)	10,000

Source: Author's compilation from UGC (2016).

Note: ST (Scheduled Tribe), OBC (Other Backward Classes), PH (Physically Handicapped), GATE (Graduate Aptitude Test in Engineering) and GPAT (Graduate Pharmacy Aptitude Test).

(or NET/JRF) qualified students belonged to the general category, 43.02 (52.28) per cent to OBC, 15.85 (or 14.43) per cent to SC and the rest 8.12 (or 5.28) per cent to ST. Within these social groups, the share of qualified female students was 47.60 (or 47.51) per cent in General, 28.21 (34.07) in OBC, 28.01 (or 30.87) in SC and 32.12 (or 38.85) per cent in ST categories. These figures show the diversity in social and gender compositions of students who are qualified to apply for UGC's JRF scholarships.

Total public expenditure and number of beneficiaries by the scholarship and fellowship schemes in 2015–2016 show interesting results in Table 9.12. Of the 17 schemes, total public expenditure on 6 schemes is above the average for all the schemes (₹68.32 crores) and the total number of beneficiaries of 4 schemes is above that for all the schemes (4,381 persons). Distribution of expenditure is more variable (coefficient of variation is 52.34%) than the distribution of beneficiaries (coefficient of variation is 66.81%). Though the simple correlation coefficient between the total expenditure and total beneficiaries of the schemes is positive and higher (0.864), the correlation coefficient between total expenditure and average expenditure per beneficiary is low (0.022) and between total beneficiaries and average expenditure per beneficiary is negative (−0.253).

In particular, Table 9.12 shows that the absolute size of public expenditure varies from ₹544 crore (or 47% of total expenditure on all schemes) for the JRF to ₹6.3 crores (or 0.54% of total expenditure on all schemes) for BSR fellowship. The number of beneficiaries varies from 21,588 persons (or 28.99% of total beneficiaries of all schemes) for the JRF to 44 persons (or 0.06% of total beneficiaries of all schemes) for the Swami Vivekananda Single Girl Child Fellowship. Consequently, average public expenditure per beneficiary of the scholarship/fellowship in 2015–2016 shows remarkable variations. The highest average expenditure is evident for Dr D. S. Kothari Post-doctoral Fellowship (₹5.78 lakh) and lowest for the Postgraduate Merit Scholarship Scheme for university rank holders at UG level (₹23,920).

Table 9.12 *Public Expenditure and Beneficiaries of Scholarships and Fellowships by the UGC: 2015–2016*

Scholarship or Fellowship Scheme	Expenditure (INR crore)	No. of Beneficiaries	Average Expenditure per Beneficiary	Share of Expenditure by Schemes	Share of Beneficiaries by Schemes
I. Post-doctoral Fellowships					
1. Post-doctoral Fellowships for SC/ST	22.61	766	295,170	1.95	1.03
2. Post-doctoral Fellowship for Women (1998)	31.14	648	480,556	2.68	0.87
3. Dr S. Radhakrishnan Post-doctoral Fellowship in Humanities and Social Sciences including languages (2014–2015)	13.57	351	386,610	1.17	0.47
4. Dr D. S. Kothari Post-doctoral Fellowship (2008–2009)	40.20	695	578,417	3.46	0.93
II. Fellowship for MPhil and PhD					
5. JRF for Indian nationals in sciences, humanities and social sciences (1957–1958)	543.58	21,588	251,797	46.81	28.99
6. Rajiv Gandhi National Fellowship for SC Candidates (2005–2006)	178.10	19,623	90,761	15.34	26.35
7. National Fellowship for Higher Education of ST Students or Rajiv Gandhi National Fellowship for ST Candidates (2005–2006)	52.13	4,929	105,762	4.49	6.62

(Continued)

Table 9.12 (Continued)

Scholarship or Fellowship Scheme	Expenditure (INR crore)	No. of Beneficiaries	Average Expenditure per Beneficiary	Share of Expenditure by Schemes	Share of Beneficiaries by Schemes
8. Maulana Azad National Fellowship for Minority Students (2009–2010)	74.26	3,609	205,763	6.39	4.85
9. National Fellowship for Students of OBCs (2014–2015)	15.12	409	369,682	1.30	0.55
10. Rajiv Gandhi National Fellowship for Students with Disabilities (2012–2013)	NR	200	NA	NA	0.27
11. Swami Vivekananda Single Girl Child Fellowship for Research in Social Sciences (2014–2015)	0.74	44	168,182	0.06	0.06
12. BSR Fellowship or Research Fellowship in Science for Meritorious Students (2006–2007)	84.41	3,918	215,442	7.27	5.26
III. Scholarship For PG Studies					
13. Postgraduate Scholarships for SC/ST Students in Professional Courses (2006–2007)	9.14	904	101,106	0.79	1.21

14. Indira Gandhi Postgraduate Scholarships Scheme for Single Girl Child (2005–2006)	11.51	4,617	24,930	0.99	6.20
15. Postgraduate Merit Scholarships for University Rank Holders at Undergraduate Level (2005–2006)	3.82	1,597	23,920	0.33	2.14
16. Postgraduate Scholarship for GATE/ GPAT-Qualified Students of ME/MTech/ MPharma	6.3	1,545	40,777	0.54	2.07
IV. Scholarship for UG Studies					
17. 'Ishan Uday' Special Scholarship Scheme for Northeastern Region (2014–2015)	74.74	9,027	82,796	6.44	12.12
All scholarships/fellowships	1,161.37	74,470	155,951	100.00	100.00

Source: Author's compilation from UGC (2016).

Notes:

1. NR refers to not reported because the expenditure is accounted by the Ministry of Social Justice and Empowerment, Department of Disability Affairs.

2. NA refers to not applicable.

State-Level Scholarship Schemes

Scholarships for UG studies are mainly offered by the state governments through the Directorate of Collegiate Education[9] and Technical Education. These schemes are diversified and include merit and loan scholarships for students in government- and private-aided courses in aided colleges of general education. For instance, Government of Karnataka's loan scholarship is called Rajiv Gandhi Loan Scholarship Scheme and it subsidises the interest cost on education loans from commercial banks.[10] Merit scholarships are (a) Sanchi Honnamma Scholarship and Kittur Rani Channamma Puraskar for girl students, (b) Sir C. V. Raman Scholarship for promotion of basic sciences and (c) Scholarship for HIV/AIDS or leprosy-infected parents' children. Table 9.13 gives a summary of these schemes by their year of inception, eligibility conditions, amount of scholarships, number of beneficiaries and size of public expenditure. All the schemes were introduced in and after 2001–2002. The highest amount of the merit scholarship (or expenditure per student) is provided for technical education (₹28,926). At present, this analysis is not extendable for other states because information on the scholarship schemes, public expenditure and coverage of students at the state level are not consolidated and available in public domain

MICRO-LEVEL ANALYSIS OF SCHOLARSHIPS FOR HIGHER EDUCATION

Micro-level analysis of the scholarships for higher education is useful to explain the individual or household-level characteristics of scholarship recipients and role of scholarships in private expenditure on higher education. The NSS 71st Round (January 2014–June 2014) on Social Consumption on Education (in short, NSS 71st Round) is the latest and nationally representative micro-level data on education in

---

[9] Government of Karnataka. http://dce.kar.nic.in/StudentScholarships.html

[10] An early objective of Government of Karnataka to encouraging the students to take education loans from the commercial banks was to reduce the budgetary subsidy to the higher education through higher student fee revisions. This objective is empirically contested by Narayana (2005) by showing that fee revision as a single instrument of reducing the budgetary subsidy to collegiate general education was inappropriate, even if the entire fee revision were to be financed by education loans.

Table 9.13 *Scholarship Schemes by State Governments: A Case of Government of Karnataka in 2015–2016*

Scholarship Scheme (Year of Inception)	Eligibility Criteria	Amount of Scholarship (INR) per Student	No. of Beneficiaries	Expenditure by Scheme (INR lakh)
Merit scholarship				
1. Sanchi Honnamma Scholarship (2002–2003)	(a) To pursue general degree education in government and aided colleges in Karnataka (b) Limited to girl students who scored high marks in II Year PUC examination (c) Must pass the degree examinations in first/one attempt.	₹2,000 per annum for the entire duration of the course	8,600	172
2. Sir C. V. Raman Scholarship (2001–2002)	(a) To pursue general degree education in basic sciences in government and private aided degree colleges in Karnataka (b) Limited to students who scored high marks in II Year PUC examination (c) Admitted to BSc course with two basic science subjects (d) Must pass the degree examinations in first/one attempt.	₹5,000 per annum for the entire duration of the course	6,380	319

(Continued)

Table 9.13 Scholarship Schemes by State Governments: A Case of Government of Karnataka in 2015–2016

Scholarship Scheme (Year of Inception)	Eligibility Criteria	Amount of Scholarship (INR) per Student	No. of Beneficiaries	Expenditure by Scheme (INR lakh)
3. Kittur Rani Channamma Puraskar (2006–2007)	(a) To pursue professional degree courses and selected by the common entrance test (CET), conducted by the Government of Karnataka (b) Limited to girl students who belong to the below-poverty-line families and scored high marks in II PUC examination (c) Must pass the degree examinations in first/one attempt (d) Number of scholarships is limited to 10 per district.	Reimbursement of college fees as they are applicable to the students who are admitted through the CET	242*	70
4. Scholarship for HIV/AIDS or Leprosy infected parents' children (2013–2014)	(a) To pursue higher education in Government or Government Aided degree Colleges in Karnataka (b) Limited to students infected from HIV/AIDS or Leprosy and students born to HIV/AIDS or Leprosy infected parents' (dead or alive) children.	(a) ₹1,500 per month as free education allowance for 12 months in a year. (b) Tuition fee reimbursement. (c) ₹3,000 per annum towards college fees, books, clothes and other necessary stationery.	Not reported	Not reported

Loan scholarship	Conditions and features of loan	Quantum of loan	Number of beneficiaries	Amount of interest subsidy (INR)
5. Rajiv Gandhi Loan Scholarship Scheme (2013–2014)	(a) Limited to interest subsidy for education loans (sanctioned from 2013–2014) up to the moratorium period on the loans taken by students from scheduled banks. (b) Interest rate as applicable to IBA Model Education Loan Scheme of the respective banks. (c) Of the total loan amount, ₹2,500 per month with a maximum amount of ₹30,000 per annum is expendable as living expenses. (d) To pursue any of the approved courses (diploma, degree, PG and integrated degree) of study in government colleges and/or aided courses in private aided degree colleges. (e) Students must belong to economically weaker section (annual family income of less than ₹250,000 from all sources). (f) Obtained 50% or more marks in II PUC examination.	Quantum of loan eligible for interest subsidy by duration of course: (a) Less than 6 months: ₹20,000. (b) 6 months or more but less than 1 year: ₹40,000. (c) More than one year but less than two year: ₹100,000. (d) Above one year: ₹60,000 per year	Not reported	Not reported

Source: Author's compilation from the Government of Karnataka (2016).

Note: * Refers to 2013–2014.

India (GoI, 2015). This data includes the socio-economic background characteristics on the current enrolled students, private expenditure on education and recipients of scholarships. Data on scholarships is limited to the amount of merit scholarships by its recipients. There is no information on the scholarships by government and private sources and amount of scholarship by schemes. Using this limited micro-level data, we analyse (a) the pattern of enrolment of students by courses, (b) age profile of recipients of merit scholarships and amount of scholarship per student by courses, (c) coverage of scholarship by courses and spread of scholarship recipients by management of institutions and (d) extent of financing of private cost of education consumption by the scholarships by courses.

Characteristics of Recipients of Scholarships in Higher Education

Table 9.14 presents the select indicators of distribution of students and amount of scholarships in 2014–2015. In total, nine courses are considered (humanities including social sciences, science, commerce, medical, engineering, agriculture, management, education and IT/computer course). There is a mismatch between the distribution of students and amount of scholarships by courses. The courses in general higher education (i.e., humanities, science and commerce) share 61.53 per cent of the total students and 12.99 per cent of the total amount of the scholarships. Engineering course shares about 18.43 per cent of the total students and 60.88 per cent of the total amount of scholarships. In a way, this comparison may not be valid because the amount of scholarships varies by courses. This is evident by the amount of scholarships per student by courses in column 4 of Table 9.14. Humanities have the lowest per student scholarship amount which is far lower than the average amount for all courses in higher education (₹18,746). In contrast, the amount of scholarships per student is ₹59,325 for agriculture, ₹36,600 for management (₹36,600), ₹29,627 for engineering and ₹59,325 for medical course. In addition, there are wide disparities across courses in the coverage of student by the scholarships. For instance, the coverage is highest for medicine (2.49%) and is followed by agriculture (1.92%) and engineering (1.84%). All the remaining courses have the

Table 9.14 Distribution of Higher Education Students and Scholarships by Courses in India: 2014–2015

Course	Distribution of Sample Students (%)	Sample Distribution of Amount of Scholarship (%)	Amount of Scholarship per Students (₹)	Coverage of Students by Scholarships (%)
1	2	3	4	5
Humanities (including social sciences)	28.95	4.04	6,082	0.38
Science	20.54	7.43	6,753	0.88
Commerce	12.04	1.52	3,487	0.60
Medical	4.27	13.74	21,358	2.49
Engineering	18.43	60.88	29,627	1.84
Agriculture	0.71	4.93	59,325	1.92
Law	0.77	0.54	26,000	0.44
Management	3.14	3.80	36,600	0.55
Education	3.20	0.33	16,000	0.11
IT/Computer course	7.93	2.79	13,450	0.53
All courses	100.00 (28,758 persons)	100.00 (₹48.18 lakh)	18,746	0.89

Source: Author's calculations using the Unit Level Data in NSS 71st Round (GoI, 2015).

coverage of less than one per cent or less than the overall coverage for all courses in higher education (0.89%).

As per the AISHE 2015–2016 (GoI, 2016), the total enrolment of students in India's higher education is equal to ₹3.46 crore. Using the coverage of students by the scholarships for all courses in higher education (0.89%) and average scholarship amount per student for all courses (₹18,746) in Table 9.14, the total amount of scholarships received by students is equal to ₹577.01 crore. This is equal to 0.004 per cent of India's gross domestic product (GDP) at current market prices in 2014–2015. Alternatively, the total amount of scholarships received by students is equal to ₹4800.24 crore or 0.035 per cent of the India's GDP if the average expenditure on the scholarships per student is equal to the UGC scholarships in Table 9.12. These results show the sensitivity of India's public-funded scholarships for the higher education in regard to the average coverage and per student amount of scholarships. In addition, the results may be sensitive if course-specific coverage of students and per student amount of scholarships are used in these calculations.

Age profile of currently enrolled students and recipients of scholarships in India's higher education in 2014–2015 is given in Figures 9.1 and 9.2, respectively. These unsmoothed profiles are calculated by using the age distribution of sample students in the NSS 71st Round discussed previously. Age profiles are calculated from age 18 to age 29 years. Both total enrolment and recipients of scholarships are heavily concentrated in age group 18–23 years. This is the prime age group of enrolment in UG courses in general higher education, technical education and other professional education. However, shapes of age profiles of total enrolment and recipients of scholarships are different. This may be due to a mismatch between the share of students and scholarship recipients in different age groups who are enrolled in different courses (as shown in Table 9.14).

Role of Scholarships in Private Expenditure on Higher Education

The NSS 71st Round is useful to estimate the extent of financing of private expenditure on education by the course-wise scholarships.

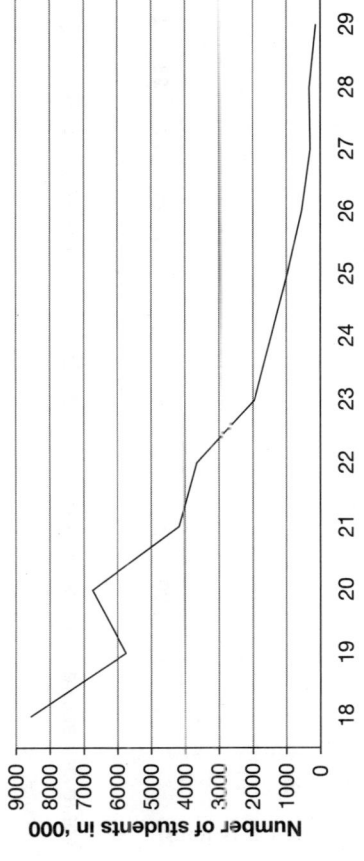

Figure 9.1 *Age Profile of Enrolled Students in India's Higher Education: 2014–2015*

Source: Author's Calculations.

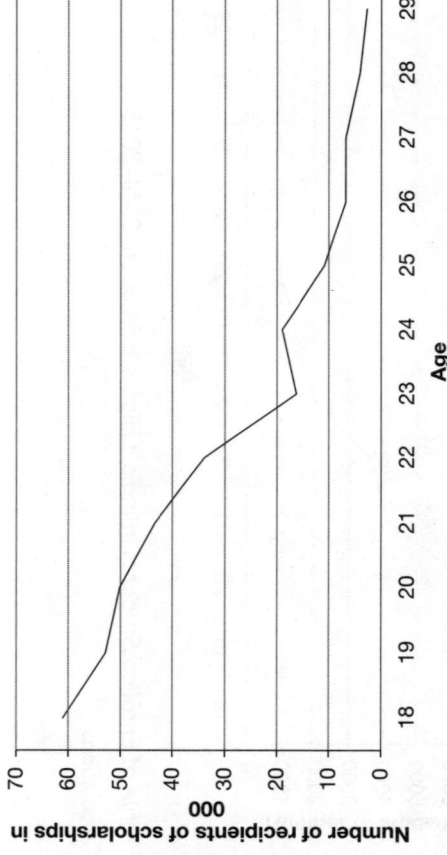

Figure 9.2 *Age Profile of Recipients of Scholarships in India's Higher Education: 2014–2015*

Source: Author's Calculations.

Private expenditure on education is that incurred by students attending educational institutions for payment of course fees (including tuition fee, college fees and examination fees), purchase of books, stationery and uniforms, expenses on conveyance and private coaching. These private expenditures may be (a) treated as cost of access and utilization of education services provided by government and private sectors and (b) related to education consumption in current academic year (2014–2015).

NSS 71st Round provides estimate of average expenditure per student pursuing general and professional education in government, private aided and unaided educational institutions in higher education. We use these estimates (rural and urban combined) to calculate the share of scholarships in total private expenditure on education by courses and by management of institutions. Throughout, we assume that per student scholarships amount by all courses in Table 9.14 is applicable for the graduate and PG courses in general education and for institutions of all management in professional education.

Table 9.15 presents the results on the share of scholarship amount in total private expenditure on higher education in India in 2014–2015. The economic interpretation of these results is as follows. In the presence of scholarships, total private expenditure on higher education is reduced by the amount of scholarships. The extent of reduction varies by courses and by management of institutions as shown by numbers in Table 9.15. For instance, among the students who received the scholarships in humanities, private expenditure on UG (or PG) level education is reduced by 45.13 (or 38.01) per cent. Of the courses in general education, the highest reduction is evident for the UG and PG courses in science. Of the professional courses, the scholarships reduce the private expenditure on education more in the government institutions than private aided institutions. This is because of the fact that tuition fee and other institutional payments are less in government colleges and public universities than in private aided colleges and private universities. Most notable reduction in government managed institutions is evident for medical, law and management courses. Thus, the scholarships have a strong impact on reduction in the private cost of access to and utilization of higher educational services in India.

Table 9.15 *Share of Scholarships Amount in Private Expenditure on Education by Courses in India: 2014–2015*

Course	Share of Scholarships Amount per Student in Average Private Expenditure per Student on Education (%)	
1	2	3
General education	UG	PG
Humanities	45.13	38.01
Science	50.10	42.21
Commerce	25.87	21.80
Profession education	Government	Private aided
Medical	69.87	42.51
Engineering	32.87	23.68
Law	66.34	81.29
Management	82.21	58.91
IT/Computer course	46.89	27.53

Source: Author's calculations using the Unit Level Data in NSS 71st Round (GoI, 2015).

In fact, GoI (2011) did recognize the importance of scholarships and fellowships as one of the instruments to overcome financial constraints faced by students to pursue higher education in India and as a way of achieving the targeted gross enrollment ratio in the Twelfth Five-Year Plan of India. The findings of this chapter offer a strong evidence for this important role of the scholarships from the demand/consumption side of financing India's higher education.

CONCLUSIONS AND IMPLICATIONS

This chapter has analysed the important role of scholarships in public education expenditure and private expenditure on education in India's higher education. On the provider's or supplier's side, expenditure on scholarships adds to the cost of provisioning of educational services to students. On the consumption side, scholarships reduce the private cost to access and utilize educational services by students. These roles signify the importance of scholarships for the entire higher education system. However, scholarships account for a lesser share in the total public expenditure on higher education in general higher education and technical education. There are marked disparities in the public expenditure on scholarships across states and UTs over time and between general higher education and technical education. In a way, these disparities are the outcome of a differential public expenditure priority on the scholarships by the union government, state governments and UTs.

At present, the national and state-level scholarship schemes are marked by diversity of eligibility criteria, objectives of social justice, amount and duration. However, all schemes ultimately aim at offering financial support for the merited students to pursue their higher education studies. This fact deserves utmost recognition for its continuity and strengthening, both at present and in future.

Scholarship has been functioning in India's higher education along with other student-based support systems. Whether or not the scholarship schemes should continue notwithstanding the availability of other instruments of student-based financing, such as, education loans, depends on future empirical evidence on the following. First, uniqueness of the scholarships as compared to other instruments of student-based financing of higher education. Second, strength of complementarily and substitutability between scholarship and other instrument of students' based financing of higher education.

Analysis of scholarship, as an instrument of student-based financing of education in India, is constrained by data limitations. First, consolidated and time series data are lacking in public domain on public expenditure on the merit and loan scholarships or scholarship schemes by student beneficiaries and courses at national and state levels. Second, there is a lack of data on private sector's financing of higher education and scholarships including management, corporate (including as part of CSR), foundations (e.g., philanthropy and charity) and others. In a way, these limitations are opportunities for future improvement of databases for deeper analysis of the scholarships in financing India's higher education.

REFERENCES

GoI (2011). *Report of the working group on higher education for XII Five-Year Plan.* New Delhi: Department of Higher Education, Ministry of Human Resource Development.

———. (2015). *Key indicators of social consumption in India—Education: NSS 71ˢᵗ Round (January–June 2014).* New Delhi: National Sample Survey Office, Ministry of Statistics and Programme Implementation.

———. (2016). *All India Survey on higher education (2015–2016).* New Delhi: Department of Higher Education, Ministry of Human Resource Development.

———. (2017a). National Scholarship Portal. Retrieved from https://scholarships.gov.in/

———. (2017b). Scholarships and education loans. Retrieved from http://mhrd.gov.in/scholarships-education-loan-0

Government of Karnataka. (2016). *Karnataka state universities rating framework: Detailed performance and analytical report 2016.* Bengaluru: Karnataka State Council for Higher Education.

Narayana, M. R. (2005). Student loan by commercial banks: A way to reduce state government support to higher education in India. *Journal of Developing Areas, 38*(2), 171–187.

Prakash, V. (2007). Trends in growth and financing of higher education in India. *Economic and Political Weekly, 42*(31), 3249–3258.

Rani, P. G. (2014). Education loans and financing higher education in India: Addressing equity. *Higher Education for the Future, 1*(2), 183–210.

———. (2002). *Financing higher education in India in the post reform period: Focus on access and equity* (NIEPA Occasional Paper No. 31). New Delhi: National Institute of Educational Planning and Administration.

UGC. (2016). *Promotion of research in annual report 2015–2016* (Chapter 6) New Delhi: University Grants Commission.

———. (2017). Scholarships and fellowships. Retrieved from http://www.ugc.ac.in/page/scholarships-and-fellowships.aspx

Varghese, N. V., Malik, G., & Gautam, D. R. (2017). *Teacher recruitment in higher education: An analysis of National Eligibility Test (NET) results* (Research Paper Series No. 8). New Delhi: Centre for Research in Higher Education, National University of Educational Planning and Administration.

Chapter 10

Student Mortgage Loans vis-à-vis Income-contingent Loans
Problems and Prospects

Mausumi Das and Tridip Ray

INTRODUCTION

The importance of higher education in an emerging economy like India cannot be overemphasized, especially at the current juncture when the country can potentially reap unprecedented demographic dividends by equipping the younger generation with appropriate skills. What is needed is to formulate policy and design strategies for massifying higher education. Financing an expanding higher education system remains a challenge in India. The pervasive inequality along with imperfect (or missing) credit market implies that privately funded education remains the prerogative of the rich. On the other hand, the oft-prescribed public education or education-subsidy policy is also not sustainable in the long run because of the large fiscal burden it imposes on the already precarious macroeconomic balance sheet of the country. Thus, the real challenge lies in designing an appropriate government policy, which is financially viable and at the same time effective in pulling out the poorer section of population of a low-education–low-skill–low-income trap.

Traditionally, financing of higher education has been the responsibility of the government. Large-scale education subsidies and publicly funded educational institutions were quite widespread during the decades of the 1950s and 1960s. However, the 1980s was a period characterized by rapidly increasing per student costs and shrinking educational budgets throughout the world. These diverging trajectories of costs and revenues were caused by rising unit cost of instruction coupled with an unprecedented increase in tertiary level participation, and an increase in the number of causes competing for the limited public budget.

With globalization and expanding knowledge economy, there is need for financial resources for both quantitative expansion and qualitative improvement of higher education. Since the costs cannot be reduced, revenue supplementation methods were the only available alternatives. This led to the advent of a phenomenon called 'cost-sharing' (Johnstone, 2004). The concept of cost-sharing begins with a presumption that the underlying costs of higher education are borne by an undefined combination of four parties: government or taxpayer (via direct or indirect taxation), parents (via savings, borrowing or current income), students (via savings, current earnings or borrowing), or philanthropists (via endowments or current contributions). Cost-sharing as a governmental policy generally refers to a shift of at least some of these costs from a substantial reliance on governments or taxpayers to a greater reliance on parents and students.

Cost-sharing is especially thought of as the introduction of, or sharp increase in, tuition fees to cover part of the costs of instruction. Some examples of countries that recently introduced tuition fees include Australia (1989), China (1997), the UK (1997), and Austria (2001). However, such increases in fees tend to make the poorer sections of society worse off and could result in exclusion of potentially beneficial investment in HC. One solution for this could be to defer the payments so that the cost of education can be recovered from the students after they get employed. Thus, came into being the student loan or education loan schemes.

We use the term education loans, henceforth, to include any repayment obligation resulting from a scheme designed especially for students (usually with some element of governmental sponsorship) to defer higher education expenses. There are two broad categories of education loans differing mainly in the denomination of the repayment obligation: (a) The fixed schedule or conventional mortgage-type loan, in which the loan obligation carries a rate of interest expressed as an annual percentage of the amount borrowed, within a pre-agreed term/schedule, and (b) Income-contingent loan (ICL), which carries a contractual obligation to repay some percentage of future earnings or income, generally until a loan is repaid at a contractual rate of interest.

In this chapter, we propose to look in detail at the problem and prospects of implementing a viable student loan programme, with special focus on ICL. The first section starts with a review of the existing student education loan schemes in India. It then introduces the concept of an income-contingent student loan scheme. The second sections closely examines the design and implementation of income-contingent student loan schemes in various developed as well as developing countries (e.g., Australia, South Africa, United Kingdom and Ghana). These country case studies are important as they provide essential benchmarks for designing and implementing an effective ICL mechanism relating to eligibility and incentives, recovery of loans and associated moral hazards, regulation and so on in the context of India. Based on these country studies, the next section of the chapter provides a template for an ICL scheme relevant for India. The concluding section of the chapter focuses on the relative merits and demerits of an ICL scheme in comparison to other existing education financing schemes, it also highlights the possible problems to its implementation and potential costs, which merit careful consideration.

EDUCATION LOAN: EXISTING LOAN SCHEMES IN INDIA

Education loans have been advocated as an effective mechanism to tackle the problem of financing higher education on several grounds. Education loans can potentially establish a revolving fund and become a self-financing scheme. Hence, in the long run, loans reduce the fiscal burden on the public exchequer caused by subsidies so that the scarce public resources can be allocated to other sectors or for other purposes (for instance quality improvement) within the higher education sector. Secondly, it is argued that since the distributions of enrolment in higher education is skewed in favour of the affluent sections of the society, public subsidization of higher education benefits the rich more at the cost of the poor. Subsidies for higher education are hence, regressive (Garcia-Penalosa & Walde, 2000; Peltzmann, 1973; Radner & Miller, 1970; Tilak, 1992; Tilak & Varghese, 1991). Therefore, it is argued that education loans would reduce the extent to which higher education subsidies transfer resources from the poor to the rich. Thirdly, student loans shift the burden of higher education investment from the present generation to the future generation. This might help the children of poor parents to break the vicious cycle of poverty (low income–low investment in education–low income) as it reduces the importance of parental income. In a well–designed education loan scheme, no poor student desirous of higher education will be prevented, for economic reasons, from pursuing higher education. Such schemes might be helpful in preventing wasteful expenditure, as only the needy students would borrow for their education, while those who can afford to pay could prefer paying the fees upfront (especially if there is a benefit involved). Finally, it is argued that loan financing would make the students more serious and responsible in making educational and career choices, which would increase the internal efficiency of the system. Thus, it is argued that student loans are superior to education subsidies both on equity and efficiency grounds (Albrecht & Ziderman, 1991; Birdsall & James, 1990; Jimenez 1987; Psacharopoulos, Tan, & Jimenez, 1986).

These equity and efficiency arguments, as well as tight budgetary pressure, have compelled many countries to opt for a policy loan financing of higher education and student loan schemes have been introduced/revamped in a major way in many developed as well as developing countries. Woodhall (1992) listed a number of countries, which already had well-established student loan programmes running since the 1950s and 1960s. The list includes many developed countries (Canada, Denmark, Sweden and the US) and a few developing countries (Colombia and India). The policy was eventually adopted in many more countries (e.g., Australia, New Zealand, South Africa,

United Kingdom, Ghana, Chile, South Korea and Thailand) and is still running with varying degrees of success.

Student loans as a means of financing higher education was introduced in India as early as in 1963. This government operated zero-interest loan scheme was not very successful and slowly disappeared. Since then various student loan schemes for financing higher education have been initiated by the Government of India (GoI) from time to time. These schemes are typically operated through the commercial banks and modes of repayment are similar to the standard mortgage-type bank loans (although the interest rates charged are sometimes lower than the market rate). Some of these bank loan schemes have been running (at least on paper) for years. But their impact has been rather limited. The problem lies both with the demand side as well as the supply side. On the supply side, there is little incentive for the commercial banks to offer these student loans unconditionally, especially to the poorer section of the population who need these most. Recovery of these loans is problematic because of lack of information and the difficulty of tracing the borrowers once they pass out of various educational institutions. On the demand side, individuals have been unwilling to take part in such schemes for the additional pressure that it creates on the borrowers to pay back even when they have been unable to secure a high-end job.

More recently, the idea of an ICL has caught the imagination of policymakers in various advanced countries. This scheme has also been implemented in countries such as Australia, New Zealand, South Africa, UK, Chile, Thailand and Ghana. An ICL—a loan scheme that staggers the repayment depending on the post-education job profile of the borrower—can take care of the demand-side problem. However, recovery of loans may still remain a problem for the banks. And this supply-side problem does not go away even when the government acts as a guarantor in case of default. The latter simply shifts the default burden from banks to the government. However, India has recently initiated a policy of issuing a unique identification number (Aadhaar) to all its citizens. With the advent of this new Aadhaar technology, the demand-side problem may also be tackled in an effective way. Linking ICLs to Aadhaar would allow the government to trace the borrowers over time and make the recovery of loans easier. Hence, it is probably time to rethink about ICLs and carefully design a viable scheme that not only takes care of the problems associated with the existing bank loan schemes but also allows more individuals to opt for higher education, thus allowing the country to move in the direction of actual realization of the demographic dividend.

India during the post-Independence period saw a dramatic rise in public investment in higher education, which increased fivefold between 1950–1951 and 1980–1981 (Tilak, 2007). However, the trend started reversing thereafter. In fact, budgetary expenditure on higher education per se, and on education as a whole, has been declining steadily over the years starting from the 1990s. For instance, education expenditure as a share of the central government's total budgeted expenditure has fallen from 4.57 per cent in 2013–2014 to 3.71 per cent in the fiscal year 2016–2017. The trend is reflected in the education expenditure as a share of gross domestic product (GDP) as well which has dipped from 0.63 per cent in the GDP in 2013–2014 to 0.47 per cent in the year 2016–2017. Rapidly growing demand for higher education, rising costs of providing quality education and fiscal constraints have led the government to seek alternative education financing policies that can relieve the pressure on the government exchequer. As a consequence, attention of policymakers has shifted towards initiating new and/or revamping the old education loan programmes in India.

We now take a closer look at some of the past and present schemes of the education loans in India and evaluate their performances in terms of extending the scope of higher education in India.

THE NATIONAL LOAN SCHOLARSHIP SCHEME

Financing of higher education via education loans is not new in India. A government-operated education loan scheme, called 'National Loan Scholarship Scheme', was initiated in 1963, with a view to improve access to higher education without government bearing the total burden of financing higher education. As highlighted by Tilak (1992, 2007), the main features of the scheme were as follows.

The National Loan Scholarship Scheme provided interest-free loans to needy and able students to help them finance full-time higher education in India, starting from post-matriculation level to the completion of higher education. The value of the loan scholarship ranged between ₹720 per annum (for pre-university and undergraduate [UG] courses) and ₹1,750 per annum for doctoral or post-second degree education in professional courses (such as medicine, engineering and technology) depending on the nature and type of education. These loans were renewable on an annual basis. The scholarships were awarded on the basis of both merit and financial means. All those who secured 50 per cent or above in the qualifying examinations, and whose parental income did not exceed ₹25,000 per annum (this limit was revised time to time; it was ₹60,000 until 1987–1988), and who did not receive any other scholarships, were eligible for the loans. The government fixed the number of loan scholarships (20,000 in 1990), and the regional distribution was based on the distribution of population. In each state, the distribution was made proportionate to the number of different qualifying examinations, subject to a minimum for each category. Selected students were required to execute a bond with the government to abide by the terms and conditions of the scheme and to repay the loan. Students and their parents, who were the guarantors in the case of default by the students, signed the bond. Students were expected to repay the loan in easy monthly instalments (EMIs), equal to one-tenth to one-sixth of the monthly income, subject to a minimum of ₹25 per month (this minimum was to be paid by even the unemployed or non-working). The repayment was expected to start one year after the scholar begins to earn an income or three years after termination of scholarship or studies. There were certain rebates or repayment concessions given to a particular category of students or graduates. Those who joined the teaching profession or armed forces were given a rebate of one-tenth of the loan amount for each year of service. Loans were written off in the case of death of the student borrower. Emigrants to foreign countries were expected to repay the loan or to obtain the consent of the government before leaving, to pay later.

The scheme was funded by the central government but administered through the state governments. The loan was actually paid through the higher education institutions (HEIs). The recovery of the loans was the responsibility of the central government, but the recovered amounts were to be shared by the central and the state governments.

Critical Evaluation of the Scheme

The National Loan Scholarship Scheme, however, did not perform well and was discontinued in 1991. Several factors have been held responsible for the same. The most important problem faced with the scheme was that of poor repayment rates. About ₹900 million were invested in all from 1963–1964 till the beginning of 1990, but the rate of recovery ranged between 8 per cent and 15 per cent between 1977–1978 and 1990 (Tilak, 2007). With zero-interest rate, the real value of money declined so fast that it was too expensive for the central government to make any special efforts to recover the outstanding amount. Even though there was increasing demand for higher education and hence for the scholarship, it was not very popular among the students because it met the needs of a small fixed fraction of students (20,000). Also, with increase in the living costs, the scholarship amount could not meet the financial requirements of many students adequately.

THE NEW EDUCATION LOAN SCHEME (IBA SCHEME)

In 2001–2002, the GoI in consultation with the Reserve Bank of India (RBI) and the Indian Banks' Association (IBA), framed a comprehensive Education Loan Scheme for pursuing higher education in India and abroad. The scheme was further modified in 2007–2008 based on experience gained in the operation of the scheme over the past years. Some salient features of the IBA's Model Educational Loan Scheme (revised version) are described below.

The main objective of the Educational Loan Scheme is to provide financial support from the banking system to meritorious students, though poor, to pursue higher education in India and abroad. The RBI advised all banks to implement the scheme on 28 April 2001. Most of the banks have formulated the scheme with their own rules and regulations under various names. The schemes differ slightly from bank to bank, but the basic flavour of the IBA Model Scheme was retained.

Any Indian National who has secured admission in recognized institutions in India and abroad is eligible. However, the banks might specify cut-offs based on the entrance/qualifying examinations. The scheme covers graduation and postgraduation as well as diploma courses that are approved by University Grants Commission (UGC) or All India Council for Technical Education (AICTE). Apart from tuition fees, expenditure on travel, examinations, stationery, books and so on are also considered for the loan. A student can borrow up to ₹10 lakhs for studies in India and up to ₹20 lakhs for studying abroad. No margin is charged for loans up to ₹4 lakhs, but loans above that are subject to a margin of 5 per cent (India) or 15 per cent (abroad), as the case may be. The collateral requirements also differ with the loan amounts. No security is required for loans up to ₹4 lakhs (only parents have to be joint borrowers). For loan amounts between ₹4 lakhs and 7.5 lakhs, besides parents being joint borrowers, a collateral security in the form of suitable third-party guarantee is taken. For a loan above ₹7.5 lakhs, tangible security of suitable value must be given to the bank. The IBA does not allow any processing charges/upfront fees in loans sanctioned under this scheme. Also, there is no age limit for a student to be eligible for the loans. Interest rate to be charged must be linked to the base rate but the details are left to the discretion of the individual banks. The repayment starts 6 months after getting a job or 1 year after completion of course, whichever is earlier. The interest accrued during the repayment holiday period is to be added to the principal and repayment is made in fixed EMIs. The loan must be repaid within 10 years (for loans up to ₹7.5 lakhs) or 15 years (above ₹7.5 lakhs).

IBA has devised a similar scheme for vocational education and training. It is broadly the same as the one mentioned earlier except that the loan amounts vary from ₹20,000 to ₹1.5 lakhs depending upon the duration of the course. Consequently, no tangible collateral is required and the loans must be repaid within 5–7 years.

To make the loans further attractive, income tax rebates are also offered on the amounts of repayment of an education loan. Also, in the framework of loan operations of the public sector banks (PSBs), education is identified as a priority sector. Recently, the government announced a scheme (applicable from the academic year 2009–2010) to provide interest subsidy for the period of moratorium on education loans taken by students from economically weaker sections (with annual parental income not more than ₹4.5 lakhs) from scheduled banks to pursue technical or professional studies from recognized institutions in India. The aim of this scheme is to ensure that nobody is denied professional education because he or she is poor. Under the scheme, interest payable by the student availing of the Educational Loan Scheme of the IBA for professional courses for the period of moratorium, that is, course period, plus one year or six months after getting job, whichever is earlier, as prescribed under the Educational Loan Scheme of the IBA, shall be borne by the government. After the period of moratorium is over, the student, in accordance with the provisions of the existing Educational Loan Scheme, shall pay the interest on the outstanding loan amount.

Critical Evaluation of the Scheme

Despite better and more careful designing, the IBA scheme has not been able to attract students in opting for the loan scheme. The uptake has been limited. According to the Annual Report of the Ministry of Finance (2014–2015), the total outstanding education loans of PSBs as on 31 March 2015 stood at ₹61,967 crores in 2,568,586 accounts. Year-wise break-up of education loans outstanding as on 31 March 2004 to as on 31 December 2015 is given in Table 10.1.

We can see from the Table 10.1 that although the loan accounts have increased in terms of absolute number over the years 2005–2015, the rate of growth of the number of loan accounts has been declining steadily. This is evident from Figure 10.1.

The interest rate charged on these loan accounts has also been quite high. The distribution of interest rates is concentrated between 12 per cent and 16 per cent, rates which are comparable to the interest rates for home loans and car loans in the country.

Table 10.1 *IBA Education Loan Scheme 2004–2015*

As on 31st March	Number of Loan Accounts	Amount Outstanding (in ₹ Crore)	Year on Year Growth (Loan Accounts)	Year on Year Growth (Amount Outstanding)
2004	3,19,337	4,550	0	
2005	4,68,207	6,713	46.62	47.54
2006	6,79,945	10,012	45.22	49.14
2007	9,44,397	14,283	38.89	42.65
2008	12,46,870	19,347	32.03	38.75
2009	16,03,385	27,646	28.59	39.51
2010	19,28,350	35,628	20.27	29.81
2011	22,37,031	43,074	16.01	20.03
2012	24,60,493	49,069	9.99	13.92
2013	25,09,465	53,520	1.99	9.07
2014	25,72,716	58,256	2.52	8.84
2015	25,68,586	61,967	–0.16	6.37
December 2015	25,44,672	65,740	–0.93	7.45

Source: Annual Report, Ministry of Finance (2015–2016).

The most important shortcoming of the IBA model is that economic backwardness does not seem to be an important criterion in granting loans by the banks. It is true that the government has provided interest subsidy for the students from economically weaker sections. However, this does not guarantee that they get the loans. If, due to the collateral and security conditions attached, the economically weaker students do not get the loans, then the interest subsidy is a self-defeating policy. Since the scheme gives a lot of leverage to the banks themselves, many private sector banks have formulated their own conditions—some offer higher or lower loan amounts, charge different interest rates and have varying conditions of repayment and collateral. To eliminate these variations, all banks must implement one comprehensive scheme.

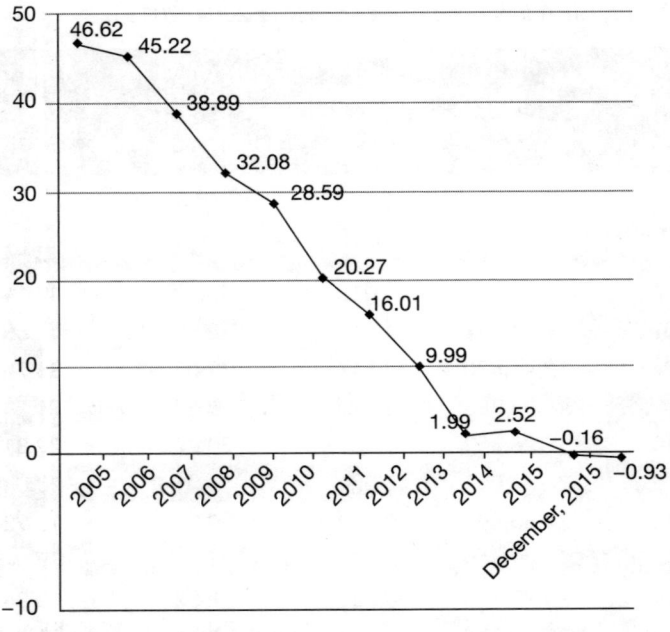

— Rate of growth of number of Loan accounts

Figure 10.1 *Rate of Growth of the Number of Loan Accounts*
Source: Annual Report, Ministry of Finance (2015–2016).

Also, the IBA scheme has not retained some of the better features of the National Loan Scholarship Scheme, such as provision for waivers and exemptions in deserving cases especially for students from economically weaker sections and for the graduates who join the teaching profession, armed forces or choose to serve in remote areas.

Very recently, the GoI has introduced some new loan schemes with the objective of promoting higher education and skill formation amongst the youth. Some of these schemes are specifically targeted towards the underprivileged sections of the population. We report the salient features of these schemes further.

OTHER RECENTLY ANNOUNCED LOAN SCHEMES
Pradhan Mantri Vidya Lakshmi Karyakram

The Pradhan Mantri Vidya Lakshmi Karyakram was launched in 2015 with the objective of easing budget constraints faced by students from poor and middle-class families aspiring for higher education. This is being done using the Vidya Lakshmi portal where students can view, apply and track applications for education loans online. Currently, 39 banks have registered 70 educational loan schemes on this web portal and integrated their systems for providing loan-processing status to students. The Vidya Lakshmi portal provides a single window for students to access information regarding and apply for educational loans that are offered by various banks. Students can apply to multiple banks for educational loans by filling the Common Education Loan Application Form (CELAF) at the portal.[1] Students can choose from among a host of education loan schemes according to their needs and eligibility and can apply to at most three banks using CELAF. The loan amount is disbursed directly by the bank once the loan request has been accepted and processed. The interest rate varies by bank and scheme; there is no blanket interest rate imposed in the Pradhan Mantri Vidya Lakshmi Karyakram.

Central Sector Interest Subsidy Scheme (2009) on Model Education Loan Scheme of IBA

In order to ensure better accessibility of student loans, the GoI approved a scheme to provide full interest subsidy during the period of moratorium, that is, during course period plus one year or six months after getting a job. This subsidy is made available to students from economically weaker sections applying for loans from scheduled banks under the Education Loan Scheme of the IBA mentioned earlier. This scheme is applicable to educational loans given by banks under the model loan scheme for students in recognized technical/professional courses in

---

[1] https://www.vidyalakshmi.co.in/Students/faq

recognized institutions in India.[2] The interest rates charged still remain the discretion of the banks depending on their base rate but are borne by the central government. After the moratorium period is over, the interest on the outstanding loan amount is borne by the student. Eligible candidates need to provide income proof of their parents/ guardians, as the benefits of this scheme are available only to students from economically weaker sections with an upper limit of ₹4.5 lakhs on gross annual family income. The disbursement of interest subsidy claims of banks is done on yearly or half-yearly basis as per the guidelines of the Ministry of Human Resource Development (MHRD).

Credit Guarantee Fund Scheme for Education Loans

This scheme was also introduced in 2015. It specifies the features of loans, which are eligible for coverage for credit guarantee by the GoI. The upper limit of covered loans is ₹7.5 lakhs without collateral and third party guarantee which are undertaken by the National Credit Guarantee Trust Company (NCGTC, set up in 2014 by GoI to operate Credit Guarantee Funds for Educational Loans [CGFSEL], Skill Development Loans and any other funds set up by GoI) to eligible borrowers by Member Lending Institutions (MLIs) as per the IBA scheme. This provision is applicable to lending institutions that apply for credit guarantee as per NCGTC procedures. The interest rate charged by the MLIs for education loans to be covered under CGFSEL should be maximum up to 2 per cent per annum over the base rate.[3] Additionally, the fund reserves the right to notify the banks regarding the courses/institutions for which the guarantee is available. The lending institution, lending education loans in accordance with the IBA procedure, is supposed to ensure linkage of every education loan with Aadhar number and register the borrower's/co-borrower's name with an appropriate credit information bureau and ensure monitoring to reduce moral hazard. For availing the guarantee coverage, the MLIs pay annual guarantee fee (AGF) of 0.50 per cent per annum of the

---

[2] http://mhrd.gov.in/sites/upload_files/mhrd/files/upload_document/IBAM. pdf

[3] http://www.ncgtc.in/sites/default/files/education_loan_one_pager.pdf

outstanding amount as on the date of application of guarantee cover, upfront to the fund within 30 days from the date of Credit Guarantee Demand Advice Note of guarantee fee. All subsequent AGFs are calculated on the basis of the outstanding loan amount as at the beginning of the financial year. According to the gazette notification of the scheme, the fund provides guarantee cover to the extent of 75 per cent of the amount in default. The guarantee cover commences from the date of payment of guarantee fee and runs through the agreed tenure of the education loan. The balance 25 per cent of the guaranteed amount is paid after obtaining a certificate from the MLI that all avenues for recovering the amount have been exhausted.[4]

National Backward Classes Finance and Development Corporation (NBCFDC)

The Skill Development Training Programme of NBCFDC aims to impart skill development training for upgradation of technical and entrepreneurial skills through government skill training institutes or sector skill councils. Members of Backward Classes living below double the poverty line (presently ₹98,000 per annum in rural areas and ₹120,000 per annum in urban areas) are eligible to avail these loans.[5] All skill development courses offered under the scheme must broadly conform to the National Skill Qualification Framework. Of the total, 100 per cent training cost or course fee of the training programme is provided by NBCFDC along with a monthly stipend of ₹1,000, subject to additional requirements. The sanctioned amount of training cost is released in two instalments of 50 per cent each. Boarding and lodging costs are also borne under this scheme. Representative of NBCFDC have the right to inspect the account books, and interaction with the trainees as well as with the trainer and officials of the training institute for better monitoring.

NBCFDC also offers Dr Ambedkar Central Sector Scheme of Interest Subsidy on Educational Loan for Overseas Studies for Other

---

[4] http://www.ncgtc.in/sites/default/files/cgfsel_gadget_notification.pdf
[5] http://nbcfdc.gov.in/res/pdf/sdtp-scheme.pdf

Backward Castes (OBCs), starting from 2014. This is a central government scheme to provide interest subsidy to the students belonging to the OBCs on the interest payable for the period of moratorium for the education loans under the scheme of interest subsidy on educational loans for overseas studies to pursue approved courses of studies abroad at masters and PhD levels.[6] This interest subsidy is linked to the IBA Model Education Loan Scheme. The designated bank maintains a separate account and records relating to the funds received from the ministry pertaining to interest subsidy on education loans. This scheme is available to employed candidates whose own income does not exceed ₹3 lakhs or unemployed candidates whose parents'/guardians' incomes do not exceed ₹3 lakhs per annum and 50 per cent subsidy is given to girl candidates. Interest payable by the students availing the education loans of the IBA for the period of moratorium (i.e., course period, plus one year or six months after getting job, whichever is earlier) is borne by the GoI. After the period of moratorium is over, the interest on the outstanding loan amount is paid by the student, in accordance with the existing educational loan scheme as may be amended from time to time. The Ministry of Social Justice and Empowerment in association with the designated banks are responsible for the monitoring of the loans. A similar scheme called Dr Ambedkar Central Sector Scheme of Interest Subsidy on Educational Loan for Overseas Studies for Economically Backward Classes is operationalized by NBCFDC. The income ceiling for eligible students is set at ₹1 lakh per annum in this case.[7] Other provisions are identical as the scheme meant for OBCs.

National SCs Finance and Development Corporation (NSCFDC)

NSCFDC, under the auspices of the Ministry of Social Justice and Empowerment also extends the Education Loan Scheme and vocation educational training loan scheme with the objective of reducing poverty through socio-economic development of Scheduled Castes (SCs)

---

[6] http://nbcfdc.gov.in/res/pdf/Guidelines%20Dr.%20Ambedkar%20Interest%20Subsidy%20OBC.pdf

[7] http://nbcfdc.gov.in/res/pdf/Guidelines%20Dr.%20Ambedkar%20Interest%20Subsidy%20EBC.pdf

living below double the poverty line. NSCFDC is an institution set up under the Ministry of Social Justice and Empowerment, GoI, for financing, facilitating and mobilizing funds for the economic empowerment of persons belonging to the SCs.[8] The Education Loan Scheme provides up to ₹10 lakhs for students who have secured admission in an institution of higher education in India and ₹20 lakhs for candidates studying abroad. The annual interest rate chargeable to beneficiaries is 4 per cent (3.5 per cent for women candidates). Educational loan is meant to cover admission fees and tuition fees, books, stationery and other instruments required for the course, examination fee, boarding lodging expenses, insurance premium for policy for insuring borrowers against loan in the case of death or permanent disability, travel expenses/passage money for studying abroad and caution money, development fund and so on.[9] The loan is repaid within 5 years in quarterly instalments, including the moratorium period. The moratorium period is considered as six months after completion of the course or getting employment, whichever is earlier. However, the total currency of loan cannot exceed 10 years from the date of first disbursement. The Vocation Educational Training Loan Scheme extends loans covering up to 100 per cent (i.e., up to ₹1 lakh for the course duration six months to one year and up to ₹1.5 lakhs for course duration above one year to two years) of the education expenditure at the same interest rate as the Education Loan Scheme. This loan is extended to eligible SC candidates to provide finance to enhance their skills and employability by pursuing vocational education and training courses in India.[10] Eligible courses are vocational education and training courses of duration of up to two years, run or supported by a ministry/department/organization of the government or a company/society/organization supported by a National Skill Development Corporation or state skills/mission/ state skill corporations. The moratorium period is six months from the completion of courses or getting employment, whichever is earlier. The loan is repaid in quarterly instalments including the applicable moratorium period of six months in 5 years for loans up to ₹1 lakh and in 7 years for loans between ₹1 lakh and ₹1.50 lakhs.

---

[8] http://www.nsfdc.nic.in/

[9] http://www.nsfdc.nic.in/uniquepage.asp?ID_PK=42

[10] http://www.nsfdc.nic.in/uniquepage.asp?ID_PK=42

National Handicapped Finance and Development Corporation (NHFDC)

The NHFDC has been set up by the Ministry of Social Justice and Empowerment under the Department of Empowerment of Persons with Disabilities to channelize funds to persons with disabilities.[11] NHFDC provides education loans to Indian citizens with 40 per cent or more disability covering their tuition and other fees such as maintenance cost, books and equipment for pursuing professional courses in a recognized educational institution in India or abroad.[12] The loan amount is a maximum of ₹10 lakhs for education in India and ₹20 lakhs abroad at an annual interest rate of 4 per cent per annum. The loan is to be repaid within 7 years after commencement of repayment and a moratorium period of 6 months after completion of course or after getting a job (whichever is earlier). NHFDC also offers financial assistance for skill and entrepreneurial development with the objective of providing training to disabled persons so that they may become self-dependent through technical training which extends to 12 months at most. This loan covers 100 per cent of the cost of training along with a monthly stipend of ₹2,000 to cover incidental expenditures. Candidates could be enrolled in government training institutes such as industrial training institutes, polytechnic or engineering colleges, agriculture Universities and National Institute for Entrepreneurship and Small Business Development.[13]

National Minorities Development and Finance Corporation (NMDFC)

The mandate of the NMDFC (A GoI Undertaking, Ministry of Minority Affairs; incorporated in 1994 as a not-for-profit company under the Companies Act) is to provide subsidized access to finance to members of minority communities for self-employment or income

---

[11] http://www.nhfdc.nic.in/about-nhfdc/our-organisation

[12] http://www.nhfdc.nic.in/schemes/schemes-implemented-through-scas-nationalised-banks

[13] http://www.nhfdc.nic.in/upload/Skill_training.pdf

generation activities. As per the National Commission of Minorities Act, 1992, the notified minorities are Muslims, Christians, Sikhs, Buddhists, Parsis and Jains.[14] Education loans are also provided by the NMDFC to students belonging to families having annual income up to ₹81,000 in rural areas and ₹103,000 in urban areas.

National Safai Karamcharis Finance and Development Corporation (NSKFDC)

NSKFDC (1997) is a GoI undertaking under the Ministry of Social Justice and Empowerment which offers a host of loans including educational loans to *safai karamcharis*/scavengers to rehabilitate them and create alternative employment opportunities and to pursue technical/ professional education or skill development. Education loan is being extended to the students from the community of safai karamcharis and their dependents for pursuing professional or technical education and also for higher study in engineering, medical, management, law, diploma in physiotherapy, pathology, nursing, diploma in hotel management and tourism and so on.[15] This scheme covers 90 per cent of the expenditure on education. Repayment can be done 5 years after termination of the course with a moratorium period of six months.

CRITICAL EVALUATION OF THE SCHEMES

All these schemes are too new to be evaluated at this point of time. Some of these are specifically targeted towards the disadvantaged sections of the society, which is a desirable feature. However, from our perspective, it is important to note that all of these are mortgage type bank loan schemes. We have already noted earlier that loan schemes that are operated through commercial banks are unlikely to cater to the poorest of the poor since it is not in their best interest. Moreover, all these student loan schemes, whether new or old, lack any insurance component that would take care of potential idiosyncratic risks (e.g., unemployment risks or health risks). What happens if after taking the

---

[14] http://www.nmdfc.org/index1.aspx?lsid=68&lev=2&lid=42&langid=1
[15] http://nskfdc.nic.in/content/schemes-programmes/loan-schemes

loan, the borrower falls sick and is unable to complete the course? Or what if the borrower fails to secure a high-paying job, which allows timely repayment? The failure to secure a high-paying job may not be due to of lack of skill or ability. Often the job market behaves in an unpredictable manner, with the job opportunities shifting from one skill-specific occupation to another. There could also be various macro-economic shocks, which may make certain skill-specific jobs obsolete, thereby leaving the population trained in that particular skill extremely vulnerable. Not having a built-in insurance component, which allows the individuals to have some fall-back option, is a serious shortcoming of all these mortgage type loans. And this is exactly where an ICL can make a big difference.

ICL: CONCEPT AND SOME CASE STUDIES

The idea of an ICL contract goes back to 1954 to Milton Friedman and Simon Kuznets who recognized that if individuals borrow money with the obligation of repaying the loan amount with the interest, the investor who loaned money could at most get back his capital and the interest; he could never realize a capital gain though he could suffer a loss. Therefore, in the absence of a collateral, the interest rate will have to be high enough to cover the risk of losses and the usual interest charges. Such a rate might exceed the returns from investments in higher education. Hence, Friedman and Kuznets suggested, 'If individuals sold "stock" in themselves, i.e., obligated themselves to pay a fixed proportion of future earnings, investors could "diversify" their holdings and balance capital appreciations against capital losses.' The purchase of such stock would be profitable so long as the expected return on investment in training exceeded the market rate of interest.

ICLs are a practical implementation of the same idea. An ICL is essentially a loan given to anyone who wants to invest in higher education and their payment, which starts once the individual gets a job, is denominated in terms of a certain percentage of the income to be paid for a stipulated time period. The distinguishing feature of an ICL is that the repayment amount is positively linked to income and could even be zero below a certain threshold income level.

The essential elements of an ICL contract are as follows: (a) The annual repayment burden, or the percentage of income or earnings that must go to loan repayment (which may be fixed for all income levels or progressive, increasing at higher incomes), (b) the stipulation of precisely what is to be counted as income and over what span of time (e.g., last year's actual taxable, or the current year's estimated gross) and (c) the provision for release from further repayments (which is generally either repayment at a contractual rate of interest or repayment for a maximum repayment period or until a maximum age). Therefore, the elements that would vary according to income or earnings are the actual monthly or yearly repayments, the repayment period and the ultimate (i.e., after the final payment is made) cost of the loan expressed as an overall effective interest rate on the original amount borrowed (Johnstone, 2004).

In contrast, in a conventional mortgage-type loan, stipulated contractual elements are (a) the required monthly or annual payments, (b) the rate of interest (either fixed or variable) and (c) the repayment period which together stipulate the cost of the loan to the borrower. All these components are fixed, irrespective of income.

One particular variant of the ICL is known as the 'graduate tax'. Graduate tax is an income tax surcharge which is imposed on the lifetime earning of students (typically graduate students) in exchange of partial or full subsidization of tuition fees and other maintenance costs. In its pure form, graduate tax is just a form of tax, which is not based on any cost-recovery principle and does not have any direct link with the beneficiary's account (Woodhall, 1989). However, in all its practical applications, graduate taxes are used as means to shift the burden of taxation from general taxpayers to the direct beneficiaries, namely the students, after they finish their education and start earning.

The financial success of the graduate tax would be measured by the discounted present value of this stream of future income surtax payments just as the financial success of a government-sponsored income-contingent student loan program, would be measured by the present discounted value of repayments that are based on a percentage of yearly income. Thus the mathematics and the practical effect on participating students of the graduate tax and the income contingent loan assuming similar terms are practically indistinguishable. (Johnstone & Marcucci, 2010)

The primary difference between income-contingent and mortgage type of loans is that the income-contingent variety serves to protect prospective students from the costs of the exigencies associated with the financial returns to educational investments. So ICLs offer a form of default insurance or insurance against unfavourable outcomes such that former students do not have to bear the costs of reneging on their debt as a result of periods of low future income. This is quite different to a mortgage-style loan, in which the costs of defaulting exist and may be very high in terms of the defaulter being locked out of other borrowing through damage to credit reputations.

Another problem for students with mortgage-type loans concerns the possible consumption difficulties associated with fixed repayments. If the expected path of future incomes has a high variance, a fixed level of a debt repayment will increase the variance of disposable income. Since ICLs are based on the capacity to repay, such consumption hardships are avoided.

Australia was the first country to institute a broadly based ICL system for higher education in 1989, and was followed by New Zealand and South Africa in 1991. The adoption of ICL has also been seen in the UK, Chile, Thailand and Ghana. All these applications have retained the basic flavour of the ICL but the other ingredients such as the repayment period, the income percentage repaid and the minimum threshold vary. In some cases, the repayment also depends on the family size and family income.

We now discuss three specific country studies where the ICL scheme has been adopted. Two of these cases (Australia and South Africa) are success stories, while in one case (United Kingdom), the response to ICL has been mixed.[16]

---

[16] Country Profiles (Australia, South Africa, UK), ICHEFAP.

Australia

Australia was the first country to combine a large-scale introduction of tuition fees with an option for the students to defer the payment by taking education loan. From the early 1970s to the late 1980s, Australian universities were financed without any direct contribution from students. In 1987, however, a conjunction of forces, discussed further, made it inevitable that the government would move financing arrangements towards increased contributions from students. First, over the 1980s, there was a significant increase in the school completion rates, so that the demand for higher education increased but there was not a commensurate expansion in supply. Second, even though there was a requirement of resources for higher education, the government at that time was intent on fiscal parsimony. Finally, there was strong political support in favour of student fees on grounds of redistribution. The political support stemmed from the view that a system that did not charge higher education students was regressive because universities were paid for by all taxpayers, yet students came from relatively privileged backgrounds, and as graduates they received relatively high personal economic benefits.

In 1989, the Australian government introduced an ICL for the payment of higher education tuition charges, known as the Higher Education Contribution Scheme (HECS).[17] This can be seen as a watershed in terms of the relationship between economic theory and education policy. In its initial years of operation, all UG students paid HECS at the rate of about 23 per cent of the average costs of study. In 1997, the uniform tuition fee aspect was removed from the scheme. HECS was increased and differentiated into three cost bands based on a combination of the relative cost of course delivery and the relative profitability (the rate of return) of certain programmes. The package of reforms introduced in 2002 includes a partial fee deregulation that starting in January 2005 has allowed institutions to set student contribution levels within a range from zero to a maximum set by the Australian government.

---

[17] http://www.studyassist.gov.au

The government administers a number of HELP-HECS loan schemes to assist students with the cost of their tuition. The repayment of the HELP debt through the taxation system starts once a student's repayment income (calculated from the information provided while filing an income tax return) is above the compulsory threshold. The compulsory repayment threshold is adjusted each year. The amount repaid each year is a percentage of the repayment income. The percentage varies positively with income. The Australian Taxation Office (ATO) calculates the compulsory repayment for the year and includes it in the income tax notice of the student. There is no real interest charged on HECS-HELP loans. However, the debt is indexed each year to reflect changes in the consumer price index to maintain its real value. Students can even make extra voluntary repayments to the ATO and receive a discount. Also, if someone believes that making the compulsory repayment would cause serious financial hardship or there are other reasons why one should not have to make a compulsory repayment, he or she can apply to the ATO to defer there payment. There is a feature in HECS called the HECS-HELP benefit, which provides incentive for graduates of particular courses (mathematics, science, nursing and education) to take up related occupations or work (primary school teacher, nurse or midwife) in specified locations thereby reducing their compulsory HECS-HELP repayments.

The HECS-HELP scheme in Australia has been quite successful in attaining the dual objective of reducing the pressure on government exchequer and drawing students from the economically and socially disadvantaged sections of the population towards higher education (Chapman, 1977, 2007; Chapman & Ryan, 2002, 2005). As Chapman and Ryan (2002) report, the ICL scheme has been able to increase government revenue substantially over a short period and income-contingent repayment through taxes now constitute a significant proportion of cost of higher education in Australia. At the same time, introduction of HECS has been associated with aggregate increases in higher education participation. In fact, the latter reforms in the HECS-HELP scheme were associated generally with increases in the participation of individuals irrespective of their family wealth. In particular, the HECS-HELP scheme did help in maintaining the rate of participation of students from relatively poor families despite sharp hike in tuition fees.

South Africa

The legacy of apartheid and its education system produced a vast preponderance of the rich among the graduate students in South Africa. It also spawned a society which showed a clear correlation between being black and being poor. There would have been no change in the status quo (gross inequalities of access and racially skewed student and graduate profiles) without serious policy intervention on the part of government, primarily because academically able black students were too poor to meet the costs of higher education without substantial assistance. Not only students had to meet living costs, but all South African HEIs charged tuition fees, and there were few private scholarships. A financial instrument was needed to be devised urgently, to make it possible for poor yet competent students, previously excluded from tertiary education, to gain access to the higher education system as soon as possible. At the same time, South Africa could not afford intervention in the form of a financial assistance scheme relying entirely on bursaries (grants), as it would not be financially sustainable. It was therefore necessary to design a financial assistance scheme that allowed deferred cost recovery by providing repayable loans with a bursary or grant element.

In 1991, the Tertiary Education Fund of South Africa (TEFSA) was established with the objective of drawing the academically able students from the historically disadvantaged groups into tertiary education. It was established as a not-for-profit company, administering a national scheme of student bursaries and loans. In 1999 the National Student Financial Aid Scheme (NSFAS) Act was passed (Act No. 56 of 1999), converting TEFSA into a statutory body called NSFAS, which was established to impact South Africa's racially skewed student and graduate populations by providing a sustainable financial aid scheme that enables academically deserving and financially needy students to meet their own and South Africa's development needs.

Although anyone can apply for a NSFAS loan, the decision to allocate funds is based on the following:

1. Financial need (determined by a national means test)
2. Having the academic potential to succeed

NSFAS does not allocate funds directly to students. Instead, its task is to raise funds and allocate them to tertiary institutions such as universities and technikons (the South African equivalent of the former polytechnics in the UK) which, in turn, allocate these funds (using the NSFAS criteria) to individual students in the form of loans, part of which can be converted into a bursary if the student achieves good results in his or her tertiary education course.

NSFAS does charge a positive real interest rate, but the interest rate charged by NSFAS is much lower than that of the bank loans as it is subsidized by donations from government, private companies and overseas donors. The student loans provided by NSFAS do not require any collateral. Depending on the student's academic performance portions of the loan can be converted into a bursary. The repayment is income-contingent and all repaid student loans are recycled to fund more needy students. The method of repayment can include a debit order, direct deposits into the NSFAS account, postal orders, cheques or employer deductions. To defer repayments in case unemployed, the borrower needs to provide written proof (in the form of affidavit valid for 3 months) to the NSFAS head office. It is the responsibility of the borrower to keep NSFAS informed about his/her employment status.

The NSFAS has made significant impact on South Africa's racially skewed student population by providing a sustainable financial aid that has enabled the academically deserving and financially needy students to join tertiary education. By 2001–2002—within 10 years of the launch of the scheme—the NSFAS awarded 587,000 disadvantaged students, 99 per cent of whom were black (African, coloured or Asian), who had collectively passed more than 73 per cent of the courses for which they had been registered during their UG years. In keeping with the philosophy which led to the establishment of the national scheme, money recovered from those who received aid in the early and mid-1990s has been effectively recycled to assist new generations of students in 2001 and 2002 (Jackson, 2002). Several factors contributed to the successful implementation of the scheme in South Africa. These factors include: (a) strong political will on part of the government to provide funds and other forms of support, (b) financial support from international donor agencies, in particular EU, in providing the funding for capitalization until the scheme became self-financing, (c) effective legislative support in empowering NSFAS in tracking the debtors and recovering the loans, and (d) the income–contingent aspect of the loan programme which allowed efficient pooling of idiosyncratic risks and made the scheme popular amongst the poorer section of the population (Jackson, 2002).

United Kingdom

Nineteenth-century British higher education was fundamentally a private endeavour. British universities were converted into state dependencies in the 20th century and are now generally considered public. Despite fiscal dependency on state funds, HEIs in the United Kingdom are legally independent and determine their own admissions policies. In the late-1960s, the government began an expansion of higher education that depended mainly on the creation of polytechnics a new, distinctly non-university sector, locally controlled and financed, featuring more practical and technical subjects. As a result, the British higher education expanded from an elite 5 per cent system in 1960 to a mass 30 per cent system by the mid-1990s. At the same time, there was pressure both to restrain expenditure and to address the issues arising from the rapid expansion of the system. Public funding of a high-quality elite system would be regressive. Hence, for a mass system, public funding needs to be supplemented on a significant scale by private funding. The policy problem, therefore, was to devise a way of bringing in private resources in a way, which simultaneously protects both quality and access. One solution was a system of ICLs.

In May 1996, the National Committee of Inquiry into Higher Education was established by agreement between the main political parties, to make recommendations for reforms in the higher education system.

In response to the Dearing Report, in 1997 the government announced means-tested contributions to the costs of instruction or tuition fees by full-time home and EU undergraduates, the introduction of ICLs and the abolition of maintenance grants. Consequently, in the 1998–1999 academic year, a tuition fee of £1,000 was introduced. How much of the fee a student paid depended on assessed family residual income students from the lowest income families did not pay. In the years that followed, it was seen that this level of tuition fee was still not providing enough funding to sustain the increasing costs.

After several proposals, protests and public consultation, the Higher Education Act was passed in 2004. This act made the following key changes: (a) It gave those universities that have signed an agreement with the office for fair access the power to charge a student contribution of between £0 and £3000 per year for each programme of study starting in September 2006; (b) The act abolished the upfront payment of tuition fees and introduced a new ICL scheme; (c) Each access agreement identified steps that the university will undertake to improve access including the provision of financial help so that students from all backgrounds apply.[18]

All student loans in the UK are disbursed through the Student Loans Company (SLC), which also collects the repayments. The SLC is a non-profit-making government-owned organization that was established in 1989 to administer the student loans scheme introduced by the Education (Student Loans) Act 1990 within the policy context and the legislative framework laid down by the government. It provides loans and non-repayable grants for living costs and studying expenses (called maintenance loans paid to the student's bank account at the start of each term) to students in universities and colleges in the UK. After the introduction of tuition fees, it also provides loans to meet the costs of tuition fees, which is paid directly to universities and colleges on behalf of students. It works with the local authorities in the four countries (England, Wales, Northern Ireland and Scotland) of the UK because they have separate policies on student finance. Before September 1998, all student loans were of the mortgage-style or fixed term loans. ICLs

---

[18] http://www.slc.co.uk

were introduced in 1998. The various functions of SLC include (a) payment of loans and grants to students and tuition fees to colleges and universities, (b) working with Her Majesty's Revenue and Customs (HMRC) to collect loan repayments, (c) collecting repayments on mortgage-style loans issued before 1998, (d) payment of bursaries and scholarships on behalf of universities and colleges and (e) running all the administrations and processing associated with these activities.

The interest rate on student loans is equal to the inflation rate, that is, a zero real interest rate; thus, the entire interest rate is subsidized. There are two modes of repayment in the UK system.

1. Repayment through PAYE

Pay as You Earn (PAYE) is the scheme in which the employers are advised by HMRC to calculate and deduct student loan repayments from the individual's salary. These deductions are shown on the pay slip. At the end of the tax year the employers are supposed to inform HMRC of the total deductions they have made and HMRC will then pass on the details to SLC. It is possible that a student deduction was made in a pay period when the earning was over the weekly or monthly threshold, but over the whole year the individual's income did not exceed the yearly threshold (this could be in the case of a bonus or overtime). The individual can then ask for a refund.

2. Repayment through self-assessment

This is meant for the self-employed. They make payment directly to the HMRC along with the usual tax payments. HMRC updates the SLC with the repayments made.

Unlike the HECS-HELP in Australia or NSFAS in South Africa, the income-contingent student loan scheme in the UK has been fraught with controversies. Barr and Johnston (2010) identified zero-interest rate on student loans and non-targeting of beneficiary groups as the two major sources of problems for the UK scheme. Zero-interest rate on loans means that the government ends up paying the interest cost of the loans even for those who are earning high enough after graduating. At the same time, there being no specific target groups for these loan schemes, everybody, even those who are financially well off, end up taking the loan and apply for admission, which puts tremendous pressure on the academic institutions. Moreover, these two features of the ICL loan scheme in the UK has meant that both the equity and efficiency aspects of the ICL loan contract have been undermined; neither has it reduced the burden on the exchequer, nor has it catered specifically to needs of the students who are academically bright but financially weak.

These case studies allow us to identify some important requirements for successful deigning and implementation of an ICL scheme. These include (a) efficient administrative and financial management systems that can disburse the loans easily and without delay and keep track of the repayments, (b) legal and judicial mechanisms which ensure that loan recovery is legally enforceable, (c) credible and politically acceptable targeting schemes such that the loans indeed reach the eligible and needy students, (d) well-developed tax networks and information networks in order to coordinate the repayment through taxation and (e) last but not the least, proactive government which provides essential support not only at the initial stage (in terms of providing the initial capital to activate the scheme) but also in actual disbursal of funds and eventual collection of repayments.

POTENTIAL FOR ICLS IN INDIA: PROBLEMS AND PROSPECTS

Designing of an ICL Scheme

The designing of an ICL scheme could vary depending on the final outcomes that are sought to be attained, the pace of implementation and the degree of coverage required. Here, we propose a tentative guideline towards designing of such a scheme based on similar systems already in practice elsewhere (e.g., Australia, South Africa, UK, Chile and so on). We must emphasize here that the actual crafting of a scheme needs a more careful consideration of various details and a closer scrutiny of possible loopholes. Our suggestions here only indicate broad directions, without going into specifics.

At the outset, it is important to point out that while an ICL scheme is extremely desirable from the perspective of an emerging economy like India, a developing economy like India also has its own sets of problems compared to the developed countries where the ICL scheme has been successfully implemented. First and foremost, the reach of taxation and information network in India is rather limited. Although it is improving over time (especially with the advent of new technology like Aadhaar), in terms of tax compliance and enforcement, we are yet to reach the level of the developed economies. Secondly, cost-sharing in higher education is a politically sensitive subject and it is not easy to garner the political wherewithal that will allow the state to move away from a system of fully subsidized education. Thirdly, the governments in developing countries, in their attempts towards cost-sharing often go to the other extreme and leave the responsibility entirely in the hands of the private players (private banks and private academic institutions), which is self-defeating. As we have argued earlier, an active government participation is required even for the implementation of an ICL scheme, without which it is bound to fail.

With these caveats in mind, let us now examine the important issues that one has to keep in mind in order to design a feasible ICL scheme for India. ICLs could be designed to serve multiple objectives pertaining to (a) reducing the burden on the public exchequer, (b) allowing poorer households to access education, (c) moving towards more direct targeting of benefits and (d) increasing higher education enrolment and skill formation for achieving higher economic growth.

All these seem to be very desirable objectives from the perspective of an emerging economy like India. Yet, in fulfilling these objectives, one has to pay attention to minute details such that the objectives can be attained without hampering the incentives of the potential beneficiaries or without compromising on the overall quality of higher education. Bruce Chapman provided a detailed roadmap towards designing a viable ICL scheme, which we revisit as follows.

1. Upon enrolment, students choose between an upfront payment, or incurring a debt, reflecting course costs and living expenses.
2. Those paying upfront do not have to be followed further, but might be later if they choose to incur debt in following years of study.

3. Those incurring the debt are issued with a social security number by the university (which has access to blocks of unused numbers).

4. The number a student receives is unique and will apply also to that student's future pension arrangement (if applicable).

5. The size of the debt is recorded and the information is communicated to the higher education unit in the Ministry of Finance.

6. A higher education debt record is set up, which will be unique for each student.

7. At the time of employment the former student is required to let the employer know what their number is, and the employer is required by law to remit debt repayments (contingent on the employees' annual income and the repayment parameters) to the relevant tax authority (this remittance could take the form of income tax).

8. The relevant tax authority is required to remit the debt repayment to the higher education unit in the Ministry of Finance, where the unique identifier allows a former students' debt to be adjusted accordingly.

9. After the debt is repaid in full, the Ministry of Finance lets the employer know that no further obligations exist, and the employer ceases collection from that former student (Chapman, 2005).

These generic guidelines are useful in planning and designing a suitable ICL scheme for India. Before we proceed further with some tentative suggestions along this line, it is imperative to note here the importance of a 'unique identifier' like a social security number for every student. Indeed, it is futile to even talk about and ICL (where recovery of loans is essentially done through future taxation) unless there is a way to identify and potentially track the borrowers in future. Until recently, this was probably the biggest hindrance towards implementation of an ICL scheme in India. Things have, however, changed in recent years with the introduction of the Aadhaar, which is a 12-digit unique identity number issued to all Indian resident based on their biometric[19] and demographic data. The data is collected by the Unique Identification Authority of India, a statutory authority established in

---

[19] https://en.wikipedia.org/wiki/Biometrics

January 2009 by the GoI. Aadhaar is the world's largest biometric ID system,[20] with over 1.19 billion enrolled members as on 30 November 2017, representing over 99 per cent of Indians. With a 'unique identifier' in place, one can now talk about the possibility of introducing an ICL scheme in India with the dual objective of extending the access to higher education to the economically disadvantaged groups and at the same time restricting the fiscal burden of the government.

In designing a suitable scheme to cater to multiple objectives of an ICL scheme, several issues need careful attention, keeping in mind the administrative as well as monetary limitations of a large developing nation such as ours. Some of these issues include financing of the initial investment required to kick-start the ICL scheme, the body responsible for the actual implementation of the scheme and collection of repayments, and whether the scheme should be universal or targeted.

FINANCING THE INITIAL SET-UP COST

In all the countries where an ICL programme for higher education has been implemented, the resources always come from the government treasury. This clearly would be a major source of concern for a developing country like India, which is already resource-constrained. Moreover, given the large size of India's young population, we may need much more resources to implement an ICL programme than the developed countries.

One possible financing option could be that the state borrows on behalf of the students from the international market. As the state has a greater credibility, it may be able to borrow at a lower rate as compared to the rate at which individuals borrow. However, there may be practical problems associated with its implementation.

An alternative could be to implement the ICL programme with help from the private sector, especially the private corporate sector. Given the high demand for technically skilled professionals in the corporate sectors, they may have an incentive to contribute in their own

---

[20] https://en.wikipedia.org/wiki/Countries_applying_biometrics

long-term interest. Such a PPP in financing ICL for higher education is not only desirable and may be easier to implement, but it also has the potential of raising much more resources, which would increase the overall access.

IMPLEMENTATION AND COLLECTION OF REPAYMENTS

The primary challenge in designing the ICL scheme lies in ensuring repayment. In Australia and the UK, recovery is done by directly linking the repayment amount to the tax payable by an individual. One could follow the same practice in India as well, whereby the recovery of loans is instituted through the tax department (which could even give a deduction on early repayment of such loans as an incentive). Needless to say, the tax collecting authority has to be efficient enough in tracking the beneficiaries once they enter the formal job market. But the tracking process may not be as difficult as it may appear. First, since majority of the population after attaining higher education would work in the formal sector and, therefore, would be under the tax-net anyway, such direct linking of taxes to repayment seems quite feasible. Secondly, if there is specific targeting, then the tracking problem becomes relatively easier, as one would be looking at a smaller set of people. Thirdly, since placements in many institutes of higher education are done through the campus, these institutes can be asked to provide information about placement of students who are under the ICL scheme.

Some other suggestions that could be adopted by the government in case the repayment is collected by the Income Tax Department are as follows: (a) The Income Tax Department could actively maintain records of the all students who have opted for ICL loans. This can be done with active support from the administrative bodies of the various institutes, which come under the purview of the ICL scheme; (b) The unique identity number (Aadhaar) could be linked to all financial transactions of the student to enforce tracking and monitoring; (c) The passport, ration card and driving license of the student could be linked to the student's records to enhance traceability and prevent evasion; (d) Filing of tax returns should be made mandatory for such students, the lack of which is to be dealt with seriously. Immediate reminders should be sent to the students via post, sms and e-mail to keep them aware that they are being tracked. In the modern computerized world, all this requires little manpower; (e) Since the concerned students, with a very high probability, will enter the formal sector after completion of the higher education degree, detailed information about the placement has to be obtained and repayment should be linked to and collected along with other tax payments. Again such tracking can easily be done with active support from the academic institutions.

Alternatively, the ICL scheme could be implemented with direct payments of all or part of fees to educational institutes. The institutes will then collect the repayments from the students and transfer the same to the government. This may require a well thought out incentive-aligned but non-intrusive (non-tax administration) method that is self-reinforcing. This could work as follows: (a) Institutions having on-campus recruitments could be asked to collect repayments from the students within a stipulated number of months after the placement; (b) The handing out of final degrees/diploma can be subjected to repayment of the loans; (c) If the educational institute fails to comply, the government could recover the loan (which it has already given to the institute as fees) directly from the institution.

It is also necessary to put in place adequate safeguards to prevent fraud either by the individuals or institutions. The direct payment of ICLs to institutions should only be done on reputational basis. Initially, only public institutions and accredited private institutions with long-standing academic and financial reputation could be made a part of the scheme. This would preclude fly-by-night operators entering to defraud individuals and government alike.

A third alternative is to explore the role of a PPP model here, where in the disbursement of loans as well as the collection of repayments is outsourced to the commercial banks. From our study, we find that the major problems that bankers face with education loans are high rates of default, problems associated with tracing of the student, problems associated with identifying the actual income of the student and unavailability of information about the quality of the institution If national, then NAAC accreditation would suffice but if internationals, quality can be a concern depending on the country. While active tax machinery used for the recovery of loans could go a long way in alleviating some of these concerns, there is also a need to bridge the information gap and smoothen some of the existing imperfections through regulatory devices. Also, since an education loan in essence is a loan taken against future earning ability (and not current assets) created by HC attainments, there is an obvious moral hazard problem. Thus, bankers concerned about the recovery of the loan, do not have the incentive to offer loans unless backed by collaterals or other such tangible means, which ensure repayment. The recovery powers of the revenue machinery may have a positive impact on the incentive structure of bankers, which in turn would make them more willing to give education loans to those with lower collaterals or with lesser parental/co-borrower incomes.

Thus, if the government can create an environment that is conducive for the private players to chip in, then an ICL scheme has the dual advantage of reducing the fiscal burden of the government as well as improving the efficiency of the market system.

UNIVERSAL VERSUS TARGETED ICL

In almost all countries (except Korea), the move to an ICL regime has been accompanied by a simultaneous move to abolish government subsidies, which then freed up resources to be used for this programme. Such a drastic step in terms of complete withdrawal of government subsidies at one go may not be politically feasible in India and may not be even necessary. It might be more appropriate to chalk out a gradual transition process such that only a specific group (say, the poorest 20%) is targeted first for the ICL scheme (like in South Africa), leaving the rest of the system unchanged. Such an interim policy, whereby the more prosperous households continue to finance education through own resources and/or mortgage type loans (as they appear to do now) while the less well-to-do households are supported by ICLs, could continue in the short and medium term until the ICL scheme becomes self-sustaining and the coverage of ICL becomes universal.

One could also think of targeting the beneficiaries on the basis of various socio-economic criteria as specified by government. In order to ensure that there is no adverse selection, targeting may also be institution-specific, such that ICL contracts can be availed only by those who are registered in specific institutions that satisfy certain quality criteria. The quality criteria can be devised in the following way. There already exists a grading mechanism whereby the UGC and the AICTE award grades based on the overall quality of the institutions and put this information on their website. This mechanism could be made more systematic and rigorous. For example, one could follow the ranking procedure of *India Today* magazine, which along with the Nielsen Company, publishes the list of top 50 colleges in India by discipline each year. They place due weight to reputation of colleges, quality of academic input, student care, infrastructure and job prospects.

Such a well-defined ranking system based on quality will have a twofold advantage. On the one hand, it will bridge the information gap between the lender and the borrower and would induce the private lenders to put in more money, since quality is now assured and therefore chances of recovery are high. At the same time it will prevent spurious institutions to misuse the benefits of the ICL financing scheme. Moreover, since this will be an indirect source of finance for various educational institutions, they would compete to get better ranks and therefore overall quality will increase. This will also encourage the private universities to offer quality education.

Advantages of ICL as a Higher Education Financing Policy

There are several advantages of an ICL contract so designed, which makes it particularly attractive for resource-strapped developing economies in comparison to measures. First, it is self-financing and therefore sustainable in the long run. Second, it is politically much easier to implement than a direct redistributive mechanism. Third, it is more equitable than general educational subsidies as it is availed only by those who need it the most. Fourth, since the government can obtain credit at more favourable terms than individuals, these credit market benefits can be passed on to the ICL-takers in the form of lower expected interest rate than the market. Finally, it provides a cushion for the poor in case they invest in higher education but fail in the labour market. This cushion effect is important as it retains the dynamic incentive for a household to keep investing in higher education even when there have been a few failures in the past.

We should emphasize at this point that the implementation of the proposed ICL scheme requires active government intervention, at least during the initial phase. In other words, this is not an argument for complete withdrawal of the government from the education sector, rather the character and direction of government intervention changes.

Since ICL is a direct contract between the student and the funding agency/government, the terms and conditions of an ICL can be suitably designed to make it more incentive compatible for the poor. Moreover ICL could be tied to other development objectives of the government. For example, lack of quality teachers in government teaching institutions and lack of quality doctors in government hospitals, especially those located in remote rural area, have been two major problems that have plagued our education and health care system for long. The repayment conditions of ICL could be modified to give special concession to those serving in these areas.

Advantages of ICL as an Anti-poverty Measure

One very attractive feature of ICL is that it acts as an anti-poverty measure and contributes to pulling people out of long-run poverty traps. In fact as an anti-poverty measure, it has certain advantages over other policies such as direct cash transfer or credit market reforms. ICL acts as a tied loan, whereby loan is provided only if the student is enrolled in an institution of higher education. Moreover, the loan is provided directly to the institutes. This prevents channelization of this loan for consumption or other purposes. Thus, it is more effective than direct cash transfer, since the latter does not come with such built-in checks and balances and therefore can be used for various wasteful expenditures. Since a household reaches a higher steady state income after attaining education, such a tied policy is welfare improving in the long run.

Since imperfection of the credit market is the primary reason why poor households get entrapped in a low education–low income trap, it has often been argued that providing easy credit to the poor will solve this problem. However, when returns to skill formation is uncertain (in the sense that even after attaining higher education a person may not find a job immediately), then a perfect credit market fails to draw people out of the long-run poverty trap. This is because under the standard credit market, the borrower has to pay back even when he is unsuccessful in getting a job. This discourages him to avail the credit in the first place, since in the event of failure, his income falls much more sharply, and is lower than his average income if he did not go for higher education. And this is precisely where ICL scores over the perfect credit market. Under an ICL contract, the borrower does not have to pay back if his income is too low. This creates an insurance, which induces risk averse agents (typically, poor people are more risk averse than the rich) to opt for the scheme and go for higher education despite chances of failure. Moreover, even when agents are not risk averse and are equally likely to opt for a loan market or an ICL as long as their expected future income is higher, ICL provides a cushion in the event of actual failure. Since the realized net income in the event of failure is higher under ICL compared to a perfect loan contract, the household may still have resources left to make a decent livelihood subsequently.

CONCLUSION

In this chapter, we have examined the origin and actual implementation of ICLs in several countries. In this context, we have also analysed the relative merits of an ICL scheme vis-à-vis other kinds of education financing schemes. Based on these analyses, there certainly seems to be a case for introducing an ICL scheme for financing higher education in India. It must, however, be noted that in developed countries such as Australia, New Zealand, South Africa and others, introducing an ICL system has been relatively easier from an administrative point of view. The reasons for this are that institutional features such as a strong legal framework, a universal and transparent regime of income taxation and/or social security collection, a smoothly functioning public administration system and an efficient repayment mechanism are already present in these countries. Ghana is an important exception in this respect, which has been able to run a successful ICL programme despite being a developing country. What may help India in tackling these kind of administrative issues is the recent introduction of a unique identity number (Aadhaar) for all its citizens and linking it to the delivery of public utilities and access to public welfare schemes (the Aadhaar Act, 2016). Given the Aadhaar technology, it is no longer difficult to identify and track individual citizens and their incomes over time and space. It is not expensive, moreover, to tack onto some existing tax collection mechanism an additional function of recollection of the loan repayments.

Notwithstanding the difficulties, it is precisely the developing countries like India which need to motivate their youth to invest in higher education and also face a binding resource constraint. What is required, therefore, is not a complete rejection of the idea of ICLs by the developing countries, but rather considering the possibility, albeit with a more cautious approach. While it is imperative to carefully evaluate the costs and benefits in designing any such scheme, a well-designed ICL scheme can overcome the problem of lack of education and lack of skill formation amongst Indian youth and help build a strong HC base for India. It is time that the ICL scheme entered the arena of public debate and discourse on higher education.

REFERENCES

Albrecht, D., & Ziderman, A. (1991). *Deferred cost recovery for higher education: Student loan programs in developing countries* (World Bank Discussion Paper No. 137). Washington, DC: The World Bank.

Barr, N., & Johnston, A. (2010). *Interest subsidies on student loans: A better class of drain.* London: London School of Economics.

Birdsall, N., & James, E. (1990). *Efficiency and equity in social spending: How and why governments misbehave* (World Bank Working Paper No. 27). Washington, DC: The World Bank.

Chapman, B. 1977. Conceptual issues and the Australian experience with income contingent charges for higher education. *The Economic Journal, 107*(442), 738–751.

————. (2007). *Higher education financing in Australia* (CESifo DICE Report). Munich: CESifo.

Chapman, B., & Ryan, C. (2002). Income contingent financing of student charges for higher education: Assessing the Australian innovation. *Welsh Journal of Education, 11*(1), 45–63.

————. (2005). The access implications of income related charges for higher education: Lessons Australia. *Economics of Education Review, 24*(5), 491–512.

Friedman, M., & Kuznets, S. (1954). Incomes in the professions and in other pursuits. In M. Friedman & S Kuznets (Eds.), *Income from Independent Professional Practice* (pp. 62–94). Cambridge, MA: NBER.

Garcia-Penalosa, C., & Walde, K. (2000). Efficiency and equity effects of subsidies to higher education. *Oxford Economic Papers, 52*(4), 702–722.

Jackson, R. (2002). The National Student Financial Aid Scheme of South Africa (NSFAS): How and why it works. *Welsh Journal of Education, 11*(1), 82–94.

Jimenez, E. (1987). *Pricing policy in the social sectors: Cost recovery for education and health in developing countries*. Baltimore, MD: Johns Hopkins University Press.

Johnstone, D. B. (2004). Cost-sharing and equity in higher education: Implications of income contingent loans. In P. Teixeira, B. Jongbloed, D. Dill, & A. Amaral (Eds.), *Markets in Higher Education* (pp. 37–59). Dordrecht: Springer.

Johnstone, D. B., & Marcucci, P. (2010). *Financing higher education in international perspective: Who pays? Who should pay?* Baltimore, MD: The Johns Hopkins University Press.

Peltzmann, S. (1973). The effect of government subsidies-in-kind on private expenditures: The case of higher education. *Journal of Political Economy, 81*(1), 1–27.

Psacharopoulos, G., Tan, J-P., & Jimenez, E. (1986). *Financing education in developing countries: An exploration of policy options*. Washington, DC: The World Bank.

Radner, R., & Miller, L. S. (1970). Demand and supply in US higher education: A progress report. *American Economics Review, 60*(2), 326–334.

Tilak, J. B. G. (1992, June). Student loans in financing higher education in India. *Higher Education, 23*(4), 389–404.

————. (2007). Student loans and financing of higher education in India. *Journal of Educational Planning and Administration, 21*(3), 231–256.

Tilak, J. B. G., & Varghese, N. V. (1991). Financing higher education in India. *Higher Education, 21*(1), 83–101.

Woodhall, M. (1989). *Financial support for students: Grants, loans or graduate tax?* (Vol. 34). Kogan Page in association with the Institute of Education, University of London.

————. (1992). Student loans in developing countries: Feasibility, experience and prospects for reform. *Higher Education, 23*(4), 347–356.

Chapter 11

Public Financing of Private Education

A Case Study of Fee Reimbursement Scheme (FRS) in Andhra Pradesh

B. Shiva Reddy and K. Anji Reddy

INTRODUCTION

Development of education is a pre-requisite for the overall development of economy and society and it requires public funding on a larger scale. Financing of education by the government is common in many countries and India is no exception to it. However, the extent of public funding varies across different levels and types of education. Not only the level of funding but also the method of funding affects the access, equity and quality, the three important parameters of education development.

Public funding to higher education takes three forms in Andhra Pradesh. First, government funds the institutions under its management. This form of funding has not been increasing significantly. Second, the institutions under private management are funded by the government in the form of grants-in-aid, mainly to meet the salary of teaching and non-teaching staff (known as private aided). This is the traditional form of public funding of private sector which is on the decline due to decrease in the number of aided institutions. The third form is the public funding of private education in the form of FRS. The public funding to higher education, including technical and professional education, is taking this form in Andhra Pradesh.

Much has been written and researched on the effects and implications of financing of higher education. Also some research is done on the issues related to the private financing of higher education. There is hardly any research related to the public financing private education through FRS. Though there are some studies related to similar methods of financing (such as voucher system), no such studies exist for India. Therefore, this chapter attempts to examine issues associated with the FRS in Andhra Pradesh. When compared to other states, Andhra Pradesh has introduced FRS on a large scale in higher education and is continuing with it even after bifurcation of the state in 2014. Compared to general higher education, professional and technical education is dominated by private sector and is funded through FRS. Within professional and technical education, engineering education is the most important component funded and affected by the FRS. This chapter focuses its analysis on financing of higher education, especially engineering education through the new modality of FRS.

The plan of this chapter is as follows. The next section examines the background and the need for the introduction of FRS in Andhra Pradesh. The salient features and implementation design and coverage of FRS are examined in second section. The third section discusses admission procedure and fee structure for engineering education in Andhra Pradesh. In the fourth section, the impact of FRS on higher education, particularly on engineering education, in Andhra Pradesh is analysed. The issues associated with the implementation of FRS are discussed in the fifth section. Summary and concluding observations are made in the last section.

BACKGROUND AND THE NEED FOR FRS

The higher education institutions (HEIs) in Andhra Pradesh were funded and managed by the government till the 1980s.

The role of private sector increased both in of the management and financing of higher education in the 1980s. Public funding to higher education declined in the subsequent period in the state partly due to the proliferation of private unaided colleges providing general and technical higher education. Further, the government believed that benefits of higher education largely accrue to the individual and hence permitted the colleges to levy fees at the level to recover full cost. This shows that higher education was not even recognized as a merit good.

As a result, the access to higher education was restricted to those willing to pay for it and hence the poor were kept away from getting access to it. The trade-off between efficiency and equity was evident with the state tacitly supporting the former by reducing the state funding and encouraging the cost recovery methods. Though statistics on the extent of private funding is not available, it may be inferred that funding of higher education through fees and other income was more than the public funding in the state till early 2000 in the state. Private sector expanded more in technical and professional education when compared to general education as the former is comparatively more rewarding both for the student and the college management.

The strategy of encouraging the private sector also helped the outflow of children from middle-class families to neighbouring states to seek technical education. The access to higher education, technical and professional education, in particular, has remained a dream for the poorer sections. Even the reservation system could not help them as their economic conditions did not permit them to study despite getting admission.

The option of taking loans from the banks, though available, is limited due to various conditions laid down by the banks. It is easier and cheaper to take loans for acquiring property (physical capital) compared to getting loans for education (human capital). Further, the uncertainty of getting economic returns from the education and consequent inability to pay back the loan also discouraged them from seeking loans.

All these issues have led to some discontentment, particularly among the backward communities (BCs) in their efforts to get access to higher education. On the one hand, the poor students from SC/ST communities got financial assistance to meet the costs of higher education. On the other hand, of those outside the reservation system some have got access to technical and professional education due to their economic position as they can get admission under management quota. Only students from BCs who have reservation were denied access to higher education, particularly technical and professional education, due to their poor economic background. At present, 29 per cent of the seats in all HEIs are reserved for BCs.

The BCs were demanding the government to bear the cost of higher education for their children admitted in private institutions. The scholarship scheme available to them was insufficient to bear the cost of technical and professional education. The efforts did not materialize till the election period where the political compulsions made the then ruling party (Indian National Congress) to promise financial assistance to children of BCs pursuing higher education. This culminated in the form of FRS introduced from the academic year 2008–2009, originally meant for children of BCs in Andhra Pradesh.

FEATURES AND IMPLEMENTATION DESIGN OF FRS

FRS is a unique method of intervention that has features different from other methods of public financing. Some of the important features of FRS are as follows.

The term 'fees reimbursement' implies that the student first pays the tuition fee and later gets the reimbursement from the government. Contrary to this, there is no need to pay the fee by the student. Government gives an assurance to pay the fees to the management after the admission, as per the guidelines. FRS covers all the eligible students (parents annual income must be less than the prescribed amount by the government along with the caste certificate, and the student should have secured a rank in common entrance test conducted by government) with no ceiling on the total number and amount. FRS is different from grant-in-aid, a common method of public funding of private education, though in both methods funding is given to the management. In the grant-in-method, the government provides funds to the private institution to meet, mainly, the salary component of teaching and non-teaching staff. The management gets the funding based on the number of teaching and non-teaching staff and not based on the number of students. In the case of FRS, the funding is based on the number of students admitted, which makes the management admit maximum number of students.

FRS appears to be similar to the voucher system, a method of public funding of education, which is prevalent in many countries (Epple, Romano, & Urquiola, 2017). Both of them cover public as well as private institutions, but the main aim of FRS is to provide access to private education. In both the cases, the institutions compete for the students as the total public funding is based on the number of students. However, they differ is several respects.

Voucher system covers only school education (foreign countries), whereas FRS is serving only higher education (India). There are instances of higher education being covered too (foreign countries). Under voucher system, the student has complete freedom to choose the institution. But under FRS, student has limited freedom and choice as the admission to the course and the college, based on merit and social background, is decided by the admission authority (known as Convener, Admissions).

The vouchers are allowed to be claimed by the institutions which are accredited and maintaining quality, but under FRS no such conditions exist. In voucher system, the school curriculum and teaching varies from school to school depending on the teachers and management but in FRS there is uniform curriculum and teaching. Voucher system encourages efficiency, while FRS emphasizes access and equity.

FRS is aimed at influencing the demand for education, unlike others which are aimed at influencing the supply. This has created an artificial demand for the courses which otherwise would not have been demanded due to high cost and less prospects. However, though aimed at the demand side, the supply side is also not completely immune to it. In fact, it was supply rather than demand that was influenced by the FRS at the later stage.

Though FRS covers both public and private institutions, it is mainly aimed at providing access to corporate and private education.

FRS is classified as a welfare activity as it is funded and administered by the welfare departments and not by the education department. FRS is administered by various welfare departments of the Government of Andhra Pradesh. The departments implementing FRS are the Department of Social Welfare for SCs, Department of Tribal Welfare for STs, Department of Backward Classes, Welfare for BCs and Economically backward communities (EBCs), Department of Minority Welfare for minorities and the Department for Welfare of Disabled. These departments reimburse the tuition fees of the students belonging to the respective categories.

Only those students admitted under convener quota are eligible for FRS and those admitted under management quota are not eligible.

Implementation Design of FRS

The Government of Andhra Pradesh has been implementing FRS for the students admitted from the academic year 2008–2009 onwards and made available to all eligible students on a 'saturation basis' among the SC/ST/BC/EBC/minority/physically challenged communities to pursue higher studies. The scheme applies to all universities and its affiliated colleges whose admission process is regulated/administered by the designated authority. Under the saturation basis, all eligible students whose family income is less than the stipulated amount are covered under the FRS. To ensure timely sanction and disbursement of post-matric scholarships, IT&C department of the government has initiated a programme called Social Benefit Management System (SBMS) in consultation with welfare departments. One of the components of the SBMS is sanction and disbursement of post-matric scholarships electronically.

The students allotted into various courses and colleges by admission authority based on the eligibility under convener quota are eligible under FRS. After the allotment, students join in their allotted course and college; the student need to apply online on the ePass website and upload the documents required and submit a hard copy of the same to the respective welfare departments through their college principal by enclosing all necessary documents for sanction of FRS. Initially, it was done manually but subsequently was made online. The welfare departments have to verify the application of students whether the student is satisfying all the conditions.

Coverage under FRS

As stated earlier, the FRS covered all the post-matric courses and all the eligible students with no ceiling on the number or the amount. Students in all the private colleges offering general, technical and professional courses, besides public institutions, have become eligible for the FRS. However, the exact number of students who benefited from the FRS is not known as it runs into millions of students. Once admitted and satisfied the conditions, the student is eligible to get financial assistance under FRS for the entire period of the course.

With the increase in the number of students year after year, the amount required under FRS also increased. The government has to make provision for it in the budget. Therefore, the budget allocation to different welfare departments has increased. However, the budget allocations made did not match with the requirements and as a result there was always a gap between the requirement and the allocation.

In Andhra Pradesh, students from various social categories get financial assistance from the government known as post-matric scholarship, including FRS. The number getting post-matric scholarship has increased significantly after the introduction of FRS (Table 11.1). The number jumped to almost two million in 2008–2009 from 1.4 million in 2007–2008. By 2012–2013, the figure crossed 2.8 million. About 80 per cent of the students in higher education were covered by the scheme. The amount spent under FRS varied from year to year. The exact amount allocated and spent for the scheme is only an approximation, as there is a delay in the release of the funds. Initially, the scheme covered first-year students admitted during 2008–2009 and all senior students were not eligible for the scheme. Therefore, the amount required was less in the beginning. But gradually the amount required increased as the first year students entered second year along with the newly admitted students. By the year 2011–2012, all the eligible

Table 11.1 Number of Beneficiaries and the Amount under Post-matric Scholarship* in Andhra Pradesh

S. No.	Year	Amount (₹ Crores)	No. of Beneficiaries (in Lakhs)
1	1997–1998	125.00	3.99
2	1998–1999	144.90	4.25
3	1999–2000	149.73	5.03
4	2000–2001	203.72	5.21
5	2001–2002	294.05	5.84
6	2002–2003	268.48	6.12
7	2003–2004	310.07	6.97
8	2004–2005	381.31	8.25
9	2005–2006	368.09	9.67
10	2006–2007	572.88	11.47
11	2007–2008	828.01	14.09
12	2008–2009	1,615.86	19.94
13	2009–2010	2,061.45	23.82
14	2010–2011	2,931.54	25.74
15	2011–2012	3,970.59	26.23
16	2012–2013	3,748.91	28.18

Source: Ramana (2014, Table 25, p. 148).
Note: * Post-matric Scholarships include both FRS and mess charges.

students came under FRS. The amount required to cover all of them increased substantially when compared to the budget allocation. One estimate suggests that amount required increased from ₹2,000 crores to ₹5,000 crores during 2008–2013 (Rao, 2012).

It may be noted that the number of students covered under FRS started declining after 2011–2012 in Telangana (Table 11.2). This is because government started imposing restrictions and plugging the loopholes to reduce the amount. After the bifurcation, both the states have continued the FRS but the Telangana government initiated

Table 11.2 *Year-Wise Number of Students Availing Reimbursement of Tuition Fee*

Year	Telangana	Andhra Pradesh	Total
2012–2013	1,444,358	1,403,771	2,848,129
2013–2014	1,432,488	1,394,951	2,827,439
2014–2015	1,377,589	1,479,914	2,857,503
2015–2016	1,411,477	1,514,197	2,925,674
2016–2017	1,365,102	1,580,181	2,945,283
2017–2018*	1,213,083	NA	1,213,083

Source: epass.cgg.gov.in (2017).

Note: * Provisional.

measures that have restricted the misuse of funds under FRS. Hence, there is drastic reduction in the number of beneficiaries in Telangana. On the other hand, the number of beneficiaries increased in the rest of Andhra Pradesh (Table 11.2).

ADMISSION AND FEE STRUCTURE IN ENGINEERING EDUCATION

The admission to the engineering courses was made on the basis of marks secured at +2 and (intermediate) level up to the year 1981. Thereafter, it was done on the basis of marks secured in the entrance examination conducted by the universities. The students need to apply separately for university and private colleges. The admissions were made university-wise, though the entrance examination was common to all the universities. In the year 1985, the government introduced Engineering and Medical Common Entrance Test (EAMCET) for admission into engineering and medical courses simultaneously. Based on the performance in the EAMCET, students were ranked. Later weightage to the performance in the intermediate examination was given to the extent of 25 per cent in awarding the ranks.

Private colleges wanted to make their own admissions but the universities did not permit them to do so. The private managements insisted for their say in the process of admission that led to the quota system in admissions. Initially managements were given the freedom to fill 10 per cent of seats while the rest (90%) were filled by admission authority (convener quota). Subsequently, owing to pressure, the management quota kept on increasing from 10 per cent to 15 per cent to 20 per cent and finally to 30 per cent. The seats under the convener quota are filled through counselling method. While filling the seats under the management quota, the norms are rarely observed. Spot admission procedure is adopted to fill vacant seats under the convener quota. However, these students are not eligible under FRS.

The government role was in the form of regulating admission and fixation of fee. During the late 1980s, government introduced the quota system where the admissions are made under the convener quota (90%) and management quota (10%). Initially, within the convener quota the government created 50 per cent free seats and 50 per cent payment seats. The fee charged for the free seat was nominal, whereas it was more under the latter (Table 11.3). Fee under the payment seat was more than five times the fees fixed under free seat. Therefore, there was cross-subsidization of those admitted under the free quota by those admitted under the payment quota. The fee fixed under the management quota was, obviously, more than the fee charged to the payment seat. Though the capitation fee was banned, it existed in different form(s); the extent depended on the demand for the course and the college.

The free quota system was removed in 2002–2003 due to controversy over subsidization of some at the cost of others. The removal followed by increase in the management quota from 10 per cent to 15 per cent. The fee fixed under the convener quota was more than the fee charged under free seat and less than the fee for payment seat, but was less than the average. For example, in 2002–2003, the fee under the free quota was ₹8,000 and ₹43,000 for the payment seat. The average worked out to be ₹25,500. But, the common fee fixed was ₹22,000 only. This arrangement continued till 2005–2006 (for 3 years only).

The managements were not satisfied either with the fees fixed or with the management quota as these did not generate sufficient income to maintain the academic standards and make profits. The government has accepted to increase the fee from ₹22,000 to ₹26,000

Table 11.3 *Fee Structure under Convener and Management Quotas* (₹ per Annum)

| | Seats | | Fee Structure | | |
Year	Convenor Quota	Management Quota	Convener Quota Free Seat	Payment Seat	Management Seat Fee
1999–2000	90	10	5,000	35,000	60,000
2000–2001	90	10	8,000	43,000	68,000
2001–2002	90	10	8,000	43,000	68,000
2002–2003	90	10	8,000	43,000	68,000
2003–2004	85	15	The free seat category was abolished	22,000	68,000
2004–2005	85	15		22,000	75,000
2005–2006	85	15		22,000	75,000
2006–2007	80	20		26,000	79,000
2007–2008	80	20		27,500	79,000
2008–2009	80	20		30,200	91,700
2009–2010	70	30		30,200	91,700
2010–2011	70	30		30,200	95,000
2011–2012	70	30		31,000	95,000
2012–2013	70	30	Common for both convener and management quotas. The minimum and maximum fee fixed by AFRC is 35,000 and ₹120,000 depending on the cost incurred by the college		
2013–2014	70	30			
2014–2015	70	30			

Source: Information compiled from various GOs issued in various years by Andhra Pradesh government.

and management quota from 15 per cent to 20 per cent. Along with increase in the management, quota the fee fixed under this category also underwent upwards revision gradually. The student admitted under the management quota had to pay more than three times the fees fixed for the convener quota. In 2002–2003, the fee under the management quota was ₹68,000 when compared to ₹22,000 under the convener quota. There was an upward revision of fee for both categories.

The managements demanded for further increase in management quota to 50 per cent to generate sufficient income for financial viability to maintain the institutions. So, these quotas changed from 80:20 per cent to 70:30 in 2009–2010. Thus, changes in the fee and the quotas had their implications for access, equity and quality.

The Supreme Court objected to the differential fee structure for the same course and directed the government to follow a uniform fee structure. The difference between fees under the convener quota (₹31,000) and management quota (₹95,000) was very high. Therefore, from the academic year 2012–2013, there is a common fee.

After the introduction of the common fee system and FRS, the managements wanted a reduction in the management quota and increase in the convener quota. The managements are at disadvantage because of uncertainty about admissions under the former and even those admitted are not eligible under FRS. But government has not taken any decision to change the quota.

The government has constituted a committee called Admission and Fee Regulation Committee (AFRC) to fix the fee under the chairmanship of a retired high court judge. The committee fixes the fee based on certain institutional norms and once fixed, valid for three academic years. Accordingly, the fee is revised from time to time. The AFRC takes into consideration the following factors while prescribing the fee—location of the institution, nature of the course, cost of available infrastructure, expenditure on administration and maintenance, a reasonable surplus required for growth and development of the institution, revenue foregone on account of waiver of fee, if any, and any other relevant factor.

IMPACT OF FRS ON ENGINEERING EDUCATION

The introduction of the FRS has brought many developments in higher education, particularly in engineering education. Some of them are explained in this section.

Access to Engineering Education

FRS has definitely increased the access to engineering education. To get admission into technical and professional courses, the candidates have to get through the entrance tests conducted for different courses. The number of candidates appeared for the entrance test increased significantly after the introduction of FRS in 2008 (Table 11.4). It suggests that candidates aspiring to study engineering increased significantly. The increase is more significant after the introduction of FRS in 2008–2009.

Table 11.4 *Year-Wise Number of Students Appeared and Qualified in EAMCET*

S. No.	Year	No. of Students Appeared	No. of Students Qualified	% of Students Qualified
1	2002–2003	191,124	160,958	84.22
2	2003–2004	170,634	123,609	72.44
3	2004–2005	162,195	136,691	84.28
4	2005–2006	192,756	154,759	80.29
5	2006–2007	234,419	177,999	75.93
6	2007–2008	282,750	265,656	93.95
7	2008–2009	350,087	327,090	93.43
8	2009–2010	365,302	294,299	80.56
9	2010–2011	367,269	304,715	82.97
10	2011–2012	321,174	278,854	86.82
12	2013–2014	376,976	282,086	74.82
13	2014–2015 AP & TS	373,216	313,628	84.03
14	2015–2016 AP & TS	375,635	298,882	79.57
15	2016–2017 AP & TS	425,222	292,716	68.84

Source: Annual Report 2011–2012 of Andhra Pradesh State Council of Higher Education (APSCHE), Hyderabad, APSCHE & TSCHE.

But after 2011–2012, the number of students appearing for the entrance tests declined. This is because the uncertainty about the continuity of FRS prevented many aspirants from opting for courses having high tuition fees. This included engineering education.

The number of engineering colleges has increased significantly after the introduction of FRS in 2008 (Table 11.5). There were very few colleges and seats in the beginning. There were just 9 engineering

Table 11.5 Number of Engineering Colleges and Intake Capacity in Andhra Pradesh

Year	Colleges	Seats
1	2	3
1996–1997	37	10,455
1997–1998	57	14,155
1998–1999	89	19,773
1999–2000	102	25,064
2000–2001	106	30,716
2001–2002	178	46,540
2002–2003	217	62,290
2003–2004	225	65,710
2004–2005	236	78,720
2005–2006	261	92,600
2006–2007	291	98,928
2007–2008	339	125,587
2008–2009	540	175,767
2009–2010	657	225,905
2010–2011	701	269,175
2011–2012	710	306,309
2012–2013	716	339,106
2013–2014	718	340,099
2014–2015	742	357,529

Source: TSCHE (2015).

colleges with 1,140 seats in 1976–1977. At first, technical education was started in public sector only and continued till 1977–1978. For the first time in 1977–1978, engineering education was permitted in private sector to a limited extent. By the year 2002–2003, the total number of colleges had gone up to 215 and the number of seats available for children also increased to 62,270. Now, another problem has cropped in, that is, opting of admission in rural engineering colleges by the children who are seeking admission in engineering course. Even before the introduction of FRS, the growth of engineering education had been significant. However, the number of engineering colleges has more than doubled after the introduction of FRS (339 in 2007–2008 to 720 in 2013–2014). With increase in the number of colleges and additional sections in the existing colleges, number of seats also increased significantly from 199 thousands to 340 thousands during the same period. Thus, access to engineering education increased significantly (Table 11.5). Within few years, the intake capacity increased by 50,000 per year due to the introduction of FRS.

Gap between Demand and Supply

In Andhra Pradesh, technical and professional education expanded so much that in almost all the courses there are vacancies (Table 11.6). The courses which were in great demand such as MCA and MBA also lost their charm. In some courses less than half seats were filled. Needless to say, students pursuing all these courses were eligible under FRS.

The expansion of engineering education has resulted in the growing number of vacant seats. Though the vacant seats existed even a decade back, the number has gone up significantly. Except in 2008–2009, the number of vacant seats also increased significantly despite the existence of FRS, accounting for one-third of the total seats in 2013–2014. In the absence of FRS, the unfiled component would have been much more. The gap between demand and supply has reversed. Earlier the demand was more than the supply till 2000, but thereafter, supply continued to exceed demand and the gap started increasing. The expectations of the managements that FRS would boost the demand did not sustain for long. When compared to 35 per cent in

Table 11.6 *Number of Colleges, Intake and Enrolment in Professional Courses: 2011–2012*

S. No.	Course	No. of Colleges	Sanctioned Intake	Enrolment	%
1	Engineering	710	306,309	178,827	58.4
2	ME/MTech	365	23,898	16,748	70.1
3	BPharm	283	27,740	22,495	81.1
4	MBA	958	93,231	57,488	61.7
5	MCA	625	44,530	13,965	31.4
6	MPharm	225	9,207	7,437	80.7
7	BEd	609	65,018	63,141	97.1
8	BArch	10	925	794	85.8
9	BPed	10	760	745	98.0
10	UG DPed	07	665	479	72.0
11	LLM	19	781	720	92.2
12	3LLB	50	7,150	4,285	59.9
13	5LLB		2,940	2,500	85.0

Source: APSCHE (2015).

2003–2004, only 5 per cent of the colleges in 2014–2015 could fill up all the seats in all the branches. If all those excluded colleges were included, the proportion would have been much less than 5 per cent.

When compared to the management quota, the percentage of seats filled is more in the convener quota (Table 11.7). It is expected as the FRS is applicable to those admitted under the former than the later. The percentage of seats filled increased in the year the FRS was introduced. But within two years, the seats filled stated declining both absolute and percentage terms.

For viability of the college, the number of seats filled should be as maximum as possible. In more than 100 colleges, the number of seats filled was less 50 in 2011–2012. About one-third of the colleges were unviable due to few admissions (Gosavi, 2013).

Table 11.7 *Number of Seats and Seats Filled under Convener and Management Quotas*

Year	Total Seats	Convener Quota Seats	Seats Filled	Surplus Seats	% Seats Filled in the Total Seats	% Seats Filled in the Convener Seats
Year-Wise Engineering Convener Quota Seats Filled and Vacant in AP						
1996–1997	9,608	8,762	8,762	0	91.19	100.00
1997–1998	14,278	12,796	12,796	0	89.62	100.00
1998–1999	20,943	18,742	16,868	1,874	80.54	90.00
1999–2000	26,246	23,310	20,690	2,620	78.83	88.76
2000–2001	31,926	27,037	24,364	2,673	76.31	90.11
2001–2002	48,307	40,283	39,049	1,234	80.84	96.94
2002–2003	64,412	52,668	51,205	1,463	79.50	97.22
2003–2004	67,590	49,891	46,668	3,223	69.05	93.54
2004–2005	82,430	64,731	50,814	13,917	61.65	78.50
2005–2006	97,450	70,792	56,866	14,432	58.35	80.33
2006–2007	104,525	67,653	61,510	6,649	58.85	90.92
2007–2008	133,912	107,130	96,324	10,806	71.93	89.91
2008–2009	192,247	144,186	129,362	6,671	67.29	89.72
2009–2010	229,560	160,693	148,720	11,973	64.78	92.55
2010–2011	262,221	185,160	144,887	40,273	55.25	78.25
2011–2012	292,616	206,207	129,897	76,310	44.39	62.99
2012–2013	340,000	234,765	134,373	100,392	39.52	57.24
2013–2014	340,099	238,069	126,862	111,207	37.30	53.29
2014–2015*	357,329	250,130	188,665	61,465	52.80	75.43
2015–2016*	283,542	198,480	124,611	73,869	43.95	62.78
2016–2017*	214,077	149,855	126,987	22,868	59.32	84.74

Source: APCHE, TSCHE and Daily News Papers (*Eenadu*, 2014).

Note: * Unpublished data collected from State Council of Higher Education of two states (Telangana and Andhra Pradesh).

Over a period of time, the position of the colleges has further worsened. The vacancy position has increased. For example, in 2003–2004, there was no vacancy in as many as 35 per cent of colleges. But by 2014–2015, only 5 per cent of the colleges got full strength. More than 100 seats were vacant in only 4.5 per cent of colleges in 2003–2004 but by 2014–2015 in almost 30 per cent of the colleges the number of vacant seats were more than 100. In few colleges, not a single admission took place (*Eenadu*, 2014).

The vacancy position is not the same for all branches of engineering. When compared to 2003, the percentage of seats filled had gone down drastically. There was hardly any vacancy in courses such as Electronics and Communication Engineering (ECE), Civil and Mechanical Branches in 2003. At present, these branches are also facing the vacancy problem (Table 11.8).

After the introduction of FRS, the number of seats in CSE and ECE increased significantly as they are more in demand than others. The increase is due to increase in the number of colleges and sections in the existing colleges. However, the number of seats available and filled declined in the last few years. This is true not only in technical and professional education but also in general higher education. For example, in the state of Telangana more than half of the seats in UG courses have remained vacant due to strict implementation of FRS (Table 11.9).

Equity in Engineering Education

The introduction of FRS has increased the educational opportunities to various sections, particularly in reputed private institutions. The tuition fees charged by them were beyond the paying capacity of the poor. Now, they could get access to it. In this respect social and economic equity is ensured by FRS.

However, the accessibility to quality engineering education to poor socio–economic groups is also not guaranteed by FRS. The admission is based on the candidates' performance in EAMCET. If the candidate gets a good rank, he/she has choice of choosing the course and the college.

Table 11.8 Course and Year-Wise Total Number of Seats and Seats Filled in Engineering Education in Andhra Pradesh

Course	2003			2008	2012			2015
	Total Seats	Seats Filled	% Filled	Seats Filled	Total Seats	Seats Filled	% Filled	Seats Filled
CSE	11,186	9,691	86.64	54,985	52,153	27,705	53.12	39,863
IT	7,526	4,417	58.69	29,330	17,338	6,212	35.83	4,342
ECE	11,359	11,342	99.85	62,570	61,135	38,912	63.65	38,926
EEE	8,867	8,720	98.34	37,755	34,797	18,433	52.97	18,539
Mech	4,201	4,160	99.02	18,285	31,879	22,541	70.71	22,904
Civil	1,220	1,217	99.75	–	22,613	15,184	67.15	19,360

Source: Information compiled from various sources.

Note: CSE = Computer Science and Engineering; EEE: Electronics and Electrical Engineering; Mech: Mechanical Engineering.

Table 11.9 *UG Courses in Telangana*

University	No. of Seats	Seats Filled	Seats Vacant	No. of Colleges
All	410,267	195,731	214,536 (52.3%)	1,092
Government	50,199	21,396	28,803 (57.4%)	122
Private	322,250	145,360	167,022 (51.8%)	992

Source: Eenadu (2017).

To get a good rank, a candidate has to spend a good amount of money as well as time to prepare for the test. For the poor students, it is beyond their paying capacity. A poor student with good rank may benefit from the present system, but this rarely happens. Most of the students studying in reputed private engineering colleges come from families where parents have better education and economic background. Wards of businessmen and professionals followed this as they can get seats under management quota. Almost all students came from high-income background that is income more than 1 lakh (DFID, 2001). Now, the poor student with not so good rank either opts for a low-quality engineering college or borrow money to get admission under the management quota in a high-quality engineering college.

It is the access to good coaching institutes that decides the rank and then the course and the college. Needless to say, paying capacity is still the main criterion for admission into such institutes. Under these circumstances, the expansion of engineering education does not guarantee equity in the long run.

Regional distribution of engineering colleges suggests that they are highly concentrated in certain districts and FRS has not helped in reducing the concentration. Rather, it has widened it to a certain extent. The number of colleges increased in almost all the districts. But the increase is more in certain districts. In absolute terms, the number of colleges are more in developed districts or districts closer to the cities. For example,

Ranga Reddy district, surrounding the capital, has the highest number of colleges exceeding the number in the entire Rayalaseema region. On the other hand, in districts like Adilabad and Srikakulam, there are very few colleges because they are far away from the capital city and backward (APSCHE).

If we look at the distribution of engineering colleges among the regions such as Coastal Andhra, Telangana and Rayalaseema, it is not equal. According to Census 2011, the proportion of distribution of engineering colleges, according to the population, is supposed to be 41.7 per cent, 40.5 per cent and 17.8 per cent, but the actual distribution is 33 per cent, 55 per cent and 12 per cent, respectively. Unlike in many other indicators, the share of Telangana is more.

When engineering colleges are opened in every district and all the rural areas have become more accessible to all students, this appears to be impressive on the face of it. It may be noted that there is no reservation for the local (district level) students. The choice of the course and then college are the important considerations and location of the college is hardly taken into consideration. Therefore, we can find many students of other areas and not the local area studying in any college. The distance is a matter of concern in school education but it is hardly important in higher education, that too in engineering education. Local students hardly prefer the college located in the vicinity unless the quality is good and the course of their choice is available. FRS has in fact discouraged the local students from opting for nearby colleges unless they ensure quality. When an industry is opened in backward areas, it is likely to be developed due to externalities in terms of providing employment opportunities and using local resources. But this may not be so when a college is opened in such areas. It may be mentioned that in some cases, both faculty and students commute every day from nearby city/town to attend the college located in backward areas. Both students and teachers commute from nearby town/city every day. Majority of students and faculty from engineering colleges in Ranga Reddy district commute from Hyderabad which is also causing traffic, pollution and road-safety problems in the city. Only for getting permission or some concession, the college is opened in remote areas and not with the intention of providing education to local students.

Quality of Engineering Education

One of the main problems faced by the education system is the quality. In whatever terms the quality is defined, the present status of engineering education is far from satisfactory. For ensuring quality, a college should fulfil minimum requirements such as buildings, classrooms, equipment and laboratory and well-trained and committed faculty. Only few colleges have all of them in place and majority lack one or the other facility.

In Andhra Pradesh, deterioration of quality in engineering education has fastened, particularly after the introduction of FRS. Though the deterioration of quality had started much before the FRS, it reached a stage where majority of the products have remained unemployable.

The most important and genuine problem for many colleges is getting the well-qualified faculty. If many colleges are opened in a given year, it is very difficult to get engineering postgraduates or doctorates to work as faculty. As such there are very few institutes offering engineering education at PG and PhD levels. According to the Academic Audit Report (2011–2012), the total requirement of faculty for 31 colleges (started before 1996) is 3,620 out of which only 1,754 faculty members are available. The number of professors available is 341 against 451, associate professors 438 against 952 and assistant professors 1,334 against 2,217. About half of the faculty positions are vacant.

The faculty strength of colleges started after 1996 is even less. Moreover, prospects of getting better jobs in the industry or service sector in India or abroad are more for them and hence, preference for teaching jobs is less. Since many of them are located away from the towns/cities, this also makes the otherwise qualified candidates to opt out of teaching jobs. Added to this, some colleges are not willing to pay the salaries suggested by the AICTE. Working conditions in some of the colleges are not satisfactory. Sometimes, control of the management over the staff also forces some of them to leave the college in the middle of the academic year. Therefore, conditions of security and job promotions are important in retaining and attracting the faculty. As far as the infrastructure is concerned, many colleges have their own buildings and laboratories but many lack proper maintenance and use, again, partly due to lack of manpower. All these lead to deterioration in the quality of engineering education.

As per the conditions, each engineering branch faculty–student ratio is 1:15 for UG courses and 1:12 for PG courses. For each department, there should be one professor, four associate professors and six assistant professors. Hardly any college satisfies these norms. According to the Task Force Committee Report (2012; it was constituted by the government to assess the facilities available in the engineering colleges as per AICTE norms; GoA, 2012), the teacher–pupil ratio was 1:28 and many of the teachers are underqualified. Further, many colleges are engaging graduates, whereas postgraduation is required. In some colleges, the faculty exists only on record. Of the 163 colleges inspected by Expert Committee, as many as 143 do not satisfy the AICTE norms laid down by the AICTE (*Eenadu*, 2015).

FRS, instead of improving the quality, has added to its deterioration. First, the tuition fee fixed by the government is not sufficient to ensure quality unless all the seats are filled. Second, even this fee is not reimbursed on time and there is inordinate delay. Even last year dues are not paid. Needless to say, many colleges are depending on income from FRS. Though the FRS has increased access to engineering education but majority of them have access to low-quality education, thus indirectly, contributing to inequality, in the long run.

In engineering education, student attendance is necessary to learn the subject skills. A student has to put in minimum 75 percentage of attendance to be eligible under FRS. It is the responsibility of college management to ensure it. Since, more than 90 per cent of colleges are in private sector and their survival is linked to FRS, obviously many colleges have ensured attendance on paper whether a student actually attended or not. Lack of proper monitoring of attendance is an important reason for the low quality of the graduates.

FRS guidelines are silent on the performance of the students which helped managements. According to the Task Force Committee Report (2012), only in 3 per cent of the colleges, the pass rate is 80 to 90 per cent and in the remaining colleges covered by FRS, the pass rate is 20 to 30 per cent only.

It is presumed that employment opportunities are brighter for engineering graduates than general graduates. It is true that unemployment is less among the former than among the latter. It may be noted that many engineering graduates are working for meagre wages. The prospects of bright future of IT graduates have become bleak with the slump in the global market. Further, the employment depends on the availability of other facilities for investment to establish factories and other establishments. The state has experienced the closure of many industrial units, including some from the public sector. The out turn from the colleges is several times the requirement and hence only those with better grades and communication skills are absorbed in the newly emerged IT sector.

FRS has led to unethical practices like some management recruiting agents to get the students. The colleges with poor infrastructure and staff, mainly located in rural areas, have indulged in these practices such as advertisement with tall claims and luring students by offering sops such as free transport and hostel facility and laptops.

FRS has created imbalances within higher education. The component of technical and professional education has increased, while the general higher education declined. FRS has indirectly encouraged many to opt for expensive courses such as engineering and management. Further, within technical and professional education, the higher (undergrauate and PG) levels increased while the lower levels (polytechnic and ITIs) have not increased much. This is contrary to the requirement in the job market where more polytechnic and ITIs than engineering graduates are needed.

The financial burden on state government has increased from about ₹1,600 crores in 2008–2009 to about ₹5,000 crores by 2013–2014. On the other side, engineering graduates benefited under FRS have remained unemployed, indicating the waste of financial resources.

PROBLEMS IN THE IMPLEMENTATION OF FRS

Initially the implementation was successful. But within no time FRS started facing problems. There are some in-built deficiencies in the design of FRS, some of which include the following.

At first, FRS was intended to financially support the BCs but subsequently extended to other sections whose parents' annual incomes are less than the prescribed amount. Many of the students could manage to get prescribed income limit certificate and were covered under FRS. Second, the fee reimbursement implies that the student has to pay the fee to the institution first and the same has to be reimbursed by the government to the student. But contrary to this, the government is giving assurance to the education institution that the tuition fee of all those eligible students will be reimbursed. This has created an artificial demand for the courses which otherwise would not have been demanded due to high cost. Third, the admission to professional, technical and other courses has two categories, that is, government quota and management quota. The government quota seats are filled by the admission authority created for the purpose and cover under FRS as per eligibility, whereas management quota seats are filled by the managements as per the government rules but are not covered under FRS. But the managements are managing the universities through lobbing, political pressure or corruption to consider the students admitted under the management quota as government quota. Once it is approved, all these eligible students are also covered under FRS. Consequently, the financial burden on state government has increased.

Fourth, the FRS is implemented on an exhaustive mode which means that every student who applied for FRS has to be sanctioned as per the eligibility. By taking this as an advantage, the managements have admitted the students who are not able to attend the college. The private managements are identifying such students and admitting them in their colleges. In the process, competition between the private managements has increased to admit such students in their college by offering incentives (mobile phones, cash and so on) to the students. If such students are admitted, there is no burden on the management to provide additional facilities related to teaching, accommodation, library, laboratory, drinking water, toilets and the likes. Even if the management spends one year fee income to offer incentive to students, the management will have two or more year's fee income with them. With this, corruption has increased for sanction of FRS.

After the bifurcation of the state, the new governments in two states (Telangana and Andhra Pradesh) are taking several measures to reduce the financial burden of the FRS as it is not producing expected results. The Telangana government is imposing new conditions such as prescribing age limit, that is, 34 years as the maximum age to receive FRS, one professional course or PG course but not both, insisting for biometric attendance for students and staff, and CC cameras at each institution and these linked to the affiliating universities to monitor. The Telangana government has constituted a task force with officials from police and revenue departments. They have inspected colleges and submitted report to government on availability of facilities in the colleges. Only after verification, the colleges are admitted under FRS. The UG courses admissions made through Degree Online Services Telangana (DOST) minimize the fictitious admissions and thereby reduce financial burden under FRS. As a result, there was significant reduction in the number of students at UG level. During the academic year 2017–2018, alone out of the 4.2 lakhs seats about 52 per cent have remained vacant at UG level. The Andhra Pradesh government department of higher education reportedly issued a circular to the engineering colleges asking to introduce skill development courses with a duration of two months for the UG BTech students. The circular asked the colleges to enrol students in the courses in civil, mechanical and computer sciences courses on payment of ₹2,000 each as admission fee. The move intends to equip the engineering students with job skills. About one-third of the colleges which do not satisfy the conditions and also due to lack of sufficient demand have either reduced the intake or closed. The political party that introduced the FRS is not in power in both the states. The two parties in power TRS in Telangana state and TDP in Andhra Pradesh do not want to continue it in the same form due to financial burden. At the same time, they cannot discontinue it owing to political compulsions.

CONCLUSION

Whether the main purpose of the FRS is achieved or not can be viewed both from students, private and social angles. Within private also, one has to examine both from the students and management angle.

From the student angle, in the narrow sense, FRS has benefited those who could not have entered into the portals of technical education. All most all categories of students SC, ST, BC, EBC, minority and disabled have access to technical education. Therefore, FRS has helped to increase the access and equity. It may be noted that, majority of them got access to low-quality education and these low-quality graduates are remaining as unemployed or underemployed.

The FRS has benefited those who could not enter into the portal of technical education but majority of them got low-quality education and have remained unemployed/underemployed.

From the management angle, many seats are filled in most of the private colleges under FRS. Otherwise many colleges would have become defunct. They have also benefited from FRS by increasing the intake capacity and admission quotas. It was done by the managements by following it with government in changing of admission quotas and fee structure and also inclusion of different categories of students under FRS.

But the college managements are benefitted from FRS by way of filling up of seats, increasing the intake capacity, changing of admission quotas and fee structure.

From the social angle, the state could produce more number of engineering graduates from all categories (SC, ST, BC, EBC and Minority). But in the process, unemployment and underemployment has increased.

Educationist late J. P. Naik remarked that there is an elusive triangle in the Indian education system. The triangle he was mentioning related to quantity, quality and equity. Generally, quantity is supposed to ensure equity as did happen in the case of India to some extent, but had an adverse effect on quality. In the case of technical education in Andhra Pradesh, both equity and quality are affected due to quantity.

FRS, though good, is a poorly designed and implemented intervention. Poorly designed interventions may reduce the overall welfare if they result in wasted resources or education that does not best meet the needs of students, institutions and the society.

In Andhra Pradesh, the higher education system in terms of quality and equity in technical education has suffered rather than benefitting from FRS. The quality and equity in technical education. FRS, though good, is poorly designed and implemented and resulted in reduction of welfare of the society by wastage of precarious financial resources as they did not meet the needs of students, institutions and the society.

The government has to establish the educational institutions to provide quality education for educationally and socially disadvantaged students. If it is not possible, FRS has to be continued by rigorously implementing conditions which include ensuring minimum 75 per cent attendance by introducing biometric machines with CC cameras directly linking to monitoring agency, ensuring minimum performance of students in each academic year, ensuring that all the institutions maintain academic standards to be made eligible for FRS, and serious punishments have to be awarded to those (institutions, officials and students) involved in unethical practices to claim funds under FRS.

REFERENCES

APSCHE. (2015). *APSCHE statistical booklet, Andhra Pradesh*. Hyderabad: Andhra Pradesh State Council of Higher Education.

DFID. (2001). *Andhra Pradesh impact and expenditure review higher education sector*. Hyderabad: Government of Andhra Pradesh.

Eenadu. (2014, September 3). Retrieved from http://epaper.eenadu.net/

———. (2015, February 1). Retrieved from http://epaper.eenadu.net/

———. (2017, August 1). Retrieved from http://epaper.eenadu.net/

ePass. (2017). Retrieved from https://telanganaepass.cgg.gov.in.

Epple, D., Romano, E. R., & Urquiola, M. (2017). School vouchers: A survey of the economics literature. *Journal of Economic Literature*. Retrieved from http://doi.org/10.1257/jel.20150679

Government of Andhra Pradesh (GoA). (2012). Report of the Task Force on availability of facilities in engineering colleges as per the AICTE norms.

Gosavi. (2013). Threat of vacant seats in engineering colleges: Reasons and remedies. *American International Journal of Research in Humanities, Arts and Social Science, 2*(1), 75–80. Retrieved from http://www.iasir.net

Ramana, V. C. (2014). *Higher education subsidies in India: A study of fee reimbursement scheme in Andhra Pradesh* (PhD Thesis). Hyderabad: University of Hyderabad.

Rao, S. A. (2012, August 3). YSR's fee reimbursement scheme hangs in limbo in Andhra Pradesh. *India Today*. Retrieved from https://www.indiatoday.in/india/south/story/ys-rajasekhara-reddy-fee-reimbursement-scheme-in-andhra-pradesh-112223-2012-03-03

TSCHE. (2015). *Tsche stastical booklet*. Masab Tank, Hyderabad: Telangana State Council of Higher Education.

PART IV

Private Higher Education

Chapter 12

Growth and Expansion of Private Higher Education

M. Muzammil

INTRODUCTION

The participation of private sector in higher education has accelerated the pace and changing composition of its development. However, the system remains publicly controlled through government rules and regulations and largely state funded. Over the last three decades, the presence of private institutions and private participation in higher education has rapidly increased in various ways. Private organizations are also helping in creation of knowledge, skill development and national advancement. Of the 799 universities in the country, as per All India Survey of Higher Education (AISHE) 2015–2016 data, 277 universities are classified as private universities. Many stand-alone institutions in the country are also privately managed.

It is due to private efforts that college density (number of colleges per lakh of population in the age group of 18–23) has gone up to 28 in the country. However, it varies from 7 in Bihar to 60 in Telangana and 26 in UP. According AISHE in 2013, average national enrolment per college comes to about 707 and 1,024 in UP. At the national level of the total enrolment in higher education, private unaided colleges accounts for 38 per cent and aided colleges for another 23 per cent (Table 12.1). Thus, private colleges account for about 61 per cent enrolment of the total. Consequently, government colleges' enrolment has come down to 39 per cent. So far, as the management-wise composition of colleges is concerned, unaided colleges in India account for 58 per cent of the total colleges, aided colleges 15 per cent and the government colleges 27 per cent.

Private colleges are now coming up in every region of the country. But the colleges are mainly concentrated in urban or semi-urban areas and are less flourishing in remote villages. In fact, top-class private institutions are concentrated in metros and urban agglomerations only. Government degree colleges are left to serve the rural population in backward and unserved areas of the country. The first section of the chapter gives a genesis of the evolution in private higher education in India. The second section elaborates about the course-wise classification of private higher education and modes of participation of the private sector. The quality, regulation and governance of private sector are discussed in the subsequent section. And the final section of the chapter gives some future prospects and implications for the Government of India (GoI).

Table 12.1 *Management-Wise Composition of Colleges and Enrolments*

Type of Management	Colleges (%)	Enrolments (%)
(1)	(2)	(3)
Private unaided	64 (58)	38
Private aided	14 (15)	23
Government	22 (27)	39
Total	100	100

Source: AISHE report of 2015–2016 (AISHE, 2016).

Note: Figures in brackets and figures in Col (3) are for the year 2012–2013 (AISHE, 2013).

EVOLUTION OF PRIVATE HIGHER EDUCATION

In ancient India, Takshashila University was the first university of the country established around 700 BC and the second was the Nalanda University in the 4th century BC. The prevailing spectrum of knowledge was comprised of Veda and philosophy, Samkhya, Yoga Shastra, medicine, astronomy and Buddhist literature. Nalanda University fascinated scholars from countries such as China, Japan, Korea, Indonesia, Turkey, Persia and other parts of the world.

The development of universities and colleges through private efforts on philanthropic basis gained momentum in the 20th century. Banaras Hindu University and Aligarh Muslim University in North India and Osmania University and Mysore University established by the princely states in the South are early examples of the beginning of private higher education. These institutions are still noteworthy. In those days, joint efforts of missionaries, people and the government gave fillip to higher education. The CMS College Kottayam founded by the Church Missionary Society of England in 1817 is said to be the first college of India.

Pre-reform Period

Development of private higher education was slow in the decade of the 1950s. The Kothari Commission (1964–1966) observed that private colleges formed the vast bulk of affiliated colleges and they were properly directed and given adequate assistance and thus the general standards in higher education exhibited improvement. The government policy to a great extent, therefore, did not discriminate between government and aided colleges from the view point of control and grants-in-aid. Following the Kothari Commission recommendation, this policy was replaced in many cases by a discriminatory pattern under which the really good institutions were given greater freedom and more liberal assistance while a firm policy of direction was adopted towards weaker institutions which did not deserve larger grants because they failed to make any attempt at self-improvement.

The government provided recurring grants to colleges to meet both the salary and other costs. This was very helpful for private colleges and these expanded significantly in the decades of the 1960s and 1970s. Management's contribution was also important in that period in running the aided colleges affiliated to universities. The management of aided colleges contributed to nonrecurring expenditure as different from the contribution of fees realized from students.

Since the mid-1980s, the policy of the government started showing a shift in the sense that government recognition was given to colleges without any financial obligation. Earlier, private institutions of higher education were largely funded by government in most of the states in India. The funding was given in the form of grants-in-aid. In the post-reform period, 'recognition' was given by government 'without any financial grant'. These were called unaided colleges or self-financed institutions.

Post-reform Period

The policy of 'recognition without grant' became lenient after economic reforms and number of unaided colleges expanded rapidly all over the country. Since the mid-1990s, mushroom growth started as green signals were given easily by the government to open private colleges/universities with enabling statutory provisions having been put in place. This was the outcome of government having refused to take any further institution on the grants-in-aid list. Thus, the self-financed private colleges became the mainstay for expanding higher education.

Consequently, enrolments increased. According to NSSO survey 71st round (2014), the enrolment in private unaided institutions has gone up to 30 per cent of the total in rural areas and 34 per cent in urban areas of the country. In South India, however, enrolment in private unaided institutions has exceeded 50 per cent of the total both in rural and urban areas. In the Northeast, the dependence on unaided institutions of higher education is the lowest (only 10% in rural and 18% in urban areas). The number of private universities in that region, however, is substantially higher.

INCREASING DEMAND FOR HIGHER EDUCATION

One of the reasons of increasing demand for higher education is that most of the pass-outs of secondary education look for higher education as if until they complete higher education their job opportunities would not open. Keeping in mind the relatively low gross enrolment ratio (GER) in higher education in the country and more so in poorer states, one can expect further increases of the new entrants into the system.

University degree is a symbol of social dignity for the youths. The value of education has led the parents to send their wards to colleges and specialized institutions. Owing to social awakening, parents are looking for new professional courses for their children. A graduation degree seems to be a must for any type of job with social recognition. Fee waiver facilities by government (for certain groups) are encouraging students' admissions because their cost in joining higher education is virtually zero. Expansion of colleges in remote areas and out of the way places also helps in attracting more students for admission.

Of late, girls' enrolment has increased rapidly. Rising urbanization has added to it. With increasing scientific temperament, the ability of the young boys and girls is increasing and naturally it is pushing up their demand for higher education. Many specialized courses often motivate the students from secondary level to go to higher education. Rich family backgrounds and employment prospects have always been pushing the demand for higher education of various types. Larger enrolments, however, affect the quality of education. The efficiency of delivery of education is also weakened. That is why some developing countries (like Tanzania) have stopped increasing enrolments in higher education for quality concerns (Ligami, 2017).

There was no private university before the Economic Reforms of 1991. The liberalization of the economy witnessed, inter alia, the entry of private universities. The Manipal Academy of Higher Education was the first institution that was accorded the status of a deemed university in 1993 and it became the first private university of India in the form of Sikkim Manipal University notified in 1995. Private universities in India are regulated by the University Grants Commission (UGC) through its (Establishment and Maintenance of Standards in Private

Universities) Regulations, 2003. Private universities grew rapidly over the last quarter of a century. Now, as per the list of the UGC, the number of private universities has gone up to 269 and the AISHE, 2016 puts the number at 277 in the country (Table 12.2).

Despite many private universities, private colleges dominate the sector of higher education. The spread has not been uniform across the country. There are other modes of participation of private sector in higher education, for example, by sponsoring courses (general and professional), collaborations and marketing (branding), earmarked financial support for creating infrastructure, special endowments and donations for specific purposes. Many private firms allow students of government institutions and the aided ones to gain practical experience and do the apprenticeship with them free of charge or at nominal rates.

GROWTH OF PRIVATE UNIVERSITIES, COLLEGES AND ENROLMENTS

Although private universities in India formally started from 1995, most of them were opened in the last 10 years. State-wise account is given further. In Arunachal Pradesh, three private universities were established in 2012 including a private open university (Venkateshwara Open University, Itanagar). It enjoys the status of being the only private open university of the country even in 2017. The other two universities were established in Namsai and Ziro. Likewise, the first private university in Assam was established in 2009 (Assam Don Bosco University, Guwahati). The first private university in Chhattisgarh was set up in 2002 at Bilaspur (Maharishi University of Management and Technology). Nirma University is the oldest private university in Gujarat which was set up in 2003. Jaypee University of Information Technology in Solan is the oldest in Himachal Pradesh established in 2002. Of the total of eight private universities in Jharkhand, the ICFAI University, Ranchi, is the oldest established in 2008 in that state.

Alliance University of Bangalore in the oldest established in 2010 in Karnataka which is having a total of 13 private universities in all. Of the eight universities in Meghalaya, two universities (Martin Luther and

Table 12.2 *Number of Private Universities in India: State-Wise*

State	Number
Arunachal Pradesh	07
Assam	05
Chhattisgarh	09
Gujarat	30
Haryana	20
Himachal Pradesh	17
Jharkhand	07
Karnataka	13
Meghalaya	08
Mizoram	01
Madhya Pradesh	24
Maharashtra	06
Manipur	01
Nagaland	03
Odisha	04
Punjab	15
Rajasthan	44
Sikkim	05
Tripura	01
Uttar Pradesh	29
Uttarakhand	11
West Bengal	09
Total	269

Source: UGC (2017; data as on 29 June 2017).

Note: The AISHE 2015–2016 gives the figure of 277 private universities in India, whereas the list of private universities provided by the UGC puts the number at 269.

William Carey) in Shillong were enacted simultaneously in 2005. The only private university in the state of Mizoram came up in Aizawl in 2006. In the state of Madhya Pradesh, there are as many as 24 private universities, the oldest among these being Maharishi Mahesh Yogi Vedic Vishwavidyalaya in Jabalpur which was established in 1995.

The state of Maharashtra has six private universities and all were established in last three years. The state of Manipur has only one private university which was established recently. Nagaland has three private universities and Odisha has four, and all these are of recent origin. Punjab has 15 private universities and the oldest (Lovely Professional University, Jalandhar) being of 2005. In Rajasthan, there are as many as 44 private universities and of these, the first one was enacted in 2008. Uttar Pradesh has a large number of private universities among the states in India. Of the 29 private universities in UP, JR Handicapped University, Chitrakoot, is the oldest established in 2001. The state of Uttarakhand has 11 universities, the oldest being Dev Sanskrit University of 2002 in Hardwar. In West Bengal, there are nine private universities and Techno India University in Kolkata is the oldest one established in 2012.

India is a large federal country with many of states having their own social and cultural identity and different levels of development. The number of state private universities differs widely from state to state. Of the 269 private universities in the country, 44 (about 16%) are located in the state of Rajasthan alone. Despite similar school education performance in Kerala and Himachal Pradesh, Kerala has no private university and in Himachal Pradesh there are 17 private universities. Even in many educationally backward states (such as Odisha and Chhattisgarh), the growth of private universities has been spectacular.

COMPOSITION OF COLLEGES: AIDED AND SELF-FINANCED

Now private colleges are offering various types of modern courses. The AICTE also approves diploma granting colleges along with the provision of online higher education. Many private institutions as stand-alone institutions have also been established in some states of India. Many private colleges command great academic prestige and

Table 12.3 *Growth of State Private Universities in India*

Year	No. of Private Universities
2010–2011	87
2011–2012	105
2012–2013	122
2013–2014	153
2014–2015	181
2015–2016	197

Source: AISHE (2016).

social recognition. Their name carries value. They are spread over in every part of the country and offer a variety of traditional and contemporary courses of study.

From 2010–2011 to 2015–2016 (Table 12.3), the number of private universities have grown by 126 per cent as against only 17 per cent growth in the number of state (government) universities. Another important feature is that a large number of private colleges are small units. Some 40 per cent of colleges in India run only a single programme of study and out of which 75 per cent are private self-financed colleges. Among these, about 30 per cent colleges run only BEd course.

COURSE-WISE CLASSIFICATION OF PRIVATE INSTITUTIONS

Government colleges and government aided colleges are generally providing what is called 'general' education, while the 'professional' courses are largely run by private colleges. One of the reasons is that the fee rates are usually very high in 'professional courses' which make these courses more viable to be run on self-financed basis and secondly, the new social class is demanding more of this type of specialized higher education than continuing with conventional learning.

Specialized private institutions provide engineering, pharmacy, hotel management, architecture, computer application, management, medicine, dentistry, physiotherapy, unani, ayurvedic and homeopathic colleges, paramedical, veterinary, physiotherapy and clinical research. Besides, teacher education institutions and physical education colleges have already been established in large number. But these institutions are not evenly distributed across the country.

Private institutions of higher education also provide learning in new courses such as office administration and professional development, beautician, electrician and mechanics and training of various types catering to the civil and defence sector requirements. With increasing role of mass media and social media in the life of people, institutions have strengthened the existing courses and started innovative programmes related with journalism and mass communication, photography and cinematography, screen writing, film-making and direction, public relations and advertising, sound engineering, acting and modelling, anchoring and presenting, video and audio editing, music composition and production, media and entertainment, and so on.

Private engineering colleges are offering various courses such as computer science and technology, electronics and communication engineering (ECE), electrical engineering, mechanical engineering, civil engineering and environmental engineering, chemical engineering, biotechnology, genetic engineering and aeronautical and aerospace engineering, and mechatronics (technology combining electronics and mechanical engineering). Management education now includes colleges and institutes in the private sector that are offering these courses: general management, HRM, financial and banking services management, corporate management, marketing (branding and advertisement) management, logistics, operations and supply chain management, family business and entrepreneurship management, agri-business and rural management, travel and tourism management, medical and hospital management, event management, media management, food production and catering management.

Private colleges offering design courses have recently been set up in large numbers. They are offering courses such as textile apparel, fashion design, visual merchandizing, fashion communication and styling, fashion technology, industrial design and product design, animation, multimedia and web designing, VFX and visual effect courses, game design and development, fashion and lifestyle business, luxury brands, media and entertainment business, and so on. With increasing air transport facilities, demand for air travel related courses have risen and consequently many intuitions have come up in the private sector that cater to the latest requirement. The courses that have become popular quickly are related with cabin crew and air hostess training, airport management, ticketing and pilot training programmes. Recognizing the value of these courses, the GoI has also set up a central university (Rajiv Gandhi National Aviation University) at Raebareli in UP.

For providing new medical education, besides the traditional medical courses such as MBBS, MD and MS, various streams at graduate and PG level and DM in cardiology and other subjects, private colleges are now offering innovative medical courses on neurosurgery and clinical genetics. In the stream of arts and social sciences, new courses like that in counselling psychology and fashion designing are also being offered in many private colleges.

MODES OF THE PARTICIPATION OF PRIVATE SECTOR

The participation of private sector comes through opening new universities and additional colleges and opening study centres in the existing institutions and sometimes through sponsoring courses. The most important form of participation of the private sector is through setting up of new institutions and it has resulted in increasing the GER of higher education in the country which is now quoted at 24.5 per cent of the higher education age group (18–23) by the AISHE 2015–2016. Many private institutions which are globally renowned have created what can be called state-of-the-art infrastructure in higher education which was not easy to be produced in government institutions. Private participation in higher education has helped in creation of capacity and competence.

Private sector has opened up new routes of collaboration with industries of various types and the sunrise industries, in particular, both in India and abroad. It has also opened up new pathways to international institutional collaborations involving foreign higher educational institutions in joining hands with Indian providers of high education

(Shankar, 2016). The private sector has helped in modernization of education and in rebuilding library facilities. They have adequately revised and updated the curricula of higher education. They have also provided better equipped libraries and online reading room facilities including creation of e-library capacity providing e-books and networking facilities for students.

PRIVATE DISTANCE HIGHER EDUCATION

Open and distance learning is now considered as an effective mode of providing higher education. It has increased access to education and helped in training and developing skills and capacity building. Many private universities in different states have been approved by the UGC to run distance programmes of learning through their distance education centres. Sikkim Manipal University started its distance education scheme in 2001 and is now offering even MSc in distance mode.

The only private open university of the country is located in the state of Arunachal Pradesh (the Venkateshwara Open University, Itanagar) which was established in 2012. It still enjoys the status of being the only private open university of the country.

A few private universities have also opened their campuses abroad. Some private universities have entered into international academic collaborations. Increasing globalization of Indian economy is witnessing increased global partnerships in higher education (Muzammil, 2010). Apart from public private partnership, private–private collaboration, marketing and brand building are coming up and gaining importance.

QUALITY OF PRIVATE HIGHER EDUCATION

The quality and excellence in private universities, aided and self-financed colleges is very debatable. There are evidences to suggest that private institutions are producing good quality education and there are contrary claims as well. Many private universities are widely known for their quality of teaching and output of well-qualified students, but larger number of private colleges in states such as Uttar Pradesh and

Bihar are exhibiting very poor quality of education (Muzammil, 2015). Naturally, they are often run down and subjected to sharp criticism by stakeholders.

Commenting on the overall status and quality in private higher education, the Draft Education Policy 2016 rightly observes:

> The quality of education provided in a large number of HEIs is a matter of great concern. There has been mushroom growth of private colleges and universities, many of them of indifferent quality. The higher education sub-sector is constrained by shortage of well qualified faculty due to vacant faculty positions; poor infrastructure in many private as well as a significant proportion of public higher educational institutions; slow progress in the renewal of higher education curriculum to align it more closely with the skills demanded in a diversified economy; and adequate funding for research and development. (GoI, 2016, p. 8)

The issue of quantitative expansion is immediately juxtaposed with quality concerns and excellence in private higher education.

PRIVATE FINANCIAL RESPONSIBILITY

The financial responsibility of the development of higher education is now significantly shared by the private sector along with the government. Even in public institutions, fee (charged from students) becomes an important source of revenue to the institution. Government, albeit, keeps surveillance. In many states, fee regulatory committees have been set up to regulate fee so that private institutions are not able to extort larger and hefty fee from students.

In Uttar Pradesh, for instance, the Admission and Fee Regulation Committee of UP (AFRCUP) has notified the fee rates for various courses and the private unaided colleges are expected to abide by its notification. However, the actual fee rates of various colleges and universities reveal that there are large variations between the fee rate recommended and the actual fee charged. Admission and Fee Regulation Committees are also in place in states such as Madhya Pradesh, Karnataka and Maharashtra.

Private educational institutions in India are run as non-profit organizations. The cost of higher education (in private institutions) is thus shared by the organization itself through its own endowment and donation and the fee charged from the students and other user charges realized from them. For-profit higher education is not yet allowed in the country (Sodha & Muzammil, 2012). If private institutions are ever allowed to earn profits in India, they may raise capital though private equity funds and stock market to mop up additional resources for investing in higher education.

Household Spending

Private participation in higher education is also rising significantly from the demand side in the form of increasing household expenditures. According to latest estimates based on NSSO data, rural households (which have at least one student in higher education) spend about 15.3 per cent and urban households about 18.4 per cent of their total expenditure on higher education (*Times of India*, 2017). Households in southern states of the country spend relatively more than in northern states. However (in terms of average household expenditure in India), spending on higher education is only 2.6 per cent in rural areas and 4.9 per cent in urban areas (Chandrasekhar et al., 2016).

The Economic Survey 2016–2017 (GoI, 2017) notes that costs of education have increased both for the general education and for technical and professional education alike. The average annual private expenditure on general education per student (primary and above) has increased from ₹2,461 in 2007–2008 to ₹6,788 per student in 2014 (p. 263). Thus, roughly threefold increase has been recorded in seven years.

Role of Fee and User Charges

Contribution of fees in private higher education is on the rise. Now, fee is being viewed not as a token payment but as a technique of financing the entire cost of education. Thus, on the one hand, high fees enable the institution to increase investment in higher education and maintain high quality, on the other, it imposes heavy financial burden on parents.

Table 12.4 *Fee Rates of a Private University in Uttar Pradesh*

Name of the Course	Annual Fee in INR
BTech	266,000
MBA	441,000
PGDM+MBA	516,000
BSc Hons	116,000
BA (3 years)	254,000
MA	118,000
BBA	353,000
BSc	103,000
MSc	101,000
BTech+MBA	432,000
BEd	82,000
BTech+MTech	251,000
BBA+MBA integrated	429,000
MCom	148,000
BCA	160,000
BCOM+LLB integrated	292,000
BCA+MCA integrated (5 years)	195,000
BArch	281,000
Bachelor of Film Technology	284,000
BBA+LLB and BA+LLB	292,000
MPhil.	253,000

Source: Amity University (2017) http://collegedunia.com/university/-amity-university-lucknow/course-fee.

Note: Figures are rounded to nearest thousand.

A reasonable balance will have to be maintained between the relative roles of internal and external sources of finance and private and public financial support to higher education (Muzammil, 2014).

The prestigious and quality educational institutions are more expensive than ordinary institutions. For instance, Amity University,

Uttar Pradesh, quotes BTech fee at ₹266,151 per year; MBA ₹440,750 per year; BSc course ₹115,591 and BA (Hons) ₹58,847 per year (Table 12.4).

Many professional courses are more expensive than other courses within the same category. For example, BTech fee differs from ₹85,000 to ₹150,000 in a private university in Uttar Pradesh depending upon the branch of the course leading to BTech degree. The related fee rates are given in Table 12.5.

In general, management courses are highly priced courses in every private university. In other courses of study that are classified as general higher education, the fee rates are relatively much lower but still several times the fee rate of the same course in state universities and government/aided colleges.

A variety of medical courses that are offered by private universities are very expensive and almost unreachable by ordinary households. For example, the MBBS course fee is quoted at ₹1,500,000 (₹15 lakh) and MD fee is a whopping ₹2,000,000 (₹20 lakhs). BSc (Nursing) fee is pegged at ₹100,000 (₹1 lakh). There are also location-wise differences in the fee structure and rates in private institutions of higher education.

Table 12.5 Fee Rates in Different BTech Courses in a Private University

Name of the Course	Fee Rate in INR
BTech CSE (Cloud Technology and Information Security)	150,000
BTech (Computer Science and Engineering)	140,000
BTech (ECE)	125,000
BTech (Bio Technology)	125,000
BTech (Lateral entry)	120,000
BTech (Biomedical Engineering)	100,000
BTech (Food Technology)	85,000
BTech (Agricultural Engineering)	80,000

Source: iul.ac.in/admissioninfo/FeeInd.aspx

Table 12.6 *Fee Rates in Different Courses in a Private University*

Name of the Course	Fee Rate in INR
MBA	125,000
BBA and MCA	70,000
BEd	65,000
MEd and BCA	60,000
MBA (agri business)	50,000
MA English	30,000
MCom (Hons)	50,000
BCom (Hons)	40,000
BSc (Agri)	40,000
Diploma (Arabic/French/German)	10,000
Certificate of proficiency in languages	6,000

Source: iul.ac.in/admissioninfo/FeeInd.aspx (accessed 15 January 2019).

Table 12.7 *Prescribed Fee Rates in Private Sector Institutions*

Name of the Course	Rate of Fee
BTech, BArch, BPharma, BFA, BFAD	55,000.00
BHMCT	73,000.00
MBA, MCA, MTech, MPharma, MArch	58,000.00

Source: Report of the AFRC of the Government of UP for 2017–2018 (GoUP, 2017).

In Amity University, for instance, fee rates differ from place to place. For example, Amity University (Noida), Uttar Pradesh, quotes fee in its Mumbai Centre for BTech course at ₹150,000 and in Noida it is put at ₹170,000 and in Patna it is pegged at ₹115,000 (for the same course).

A new fee structure is coming up in some states. For instance, in Uttar Pradesh, the AFRCUP has recommended (in its order dated 5 July 2017) the fee structure shown in Table 12.7 for degree-level engineering and professional institutions.

But in actual practice, fee rates charged by institutions in the private sector are much higher than the prescribed fee rates. There are several types of BTech programmes in private institutions and the government fee committee has recommended one rate across the board. This creates practical problems in deciding the course-related actual fee rates.

In view of high fee charged in certain private institutions, the Draft National Policy on Education, 2016, has observed: 'Commercialization is rampant both in school and higher education sub sectors as reflected in the (high) charges levied for admissions in private higher educational institutions. The proliferation of substandard educational institutions has contributed to the diminished credibility of the education system' (GoI, 2016, p. 12).

A suggestion has also been made that fee rates in quality institutions of higher education may be linked with the earnings of the pass-outs as has been done in UK (Muzammil, 2013). This alternative mode will provide much relief to parents.

Private Voluntary Contribution

Sadly, voluntary contribution is on a decline. It has been a very noble tradition to support the cause of higher education generously. But now that gracious spirit is dwindling. Private voluntary contribution came in two forms—endowments and donations. Historically, landed property was donated for setting up colleges and universities. History is a witness that the rulers and landlords in the British India donated their might willingly and very generously for setting up colleges and institutions of higher learning. Gradually, that generosity of giving out parts of their land for education slowly waned out. One of the reasons was the legislation of Zamindari Abolition almost in all states soon after the independence of the country. Later on, ceilings on land holdings were imposed. Consequent upon these two legislations, the land-donating capacity was seriously eroded. Sensing the predicament, government also reduced the limit of minimum land required for setting up of a college in rural and urban areas!

CORPORATE SECTOR PARTICIPATION

The main argument for corporate sector participation has been that India cannot produce world class higher educational institutions without the contribution of the corporate sector in improving infrastructure. The NR Narayana Murthy Committee (Murthy, 2012) on Corporate Participation in Higher Education in India opens its report with the logic that the massive growth of Indian economy required to push the GER to 30 per cent and make commensurate heavy capital investment in trained faculty and research in higher education cannot be expected to come from the resources-starved public sector. Since corporate sector is a key stakeholder, it must assume a substantial role for improving the condition of higher education. This can be done by (a) making the higher education sector robust, (b) creating conducive conditions for attracting heavy investment, (c) improving faculty and research with corporate sector investment and (d) engaging the corporate sector in improving existing institutions, setting up new ones and creating education clusters.

Luckily the corporate sector has shown readiness and subsequently good performance has come up. The contributions of Tata and Birla corporate houses in India are widely known and they had a very early beginning in India. Later on, many other business houses invested in higher education by setting up renowned institutions of higher and specialized education. With increasing pressure of heavy investment in education, the role of the corporate sector in future will become more important (FICCI, 2011). Corporate houses will be helping in two ways, through direct investment and through corporate social responsibility (CSR) contributions.

The entry of the corporate sector has given further boost to quantitative expansion and quality learning. Education in posh educational institutions is expensive but still patronized by students as money here buys good quality education.

CSR IN HIGHER EDUCATION

CSR is meant to guide organizations whether business or educational, to act in an ethical and transparent manner that contributes to the health and welfare of the society. It has been reported (Weiss, 2016) that 363 universities in 77 countries of the world have stated themselves as engaged institutions involved in civil and community service. It has also been observed that universities cannot be sustainable without being socially responsible. Governments in many countries are urging the universities to adopt CSR and it is also felt that if they do not adopt voluntarily, it will be forced upon them.

Higher education is sometimes, not considered as a social good and is deemed as private good to be made available through the market mechanism in the strict sense of the word (Muzammil, 1998). In this case, it will require CSR to be put in place with a built-in mechanism of fee waivers and scholarships. Universities should also be contributing positively to the society. CSR demands that since universities are also in a position to generate surpluses, part of it should be used for social welfare function. Such type of provision is on the rise across the world and many universities are shouldering their responsibilities to this end. India is no exception. Here also it has been stressed that universities should set aside CSR budget to be used for the welfare of the society in the year concerned and it should be fixed for each financial year and should not be allowed to lapse (Chopra & Marriya, 2013). The value of CSR is so important that it must be made functional in all institutions and should not remain only on paper.

The rationale of CSR is that the profit of the organizations should also be used for generating social benefits like promoting education. But as of now the status of CSR leaves much to be desired and efforts be made to make it widely applicable and useful. The provision of CSR is in the interest of the private universities themselves and the corporate houses that offer to open private universities. Higher education largely benefits the industries and thus the direct output of educational institutions and the indirect benefits both accrue to the business sector. The indirect benefits of higher education that accrue to the industry is through the scientific temperament that is created by higher education in the society and the impact on peoples' choices to go for new products of the industry which is often seen as the impact of education-led awakening and increase in demand.

The business sector is also encouraged to be involved in higher education as it increases its reputation and goodwill and also commands respect from the society at large. Those business houses that have reputed institutions of higher learning in the country (such as TISS and BITS) command great respect in the house itself and the society. The popular feeling is (and it is also substantiated with survey data) that business should play a positive role in education in the form of helping financially and CSR is in fact a step ahead of it that universities and institutions so established by the private sector should also set aside the stipulated amount for social welfare activities. Many private universities (like Integral University, in Uttar Pradesh) have already taken up social welfare functions in the form of free medical check-up of patients and free medicines to the poor in those universities that are running medical courses of education.

Thus, for ensuring an equitable system, private higher educational institutions will need to own the CSR that would help the poorer students and also save them (institutions) from criticisms. It will serve a great social cause. Therefore, surplus-generating top private universities should keep aside a minimum of 2 per cent (as statutorily ordained) of their surpluses for helping the poor and deserving students through fee waivers or offering scholarships.

REGULATION AND GOVERNANCE OF PRIVATE INSTITUTIONS

The regulatory mechanism of higher education in India is wanting. Governance within the institution is better ensured in private institutions than in public organizations. Teacher absenteeism is an important issue in government colleges and universities, but it is well taken care of in private organizations.

The Draft New Education Policy, 2016, observes:

The Governance and management of education system and institutions, especially at the tertiary stage has assumed complexity with the advent of a multiplicity of providers, programmes and modes of financing. While it is true that some states have displayed encouraging initiatives and innovative management, the overall picture in the country is mixed. A renewed look at governance and management policies both at the system as well at the institutional level has become imperatively urgent. (GoI, 2016)

A new mechanism of monitoring, regulation and governance will be needed in the country in future when the number of private HEIs increase beyond a limit with a complex composition. As of now, only National Assessment and Accreditation Council (NAAC) is the organization in the country to assess and grade the universities and colleges of the country. It also covers private universities and colleges and other institutions. Now, Ministry of Human Resource Development (MHRD) is also contemplating to assign the task of assessment and accreditation to private organizations as well (Pandey, 2017).

NITI Aayog has impressed upon the MHRD to allow accreditation by reputed private players. Thus, in future along with NAAC, there will be private agencies too to carry out assessment as per the protocol prescribed by the UGC.

PROSPECTS AND IMPLICATIONS FOR GOVERNMENT

Future opportunities and prospects for expanding private higher education in India are enormous. It will have to be helping itself by developing competitive curricula, having trained faculty, embarking upon the frontiers of research in science and technology, strengthening infrastructure and developing partnerships (nationally and globally), discovering a comprehensive mechanism of internal governance along with financial sustainability.

The National Knowledge Commission (GoI, 2006), estimated that the country would require some 800 new universities and about 35,000 additional colleges by 2020 to meet the demand for higher education of about 36 million students by then at an assumed rate of GER of 25 per cent. Most of the required facilities will be generated by the private sector.

It is, therefore, heartening that private higher education is flourishing and growing rapidly. It has expanded in all domains of knowledge and has taken strides in specializations in which no central or state university could venture into. The implication of this development is largely twofold for the government. First, government can save on resources and use them in improving law and order, human security and the likes. Second, government can exclusively concentrate on effective management and good governance of private higher education to improve quality.

REFERENCES

AISHE. (2013). *Report of the All India Survey of Higher Education 2013–2014*. New Delhi: MHRD, GoI. Retrieved from http://mhrd.gov.in/sites/upload_files/mhrd/files/document-reports/AR2013-14.pdf.

———. (2016). *Report of All India Survey of Higher Education 2015–2016*. New Delhi: MHRD, GoI. Retrieved from http://mhrd.gov.in/sites/upload_files/mhrd/files/statistics/AISHE2015-16.pdf.

Amity University. (2017). Website of the university, Uttar Pradesh. Retrieved from http://www.amity.edu/un/fee-structure.asp

Chopra, A., & Marriya, S. (2013, March). Corporate social responsibility and education in India. *Issues and Ideas in Education, 1*(1), 13–22. Retrieved from http://www.iie.chitkara.edu.in/pdf/Sample%20Paper%20IIE.pdf

FICCI. (2011). *Private sector participation in Indian higher education* (FICCI Higher Education Summit 2011). New Delhi: Federation of Indian Chambers of Commerce and Industry. Retrieved from http://www.ey.com/Publication/vwLUAssets/Private_sector_participation_in_Indian_higher_education/%24FILE/Private_sector_participation_in_Indian_higher_education.pdf

GoI. (2006). *Report of the National Knowledge Commission*. MHRD Retrieved from http://knowledgecommissionarchive.nic.in/downloads/report2009/eng/report09.pdf.

———. (2016). *Some inputs for draft new education policy-2016*. MHRD. Retrieved from http://mhrd.gov.in/sites/upload_files/mhrd/files/nep/Inputs_Draft_NEP_2016.pdf

———. (2017). *Economic survey, 2016–2017*. Ministry of Finance. Retrieved from http://indiabudget.nic.in/es2016-17/echap10_vol2.pdf

Government of Uttar Pradesh (GoUP). (2017). *Report/Order of the Admissions and Fee Regulation Committee of Uttar Pradesh*. Retrieved from https://www.google.co.in/search?q=afrcup&oq=afrc&gs_l=psy-ab.1.0.0j0i67k1l2j0.1818.5207.0.8141.33.11.0.0.0.0.839.1961.3-2j1j0j1.4.0....0...1.1.64.psy-ab..29.4.1958...0i131k1.s7DfAnHLGRk

Integral University. (2017). *Website of the university*. Retrieved from http://iul.ac.in/admissioninfo/FeeInd.aspx.

Ligami, C. (2017, September 1). Commission stops new enrollments in 19 universities. *University World News*, p. 472. Retrieved from http://www.universityworldnews.com/article.php?story=2017090106541960

Murthy, N. R. (2012). *Report of the Committee on Corporate Participation in Higher Education*. New Delhi: Planning Commission, GoI. Retrieved from http://fi.ge.pgstatic.net/attachments/d470eba1383043ffbb7d42dfe513d27a.pdf

Muzammil, M. (1998, June 15). Leading issues in economics of higher education. *University News* (Special number on higher education as a merit good), *36*(24), 4.

———. (2010, September 13). Foreign providers in Indian higher education: Motivation and implications. *University News*, *48*(37), 37.

———. (2013). Financing of British universities: What India can learn. *University News* (reproduced in *Education India Journal*). Retrieved from http://educationindiajournal.org/home_art_avi.php?path=&id=81.

———. (2014, February). Universities in Uttar Pradesh—Administrative and financial problems: Review and suggestions. *University News*, *52*(7), 58–64.

———. (2015). Ensuring quality and excellence in quantitatively growing affiliating universities of Uttar Pradesh. *University News*, *53*(Special Issue), 20.

Pandey, N. (2017, June 30). Accreditation to universities could soon be given to private players. *Hindustan Times*, New Delhi. Retrieved from http://www.hindustantimes.com/education/accreditation-to-universities-could-soon-be-given-by-private-players/story-OISDRRuDAtjl0Sfat6kr0H.html

Shankar, A. (2016, January). *Role of private sector in higher education*. Retrieved fromhttp://www.prsindia.org/administrator/uploads/general/1453203086_Role%20of%20Private%20Sector%20in%20Higher%20Education.pdf

Sodha, M. S., & Muzammil, M. (2012). For-profit provision of higher education. In Vijaya Deshmukh (Ed.), *Education for human resource development*. New Delhi: Atlantic Publishers and Distributors.

Times of India. (2017, June 13). South India spends most on higher education. Mumbai. Retrieved from http://timesofindia.indiatimes.com/home/education/news/south-india-spends-most-on-higher-education/articleshow/59116448.cms

University Grants Commission. (2017). *List of the private universities in India*. New Delhi. Retrieved from http://www.ugc.ac.in/oldpdf/Private%20University/Consolidated%20List%20Private%20Universities%20as%20on%2029.06.2017.pdf

Chapter 13

Financing of Private Higher Education Institutions in India

Sangeeta Angom

INTRODUCTION

The process of development of universities in India is only 160 years old. With the establishment of its first three universities in Bombay, Calcutta and Madras by the British Government in 1857 along the lines of the then London University, an organized system of higher education was introduced and the pace of development of higher education was boosted with setting up of more colleges for enrolling a larger number of students. Higher education in India has grown since Independence and witnessed increase in the institutional capacity. During 1950 and 2016–2017, the number of universities increased from 21 to 864, number of colleges from 700 to 40,026 and number of teachers from 15,000 to about 13.65 lakhs. The number of students in higher education institutions (HEIs) is from mere 1 lakh to 35.7 million. Around 36 per cent of the universities and 75 per cent of the colleges are privately managed (AISHE, 2016–2017). Despite considerable progress, the enrolment of students in HEIs in India is well below the world average of 26 per cent and, moreover, the unprecedented expansion has been extremely uneven which resulted in the neglect of quality, research and managements aspects. Taking into consideration the 'Three Es', the 12th Five-Year Plan adopts a holistic approach to the issues of expansion, equity and excellence.

In fact, higher education in India is now at a crossroad and the institutions are facing challenges for its development relating to limited access despite the recent expansion, regional imbalance, questionable quality and relevance to the job market and national development priorities, shortage of well-trained faculty, poor infrastructure and outdated and irrelevant curricula. Moreover, with privatization, the system has expanded further leading to commodification, commercialization and urban-centric growth. According to Johnstone (1999), the idea of privatization in higher education entails any or all of the following: (a) more autonomy from government in financial matters, (b) enhancing resources through tuition fees, (c) Paying attention towards marketing, (d) management of student enrolment and considering fee discounts to select groups, (e) serving students, (f) raising fund and outsourcing the ancillary functions and (g) introducing study areas following contemporary market demands and scrapping non-sought-after subjects. While reflecting on his view on privatization of higher education, one could very well relate it with the nature of private universities in India. However, empirically it is not easy to analyse the very aspect of financing of the private universities.

This chapter attempts to analyse the private university financing based on the data obtained through university representative questionnaire and interview with few officials administered as part of the NIEPA research study.[1] The first section discusses about expansion the of private sector, universities and colleges in India which is followed by a section analysing the financing and expenditure patterns of selected private HEIs. The chapter concludes with a section depicting the cost of education and financial incentive for students and teachers.

PRIVATIZATION AND PRIVATE SECTOR EXPANSION IN HIGHER EDUCATION

According to Belfield and Levin (2002), the term 'privatization' is an umbrella term referring to many different educational programmes and

---

[1] A study of private universities in India of NIEPA completed in 2013 and conducted by the author.

policies. They give an overall definition, 'privatisation is the transfer of activities, assets and responsibilities from government/public institutions and organisations to private individuals and agencies'. Studies have found that the rapid spread of privatization in higher education globally and the growing variations of its forms and practices raise a set of complex issues for researchers, practitioners and policymakers in higher education.

There has been a long tradition of private education in India but mostly through the philanthropic efforts. Today, this form has taken shape of non-philanthropic efforts and the expansion is taking place in the private higher education sector which is more into 'profiteering', market-driven than philanthropy (Tilak, 2006, pp. 114–119) and many believed it to be a money-spinning enterprise than one into philanthropy.

TREND OF PRIVATE SECTOR EXPANSION IN UNIVERSITIES AND COLLEGES

Altbach (2005) rightly pointed out that private higher education is expanding worldwide and, without question, will continue to grow. In this context, Levy (2009) stated that in reality the growth of private higher education differs within and across regions and countries as well as across time. Further, he expressed that both the expansion and breadth of private higher education can be seen as an exploration of increased higher education access. On enrolment, he finds no clearly developed countries in the 35–60 per cent private enrolment range and most still under 10 per cent. In contrast, few developing countries remain under 10 per cent and many are over 60 per cent.

Over the years, the private sector presence in higher education has been witnessing growth in terms of number of universities and colleges in India. Student enrolment is also increasing in these institutions. A comparative picture of institutes of private higher education, by considering state private universities, deemed universities—private and private colleges across states, is being discussed.

As per AISHE (2016–2017), out of 40,026 colleges in the country, 64 per cent are 'private unaided' and 14 per cent are 'private aided' colleges. The top five states having the highest number of private colleges are Telangana (89%), Andhra Pradesh (88%), Uttar Pradesh (87%), Tamil Nadu (86.3%) and Gujarat (86.1%). At all-India level, in terms of having the highest share of private colleges, Uttar Pradesh is the leading state with 19.5 per cent share of private colleges of the country followed by Maharashtra (11.3%), Karnataka (9.7%), Andhra Pradesh (7.9%) and Tamil Nadu (7.8%). The states having the least number of private colleges are Mizoram, Daman and Diu, Dadra and Nagar Haveli, Sikkim, and Arunachal Pradesh. Further, enrolment pattern for the year 2016–2017 shows that 67.3 per cent of students enrolled in private colleges, out of that 46 per cent of students enrolled in private un-aided colleges.

The top five states in terms of having highest number of enrolment in private colleges are Uttar Pradesh, Maharashtra, Tamil Nadu, Andhra Pradesh and Karnataka, while Uttar Pradesh is the leading state in terms of having the highest number of enrolment in private unaided colleges followed by Tamil Nadu, Maharashtra, Andhra Pradesh and Telangana. The top six states having the lowest number of enrolment in private colleges are Mizoram, Daman and Diu, Sikkim, Arunachal Pradesh, Dadra and Nagar Haveli, and Tripura. In general, the enrolment in private unaided colleges is more than that in the private aided colleges.

There are 313 privately managed universities in India (AISHE, 2017) and the number of private universities varies greatly across the states. As per the latest University Grants Commission (UGC) consolidated list of state private universities (Figure 13.1), 23 states in the country are with state private universities and the leading states in term of having larger number of such universities are Rajasthan (46), Gujarat (31), Uttar Pradesh (29), Madhya Pradesh (24) and Haryana (20). Also, 16 states in the country are with deemed universities (private) and Tamil Nadu (26) has the largest number of deemed private universities (Figure 13.2). Besides, there are around 11 deemed universities that are government aided in the country too. The number of state open private universities is almost negligible in the country with the exception in Arunachal Pradesh.

Referring to Table 13.1, an increasing enrolment trend is seen in state private universities from 9.03 per cent in 2015–2016 to 11 per cent

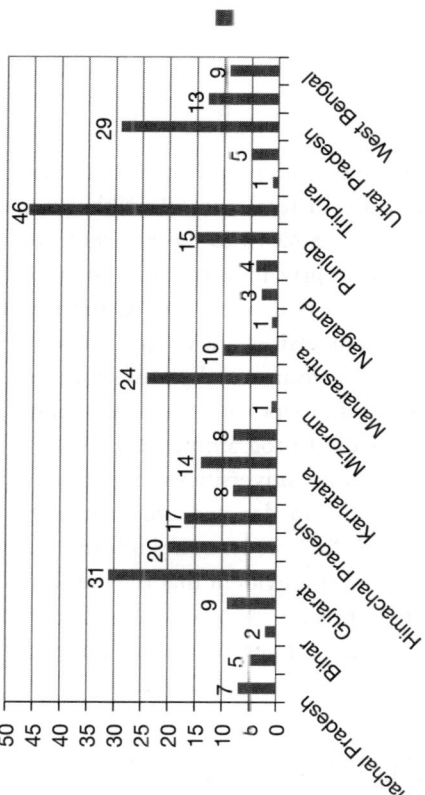

Figure 13.1 *Number of Private Universities in India (as on 6 October 2017)*

Source: UGC (2017).

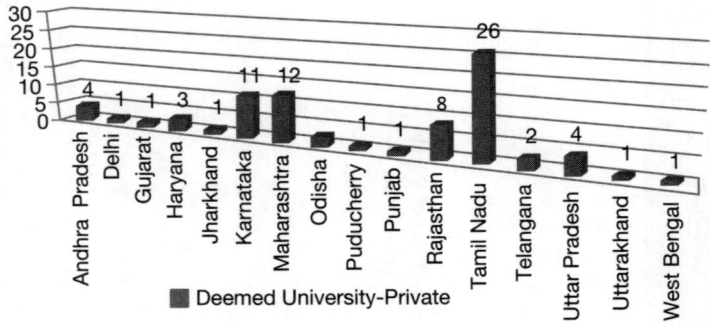

Figure 13.2 *Deemed University—Private*

Source: AISHE (2017).

in 2016–2017. In deemed universities—private too, the enrolment has increased; however, its share in total enrolment shows a decreasing trend from 9.2 per cent in 2015–2016 to 8.6 per cent in 2016–2017. Enrolment share of open state private universities is almost negligible and remains at 26 per cent in both the years. Currently, level-wise enrolment in state private universities shows an increasing trend and the highest enrolment share is found in diploma and integrated programmes. In deemed universities—private, the highest enrolment share is found in integrated and PhD programmes. At all-India university level, enrolment share of private universities is highest in diploma and integrated programmes, while in deemed universities—private, the enrolment in integrated and PhD programmes is found comparatively better than the other courses. It is evident that the enrolment number, though increasing, in these private universities is still low. Moreover, Angom's (2013) study reveals that getting quality students enrolled in state private universities still remains a challenge.

EMERGENCE OF PRIVATE UNIVERSITIES IN INDIA

Tilak (1999) and Agarwal (2006, p. 13) are of the view that till 1980, the higher education sector was controlled by government and thereafter there has been a trend towards privatization of higher education. Primarily, expansion of private higher education has been due to increase in the number of newly established institutions on self-finance basis and

Table 13.1 *Enrolment in Private Universities Level-Wise, 2015–2016 to 2016–2017*

Universities/ Level-Wise	State Private Universities		State Open Private Universities		Deemed Universities—Private		Total All-India	
	2015–2016	2016–2017	2015–2016	2016–2017	2015–2016	2016–2017	2015–2016	2016–2017
PhD	7,164 (6.5)	10,155 (8.2)	0	0	13,878 (13)	16,595 (13.4)	109,552	123,712
MPhil	864 (3.5)	851 (3.4)	0	0	1,156 (4.6)	1,539 (6.1)	24,878	25,035
PG	111,056 (5.9)	141,474 (7.2)	11 (0.0006)	11	99,129 (5.3)	95,813 (5)	1,876,565	1,958,125
UG	385,396 (9.4)	503,256 (11.4)	15 (0.0004)	15	451,916 (11)	466,354 (10.6)	4,098,936	4,413,539
PG diploma	14,585 (9.2)	17,137 (12.5)	0	0	12,042 (7.5)	7,623 (5.7)	159,373	137,013
Diploma	67,597 (24.3)	70,891 (18.6)	0	0	10,492 (4)	7,468 (3.02)	277,964	247,229
Certificate	675 (1.4)	502 (0.76)	0	0	733 (2)	576 (0.9)	49,104	65,693
Integrated	16,539 (18)	24,123 (23.6)	0	0	14,414 (16)	15,997 (16)	92,824	101,938
Grand total	603,876 (9.03)	768,389 (11)	26 (0)	26 (0)	603,760 (9.2)	611,965 (8.6)	6,689,196	7,072,284

Source: AISHE (2017).

Note: Figures within the brackets are the percentage share of each item.

also due to newly added self-financing courses in the existing institutions. Moreover, the inclusion of market-driven need-based newly inducted courses is also responsible for the exponential growth of institutions in private higher education. The growth on the enrolment in private unaided institutions offering professional courses was at the rate of 30 per cent during the period 2000–201 to 2005–2006. An emerging trend of private universities and foreign providers, that are financially independent, was also seen during the period (Agarwal, 2006, p. 13). Of all the forms of privatization of higher education in India, setting up of private universities under the State Private University Act by individuals and private trusts is a new trend of privatization of higher education witnessed during the 21st century. The concept of a private university established by the state act has been pioneered by Chhattisgarh with its Act in 2002 (Angom, 2015). As per this Act, Chhattisgarh government may, by notification in the Gazette, establish a university with the recognition and authorization to conduct a syllabus or to grant degrees or diplomas or awards. Subsequently, many states have established private universities through separate acts. These private universities are regulated by the UGC (Establishment of and Maintenance of Standards in Private Universities) Regulations, 2003. According to the UGC, there are 282 private universities (as on 10 June 2017) approved by the commission under Section 2(f) of the UGC Act 1956. It is also a fact that the exponential growth of private universities in recent years has posed challenges to provide quality and equity in education.

GROWTH PATTERN OF PRIVATE UNIVERSITIES

In many developing countries, private sector in higher education is the fastest growing segment. In African countries, in fact, the numbers of private universities are outnumbering the public universities. However, in terms of enrolment, the public institutions still dominate the scene in Africa (Varghese, 2004). In India, public institutions, especially university and university level institutions, are still dominating the private institutions in terms of size and enrolment but private colleges dominate government ones both in terms of size and enrolment. The pattern of growth of private universities during the last five years, from 2012 to 2017, across the state shows an interesting trend (Table 13.2).

Table 13.2 *Growth of Private Universities from 2012 to 2017 (in %)*

States	Private Universities	
	2012	2017
1. Arunachal Pradesh	0	2.5
2. Assam	1.9	1.7
3. Bihar	0	0.7
4. Chhattisgarh	3.7	3.2
5. Gujarat	8.4	10.9
6. Haryana	4.8	7.1
7. Himachal Pradesh	11.2	6
8. Jharkhand	0.93	2.8
9. Karnataka	1.9	4.9
10. Madhya Pradesh	6.5	8.5
11. Meghalaya	6.5	2.8
12. Mizoram	0.93	0.35
13. Maharashtra	0	3.5
14. Manipur	0	0.35
15. Nagaland	1.9	1.1
16. Orissa	0.93	1.4
17. Punjab	2.8	5.3
18. Rajasthan	22.4	16.3
19. Sikkim	3.7	1.8
20. Tripura	0.93	0.35
21. Uttar Pradesh	14.9	10.3
22. Uttarakhand	5.6	4.6
23. West Bengal	0	3.2
24. Total	107	282

Source: UGC (2012, 2017).

In the year 2012, there were only 107 private universities in 18 states (UGC, 2012). The top five private universities in terms of number were Rajasthan (22.4 5%), Uttar Pradesh (14.9%), Himachal Pradesh (11.2%) and Gujarat (8.4%); however, Madhya Pradesh and Meghalaya share 6.5 per cent universities each. In the year 2017, the total number of private universities reached 282 with the addition of five more states in the list. Further, an increasing trend of the number of universities is seen in many states, except Tripura and Mizoram, with Rajasthan sharing 16.3 per cent of the total private universities still in the top list. And these private universities are competent to award degrees as specified by UGC under Section 22 of the UGC Act with the approval of the statutory councils, wherever required through their main campuses. Table 13.3 presents a summary of the size and ownership structure of universities in India.

OVERVIEW OF RELATIVE SIZE OF INDIA'S PUBLIC AND PRIVATE UNIVERSITY SECTORS

Public universities are still dominating the higher education landscape in India for several decades. However, in the recent years, the private universities have been attracting students by offering courses mostly in engineering and management. The number of central government

Table 13.3 Overview of the Relative Size of India's Public and Private Universities Sector

Type of Universities	Universities		% of Total	
	2014	2017	2014	2017
Central government	45	47	8.54%	6.7%
State government	311	365	59.01%	52.6%
Private (individual and corporate bodies)	171	282	32.45%	40.6%
*Total	527	694	100	100

Source: UGC (2014, 2017).

Note: * The figure does not include deemed universities.

owned universities remained stagnant at 25 till 2007. But in 2009, it grew to 40 and in the succeeding years the number has increased steadily and reached up to 47 in 2017. Table 13.3 shows that presently, there is relatively no balance in the number of universities owned by the central, state and private entities. However, in terms of public–private sector divide, the size of the public sector predominates as it controls 59.3 per cent while the private sector controls 40.6 per cent. If we compare this with the figure of 2014, we find a decreasing trend of public sector expansion which was 67.6 per cent while an increasing trend in private sector expansion of 33 per cent. In this context, it has been rightly mentioned that considering the rate at which the private universities are growing during the last 2–3 years, there is a prospect of more private universities in the near future (Angom, 2014). According to Obasi's (2007) observation about private universities in Nigeria, in India too, the size of private universities may dominate in future as already happening in countries like Japan. The average growth rate of private universities during the last four or five years is considered to be much higher than that of the state universities in the country (Angom, 2015).

UNDERSTANDING FINANCING IN PRIVATE UNIVERSITIES

For many reasons, finance occupies an important place in the functioning of an institution. Financing of universities has multi-dimensional problems as while the sources are extremely limited, the needs are disproportionately too many, creating hurdles to fulfil the objectives of an institution, particularly in the context of demands of the developing society and the role that such institutions have to play to meet the various needs of the country (Ghosh, 1983). Historically, universities in India have always depended in varying degrees on government fund. Some are of the view that, in early days, private donations met many developmental needs of the universities which have almost come to a stay in the post-Independence period.

Conceptually, universities are not expected to function on commercial organizations but are meant to provide intellectuals to the society so that the need for trained manpower could be fulfilled for country's proper development. Precisely, in financing the universities, the basic approach should not be the profit or loss, but the needs of the university to function without financial stress and strain so as to enable the functionaries to devote freely to achieve the academic objectives which are national in character. Altbach (1999, pp. 1–14) rightly mentions that tuition payment is the financial basis of the private institutions and without that their survival would be impossible. Therefore, tuition levels must be adequate to provide sufficient funds for institutional survival, which requires careful planning relating to student numbers, the cost per student and expenditure levels. Government finances government colleges substantially while private government aided colleges partially. However, for private unaided colleges, 80 per cent of income is from the fees. Government supports public universities; therefore, they receive a major share of funding, while private universities in India seldom receive financial aid from public authorities. Tuition fees formed the financial backbone of many private institutions. The total income of private institutions is, therefore, determined by the number of students and the rate of tuition levied. Private universities try to attract students through introducing courses that are popular in the employment market and not offered by public/traditional universities. Accounts of the private universities in India are required to be audited by a statutory auditor who shall be a chartered accountant or a firm of chartered accountants and the report of such accounts are submitted to the governing board. Private universities under the study are reluctant to share their financial information with outsiders. Before going into detail on financing of private universities, the state profile of the six sampled universities and courses offered by them are being discussed here.

STATE PROFILE OF SAMPLE PRIVATE UNIVERSITIES

Sikkim, the least populated state, became India's 22nd state in 1975 (GoI, 2013–2014). It occupies the 13th position at national level and 3rd position among northeastern states in literacy with 82.29 per cent (male—87.29%, female—76.43%) in 2011. A tiny highland state has not only progressed remarkably in literacy, but has well addressed to gender parity. Kumar (2014) mentions that by 1975, not even one college of permanent nature was operational in Sikkim and annals of history shed lights on three institutions set up in the years 1957, 1963 and 1972 which have proven their worth. By 1995, the state could establish only 10 colleges with the contribution of private investors. By the 21st century, a few pioneering efforts were witnessed in the form of colleges and the first and foremost university, the Sikkim Manipal University was established in 1995, followed by the ICFAI University (2004), the EIILM University (2006), the Vinayak Mission (2008) and the SRM University (2013). The establishment of NIT and Central University has brought change in state's higher education scenario. Despite the fact that colleges, technical training institutions and universities are showing an upward trend, yet these could hardly accommodate all those who have desire for tertiary level education. Sikkim's most colleges are responsible for offering general courses and programmes and there are technical institutes which provide wide ranges of on-campus facilities. Development of universities in the state is rather late and surprisingly low.

Himachal Pradesh came into being on 15 April 1948 as a centrally administered territory by the integration of 30 erstwhile princely states. It is one of the most dynamic hill states of India that scored significantly high on human development indicators. The state extends over an area of 55,673 sq km with total population of 6,864,602 (Census 2011) and ranks 17th among the states and UTs in terms of area. Sikkim's literacy percentage has increased from 76.48 in 2001 to 82.80 in 2011 as against all-India literacy rate (Planning Commission, 2014). According to the GoI (2015) report, the state has one National Institute of Technology (NIT) at Hamirpur and one at Mandi, 20 engineering colleges, 34 polytechnic institutions and 13 B. pharmacy colleges under the department of technical education. Besides, the state has 222 ITIs catering to the need of the industrial sector. Four public universities and 10 private universities are also functioning in the state to meet the educational needs of the students of Himachal Pradesh as well as of other states. Presently, there are two medical colleges, one government dental college, five private dental colleges, 33 general nursing and midwifery schools and 13 BSc nursing colleges (Government of Himachal Pradesh, 2017).

Gujarat was created out of 17 northern districts of the former state of Bombay, located in the western coast of India. Gujarat with 33 districts, 6.03 population and literacy rate of 79.31 per cent (87.23%

male and 70.33% female) has made tremendous progress in terms of industrial development and is considered to be one of the fastest developing states. Gujarat has over 2,000 colleges (AISHE, 2016) and about 61 universities of which 31 are state private universities (UGC, 2018). However, some are of the view that Gujarat's higher education system has been unable to deliver graduates fit to be readily employed in the market. While there has been improvement in the primary and secondary education sector, the higher education scenario needs further augmentation. However, the state government is taking aggressive steps to enhance both the infrastructure and quality of higher and technical education within the state (Gujarat Infrastructure Development Board, 2016).

Meghalaya, known as the 'Scotland of East' of the northeast region of India, marked the beginning of a new era of the geopolitical history of the region after becoming a full-fledged state in 1972. The state having an area of 22,429 sq km, population of 2,964,007 and literacy rate of 75.48 still retains influences of the British in its architecture, lifestyle and language. Shillong has been the education hub of the region through ages. This historical legacy coupled with an enabling environment has been instrumental in the state being able to host several national institutes of repute. One little known feature in the state's education scenario is the large number of out-of-state students who contribute significantly not only to the vibrancy and cosmopolitan nature of the student community but also to the state's domestic product figures (Government of Meghalaya, 2018). It was reported that poor quality of higher education in the state can be attributed to variety of reasons, spanning from under-investment to inadequate faculty resources and deficiency in teaching-learning process (Government of Meghalaya, 2016).

Rajasthan, 'Land of Kingdom' and the largest state by area located on the northwestern part of the country, is a home of cultural diversity. Its features include the ruins of the Indus Valley Civilization, temples, forts and fortresses, and its nine regions are equally rich in its heritage and artistic contribution. The state was formed on 30 March 1949 when Rajputana was merged into the Dominion of India with Jaipur declared the state capital. The total population of Rajasthan shares 5.66

per cent of India of which 52 per cent are males showing a decreasing trend from the previous decade (Census 2011). Rajasthan's literacy rate has witnessed a steep rise to 67.06 per cent against 38.55 per cent and 60.41 per cent during the years 1991 and 2001, respectively. The state has more than 150 government colleges and also has more number of private colleges catering the society's need. Majority of the universities are privately managed, thus, the state is recorded as the one with the largest number of private universities. It was reported that the state government has taken many new initiatives particularly for education of the rural population and people of weaker society. Moreover, with increasing literacy rate, the state is attaining new heights in education day by day and with growing number of universities, being able to get higher education here will not be a dream in future (Government of Rajasthan, 2017).

Uttarakhand, known for the Chipko Environmental Movement during the 1970s, has total area of 53,483 sq km of which 86 per cent is mountainous. It has a population of 10,086,292 comprising 5,137,773 males and 4,948,519 females, with 69.77 per cent of the total population living in rural areas. The higher education scenario in the state has changed drastically since 1995 with increasing number of colleges and universities. The number of self-financed degree colleges and institutions are constantly increasing. Predominantly being a hilly state, various constraints are obvious in imparting higher education. Keeping in view the skill deficit, vocationalization of higher education is a priority area of investment for the state. Providing basic minimum infrastructure for newly established colleges and strengthening the facilities, including expansion of subjects and ensuring the availability of faculties are accorded priority (Government of Uttarakhand, 2017).

The state, most importantly Dehradun, is growing as an education hub. However, Todaria (2015) states that many of the self-financing colleges in the state are running on profit motive affecting the quality of education.

To summarize, all the six states have central universities and also have a good number of state universities except Meghalaya and Sikkim (UGC, 2017). Gujarat has the highest numbers of state universities (29), followed by Rajasthan (22) and Uttarakhand (11). Further, Rajasthan has the largest number of private universities (46), followed by Gujarat (31), Himachal Pradesh (17), Uttarakhand (13), Meghalaya (8) and Sikkim (5). As per AISHE (2016–2017), private colleges dominate the scenario of college education in the states except Sikkim, 80 per cent colleges in Gujarat and Rajasthan are the privately managed and more than 45 per cent colleges in Himachal Pradesh and Meghalaya are managed by the government. However, 64 per cent colleges in Sikkim are government managed with highest 92.5 per cent enrolment followed by Himachal Pradesh (76.2%), Uttarakhand (51.2%), Meghalaya (46.3%) and Rajasthan (44.5%). However, Gujarat has the least number of students enrolment (17.3%) in government colleges. Enrolment in private unaided colleges is higher than in private aided colleges in the states of Sikkim (98.5%), Himachal Pradesh (71.2%), Rajasthan (91.7%), Gujarat (50.3%) and Uttarakhand (58.9%), while Meghalaya has more enrolment in private aided colleges. Overall, Rajasthan has the highest enrolment in colleges while Sikkim has the least.

COURSES OFFERED IN SAMPLE PRIVATE UNIVERSITIES

One of the important features of private universities in India is that a majority of them offer courses which are market driven with less focus on traditional subjects. Unlike public universities, most of the private universities under study offer courses mostly leading to UG and PG courses in engineering, pharmacy, business management, IT, and very few on medical and allied subjects, law and master in science or arts. It is also evident that the private universities focus more on limited market-oriented courses than humanities and social sciences. Of the sample universities, 50 per cent offer diploma course in engineering, information sciences, IT and business law. All the sample universities offer PhD in any of the subjects of engineering/technology, medical, business management, pharmacy, social work, social sciences or humanities.

SOURCES OF PRIVATE UNIVERSITY FINANCE

The main sources of finance for surveyed private universities include tuition and other fees. Though tuition fees formed the financial backbone of the private universities, there are other sources of funding, namely funds from the sponsoring body or charitable trust, bank loans, health care services, charities from group of companies, interest on fixed deposits with banks, income from conducting various programmes relating to academic, relief bond and recovery of past salary. Main sources of income of the surveyed universities are fees and funds from the sponsors (Table 13.4). Bank loan and interest on fixed deposits with bank also form an important source of fund. Both the private university of Gujarat and Rajasthan received income from consultancy and other works. Private university in Sikkim has received government financial support and it formed an important source of income, besides fees, interest and other income including health care services. Moreover,

Table 13.4 *Sources of Fund of Private Universities under Study*

University	Sources of Fund
Private University—Meghalaya	Fees and income from the sponsors
Private University—Himachal Pradesh	Student fee, fund from Jaypee Group through charitable trust Jaiprakash Sewa Sansthan and bank loan
Private University—Sikkim	Fees, grants from state government, health care services, interest and other income
Private University—Gujarat	Fees, bank loan, interest on fixed deposits with bank, interest on RBI relief bond, income from testing and consultancy, income from Management Development Programmes (MDPs), recovery of past salaries and income from conducting seminar, workshop/training
Private University—Rajasthan	Fees and other charges received by the university, contributions made by the sponsoring body, income received from the consultancy and other works, income from endowment fund and other sums received by the university
Private University—Uttarakhand	Fees, bank loans and other endowments

Source: Angom (2013).

the private university in Sikkim is the only exception providing details on trend of sources of income for the years 2006–2007 to 2008–2009 (Figure 13.3).

It is evident that the major share of income of the university is shared by students' fee at an average of 84 per cent of the total income. However, the income from fees show a decreasing trend from an amount of ₹16,980.70 (in lakhs) in 2006–2007 to ₹3,419 (in lakhs) in 2008–2009. It further shows that the income from the government grants remains the same amounted of ₹225.00 (in lakhs) for the years 2006–2007 to 2008–2009. The income from health care service shows an increasing trend from ₹353.64 (in lakhs) in 2006–2007 to ₹780.63 (lakhs) in 2008–2009. The income from interest and other income also show an increasing trend. The total income shows a decreasing trend from ₹17, 676.57 lakhs in 2006–2007 to ₹4,718.93 lakhs in 2008–2009. So the maximum source of income is students' fee charged on various items.

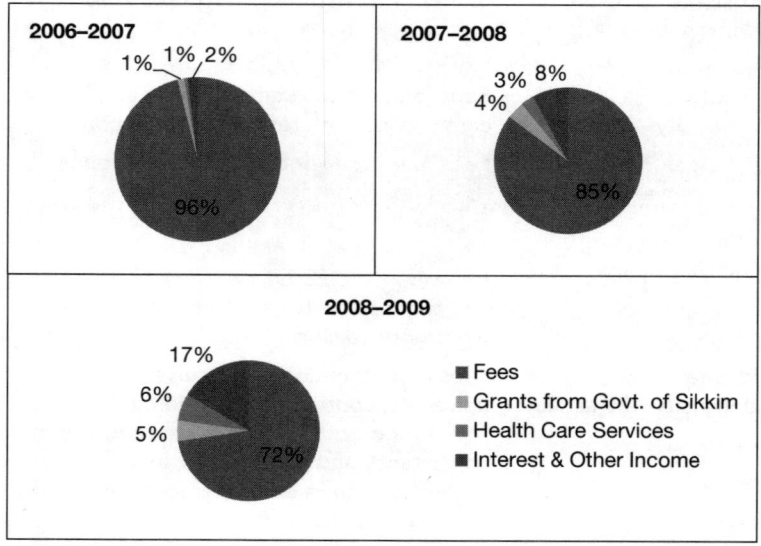

Figure 13.3 *Private University—Sikkim's Trend of Source of Income for the Years 2006–2007 to 2008–2009*

Source: Angom (2013).

EXPENDITURE PATTERN IN THE PRIVATE UNIVERSITIES

It is a well-known fact that recurrent expenditure drives the cost of private university education in most of the countries including India. How an institution uses its funds to purchase various goods and services to support its current operations is reflected in its overall expenditure structure. The trends of an institution's recurrent expenditure structure can signal financial strength or financial vulnerability. The recurrent expenditure of three surveyed universities is analysed over time separately. Figure 13.4 shows the comparative patterns of expenditure between two universities, namely Private University—Gujarat and Private University—Himachal Pradesh for the years 2003–2004 to 2007–2008. This is given in share percentage of the total expenditure item-wise.

In the case of Private University of Gujarat, expenditure for the last five years from 2003–2004 to 2007–2008 shows an increasing trend (Figure 13.4). The university kept its share of recurrent expenditure on salaries at or below 28 per cent over the study period 2003–2004 to 2008–2009. On an average, personal emoluments consumed 24 per cent of the operational budget every year during that period. The university's second most important recurrent expenditure item was library. This item accounted for an average of 1.9 per cent of annual recurrent expenditure during the year 2003–2008, which is a very small amount. This shows that private universities spend almost negligible amount on library. The average expenditure on equipment is 4.2 per cent that shows an increasing trend during that period. Private University—Himachal Pradesh's expenditure on salaries has been growing. Whereas it was a modest 11.5 per cent in 2003–2004, it went up to 16.5 per cent in 2007–2008. On an average, the university's salaries bill accounted for 15.2 per cent of its recurrent budget between 2003 and 2008. A university spends on an average 12 per cent on equipment, whereas only 2.8 per cent on library.

As given in Figure 13.5, Private University—Uttarakhand has spent the maximum on salaries of all the three universities under study on expenditure pattern. Its average expenditure on emoluments during 2005–2010 was 30.5 per cent, about 15.3 per cent higher than Private

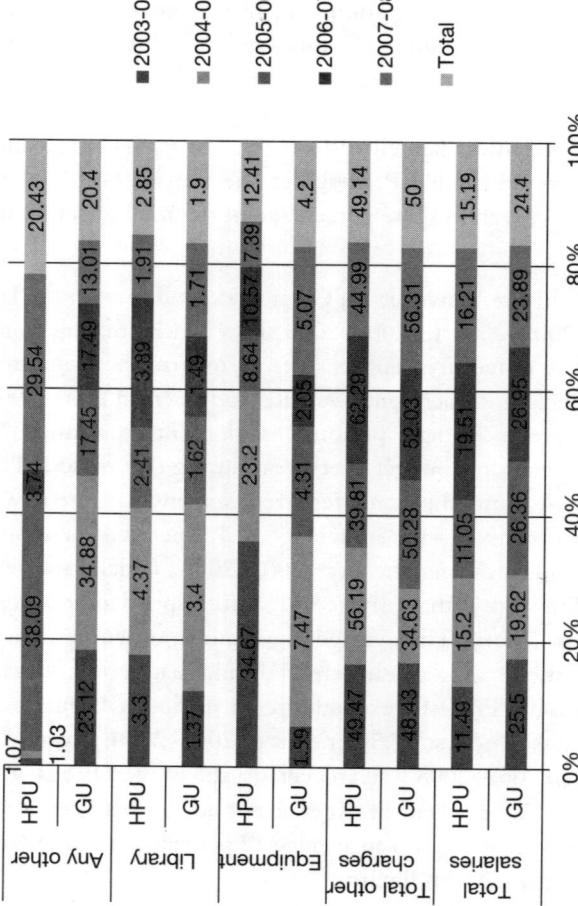

Figure 13.4 *Expenditure Pattern for Private University—Gujarat and Private University—Himachal Pradesh, 2003–2004 to 2007–2008 (Figures in %)*

Source: Angom (2013).

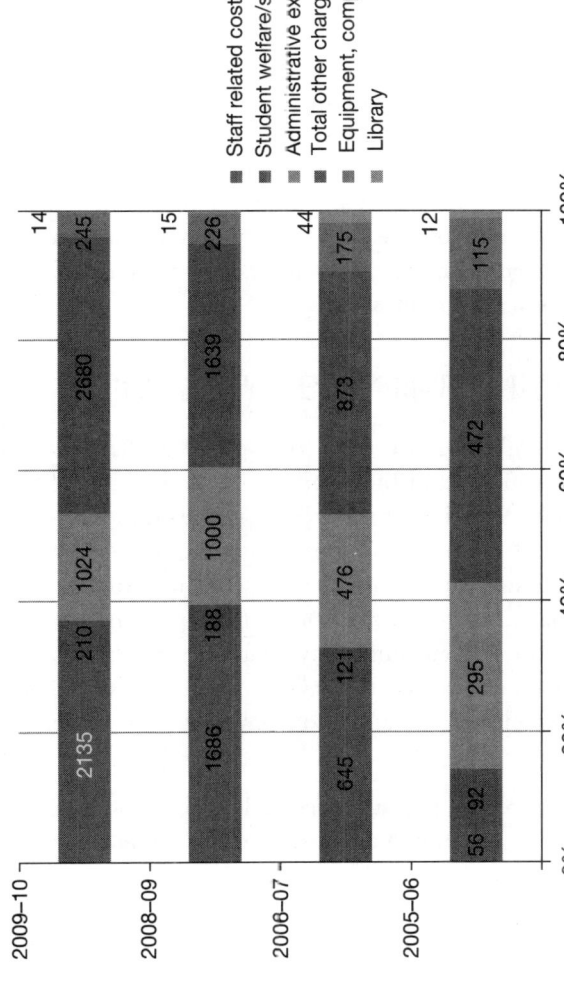

Figure 13.5 *Expenditure Pattern for Private University—Uttarakhand (Amount in Lakh)*
Source: Angom (2013).

University—Himachal Pradesh. Its expenditure on students' welfare and scholarship and also administrative expenses trend was unsteady. Private University—Uttarakhand has spent the least on libraries of all the three universities under study at an average 0.6 per cent between 2005 and 2010 and its expenditure on library also shows a decreasing trend from 0.9 per cent in 2005 to 0.21 per cent in 2010.

To summarize, total expenditure in all the three universities under study shows an increasing trend. Expenditure on salary shows an increasing trend, however expenditure on library by the universities is almost negligible. As per teachers' responses, expenditure on research in all the sample private universities is also negligible. It has been observed that most of the universities were in the early period of their existence; the universities seemed to have been spending more on infrastructure such as development of library, laboratory, buying laboratory equipment, construction of buildings and so on.

COST OF PRIVATE UNIVERSITY EDUCATION

Like in other developing countries, one of the challenges faced by educational policymakers in India today is determination of the unit cost of education. Officials of the private universities indicated that that they used cost estimates based on experience and/or anticipated expenditure and student enrolments to determine tuition charges. They also compare their fees with what their competitors charge before making a decision. Private university unit costs are largely course-based. Students are charged on the basis of course. These charges vary from university to university and also from student to student of the same course.

The cost of university education per student per year (annual recurrent expenditure) for the three universities under study was calculated and it was found that all the three universities have increased unit cost per students during the period 2005–2007 (Table 13.5). Private University—Uttarakhand has the highest cost of university per student, whereas Private University—Gujarat has the least. Table 13.6 confirmed that the average unit cost per student varies from university to university from ₹242,739 to ₹94,982.

Table 13.5 *Recurrent Unit Costs per Students (Amount in Lakh)*

Year/University	Annual Recurrent Expenditure	Enrolment	Recurrent Unit Cost per Year
2005			
Private University—Himachal Pradesh	1,918.04	1,134	169,139
Private University—Gujarat	3,802.66	5,071	74,988
Private University—Uttarakhand	134,198,631	672	199,700
2006			
Private University—Himachal Pradesh	1,718.22	1,474	116,568
Private University—Gujarat	4,430.98	5,070	87,396
Private University—Uttarakhand	233,446,561	893	261,418
2007			
Private University—Himachal Pradesh	2,791.96	1,475	189,285
Private University—Gujarat	6,213.90	5,070	122,562
Private University—Uttarakhand	325,062,704	1,217	267,101

Source: Prepared by author from response of sampled students (2010–2011).

TUITION FEE, FINANCIAL ASSISTANT TO STUDENTS AND SALARY STRUCTURE

Tuition Fee in Private Universities

Tuition fees do vary among private universities in India, and at times, the variation is substantial like the case in African private HEIs (Varghese, 2004). The study also found that tuition fees do vary between

Table 13.6 *Average Unit Cost per Student (Figures in Rupees)*

| University | Recurrent Unit Cost per Year | | | |
	2005	2006	2007	Average
Private University—Himachal Pradesh	169,139	116,568	189,285	158,330
Private University—Gujarat	74,988	87,396	122,562	94,982
Private University—Uttarakhand	199,700	261,418	267,101	242,739

Source: Prepared by author from response of sampled students (2010–2011).

the private universities. Some officials of the private universities under study indicated that they do compare their fee structures, with what their competitors have, before making a decision on the fee structure. Moreover, the fee structure is determined by the respective institution itself. In some sample universities, the structure of fee needs to be recommended by university fee committee as well as reviewed by the finance committee before its final approval by the board of management. Available statistics on the fee structure of the universities under study revealed that the fees charged differ across universities and across disciplines in the same universities. Data revealed that in a private university, a student has to spend ₹280,000 per annum for MBA course in Private University—Gujarat but a student has to spend as low as ₹7,000 in Private University—Uttar Pradesh (special concession for the physically challenged students). In Private University—Sikkim, a student has to spend a sum of ₹343,050 for the course of MBBS, whereas in Private University—Rajasthan, a student has to spend at least ₹2.3 lakhs per annum. For a professional course like Master of Education, a student has to spend as low as ₹25,000 in Private University—Uttar Pradesh to as high as ₹1 lakh in Private University—Gujarat. Though the students pay higher fee at private universities, only 53 per cent of the sample students agreed that the fees for the course are justified with the teaching quality provided by the universities. Further, the maximum number of students that responded (77%) from the sample universities expressed that their parents support their tuition fees, 11 per cent of the students expressed the support of their fees by bank loan. However, very few of them (6%) were found enjoying scholarship to complete their education.

An attempt has been made to understand the fee structure of a private university for a course. For instance, Private University—Gujarat had charged ₹230,000 per annum for MBA for national students, whereas for foreign nationals/PIO/NRIs/Gulf quota, it charged US$ 20,000 or equivalent in Indian Rupees for the entire course. Further, the university charged ₹30,000, ₹15,000 and ₹8,000 as hostel fee, activity fee and examination fee, respectively, per annum. So, a student pays more than 280,000 per annum as the total annual fee for a MBA course. Tuition and hostel fees in the second year may be revised upwards by about 10 per cent. At the university, for a Master in Technology (MTech) course, a student has to pay ₹60,000 annually if he is a sponsored applicant, if not then he has to pay ₹55,000. However, a student of MTech in Computer Science and Engineering has to pay ₹65,000 annually as the course fee. Tuition fees can be paid in two instalments (semester-wise). An applicant is required to pay ₹5,000 as a deposit on the day on which the admission is offered and this deposit will be adjusted against payment of fees. The break-up tuition and other fees of the University for MTech course including hostel fees are given in Box 13.1.

Box 13.1 *Private University—Gujarat: Tuition and other Fees for MTech Course*

Tuition fee per annum: ₹60,000 (sponsored applicants)
                        : ₹55,000 (others)
Other charges/deposits
Library deposit: ₹5,000 refundable
Caution money deposit: ₹2,500 refundable
Other charges

1. Registration PG: ₹500 (one time)
2. University fee: ₹8,000 (per annum)
3. Enrolment fee: ₹400 (one time)

Hostel fees: ₹25,000 per annum
Hostel and electricity advance: ₹5,000
Hostel internet charges: ₹5,000 (per year)

Source: Prospectus 2009, Private University—Gujarat (PG programmes).

University Financial Assistance to Students

It has been evident from the study that some of the private universities offer financial assistance to students in some form or other. For instance, in a selected private university in Gujarat, the research education and research foundation offers different kinds of scholarships to the needy student to be admitted in the school of science and technology on the basis of merits and means as per the rule: (a) The students in each programme limited 5 per cent of the intake will be assisted by the way of paying 100 per cent interest on the loan taken from the scheduled bank. The financial ceiling of the earning of the family per annum will be ₹2 lakhs and (b) The students in each programme limited 5 per cent of the intake will also be partially assisted by the way of paying 50 per cent interest on the loan of the student concerned from the scheduled bank. The financial ceiling for this category is ₹4 lakhs programme. In another case, a private university in Uttarakhand has offered fee concession to all domicile students of the state for MBA courses. This may be the reason for attracting students to pursue the offered course in the university.

Salary Structure

It is true that in many countries, private universities' remuneration/ salary structure reflects competitive market rates in order to attract, motivate and retain qualified academic and senior administrative staff. Like the case in countries like Vietnam, private universities in India enjoy flexible payment policy. Mwiria (2007) on 'Public and Private Universities in Kenya' reported that among the Kenyan private universities, the United States International University (USIU) was the only exception to the pattern of low salaries and its remuneration structure reflects competitive market rates. Therefore, out of 41 per cent teaching staff, about half have been recruited from the public universities. Over 80–85 per cent part-time lecturers are also drawn from the public universities. The study revealed that few private universities in India are also able to design attractive salaries, allowances and bonuses which are considered as effective incentives to draw qualified professors.

However, in the case of some private universities, the salary packages are not attractive enough to draw qualified professors from the public institutions/universities to work for them as per the information provided by the sample universities. No doubt, there is even competition among private universities within the state to attract better professors.

Though author made an attempt to capture the remuneration structure of Indian private universities, it was not possible to extract the exact data on salary structure from majority of the universities under study as the universities kept this information confidential. Though adequate remuneration is paramount in attracting and retaining high-quality academic staff, majority of teachers have responded that there is no proper pay scale in their university. And there could even be negotiation for their pay scale at the time of interview. They also reported that staff salaries and allowances are much lower in private universities than the public universities. However, very few universities have been found to pay higher salary at par with the UGC scale to the teachers. Except a private university from Himachal Pradesh, the rest of the universities under study were reluctant to share the exact information on salary structure of the staffs. The study further reveals that a private university from Rajasthan has not uniformly implemented the salary scale, not even the pre-revised UGC scales so far. This may be the case for many private universities.

CONCLUDING REMARKS

Private universities in India are self-financed institutions and their main sources of income are fees from the students, endowments, bank loans and donations and so on. They are not getting any financial grant from the state government, central government or UGC. However, very few universities get fund from governmental organizations in the form of research fund for conducting projects. Many of such universities are in the initial stage of their growth and so taking up many developmental works. Therefore, beyond meeting payments to the staffs and day-to-day maintenance fund, many of these universities are not in the position to undertake research work. The study revealed that a private university's fee structure is much higher than the public university and also differ among them. It is also observed that not all the private universities pay higher salary at par with Sixth Pay Commission, but many of them pay much lower than the Fifth Pay Scale. Teachers from the sample university opined that there is no proper pay scale in the university. Most of the sample private universities have kept their salary bills within balance and were able to release resources for the purchase of other instructional support materials. The accounting and financial records of the universities were computerized. It should be mentioned that private universities are reluctant to share their financial information with outsiders, therefore it is quite difficult to get the complete information about the financing of the university. It was also found that accounts of the private universities in India are required to be audited by a statutory auditor who shall be a chartered accountant or a firm of chartered accountants and the report of such accounts are submitted to the governing board. Through the present study, it can be suggested that funds of private universities must be earmarked for regular upgradation of facilities. Universities must try to increase the funding for research through external funding agencies with proper authentic research proposals. University administrators should have some policies to generate income. Some financial support from the bank/state in the form of low interest bearing loans may be given to deserving institutions based on some performance indicators of inputs and teaching-learning processes. It is suggested that further research study focusing only on fee structure, salary and income expenditure pattern of private universities needs to be undertaken.

REFERENCES

Agarwal, P. (2006). *Higher education in India: The need for change* (ICRIER Working Paper No. 180). Retrieved from www.icrier.org/pdf/ICRIER_WP180__ Higher_Education_in_India_.pdf

AISHE. (2016). *All India survey on higher education (2015–2016)*.Retrieved from http://aishe.nic.in/aishe/viewDocument.action?documentId=227

AISHE. (2017). *All India survey on higher education (2016–2017)*. Retrieved from http://aishe.nic.in/aishe/viewDocument.action?documentId=239

Altbach, P. G. (1999). *Private Prometheus: Private higher education and development in the 21st century*. London: Greenwood Press.

————. (Ed.). (2005). *Private higher education: A global revolution*. Dordrecht: Sense Publishers.

Angom, S. (2013). *A study of private universities in India* (Unpublished Research Report). New Delhi: NUEPA.

————. (2014, February). Private universities in India: Status and policy perspective. *University News*, Association of Indian Universities, Special Issue, 167.

————. (2015). Private higher education in India: A study of two private universities. *Higher Education for the Future, 2*(1), 93 and 105.

Belfield, C. R., & Levin, H. M. (2002). *Education privatisation: Causes, consequences and planning implications*. Paris: International Institute for Educational Planning (IIEP), UNESCO, International Institute for Educational Planning, 19 Retrieved from http://unesdoc.unesco.org/images/0013/001330/133075e.pdf

Ghosh, D. K. (1983). *University system in India*. Jabalpur: Rahul Publication, MP Jaypee University of Information and Technology, Annual Report 2008–2009.

GoI. (2013–2014). *State industrial profile of Sikkim, Ministry of MCSM*. Retrieved from http://sikkim.nic.in/msme-di/documents/State%20Profile%20of%20 Sikkim.pdf

————. (2015). *State industrial profile of Himachal Pradesh, 2014–2015*. Retrieved from http://dcmsme.gov.in/dips/state_wise_dips/Himachal%20Pradesh.pdf

Government of Meghalaya. (2016). *State higher education plan: SHEP—Meghalaya*. Retrieved from usa.nic.in/download/151/shep/.../state-higher-education-plan-meghalaya-shep-final.pdf

————. (2018). *Education and literacy, official web portal*. Retrieved from http://megeducation.gov.in/about.html

Government of Rajasthan. (2017). *Official web portal pages on education*. Retrieved from https://rajasthan.gov.in/Education/Pages/default.aspx and https://rajasthan.gov.in/Education/CollegesAndUniversities/Pages/default.aspx.

Government of Uttarakhand. (2017). *Directorate of education, Uttarakhand*. Retrieved from http://directorateheuk org/index.php?mod=content&page=105

Gujarat Infrastructure Development Board (GIDB). (2016). *Education in Gujarat—A fact file*. Retrieved from http://www.gidb.org/education-afact-file

Johnstone, B. (1999). *Privatisation in and of higher education in the US*. Retrieved from http://gse.buffalo.edu/FAS/Johnston/privatization.html

Kumar, S. (2014). Sikkim State Higher Education (SSHE) in India—Visionary monologues of Koottathuppatty Natarajan Sundaram Mudaliar (Book review). *European Academic Research, II*(3), 3845. Retrieved from http://euacademic.org/UploadArticle/652.pdf

Levy, D. C. (2009). Growth and typology. In Svava Bjarnason, Kai-Ming Cheng, John Fielden, María José Lemaitre, Daniel C. Levy, N. V. Varghese (Eds.), *A new dynamic: Private higher education*. Paris: International Institute for Educational Planning (IIEP), UNESCO, 7–8.

Mwiria, K. (2007). *Public and private universities in Kenya*. Oxford: James Curry Limited.

Obasi, I. N. (2007). Analysis of the emergence and development of private universities in Nigeria, *JHEA/RESA*, *5*(2–3), 39–66.

Planning Commission. (2014). Himachal Pradesh: A profile. GoI. Retrieved from http://planningcommission.nic.in/plans/stateplan/index.php?state=sp_sdrhp.htm

Tilak, J. B. G. (1999). Emerging trends and evolving public policies in India. In P. G. Altback (Ed.), *Private Prometheus* (pp. 113–132). London: Greenwood Press.

———. (2006). *Private higher education: Philanthropy to profits, higher education in the world*. Retrieved from https://upcommons.upc.edu/bitstream/handle/2099/6956/2006-02_eng_tilak.pdf

University Grant Commission (UGC). (2012, March 6). *Public notice on private universities*. New Delhi: University Grant Commission.

———. (2014). *Private universities list*. Retrieved from http://www.ugc.ac.in/privatuniversity.aspx.

———. (2017). *Consolidated list of private universities*. Retrieved from https://www.ugc.ac.in/privatuniversity.aspx

———. (2018). *Consolidated list of universities*. Retrieved from https://www.ugc.ac.in/oldpdf/Consolidated%20list%20of%20All%20Universities.pdf

Todaria, N. (2015). *Higher education in doldrum in Uttarakhand*. Retrieved from https://timesofindia.indiatimes.com/city/dehradun/Higher-education-in-doldrums-in- Uttarakhand/articleshow/49835578.cms

Varghese, N. V. (Ed). (2004). *Private higher education in Africa*. Paris: International Institute for Educational Planning (IIEP), UNESCO, 13, 21–22 February; 9/05/2015. Retrieved from www.unesco.org/iiep/PDF/pubs/PrivatHEAfr.pdf

About the Editors and Contributors

EDITORS

N. V. Varghese is Vice Chancellor, National Institute of Educational Planning and Administration (NIEPA) and also the founding director of the Centre for Policy Research in Higher Education (CPRHE) at NIEPA. Formerly, he was the Head, Governance and Management of Education, International Institute of Educational Planning (IIEP/ UNESCO), Paris.

Jinusha Panigrahi is Assistant Professor at the CPRHE at NIEPA. She is serving as the Co-chairperson of Economics and Finance of Education, Special Interest Group (EFE-SIG), Comparative International Education Society (CIES), USA.

CONTRIBUTORS

Sangeeta Angom is an Assistant Professor at the Department of Higher and Professional Education, NIEPA. She was a guest lecturer in Education Department, North Eastern Hill University, Tura campus.

M. M. Ansari is former member of University Grants Commission (UGC), New Delhi; an interlocutor for Jammu and Kashmir, Government of India; and former Information Commissioner of the Central Information Commission, Government of India.

Saumen Chattopadhyay is currently Chairperson of the Zakir Husain Centre for Educational Studies, School of Social Sciences, Jawaharlal Nehru University (JNU), New Delhi. He is President of Comparative Education Society of India (CESI), affiliated to the World Council of Comparative Education Society (WCCES).

Mausumi Das is an Associate Professor at Delhi School of Economics, University of Delhi.

Sailabala Debi is former Director of the Centre for Multi-disciplinary Development Research, Dharwad, Karnataka. She was professor at the Department of Analytical and Applied Economics, Utkal University, Bhubaneswar, Odisha.

Harvinder Kaur is Professor of Economics at the Punjabi University, Patiala.

Mona Khare is Professor and Head at the Department of Educational Finance, CPRHE, NIEPA, New Delhi. Previously, she was a Professor at Barkatullah University, Bhopal, Madhya Pradesh.

Subir Maitra is an Associate Professor and Head of the Department of Economics in Heramba Chandra College. He is also Guest Professor at ICFAI, Kolkata; Narula Institute of Technology, Kolkata; Institute for Civil Services Aspirants (promoted by Confederation of Indian Industries) and Civil Services Study Centre under Administrative Training Institute, Government of West Bengal, Salt Lake.

M. Muzammil is Ex Vice Chancellor M. J. P. Rohilkhand University, Bareilly, and Dr B. R. Ambedkar University, Agra; and Professor of Economics, Lucknow University, Lucknow. He was conferred with the All India Govind Ballabh Pant Economics Award in 2000 for his book on agricultural economics. Besides this he has been the chairperson and the member of several committees appointed by the Government of India and Uttar Pradesh state government.

M. R. Narayana is faculty and Editor-in-Chief of *Aarthika Charche*, the FPI Journal of Economics and Governance, Fiscal Policy Institute of Government of Karnataka, Bengaluru. He is former Professor of Economics in the Centre for Economic Studies and Policy at the Institute for Social and Economic Change, Bengaluru.

Tridip Ray is a Professor of economics at the Economics and Planning Unit of the Indian Statistical Institute, Delhi. He was formerly with the Department of Economics of the Hong Kong University of Science and Technology.

K. Anji Reddy is an Assistant Professor, Department of Economics, Mahatma Gandhi University, Nalgonda, Telangana.

B. Shiva Reddy was former Head of the Department of Economics and the Chairman Board of Studies in Economics of Osmania University. He was a Member of Tapas Majumdar Committee and Member of National Council of Teacher Education (Southern Region), Member of DPEP Appraisal Committee at state and national level.

Index